D0893424

SCHIZOPHRENIC DISORDERS

SCHIZOPHRENIC DISORDERS

Theory and Treatment from a Psychodynamic Point of View

PING-NIE PAO, M.D.

INTERNATIONAL UNIVERSITIES PRESS, INC.
Madison   Connecticut

Fourth Printing, 1994

Library of Congress Cataloging in Publication Data

Pao, Ping-Nie.
    Schizophrenic disorders: theory and treatment
from a psychodynamic point of view.

    Includes bibliographical references and index
    1. Schizophrenia. 2. Psychoanalysis. I. Title.
RC514.P284   616.8′982   77-92180
ISBN 0-8236-5990-9

Manufactured in the United States of America

To Pearl, Maryland, and William

Contents

Preface

At Chestnut Lodge, my colleagues and I spend a good portion of each day in the long-term, intensive, psychoanalytic psychotherapy of severely emotionally incapacitated patients, many of whom are schizophrenics. After a number of years of being ill, and feeling disappointed with the help previously received, these schizophrenic patients have become settled in their way of life. As much as they still long for people to stay close by them, they play a "distance" game with others. In the proximity of others, they appear aloof, indifferent, and distant. They talk in "schizophrenese," which makes their communication difficult to comprehend. They allow themselves minimal affective experience, so that others can hardly empathize with how they feel. As they withdraw from real persons, they place themselves among delusional, persecutory figures.

In treating these patients, the therapist learns that they live in the throes of terrors and panics. To minimize the terror, such patients create the schizophrenic existence of isolation. To help such patients in psychotherapy, the therapist must understand the workings of the patient's mind, as well as his own, so that he can assess from moment to moment when and how the distance between him and his patient has decreased or increased. In addition to this intellectual understanding, the therapist must have a special tolerance for bizarreness: He must be willing to step into his patient's bizarre world and stay with him in his distorted world. The therapist must have sufficient interest in the patient as a person, not as a patient of a certain diagnostic category, and he must be willing to stick it out, regardless of how the patient behaves and how much time may be required. He must be able to tolerate those moments when his patient radically and absolutely rejects him. While he must be genuinely optimistic about what he is attempting to achieve, he must also be able to accept disappointment, as his job can at times be likened to that of Sisyphus who, rolling the boulder uphill, repeatedly found his effort thwarted near the top and had to start all over again. He must realize that the therapeutic process tends to be long and tedious, and can be extremely taxing. Often the supporting person, namely the therapist, may himself need support from others. A hospital designed to treat schizophrenic patients in long-term, intensive psychoanalytic psychotherapy must therefore have available a sophisticated supportive system for therapists (as well as for other members of the therapeutic team).

Each person is unique. The psychopathology of one patient is very different from that of another. In the psychotherapy of each patient, the therapist has to ferret out his specific conflicts and find specific ways to help him resolve them. A statement or an action by the therapist that engenders panic in one patient may have a soothing, curative effect for another. But however much the clinical manifestations and underlying psychopathology differ from one patient to another, all schizophrenic patients do share certain conflicts and fears, likes and dislikes. Because of the similarities among them, the experience the therapist acquires from working with his patients is cumulative, and what is learned from one patient may be somehow applicable to another. And because of the similarities among schizophrenic patients, the knowledge we have accumulated at Chestnut Lodge may be useful to others who choose to devote their energy and time in a way similar to ours. Hence the impetus to organize this book.

Some years ago one of my colleagues at the Lodge presented a taped session in a group of 11. At one juncture, every one of the 11 agreed that the therapist should make some therapeutic intervention, yet no two agreed on the content of the intervention. This led to the realization that the most

central of the sundry curative factors in any psychic therapeutic intervention is perhaps the therapist's ability to use
freely his innate capacity to empathize with the patient. But
the use of empathy must be guided by the therapist's *conscious* knowledge of the patient's conflicts, psychodynamics,
and psychic functioning; otherwise the empathy can be mis-
directed. This realization in turn led to the notion that in
undertaking psychotherapy with his patient each therapist
should possess a working hypothesis or theory about his patient, for without such a hypothesis the therapist may get lost
in a mass of seemingly irrelevant, irrational, and disjointed
information.

My working hypothesis or theory of schizophrenia is based
on psychoanalytic contributions made by Freud and others.
Accordingly, I conceptualize schizophrenia in terms of human
development; that is, a certain combination of nature and
nurture in the first weeks of life results in a poor tolerance
of affective experience and a deficient capacity for adaptation,
which become increasingly worse and eventuate in schizophrenic illness.

My theory of schizophrenia, the exposition of which is the
primary aim of this book, integrates various viewpoints. This
integrated theory of schizophrenia not only offers guidelines
for the psychoanalytic treatment of schizophrenic patients,
but also provides new systems for subgrouping the schizophrenias. These new systems of subgrouping or classification
make prognostic evaluation possible and aid in the therapeutic planning for any given patient at the time of initial consultation.

The book is divided into four parts. In Part I, after giving
due consideration to the term "schizophrenia," the discussion
focuses on how diagnostically to class schizophrenia into
subgroups I, II, III, and IV, and how clinically to subdivide
the course of illness into acute, subacute, and chronic phases.
Part II reviews some of the widely acclaimed early psychoanalytic theoretical conceptualizations, and critically evaluates
their importance in explaining schizophrenia I, II, III, and IV

as well as the acute, subacute, and chronic phases of the illness. In Part III of the book contributions of other authors are integrated into a cohesive psychoanalytic theory of schizophrenia that explains schizophrenias in all the categories listed above. Here, such issues as nature versus nurture, early object relations, basic adaptive defects, steady worsening of adaptive capacity, and mechanisms of symptom formation are discussed in detail. Part IV is essentially the clinical application of the formulation advanced in Part III.

In the section on treatment, I have offered only some guidelines. Details of the intricacies of psychotherapeutic interactions would have expanded the book enormously. Nor have I done justice to such important issues as administrative care, nursing care, family work, and the use of drugs. All these deficiencies must be remedied on another occasion.

In the preparation of this book, I owe an immense debt to Dr. Dexter M. Bullard, Jr., the Medical Director of Chestnut Lodge, for his ceaseless support and interest. So very often did he and I talk about the content of the book that he in fact helped organize it. I also want to thank Dr. Joseph Sandler, my good friend from England, and Dr. Otto A. Will, Jr., my predecessor as Director of Psychotherapy at Chestnut Lodge, for their continuous encouragement.

As for the content of the book, I am most indebted to all of my patients, past and present: Each of them taught me something different, and together they taught me immensely. I am also indebted to Drs. Frieda Fromm-Reichmann, Lewis B. Hill, and Harold F. Searles. It was from their pioneer work in the psychotherapy of hospitalized schizophrenics that my own knowledge and skill have evolved. Among my many teachers the most important has been Dr. Dexter M. Bullard, Sr., who taught me *how* to say what must be said to the patient. We all know that anything we say to our patients must be relevant, timely, and understandable. But proper and timely interpretations are not good enough for patients with severe narcissistic problems. Dr. Bullard has always been concerned with how to say what must be said without shattering the patient's already very fragile self-esteem. I am also beholden to all of my colleagues who have worked and are still working at Chestnut Lodge. Without their open exchanges of ideas with me, my views on many clinical and theoretical issues could not have been clarified. I regret that I cannot here list all their names.

Dr. Joseph D. Lichtenberg, a distinguished contributor to the psychoanalytic literature and a dear friend since our residency days, must be specifically mentioned for his tireless efforts in reading several versions of each chapter and for his generous and critical suggestions, many of which I have incorporated. Drs. Erich Heydt and Samuel V. Thompson have also read versions of some of the chapters and have offered their opinions. Dr. Pearl Shen, my wife and colleague, contributed immensely to every phase of the writing of this book. She not only allowed me to become totally absorbed in my work for long periods of time, but also offered me enormous encouragement when I felt bogged down in the writing and rewriting of certain passages.

The book could not have been completed without my secretary, Mrs. Sarann Barnsley, who not only typed and retyped the manuscript, but saved tremendous amounts of my time by learning to "decode" my rough handwritten drafts. Mrs. Hilma Beall, the librarian at Chestnut Lodge, was most helpful in locating reference material and in preparing the reference list. Ms. Norma Player helped to prepare the index.

I am extremely appreciative of Miss Suzette Annin's contributions in the preparation of the manuscript for publication. Her perceptive questions and valuable suggestions have removed many unclarities and inconsistencies. I enjoyed our cooperative work. I also want to thank Ms. Laura Kosden and Ms. Susan Heinemann of International Universities Press for their editorial assistance.

PART I

Diagnostic Considerations

CHAPTER 1

On the Diagnostic Term "Schizophrenia"

Although physicians generally assume that a clear-cut, widely agreed-upon definition of schizophrenia exists, unfortunately, that is not the case. In ordinary medical and psychiatric practice, the term schizophrenia is applied to many groupings of clinical symptoms and aberrant behaviors. For example, patients with the following manifestations of mental illness are regarded as schizophrenic: an old man who for 20 years has inhabited the back ward of a state hospital, sitting in one spot grimacing and gesticulating; a young college student who was found in his car completely oblivious to his surroundings and the activities going on around him; a middle-aged woman who is violent, disoriented, incontinent of urine and feces, smearing, drinking, and eating her own discharges; a young woman who exhibits a mixed clinical picture of hysteria, obsessional and hypochondriacal symptoms, and evidence of transient looseness of thought processes; a 35-year-old man of limited intelligence who is aloof, arrogant, and little involved with others, but nevertheless able to function in a nondemanding routine job. Clearly, as long as the term schizophrenia can be

This chapter is based on a paper of the same title published in *The Annual of Psychoanalysis*, 3:221-238, 1975. New York: International Universities Press.

used to cover such a wide range of clinical entities, it not only has limited value as a diagnostic term, but also creates a great deal of confusion in communication among professionals.

In writing about schizophrenia, the task of establishing a precise definition and a clear set of criteria for diagnosis is essential. In this chapter, I shall take a fresh look at an old familiar problem—the diagnosing of schizophrenia. Through the broad application of the psychoanalytic approach, we have increased our awareness of empathy and introspection as means for one person to penetrate the most defended psychological barriers of another. To the skills of careful observation used in natural sciences we have added the sensitive trained clinician's awareness of his responsiveness to the patient. This chapter deals with methods for making a diagnosis of schizophrenia using both vantage points—the discerning discriminations of natural science and the awareness gained from sensitized empathy and introspection.

The Origin of the Term

Before describing my criteria for making a diagnosis of schizophrenia, I shall review the origin and history of the present usage. From even a brief survey of the ways in which physicians have attempted to define and clarify the confusing and varied symptoms presented by the schizophrenic patient, we can appreciate the complexity of the problem.

Definitions and classifications of mental illnesses had been made as early as the middle of the nineteenth century. Not until 1899, however, did Kraepelin's system bring an initial order to classification. In his system, a psychosis is endogenous if it is not caused by a demonstrable anatomic lesion in the brain, by the existence of an identifiable toxic or chemical agent, or by metabolical or hormonal disturbances, traceable in the human organism, that could affect the function of the brain. This system divides endogenous psychoses into two broad categories: dementia praecox[1] and manic-depressive psychosis. Manic-depressive psychosis is manifested in self-terminating episodes of exaggerated "normal" affects and behavior; dementia praecox is characterized by bizarre behavioral and affective manifestations and steady personality deterioration.

In the history of psychiatry, Kraepelin's contribution is a significant one. As Bleuler (1911) wrote, "Hand in hand with the elaboration of the dementia praecox concept other disease-entities were defined, particularly the manic-depressive psychosis. In this way, dementia praecox was thrown into bold relief; and its delimitations were no longer drawn unilaterally from within but also solidly from without" (p. 7). On the other hand, the advantages of Kraepelin's contribution were outweighed by disadvantages. As Zilboorg (1941) said, Kraepelin's belief in the inevitability of deterioration unavoidably led to "the ultimate achievement of an attitude which expected little from man once he was mentally ill; it stood ready to take him into the kindly custody of a well-organized and well-conducted hospital where he could await his fate with the maximum comfort his psychological condition, social position, and financial ability would allow" (p. 461).

In 1903, Bleuler said of dementia praecox, "Twenty years' experience has taught me to delineate the disease in the same manner as Kraepelin has done" (p. 113), but, he noted, "dementia is not always an accompaniment of the disease, nor is the disease always praecox. To be sure, the name is not well chosen" (p. 120). Five years later Bleuler suggested the new term "schizophrenia." In his monograph *Dementia Praecox or the Group of Schizophrenias* (for the most part written in 1908, but not published until 1911), he offered his reasons

[1] Zilboorg (1941, p. 438) has said that Kraepelin's use of "dementia praecox" differed from that of Morel, who had, in 1860, coined the term to describe a clinical phenomenon of very limited scope. Kraepelin, as Bleuler (1911) says, "subsumes the whole deteriorating group under the term [dementia praecox]" (p. 6). In Kraepelin's usage, dementia praecox includes not only Morel's dementia praecox, but also Kahlbaum's catatonia, Hecker's hebephrenia, Pick's simple deterioration, and paranoia hallucinatoria or phantastica.

for introducing the new term: (1) The term dementia praecox describes the disease, not the person who is afflicted with it. From the term, no adjective can possibly be derived. To write a differential diagnosis, the clinician finds it extremely awkward and cumbersome to be writing about the disease and not about the person afflicted with it. (2) The term dementia praecox tends to lead to a misconception that the disease must begin during adolescence and end in a state of dementia. Clinically, that need not be so. (3) The new term schizophrenia (from the Greek roots for "split" and "mind") not only does away with the above problems but also clearly reflects characteristics of the illness, namely the phenomenon of "splitting" of the mind or personality, characterized by Kraepelin as the "peculiar destruction of internal connections of the psychic personality" (1919, p.1).

Because of its many advantages over "dementia praecox," the term "schizophrenia" achieved instant popularity. In fact, it continued to be used in spite of Freud's attempts to replace it with the term "paraphrenia." Partly because he never attempted to convince others why paraphrenia was a better term, Freud was the only one to use it for a decade.[2] In the end he accepted the term schizophrenia. Expounding a psychobiological (or a biological and adaptive) point of view, Meyer (1938) introduced the term "paraergasia" to replace schizophrenia or dementia praecox in order to emphasize that mental illness is a reaction to the stress of life and not a "disease" that affects the brain. But despite his great influence in American psychiatry, Meyer's effort was as futile as Freud's had been.

According to the Kraepelinian system, a diagnosis of dementia praecox is ultimately dependent on mental deterioration. Since dementia might take time to appear, an immediate diagnosis of dementia praecox could occasionally be difficult. By stressing that schizophrenia is recognized by "a specific type of alteration of thinking, feeling, and relation

---

[2] See Strachey's footnote to Freud (1911, p. 76, n.1).

to the external world which appears nowhere else in this particular fashion," Bleuler (1911, p. 9) remedied this shortcoming in Kraepelin's approach. At a time when psychiatry was still dominated by neurology, and an immediate diagnosis was paramount, the importance of Bleuler's contribution was unequivocal. Later, when Freud and Meyer suggested their preferred new terms, they were striving to convey important messages through them. But because these terms did not facilitate the process of diagnosis, in a period when clinical diagnosis was considered vital, they had little chance of competing with Bleuler's.

Notwithstanding their disagreements about nomenclature, Kraepelin, Bleuler, Freud, and Meyer seem to have agreed that dementia praecox, schizophrenia, paraphrenia, and paraergasia are different terms for one and the same discrete clinical entity, which has its own boundary (e.g., it is distinguished from manic-depressive psychosis) and for which a definitive criterion for a diagnosis can be established.

The Usefulness of Establishing a Diagnosis

Before delineating the criteria for a diagnosis of schizophrenia, let us first consider the usefulness of establishing a diagnosis. In recent years, many authors have objected to the use of the term schizophrenia. Some believe that it is so generalized that it is devoid of meaning. Some, like Szasz (1961) and Laing (1967), regard affixing a diagnosis of schizophrenia as equivalent to assaulting the personal integrity of the patient. Others, like Hay and Forrest (1972), believe that for a psychotherapist a formal diagnosis is a luxury. Their arguments are eloquent, convincing, and humanistic, but they do not seem to benefit clinicians. From the clinician's point of view, a diagnosis can be extremely useful. It enables professionals to communicate multilevel information in an economical way. For instance, a diagnosis of hysteria not only tells of the patient's symptoms, it also reveals conflicts, early object relations, etc., of a certain specificity. In addition, if psycho-analysis is to be recommended as the preferred method of treatment, the therapist can be assured that the hysteric will be able to sustain the anxieties aroused in the course of the treatment without a total collapse of his ego functions or a loss of his sense of self-cohesion outside the therapeutic sessions. Similarly, a diagnosis of schizophrenia is not limited to the recognition of the fundamental and accessory symptoms that Bleuler spoke of. It informs us further that the patient suffered from disturbed early object relations with resultant ego and superego defects that predisposed him to panic, a collapse of ego functions, and a loss of self-cohesion. Such information warns us that psychoanalytic treatment cannot be used profitably without the adoption of parameters (Eissler, 1953a), at least in the early phases.

Speaking as clinicians, Menninger et al. (1963) said, "our concern now is not so much what to call something as what to do about it" (p. 2), and "it is still necessary to know [the diagnosis] in advance, to plan as logically as we can" (p. 6). In line with this viewpoint, Frosch (1964, 1970) has laboriously delineated "psychotic character," Kernberg (1967) the "borderline personality organization," and Kohut (1971) the "narcissistic personality disturbances." Clinical considerations prompted Anna Freud (1965b) to design the metapsychological diagnostic profile, which allows the study of pathology against the background of normal development, and Freeman (1972) to outline a profile for use in evaluating schizophrenic cases.

Thus a diagnosis of schizophrenia is neither a luxury for the clinician nor a derogatory label attached to the patient. The benefits that can accrue in transmitting multilevel information economically, in establishing a prerequisite for sound therapeutic planning, in assessing various developmental lines and deviations, and in developing a theory of schizophrenia from which consistent therapeutic endeavor can follow, make a sound diagnosis an essential and significant aspect of research on and treatment of mental illness.

Criteria for a Diagnosis of Schizophrenia

Descriptive and Symptomatic Approach

I have mentioned that although Kraepelin differentiated dementia praecox from manic-depressive psychosis, Bleuler was the first to use symptoms as criteria for the diagnosis of schizophrenia. According to Bleuler, schizophrenic symptoms can be divided into two groups: fundamental and accessory.[3] The fundamental symptoms, which are essential and conclusive for a diagnosis, consist of "a specific type of alteration of thinking, feeling, and relation to the external world" (1911, p. 9). More specifically, they are disturbances in associative processes, dissociation between affect and thoughts, ambivalence, and autism. Delusions, hallucinations, ideas of reference, experiences of being directed, experiences of bodily changes in the form of hypochondriasis, feelings of depersonalization and unreality, loss of a sense of the past, merging of self with others, are conceived as accessory symptoms. Although not a prerequisite for a diagnosis, the accessory symptoms often dominate the clinical picture. "It is not often that the fundamental symptoms are so markedly exhibited as to cause the patient to be hospitalized in a mental institution. It is primarily the accessory phenomena which make his retention at home impossible, or it is they which make the psychosis manifest and give occasion to require psychiatric help" (p. 94).

Today, if the diagnosis of schizophrenia is approached from the symptomatic and descriptive level, Bleuler's criterion of fundamental symptoms is still adhered to (see American Psychiatric Association, *DMS-II*, 1968). Anna Freud (1965a) has demonstrated that deeper understanding of the patient can often be deduced from the surface data. But relying on symp-

---

[3] Bleuler's definitions of fundamental and accessory symptoms are not to be confused with his definitions of primary and secondary symptoms. Bleuler believed that schizophrenia was basically a disease of the brain that caused the associational disturbance. Thus, to him, the associational disturbance was the primary symptom and the other symptoms were secondary to it.

toms or surface data alone can be fraught with complications. The following case illustrates this diagnostic problem.

Debra was considered an ideal daughter by her mother until Debra reached 16 and became involved with boys. She no longer reported every detail of her daily life to her mother as she had previously done. Distressed, the mother took Debra to a woman psychiatrist. After a seemingly promising start, the patient refused to talk in her therapy sessions. She was then taken to a male therapist, with whom she repeated the same pattern. Because of her silence and general appearance of depression, Debra was hospitalized. After a flight from the hospital, the patient was reported as displaying bizarre behavior, such as hiding herself behind a chair in the doctor's office. Diagnosed as schizophrenic, she was transferred to a second hospital a long way from her home. Here, relatively free from her mother's influence, her symptoms disappeared. Her previous silence and bizarre behavior, which had presumably earned her the diagnosis of schizophrenia, were now determined to be the result of willful nonengagement rather than of autistic withdrawal. Thus a diagnosis based on behavior and accessory symptoms proved unsound, and resulted in inappropriate plans for treatment.

Along the same diagnostic lines, Bleuler's (1911) dictum that "definite schizophrenic disturbances of association alone are sufficient for the diagnosis" (p. 298) resulted in many patients being labeled schizophrenic when associational disturbances occurred in no circumstances other than the psychological testing process (cf. Rapaport et al., 1945-1946). In an attempt to resolve this problem, later writers tended to subdivide schizophrenia into two classes: reactive versus process schizophrenia, or schizophrenialike psychosis versus schizophrenia. The implication is that, although they have similar symptomatic manifestations, one class has a better prognosis than the other. This approach reintroduces Kraepelin's idea of using the outcome of the illness or prognosis as a criterion, with the resultant feeling of hopelessness that often derives from such a view.

A Psychoanalytic Approach

In concentrating their effort on an understanding of the hows and whys of the schizophrenic phenomenon, psychoanalysts do not as a rule concern themselves with the diagnostic criteria. When diagnosis becomes an issue, they simply accept the descriptive or symptomatic approach. The earliest analysts, however, such as Freud, Tausk, Federn, perhaps less influenced by Bleuler, tended to use stricter criteria for the diagnosis of schizophrenia. The schizophrenic patients on whom Freud, Tausk, and Federn formulated their theories were distinctly sicker than those discussed in recent literature (e.g., Boyer and Giovacchini, 1967; Arlow and Brenner, 1969).[4] In spite of a lack of explicit effort to define the diagnosis, each of these psychoanalysts, in his theoretical formulation about schizophrenia, did lay down his own criteria in one form or another. When Freud formulated his theory of schizophrenia (1911), he ascribed all the schizophrenic symptoms to (1) withdrawal of libidinal cathexis from the outer world and from the representation of the objects, and (2) libidinal recathexis of the objects. The implication of the theory is that a "break with reality" consequent on withdrawal of cathexis is an implicit criterion for a diagnosis of schizophrenia. The major drawback of this criterion is that the break often belongs to the history; we are then asked to rely on the history, rather than on the examination of the patient, to reach a diagnosis.

Tausk (1919) was the first to use the expression "loss of ego boundaries" to describe the phenomenon that Bleuler called "merging of self with others." Federn (1936, 1949b) gave new meaning to the term loss of ego boundaries by suggesting that it leads to misinterpretation of events, ideas of reference, delusional formation, and so on. Thus he seemed

---

[4] Reichard (1956) suggests that two of the five cases Freud described in *Studies on Hysteria* (Breuer and Freud, 1893-1895) could be diagnosed as schizophrenic. And in his recent review of the Wolf Man's childhood, Blum (1974) suggests that Freud's "From the History of an Infantile Neurosis" would be more appropriately entitled "From the History of an Infantile Psychosis."

to consider the loss of ego boundaries an implicit criterion for a diagnosis of schizophrenia. Although such later observers as Nunberg (1920), Hartmann (1953), Jacobson (1954a), Freeman et al. (1958), and Searles (1965) have all recognized that the loss of ego boundaries is a consistent manifestation of schizophrenia, the phenomenon tends to be more evident in the treatment setting than in the diagnostic setting. Talking to a stranger, the patient may not show any such disturbance at all. Furthermore, a transient loss of ego boundaries can often be witnessed in borderline psychotics and, sometimes, in neurotics in analysis—sometimes even in normal persons in states of ecstasy or states induced by consciousness-altering drugs. If the loss of ego boundaries is to be used as a criterion for a diagnosis of schizophrenia, some qualifications must be made.

Melanie Klein (1946) identified the tendency of schizophrenic patients toward ego fragmentation and projective identification. Bion (1957) adds to the list of diagnostic criteria the patients' propensity for aggression and inability to sustain object relations. But these criteria, like the loss of ego boundaries, are more readily discernible in the treatment setting than in the diagnostic setting.

In 1917, Freud described how the thought processes of schizophrenic patients are dominated by primary-process functioning. Unlike the loss of ego boundaries or projective identification, this phenomenon does not require an analytic setting to be revealed; in other words, primary-process functioning can often be discerned in a diagnostic situation where patient and doctor are meeting for the first time. Hence later writers have used "reverting to primary-process functioning" as one criterion for a diagnosis of schizophrenia. However, we must certainly not give a diagnosis of schizophrenia to those patients who, as Rapaport et al. (1945-1946) demonstrated, show primary-process functioning only in stressful situations, such as during psychological testing. Primary-process functioning as a diagnostic criterion must therefore include the circumstances and duration of its occurrence.

An Empirical Approach

At Chestnut Lodge, since 1967, I have interviewed each new patient within a few days after admission. This privilege has allowed me to develop, among other things, a way to assess each patient diagnostically. Such assessment is by no means infallible, but it has yielded significant guidelines for diagnosing schizophrenia.

Before their admission to Chestnut Lodge, most "schizophrenic" patients had been placed on psychotropic medications in other hospitals, often for many years. Most of them had been made "rational" by the drugs. Others, despite large daily doses of medication, still demonstrated the fundamental or accessory symptoms described by Bleuler or the primary-process functioning described by Freud. In an interview setting, however, both "rational" and "irrational" patients sooner or later exhibited the same kind of special aura that became an identifying tool for diagnosis.

Ordinarily, in the interpersonal setting of an interview, we feel that we and the interviewee are in contact with each other if we are engaged in a conversation; there is an interaction of a live, lively, friendly or unfriendly nature between us. However, we feel very little of this contact or engagement in an interview with a schizophrenic. With him we are never certain whether we are in contact emotionally; we intermittently sense that a barrier exists between us; we sometimes feel as if we are meeting with a robot; we may observe that the patient's movements, facial expressions, and words are stereotypic; and we may find fragments of his interactional modes—his gestures, phrases, and manners—detached and disengaged from their cohesive purposiveness in human interaction. All these qualities give us the feeling that the patient is both there and not there. In other words, two people are exchanging rituals, but their minds are miles apart.

This peculiar atmosphere is created by the patient.[5] Usu-

---

[5] If the therapist is anxious at the start of an interview, he may precipitate the patient's specifically schizophrenic response.

ally it is created before he begins to talk; that is, its existence does not depend on his speech. His stream of speech, however, his intonations and choice of words, further enhance it. The atmosphere may seem very "thick" in the beginning, appearing more relaxed as the interview progresses; or it may grow thicker as the interview goes on; or it may remain static throughout the interview. The fluctuation or lack of fluctuation may be due either to the degree of the patient's sickness or to the interviewer's success or failure in eliciting empathic trust. When the patient is gravely ill (i.e., acutely distressed and very self-engrossed) the peculiar atmosphere tends to be maintained throughout the interview. Whenever a fluctuation does occur, it may be fair to say that the patient dispels the peculiar atmosphere because he considers the conversation with the interviewer worthwhile, or he hides behind the peculiar atmosphere because he distrusts the interviewer as he has distrusted others in his life.

Speech, as indicated, helps to enhance the special atmosphere. For instance, after he has admitted that he needs to be in the hospital, the patient may then declare that nothing is wrong with him, or, after saying he has been in various hospitals before, he may say he never committed a crime and should not have been imprisoned. On the surface, the speech appears to be senseless, but careful scrutiny reveals that a second thought tends to invalidate the first thought. The patient's primary purpose in such speech is simultaneously to engage and disengage in the conversation with the interviewer. That schizophrenic speech shows a special kind of peculiarity in itself has been beautifully described by Bleuler (1911), Storch (1924), and Kasanin (1944). A simple interpretation of these observations is that the patient's language is affected by his conflicting efforts to communicate and not to communicate with the interviewer. In schizophrenic language crucial words are replaced by others, so that on the surface the patient's speech is irrelevant and impossible to comprehend. The word replacement is accomplished without the patient's awareness and is subject to the primary process.

For example, on entering the office for the first time, Anna (she was one of the rare cases who was not on medication) paced the room and screamed at the top of her lungs, protesting vehemently at having just been brought to the hospital against her will. Continuing to pace, she occasionally stopped screaming, and listened to the doctor's short comments on her distress at being rehospitalized (she had been in a hospital several years previously), and on her complex emotions before the current need for rehospitalization. The pacing and intermittent screaming continued for over 25 minutes. Suddenly she declared she was tired, and readily accepted an invitation to sit. Slouching in her chair, she closed her eyes and was quiet and motionless. Five minutes later she opened her eyes, but otherwise made no movement. Fixing her eyes on a picture on the wall, she said, "The picture is very *peaceful.* I like it." Having followed her eyes to the painting of a countryside landscape, the doctor said, "It is. And you may find your inner peace around here, in this office." Thereupon, the patient responded with a clear "yes."

Ben, after 10 months of treatment (he was not in treatment with me), lapsed into apparent apathy after the doctor's summer vacation. Although previously he had talked enough to make himself clear, now he was practically mute. The doctor, after having made a connection between his vacation and the patient's behavior, and having sat through many silent sessions with the patient, felt particularly irritated one day and expressed his dismay about the patient's silence and general attitude. For the rest of the session, although the doctor felt a bit relieved, the patient remained silent. The patient opened the next session, however, by saying desultorily that when he was in high school he was in love with Leslie. The doctor said nothing, and the patient, after pausing a couple of minutes, continued, again in a desultory manner, "I couldn't talk to Leslie."

Anna had said, "The picture is very peaceful," when she could have said, "You give me a very peaceful feeling." Ben could have said, "My anger or hatred for you, or even my

attachment to you, has made me tongue-tied," but instead
had to make his point via a long-past experience of being in
love with Leslie. This kind of word replacement has been
called "schizophrenese" (Hill, 1955). Talking schizophrenese,
any patient may give the impression of what Bleuler (1911)
called "loose association." Ben, in addition, used intonation
and affect to achieve his purpose of creating the special atmosphere. By flattening his affect and talking in a desultory
manner and then pausing, he had told, but at the same time
not told, his therapist why he had been silent.

I think it can be said that the special atmosphere I have
described is experienced only with schizophrenic patients. This
atmosphere is not created consciously; it is quite beyond the
patient's awareness. Once created, it tends to make others
feel estranged, bewildered, confused, and incapable of empathy for the patient's preoccupation or mood. Consequently, in
treating such a patient, the psychiatrist may resort to a technique or defense in order to remove himself from the patient:
He may end the interview, or keep his own thoughts unrelated to the interpersonal setting. Judging from his own feelings and activities, he may conclude that his patient is
extremely hostile and is making "attacks on linking" (Bion,
1959). But hostility explains only half of the phenomenon,
even in the case of Ben. The doctor's long absence no doubt
produced in Ben extreme feelings of hurt and abandonment.
As the result of his narcissistic rage, Ben became silent. When
frightened by his doctor's angry remarks, he felt compelled to
talk, grudgingly, and therefore cryptically. Still, the hostility
fails to explain the totality of the condensed act of telling and
not telling (or getting close to and yet away from) the therapist. The act is not the result of ambivalence or ambitendency; it transcends ordinary ambivalence—where the patient
is still completely related to the other person. In the act that
creates this special atmosphere, the patient seals off his feelings, libidinal and/or aggressive. He simply turns on one of
the defensive devices that he originally adopted with his
mother in order to cope simultaneously with two or more con-

tradictory messages, and that he now uses in any ambiguous situation when he is reminded of the confrontation with his mother (cf. the "double-bind" concept [Bateson et al., 1956; Kafka, 1971]).

My emphasis is that diagnosis should begin with the interviewer's study of his own emotional reactions in the interaction between himself and the patient. Here we may discover the patient's tendency to create a special atmosphere that conveys his simultaneous expression of two diametrically opposite wishes—to move toward and to move away. This atmosphere interferes with the interviewer's empathic understanding of the patient and often incurs a narcissistic hurt to the interviewer's ideal image of himself as a savior. Because of this hurt, the interviewer then thinks of the patient as being hostile, as having suspended his trust in the whole human race, and consequently as being subhuman.

The interviewer's study of his own emotional response to the patient is subjective and personal. It should never be used *alone* as a *single* diagnostic criterion. It must be objectified. To achieve this objectification, the interviewer may need to spend more time with the patient. A series of interviews may give him a chance to learn,[6] through the patient's report, something about the patient's inner experience. Such reports may reveal the first-rank symptoms (e.g., audible thoughts, experiences of impulses and volitional acts under outside influence, delusional perception, experience of thoughts as being controlled by others), as described by Schneider (1959). I do not, however, agree with Schneider's claim that a diagnosis of schizophrenia can be made with certainty in the presence of only first-rank symptoms.

Anna Freud (1965a) says that when doing diagnostic work, the analyst

has to proceed as a comparative stranger to the patient, with no established transference coming to his help, and he has in

___

[6] He may also observe a loss of ego boundaries, a reversion to the use of primary-process functioning, or projective identification.

his field of observation no more than overt behaviour, conscious manifestations, descriptions of symptomatology and suffering often inadequate, in short the surface of the patient's mind. With child patients . . . he has to proceed even without their cooperation or in the face of their opposition which implies that these surface appearances, symptoms, etc., are also obscured by the subject's fears, distrust, avoidances, denials. To compensate for the paucity of material elicited under such conditions with child patients, the diagnostician finds himself forced to go beyond the subjective account which the patient is able or willing to give of himself and to turn to allegedly objective sources as provided by information about the individual's historical and social background, the environment's or parents' descriptions and complaints, as well as to the technical help offered by a battery of tests [p. 32].

This statement can easily be applied to schizophrenic patients. If we regard diagnosis as being quite important (as the prerequisite for planning a sound treatment program), we must not only pay attention to the special atmosphere and to symptoms and other surface data, but must also scrutinize carefully the patient's developmental history, his capacity to endure anxiety, his propensity for regression, his adaptive capacity, and the environment he lives in. Such information may be elicited from all available sources—the patient himself, members of his family,[7] the family physician, pediatricians, school reports, previous psychiatrists, previous psychiatric hospitals, etc.

If a diagnosis is approached in this fashion,[8] no differential diagnosis is called for. Neither manic-depressives nor borderlines create the "special atmosphere." In the interview setting, the depressed patient tends to squeeze as much sympathy as possible from the other person; in the process he causes the interviewer to feel depleted and therefore irritated at the pa-

[7] Empirically we know that the mothers of schizophrenic patients also have an air about them that the mothers of borderlines do not have.

[8] Over 90 percent of the patients admitted to Chestnut Lodge have been previously diagnosed as schizophrenic. Using our method of scrutiny five to six percent of these patients are rediagnosed as borderline.

tient for his greediness. The manic patient often feels frustrated and attacks the other person—creating in the latter a feeling of outrage. Or he tries so hard to entertain the interviewer as to overwhelm him, causing him to become bored and, consequently, irritated and eager to leave. Borderline patients display a wide spectrum of behavior (Kernberg, 1970), but even the sickest do not create the described special atmosphere. They may evoke a wide variety of emotional responses in the other person, but they always make him feel he is with the patient. Aside from the transience of the "psychotic symptoms" and the ability to identify the cause of symptoms, the lack of the special atmosphere is perhaps another characteristic difference between borderline and schizophrenic patients.

My own approach to the diagnosis of schizophrenia consists of three steps. First, I serve as a stimulator of affective responses from the patient. Second, I serve as a receptor for these responses.[9] Finally, I objectify my subjective experience with additional information about the patient, including his developmental history, family background, etc. But however stringent the criteria may be for a diagnosis of schizophrenia, the term still covers a broad spectrum of clinical phenomena. In the next chapter, I shall describe a method of categorizing schizophrenic patients into subgroups. Subgrouping removes some existing confusion in nomenclature and facilitates recommendations for therapy.

[9] Others (e.g., Kohut, Kernberg, Modell) have also scrutinized affective reverberations between patient and interviewer in attempting to reach a diagnosis. Modell (1975) has made it explicit that he resorts to the study of the affective exchange between himself and his patients to make a differential diagnosis between borderline cases and narcissistic personality disorders.

CHAPTER 2

On Schizophrenic Subtypes

Because the diagnosis of schizophrenia can be affixed to a wide variety of clinical conditions, Kraepelin, Bleuler, and others attempted to subgroup schizophrenia. Since Kraepelin's and Bleuler's time, the manifest symptoms have traditionally been used as the criteria for subgrouping. For instance, the American Psychiatric Association's *DMS-II* (1968) is based on this tradition. The recent suggestion (by Carpenter et al., 1976) to divide schizophrenia into four subtypes—typical, flagrant, insightful, and hypochondriacal—is also primarily based on symptoms.

The purpose of subgrouping is to clarify and delineate the characteristics of schizophrenic illness, thus to improve communication between doctors, nurses, social workers, and psychologists, and to allow for more effective determination of prognosis and more accurate and useful setting of short- and long-term goals and methods of treatment. The current system (or traditional method) of subgrouping does not really achieve that purpose. In this chapter, therefore, after a brief review of current forms of subgrouping, I shall propose two systems for subgrouping schizophrenic patients. The point of reference of the first system is developmental, of the second system, the sense of self-cohesion.

Symptoms as a Point of Reference

A point of reference is essential in classification. To divide schizophrenia into subtypes, Bleuler used the manifest symptoms. The choice of this point of reference was natural for Bleuler, whose primary interest was to arrive at an immediate diagnosis. In terms of the clinical picture, Bleuler (1911) conceived that the schizophrenias "are most easily arranged in four main categories"—namely, the paranoid, the catatonic, the hebephrenic, and the simple. He recognized that this approach had flaws, for "a case which begins as a hebephrenic may be a paranoid several years later" (p. 227). But he also knew that his approach served his main purpose of arriving at a diagnosis.

Over the years, Bleuler's classification was endorsed and then modified. The American Psychiatric Association (1968) lists Bleuler's basic subtypes, and also the latent, the schizoaffective, the childhood, the acute, and the chronic undifferentiated, and other types. Although the list of subtypes has been greatly lengthened in *DMS-II,* it must be noted that this manual has retained the use of symptoms as the point of reference.

At the turn of the century, Bleuler's major preoccupation was not the treatment of schizophrenics, but the identification and classification of schizophrenia. For this purpose, his four subtypes seemed both adequate and appropriate. However, when choice of treatment method is considered, Bleuler's classification (or the modification of it) is deficient. If we inform a colleague that a certain patient belongs to the simple, hebephrenic, or schizoaffective type, we have actually said little about the choice of treatment for this patient. We are therefore compelled to consider factors other than manifest symptoms as a point of reference.

Developmental Review as a Point of Reference

In 1970, the staff at Chestnut Lodge began an ongoing review of all patients who were discharged from that hospital. The review paid particular attention to: (1) the symptoms that led to their admission to other hospitals and finally to Chest-

nut Lodge; (2) the course of illness during previous hospitalizations as well as at Chestnut Lodge, to determine the ways
in which patients did or did not respond to the treatment
program; (3) the transference manifestations, as summarized
by each Chestnut Lodge therapist in his running notes; (4) a
longitudinal study of each patient's past to determine his or
her pathological deviation from the normal maturational-developmental sequence; (5) an assessment of the family dynamics throughout the patient's life, including the current
status (e.g., whether the patient is entrapped by the family
pathology or is allowed to grow away from the family). A new
classification of schizophrenia has evolved out of this review,
using the patient's development as the point of reference. According to this new classification, the illness is categorized
into schizophrenia I, II, III, and IV.[1]

Schizophrenia I

While there may have been identifiable cumulative traumata in the patient's earliest years, the personality of the
mothering person does not usually show marked pathology of
a schizoid nature. The patient's history reveals near-adequate
development and functioning, including satisfactory subli-
matory activities, until the late teens. Faced with the final
steps of the second separation-individuation process, the patient develops acute symptoms. Once the patient is sick, his
symptoms tend to be floridly psychotic. In addition to bodily
and hypochondriacal preoccupations, delusions, hallucinations, looseness of association, fragmentation of thought processes, and loss of contact with reality, the patient may even
lose sphincter control and smear urine and feces. On the surface, the florid symptoms seem to be indicators of a poor prognosis. On closer scrutiny, however, they reflect the patient's
lack of need to hide his distress from the mothering person.
From very early in life, the schizophrenic patient tends to
hide his needs and distress from his mothering person lest

---

[1] See Fort's preliminary report (1973).

the expression of difficulties demolish her. Thus the schizo-phrenic-I patient's lesser need to hide distress portends a bet-ter prognosis. As a rule, even during his most disturbed moments, there is clear evidence that the schizophrenic-I pa-tient knows what is going on around him. If the therapeutic environment is "favorable," he responds readily. Usually within a period of months, symptoms recede and a "social" recovery follows, that is, the patient's conflicts are sealed over but not necessarily resolved. Whatever his ego deficiencies may be, they are not compensated for. Should the patient henceforth be left alone (that is, untreated), he may remain vulnerable to a recurrence. In other words, he may be leading a seemingly "normal" life, but a relapse into illness is likely to occur.

For example, Mark, a bright young man, began to have recurrent bronchitis at 17 when he learned that he had enough credits to enter college a year before his scheduled high-school graduation. He chose, however, to remain in prep school in order to be with his school friends. The next year, shortly after graduation, he became acutely perplexed, frightened, and confused. He hallucinated with many ideas of reference and paranoid ideation. A week later, he was admitted to a hospital where he made a "miraculous recovery" in less than a month. Two months later he was discharged from the hos-pital. He immediately enrolled at the college where he had originally been accepted, and for the next three years did well. Just at the time everyone close to him was jubilant about how well he was doing, he fell ill again in his senior year when he was about to become engaged to be married. He was hospi-talized again, but this time for a prolonged period.

The schizophrenic-I patient's major problem lies toward the conflict side of the conflict-deficiency continuum, and he has the potential for developing a satisfactory therapeutic re-lationship. The treatment mode of choice is therefore modified psychoanalytic psychotherapy.[2] In treatment, the patient may

[2] His cognitive development is usually at a level that makes him amenable to modified psychoanalytic psychotherapy.

actually resolve his conflict and make up his ego deficiencies. His parents are usually so alarmed by the suddenness and floridity of the patient's symptoms that they are willing to do anything to get him into treatment. But when he has recovered "socially," the parents may want to treat the illness like a bout of pneumonia, to be forgotten altogether. If this parental attitude is not corrected, it can reinforce the patient's need for denial, leading him to avoid the necessary treatment. Since the parents themselves are not severely handicapped emotionally, however, they can usually be educated about the seriousness of their child's illness. They will often lend their sincere support to the treatment program so as to avert an irreversible relapse at a later date.

Schizophrenia II

Generally, the patient has had a more disturbed infancy and childhood than the schizophrenic-I patient. Despite early difficulties, the patient had a relatively uneventful latency. There is, however, a definite lag in each phase of development. Then, in the middle of adolescence, in the process of loosening the ties with the primary object, old conflicts arise again. At such times, symptoms appear. The gradual nature of the onset of the symptoms may indicate that the patient has made a sincere, strenuous effort to overcome his conflicts. Such efforts are usually ineffectual. Once such a patient becomes psychotic, the chances of his emerging from the illness are reduced. When and if the psychotic symptoms are interrupted by the use of drugs (as is usually the case), the patient may function adequately in a protected environment, but, by and large, he appears to be indifferent to the future. He seems to settle into a regressive mode of existence, as if the illness had taken something vital out of him. Psychoanalytically oriented intensive psychotherapy can be useful in improving his outlook and should be recommended.

The parents of schizophrenic-II patients are often extremely troubled persons themselves. As much as they react to the patient's overt symptoms with acute distress, and perhaps wish to do everything possible for his recovery, they do not seem able to lend much support to his treatment program. Unless intensive family work is attempted, it is not unusual to witness a parental effort to sabotage the treatment. More often than not, the parents tend to include the patient in their own struggles with each other. This tendency may become even more evident once the patient is psychotic. Frequently, the prognosis is determined solely by whether or not the patient can be extricated from the parents' hold.

For example, Philip's father, while engaged to his mother, felt "he had been had" and wanted to break the engagement, but was pressed into the marriage by his future mother-in-law. In the marriage, the father contributed little. The mother, who developed ulcerative colitis, was pleased to have a son and developed a close tie to him. When Philip became increasingly psychotic at the age of 16 and was finally hospitalized at 17, his mother became distressed and constantly worried about him. Her periodic phone calls to him caused his hospital stay to be stormy. After a great deal of preparatory work with the mother, she finally agreed to seek psychiatric help for herself. Some months later, as she settled into her own treatment, she was better able to leave her son alone. Without her agitation, the patient gradually calmed down without the use of antipsychotic drugs, was able to leave the hospital, and could work out his problems in continued treatment.

Schizophrenia III

The patient has had a very disturbed infancy and childhood. (Such information is usually obtained not from the parents, but from such sources as medical reports). He shows distinctly defective ego functioning, noticeable from the early developmental phases on (as indicated by school records, etc.). Although he may flourish during latency, he is swept off his feet at the slightest drive intensification. The onset of symptoms at the dawn of puberty tends to be insidious, taking the form of flattened affect, silly laughter, autistic thinking, preoccupation with incest, with religion, and with life and death. The prognosis for this type of patient is grave. In treatment, work with his conflicts must not be emphasized. His ego deviation and ego arrest may not allow him to undertake intensive psychotherapy immediately. Although antipsychotic drugs may ameliorate or even correct the patient's overt psychotic manifestations, psychotherapeutic intervention may be necessary to modify his delusional conceptualization of his self.

The family members of a schizophrenic-III patient are usually quite disturbed. The general description of a schizophrenogenic mother or a schizophrenogenic family may be applicable here. Long before the patient was overtly sick, the family dynamics may have been organized in such a way that the mother (occasionally the father) has formed an unbreakable tie with the patient. Early in life, the patient learned that establishing emotional separateness from his mother could mean her emotional demise, and he would choose to remain sick rather than recover and thereby "kill off" his mother.

Schizophrenia IV

The patient may have begun as a schizophrenic-I, -II, or -III.[3] After repeated hospitalizations and/or prolonged periods of confinement in an institution, however, he can no longer be designated as still belonging to the subgroup to which he was originally assigned. Being sick for many years seems to have robbed him of hope. He is now in utter despair, and resigned to sickness as a way of life. Yet the prognosis for a schizophrenic-IV patient is not generally poor. An originally schizophrenic-I or -II patient may, in favorable therapeutic

[3] Then why not leave out schizophrenia IV altogether? The fact is that chronicity does make a difference for prognosis and treatment plan. Moreover, if schizophrenia IV were left out, schizophrenia I, II, and III would each have to be subdivided into new and chronic categories.

circumstances, be able to resume normal living outside the hospital.

As an example, Helen, who had been making a generally satisfactory adjustment, was depressed and withdrawn on graduation from high school, and for the next five years made a marginal adjustment. By then, she was noticeably withdrawn, with flattened emotionality and delusional ideas. For the next five years she was hospitalized successively in four different hospitals, made many attempts at psychotherapy, and underwent many courses of electric and insulin therapy without obvious improvement. An oncoming "rapid deterioration" was predicted for her, at which time she was transferred to Chestnut Lodge. There, with the help of lengthy intensive psychotherapy, she recovered from her illness. Ten years after her admission, she was able to leave the hospital, finish college, and become gainfully employed. (In this case, psychotropic drugs were not used.)

In this proposed new classification of schizophrenia into I, II, III, and IV, the point of reference is a review of the patient's development. It is different from Bleuler's classification (or the American Psychiatric Association's [1968] *DMS-II*), in which manifest symptoms are the point of reference. Because the new classification takes into consideration the dynamic, economic, structural, and adaptive viewpoints as well as the developmental, it has many advantages over the American Psychiatric Association's (1968) *DMS-II* classification. First, when schizophrenics are classified as simple, catatonic, hebephrenic, etc., we are often unable to place the patient in one category or another because of mixed symptoms. This is especially true when the patient is undergoing intensive psychotherapy. In the course of treatment, we often see the patient's symptoms change from hebephrenic to paranoid to catatonic, etc. Second, the new classification pinpoints such information as the severity of the illness, the factors that influence prognosis, the rationale for a particular treatment plan for a given patient, and the nature of work to be done with the patient's family, thus reducing confusion.

With the standard classification, when informed that a certain patient is hebephrenic or paranoid, we simply cannot be certain whether he is hopelessly ill or stands a chance of recovery. Similarly, when a colleague tells us that he is treating a schizophrenic patient with classical analysis, we feel at a loss, wondering why we, unlike our colleague, must introduce parameters. With the new classification such doubts can be dispelled, for we know that classical analysis can be attempted with many schizophrenic-I patients and perhaps a handful of schizophrenic-II and -IV patients, but that it is not the appropriate therapy for a schizophrenic-III patient.

According to the new classification of schizophrenia into I, II, III, and IV, symptoms appear either in early, middle, or late adolescence. On the surface, this emphasis seems to contradict the clinical observation that schizophrenic illness can begin at any age. As a matter of fact, Bleuler's most basic objection to the term dementia praecox was that the disease did not always result in dementia, nor was it always *praecox* (1903). On careful scrutiny, however, we find that in most cases where symptoms are reported as appearing at a later age, the patient had, in fact, experienced a brief psychosis during adolescence. These patients had "reintegrated" rapidly, only to break down again at a later date.

The case of Helen is an example. Although she had had a series of disabling symptoms since her graduation from high school, Helen was diagnosed as psychoneurotic for three or four years, until she was too withdrawn and too difficult to be understood. Another example is Florette. She was the only person in the family who did not display any grief following the death of her father (when she was 14 years old). Yet she locked herself in her room and staged peculiar dances that she called "sun dances." Shortly after these episodes she was declared to be "normal," despite the fact that she was increasingly isolated and withdrawn and had lost all of her previous girl friends. Because she was able to finish college at a marginal level, she was not diagnosed as a schizophrenic until she was 22. At that time, she was striking out at her brother-in-law or any other man who happened to be standing near her, claiming that men were transmitting vile thoughts to her. In addition, other behavior patterns suggested that she was having hallucinatory experiences. For instance, she grimaced frequently, often ordering invisible persons to be quiet.

John, another patient, was in his 30's when he was first diagnosed as schizophrenic. Following an encounter with a go-go girl at a bar, he became confused, communicated with God, and was admitted to a hospital in a catatonic state. But almost 20 years earlier he had dropped out of the second year of college after panicking on a suspension bridge. From then on he had led an isolated life and worked at a job far below his educational level.

Still another example is Peggy. She was not diagnosed as schizophrenic until she was in her 30's, when letters she wrote to the President of the United States and to senators aroused suspicion that she was a security risk. Yet 20 years earlier, following her society debut during her first year of college, she was (supposedly) mysteriously ill for a few months. On what was called a "full" recovery from this mysterious debility, she had not been able to continue college and for many years lived as a drifter. Because of her family's wealth and because her general behavior fitted in with the family life style, she was never thought of as sick.

The list of examples could be lengthened. Suffice it to say that the diagnosis of schizophrenia I, II, or III should have been made much earlier in these patients' lives. Their escape from a diagnosis of schizophrenia seems to have been determined simply by the fact that after a brief appearance of what Bleuler termed fundamental or accessory symptoms, they made a "spontaneous recovery" and were not hospitalized. In my view, a diagnosis of schizophrenia may be affixed when and if, following an upset of psychic equilibrium accompanied by panic and the formation of bizarre symptoms of varying duration, there is a *drastic* reorganization of the self accompanied by emotional withdrawal, social isolation, and a regressed level of ego functioning. On the basis of this view, in most instances schizophrenic illness actually begins during adolescence.[4]

At this point it is worth noting the correlation between the classification of schizophrenia into I, II, III, and IV and the "special atmosphere" I described in Chapter 1. In the interpersonal setting, a schizophrenic patient often gives the impression that he is both there and not there. This unique, defensive way of relating to others, this peculiar aura, is characteristic of all schizophrenic patients. As I mentioned in Chapter 1, some schizophrenic patients create denser special atmospheres than others. The degree of density of the special atmosphere is directly correlated with the severity of the patient's illness. Consequently, classification of a patient as belonging in subgroup I, II, III, or IV is aided by an awareness of the density of the atmosphere he creates. For instance, we can easily detect a denser atmosphere during an interview with a schizophrenic-III patient than with a schizophrenic-I patient, and the atmosphere created by the former is invariably more difficult to break through than the atmosphere created by the latter. But as much as we may use density as an aid in determining the severity of the patient's illness and as a guide for classification, we must not rely solely on such subjective experiences. The necessity to objectify this experience has been discussed in Chapter 1.

Passage of Time as a Point of Reference

I have suggested that the new classification of schizophrenics as belonging to subgroup I, II, III, or IV not only conveys immediate wide-ranging knowledge about the pa-

[4] Childhood schizophrenia is not included in the proposed new subgrouping of schizophrenia. Since my own experience has been limited to working with adult schizophrenic patients, I cannot be certain of the connection between childhood and adult schizophrenia. Research in that area has only recently been initiated at Chestnut Lodge through the opening of the Adolescent and Child Service in October, 1975. As of now, I would classify patients who became manifestly psychotic during childhood and who came to Chestnut Lodge for treatment as adults under the heading of schizophrenia IV.

tient's developmental profile, personality structure, adaptive capacity, and family dynamics, but also offers a tentative plan for therapy and a fairly reliable prediction of the course of his illness.

An obvious question is, when does a schizophrenic-I, -II, or -III patient become a schizophrenic-IV patient? For example, let us look at the case of Helen (see above). If we had seen Helen a few months after she had graduated from high school, we would probably have diagnosed her as a schizophrenic-I. But we first saw her 10 years after her graduation (i.e., after five years of continuous hospitalization), at which time we unequivocally diagnosed her as a schizophrenic-IV. Now, what determines the change of diagnosis from schizophrenic-I to schizophrenic-IV? Is the change determined simply by the passage of time? Or do some other factors enter into consideration?

In practice, the passage of time is actually used as a diagnostic criterion. When our colleagues refer to a certain schizophrenic patient as an acute or a chronic case, they are essentially using the passage of time as the criterion for the distinction between acute and chronic. The American Psychiatric Association (1952, 1968) recommends distinguishing between the acute and the chronic undifferentiated types. But it also advocates using the passage of time as a criterion. As much as the passage of time is popularly used, the problem inherent in the choice of this criterion is that there has been no agreement about what length of time is required to make the distinction between acute and chronic. The matter is further complicated by the fact that the passage of time implies a beginning. The beginning of a schizophrenic illness is usually assigned to the outbreak of symptoms. Often, however, there is no agreement about the onset of the illness. The following vignette from Bleuler (1911) illustrates the second point:

> . . . throughout her entire school career a young girl exhibited only average scholarship with the exception of brilliant work in music. Suddenly, immediately after the onset of puberty, she

developed a passionate interest in her studies, an energy and drive which was totally unknown to her before, until an abruptly starting catatonic delirium ushered in the subsequent deterioration. Yet, it is impossible to say whether the personality changes had already belonged to the disease picture itself or not [p. 251].[5]

Thus we must recognize that to explain acuteness or chronicity only in terms of the passage of time is not a satisfactory procedure.

Levels of Regression as a Point of Reference

Arieti (1974) suggests that by studying the patient's behavior in terms of regression, the course of schizophrenia can be divided into four substages: (1) the initial stage where the patient is not yet severely regressed; (2) the advanced stage where the patient is "more completely regressed to a lower level"; (3) the preterminal stage where further regression leads to impoverishment of volitional life and the ascendance of certain primitive habits, like hoarding and self-decoration; (4) the terminal stage where neurological and psychological distinctions become blurred and there is impairment of the most primitive capacities (e.g., insensitivity to pain or temperature). Although the unfolding of the four substages is intimately related to the passage of time, Arieti emphasizes the study of the patient's behavior in terms of regression. With this shift of emphasis, Arieti illustrates with great clarity what may happen to a schizophrenic patient who is left untreated. His concept of "self-perpetuating regression" also serves as an important reminder that the proper treatment must be given to the patient in the early phases of the illness.

Returning to Helen as an example, she would probably be assigned to Arieti's initial substage at the appearance of her

---

[5] From my own point of view, this so-called personality change is a part of the illness.

symptoms following her graduation, and she might be assigned to the advanced substage 10 years afterward. All is well so far. Now, suppose that in the fifth hospital (as was the case) modified psychoanalytic psychotherapy was recommended for her, and, six months later, the therapist was asked, "How is Helen?" How should the therapist answer the question? Obviously it would be meaningless for him to think of the answer in terms of any of the classifying descriptions (e.g., schizophrenic-I, -II, -III, or -IV; acute or chronic; one of Arieti's four substages). Yet, in such a situation, the therapist somehow knows how to answer the question intuitively. For instance, he will say: The patient is still living in terror to a great degree; she is beginning to have good days now; she was better, but her condition was worsened because . . . ; she is much better now, but is still easily upset; her condition is stabilized now; she is in a rut; and so on. In these answers the therapist is using a definite point of reference even though it is of a preverbal nature and has not been explicitly articulated. That specific point of reference is related to a concept that can be referred to as the reorganization of the self.

Reorganization of the Self as a Point of Reference

At this juncture, it is helpful to make a phenomenological study of the course of the illness. Generally speaking, when the schizophrenic patient can no longer contain his conflicts, he begins to live in terror. What is experienced by average people as anxiety is experienced by the schizophrenic as panic. Now the symptoms break out. If he is instantly placed in a good-enough holding environment, his terror will gradually lessen or become intermittent. If he stays in that setting, the terror will one day disappear altogether. In the meantime, as the terror ebbs, the patient may reveal fewer psychotic symptoms (such as hallucinations), but more gross personality changes (for instance, increasing apathy, little effort to relate to others). Along with the observable personality changes there will be a definitely altered view (if this can in any way be determined) of himself and of the people he knows well. It is these alterations that make others think of him as "no longer himself." He is no longer the same person he was before the breaking out of panic or symptoms. If, at this stage, he is engaged in psychoanalytically oriented intensive psycho-therapy, he will repeatedly re-experience the terror—though each time to a lesser degree. In connection with this recurring but attenuated terror, he may gradually modify his views about himself and others. Simultaneously, his symptoms will abate; he will become less apathetic or more related to others. Of course, whether or not he improves in treatment has a lot to do with his being a schizophrenic-I patient or a schizo-phrenic-III patient to begin with. Yet if psychotherapy is put off too long, even a schizophrenic-I patient may not respond at all, even to the efforts of an extremely competent therapist.

This observation suggests that (1) a drastic change of per-sonality has occurred during the rise and fall of the terror phase, and (2) the altered views of self and others may no longer be modifiable after a long period of time.

How can these observations be explained in metapsychol-ogical terms? That terror is associated with a loss of ego, ego fragmentation, ego disintegration, has been stressed repeat-edly in the literature. Although ego reintegration is consid-ered, its relation to terror has not been carefully studied. With the concepts of ego, self, and sense of self-cohesion more clearly defined by Hartmann (1950a, 1953), Jacobson (1954c, 1964), and Kohut (1971), we may now speak of a loss or fragmen-tation of the sense of self-cohesion (in place of loss or frag-mentation of the ego) and a re-establishment of a sense of self-cohesion or reorganization of the self (in place of ego rein-tegration). In Chapter 14, I shall have more to say about the re-establishment of a sense of self-continuity or -cohesion. Here it is enough to say that man uses his self as the most reliable reference in the changing world. If he loses his sense of self-cohesion, he will strive to re-establish it even though, in the process, he organizes a "false self" (Winnicott, 1960b) or a regressed self.

Observation bears out that terror is associated with a loss of self-cohesion, and it is generally theorized that the terror is generated by a preconscious awareness that self-cohesion is threatened. Such an awareness may contribute to the terror, but it is not the moving force behind it. Rather, the process operates the other way around; that is, terror generates a loss of self-cohesion. Observation has also borne out that terror reigns as long as a sense of self-cohesion is absent or poorly re-established, and subsides when self-cohesion is re-established. The most extreme form of this process is seen in the acute paranoid formation. After a period of intense terror, the patient suddenly "understands everything." With this understanding, a sense of self-cohesion is re-established in which the paranoid ideation is crystallized and most of the patient's terror is dispelled (though the paranoid fear of persecution still reflects an attenuated degree of terror). Consequently the patient can be much more at ease with himself and his object world.

This observation not only underlines the importance of a sense of self-cohesion for being oriented in the ever-changing world, but also offers the possibility of distinguishing three phases in the course of schizophrenia: acute, subacute, and chronic.

The *acute* phase refers to a period of varying duration, which begins with the eruption of conflicts, the onset of symptoms, and the loss of the sense of self-cohesion. It ends when a sense of self-cohesion is tentatively re-established (whereupon a new self is being organized). During this phase terror reigns, and the ego functions at an extremely regressed level.

The *subacute* phase refers to a period of varying duration during which the patient begins to re-establish a sense of self-cohesion. Terror is now on the wane (as long as the conflicts are not resolved, it does not disappear altogether—it is only attenuated), and the ego functions more stably at a less regressed level. Being tentative, the sense of self-cohesion is easily disrupted, and disruption may be followed by terror. During this precarious state of affairs the patient begins to reinforce certain views about himself (the result will be the organization of a new self) and about other people that are very different from his views before his illness.

The *chronic* phase begins when the subacute phase ends. While during the subacute phase the altered views about self (hence the new self) and others are still subject to modification, after a certain length of time—different for different patients—the altered viewpoints, reinforced through repetition, become increasingly unmodifiable or fixated. The illness may then be considered chronic.

According to this schema, the subacute and the chronic may be further divided into subphases. Thus Helen would be considered to be in the late subacute phase when she was admitted to the fifth hospital. Under the therapeutic program devised for her there, she lived through a long, tortuous, fluctuating course of many years' duration until she finally "recovered": Her distorted views about herself and others were sufficiently modified to enable her to get along with herself and others.

One additional value of the subdivision of schizophrenia into acute, subacute, and chronic phases is that it informs us about what to do for a given patient. For instance, during the acute phase, treatment should consist of creating a situation in which terror may be minimized so as to enable the patient to re-establish a sense of self-cohesion. For a patient in the subacute phase, treatment must aim at modifying his view about himself and others without subjecting him to more than moderate terror. In order to head off the "self-perpetuating regression," intensive psychotherapy is almost a must. For a patient in the chronic phase, the aim of treatment is not primarily or immediately to modify his pathological views about himself, but to help him learn to adjust, that is, to modify his views about others. As a result, he must also make some alterations in his view of himself. In general, the extent of that modification is limited.

It must be stressed that the classification of schizophrenia into I, II, III, and IV on the one hand and the classification into acute, subacute, and chronic phases on the other use entirely different points of reference. A schizophrenic-I, -II, -III, or -IV patient can therefore be classified as in an acute, subacute, or chronic phase. For instance, Helen was a schizophrenic-IV patient in the late subacute phase when she began intensive psychotherapy. In the course of treatment she became acutely disorganized, and for a while fell briefly into the acute phase.

In this chapter, I have proposed two systems of classification, using a developmental review and self-cohesion as points of reference. In subsequent chapters, I hope to show the usefulness of these systems for clinical practice as well as for the formulation of a theory of schizophrenia.

PART II

Early Psychoanalytic Theory of Schizophrenia

CHAPTER 3

Freud's Theory of Schizophrenia

When the honor of the Goethe Prize was bestowed on him, Freud said, "My life's work has been directed to a single aim. I have observed the more subtle disturbances of mental function in healthy and sick people and have sought to infer—or, if you prefer it, to guess—from signs of this kind how the apparatus which serves these functions is constructed and what concurrent and mutually opposing forces are at work in it" (1930, p. 208). In keeping with this aim, Freud had steadfastly sought to understand and interpret various manifestations of schizophrenic illness.

Broadly speaking, in his attempt to understand schizophrenia, Freud consistently applied a point of view that had proved to be illuminating in the study of neurosis. His theory of schizophrenia can be divided into three phases:

Phase One (1890's). During this phase, Freud observed that both neurosis and psychosis were defenses[1] against the return of the repressed, and that the difference between them

---

This chapter is based on a paper entitled "Notes on Freud's Theory of Schizophrenia," published in the *International Journal of Psycho-Analysis,* 54:469-476, 1973.

[1] Rapaport (1959) has pointed out that this early concept of defense differs from the present one. Although both imply that a quantitative factor is dammed up and displaced, in the early defense concept this quantity was "affect" associated with the disowned memory, not "drive cathexis" (p. 6).

lay in the different defensive devices that are adopted. While the hysteric adopts conversion and the obsessional uses substitute thought where he would otherwise experience an unpleasant thought or feeling, the paranoid person uses projection (1894, 1895, 1896a, 1896b).

Phase Two (1897-1922). At the turn of the century, Freud was formulating the libido theory. Although he mentioned fragments of his ideas in letters[2] to Fliess, Abraham, Jung, and Ferenczi, he did not formally apply libido theory to schizophrenia until 1911, when he published "Psycho-Analytic Notes on an Autobiographical Account of a Case of Paranoia (Dementia Paranoides)."[3] He elaborated further on this theory of paranoia or schizophrenia in a series of subsequent works (1914b, 1915b, 1915c, 1916-1917, 1922).

It is worth noting that what Freud perceived as "more essential" was "that paranoia should be maintained as an independent clinical type,[4] however frequently the picture it offers may be complicated by the presence of schizophrenic features" (1911, p. 76). Yet he considered that, with only slight modifications, one theory could be used to explain the clinical phenomena of both paranoia and schizophrenia.

The theory Freud put forward in the second phase can be summarized as follows: (1) Libidinal development proceeds from autoerotism to narcissism and finally to object love. In the progression, certain portions of libido may lag behind, resulting in fixation points. He postulated that in paranoia the fixation point is at the narcissistic stage, and in schizo-

[2] Freud told Fliess in 1899 that paranoia represents a return to "autoerotism"; he wrote and discussed with Abraham on July 26, 1907, and on December 18, 1910, the concepts of libidinal withdrawal, megalomania, and fixation at the "autoerotic" level; and he informed Jung on January 27, 1908, and Ferenczi on February 11, 1908, that there is a connection between paranoia and passive homosexuality (Strachey, 1958).

[3] It is clear that the "the case of Schreber" was not the sole source of raw data on which Freud built his theory of paranoia; he said, "I had developed my theory of paranoia before I became acquainted with the contents of Schreber's book" (1911, p. 79).

[4] Although Freud spoke of paranoia and schizophrenia together, he continually thought of them as separate clinical entities (see Freud, 1914b, 1915, 1916-1917, 1922).

phrenia it is at the autoerotic stage.[5] (2) In paranoia, the conflicts involve homosexual wishful fantasy. In schizophrenia, the conflicts are not necessarily homosexual, but their actual nature is undefined. (3) In the face of conflicted object relations, a paranoid or a schizophrenic patient withdraws his libidinal attachment from the people in his environment and from the external world and invests it in the "ego." Similar withdrawal occurs in neurotics as well, but the libido, after its withdrawal, remains invested in the object in fantasy. In neurosis, after the failure of repression, an attempt at re-repression will ensue, which, as a result of the nature of the "defenses," brings about specific neurotic symptom formation.[6] A parallel process is observable in schizophrenia: The detachment of the libido is perceived as equivalent to repression proper; it is accompanied by a process of reconstruction or an attempt at recovery, which undoes the work of repression and reinvests the libido in the people from whom it had been withdrawn. In paranoia, the reconstruction is accomplished through the mechanism of projection; the patient now experiences the object as one who hates him, and himself as being persecuted and attacked by the object. In schizophrenia, hallucinatory mechanisms are attempts at recovery. While the detachment is a silent process that can only be inferred from subsequent events, the process of recovery, accompanied by delusion and hallucination, is what forces itself so blatantly on others' attention (1911, p. 69). (4) At this stage the clinical phenomenon of an end-of-the-world experience is seen as "the projection of this internal catastrophe" (191, p. 70), which is, however, conceptualized as an accompaniment of withdrawal of libido. (5) The aggrandizement of self or megalomania is conceived as the withdrawn libido being heavily invested in the "ego." (6) Because of the nature of the libidinal withdrawal, the paranoid or schizophrenic patient cannot establish a transference; therefore, he cannot be treated by psy-

[5] As early as 1899, Freud wrote in a letter to Fliess that paranoia was a return to autoerotism. Obviously the definition of autoerotism is now slightly modified.

[6] That is essentially the theory of the first phase.

choanalysis. Nevertheless, transference phenomena may be observed after libidinal recathexis, or if the decathexis was not a complete one.

In "On Narcissism: An Introduction" (1914b), Freud introduced two new ideas. (1) With respect to hypochondriasis, he said, "Megalomania would accordingly correspond to the psychical mastering of this latter amount of libido, and would thus be the counterpart of the introversion on to phantasies that is found in the transference neuroses; a failure of this psychical function gives rise to the hypochondria of paraphrenia and this is homologous to the anxiety of the transference neuroses" (p. 86). (2) Regarding the delusion of being watched and the "voices," he supposed that both were related to a process in which "the evolution of conscience is reproduced regressively" (p. 96).

Freud dealt with thought disorders in schizophrenia in two later papers, "The Unconscious" (1915a) and "A Metapsychological Supplement to the Theory of Dreams" (1915b). In these papers, he distinguished between "thing-presentation" and "word-presentation" of an object and suggested that in schizophrenia *words* and not things are subjected to the primary process. That is, words (not things) are condensed and substituted, resulting in the characteristic disorder of schizophrenic thought process. He explained that in schizophrenia, after object cathexis is withdrawn, both the thing presentation and word presentation of the object are decathected. But in the attempt at recovery, the schizophrenic sets "off on a path that leads to the object *via* the verbal part of it, but [is] then . . . obliged to be content with words instead of things" (1915a, p. 204).[7] Characteristic of schizophrenia is that free communication between preconscious (word cathexis) and unconscious (thing cathexis) is cut off (1915b, p. 229).

[7] Elsewhere, Freud gives the impression that libidinal cathexis is withdrawn from external objects and things. This led to Jung's criticism that libidinal decathexis " 'would result in the psychology of an ascetic anchorite, not in a dementia praecox' " (Freud, 1914b, p. 80). Here Freud makes clear that decathexis involves the *representations* of persons and things in the mind of the patient.

In 1920 Freud formulated his theory of aggression, but did not apply it to schizophrenia until 1925. In "Negation," he said: "The general wish to negate, the negativism which is displayed by some psychotics, is probably to be regarded as a sign of a defusion of instincts that has taken place through a withdrawal of the libidinal components" (1925, p. 239).

Phase Three (1923-1939). This phase is arbitrarily considered as beginning with the publication of "The Ego and the Id" (1923). During this phase Freud wrote two papers (1924a, 1924b) primarily on schizophrenia. In the meantime, in applying his structural model to neurosis, he made many pithy remarks about schizophrenia to illustrate the structural differences between it and neurosis (1925, 1926a, 1926b, 1927a, 1937a, 1938a, 1938b, 1939).

In "Neurosis and Psychosis" (1924a) he described how when the ego is in conflict with the id, superego, and reality, "The pathogenic effect depends on whether ... the ego remains true to its dependence on the external world and attempts to silence the id, or whether it lets itself be overcome by the id and thus torn away from reality" (p. 151). In the former case a neurosis results, in the latter, a psychosis. In the same paper he said, "Transference neuroses correspond to a conflict between the ego and the id; narcissistic neuroses,[8] to a conflict between the ego and the super-ego; and psychoses, to one between the ego and the external world" (p. 152).

In "The Loss of Reality in Neurosis and Psychosis" (1924b) he contrasted the two by saying, "in psychosis, the initial flight [from reality] is succeeded by an active phase of remodelling; in neurosis, the initial obedience [to the reality] is succeeded by a deferred attempt at flight"; and, "neurosis does not disavow the reality, it only ignores it; psychosis disavows it and tries to replace it" (p. 185). Here Freud introduced the concept that psychosis uses disavowal as a defense.

In "Fetishism" (1927a), Freud expressed dissatisfaction at

---

[8] Here, "narcissistic neuroses" refers to melancholia; earlier, Freud had also referred to schizophrenia as a narcissistic neurosis (see 1915a, 1915b, 1916-1917).

what he had postulated in the two earlier (1924a, 1924b) papers, and attempted to explain the difference between neurosis and psychosis in terms of the concept of splitting (i.e., the coexistence of two contradictory attitudes, one of which conforms to a wish and the other to reality. He indicated that splitting, like disavowal, could be another defense adopted by the schizophrenic ego. "The issue depends on their relative strength. [If the attitude that fits in with the wish] is or becomes the stronger, the necessary precondition for a psychosis is present. If the relation is reversed, then there is an apparent cure of the delusional disorder" (1938a, p. 202). But, when he reconsidered "splitting" (1938b), he conceived the mechanism as being less specific to the genesis of psychosis.

Freud discussed "alteration of the ego" broadly in terms of "the effect brought about in the ego by the defences" (1937a, p. 239). The application of this viewpoint to psychosis can only be inferred, even though long before the concept of ego in the structural sense was formed, Freud applied a similar view strictly to psychosis: "The delusional ideas which have arrived in consciousness by means of a compromise . . . make demands on the thought-activity of the ego until they can be accepted without contradiction. Since they are not themselves open to influence, the ego must adapt itself to them" (1896b, p. 185).

In 1939, Freud considered "a State within a State":

> All these phenomena, the symptoms as well as the restrictions on the ego and the stable character-changes, have a *compulsive* quality: that is to say that they have great psychical intensity and at the same time exhibit a far-reaching independence of the organization of the other mental processes, which are adjusted to the demands of the real external world and obey the laws of logical thinking. They [the pathological phenomena] are insufficiently or not at all influenced by external reality, pay no attention to it or to its psychical representatives, so that they may easily come into active opposition to both of them. They are, one might say, a State within a State, an inaccessible party, with which co-operation is impossible, but which may

succeed in overcoming what is known as the normal party and forcing it into its service. If this happens, it implies a domination by an internal psychical reality over the reality of the external world and the path to a psychosis lies open [p. 76].

He had described a similar concept in 1922 when he said, "classical persecutory ideas may be present without finding belief or acceptance . . . ; it may be that the delusions which we regard as new formations when the disease breaks out have already long been in existence" (p. 228).

In summary, Freud added many new theoretical constructs during phase three. He could have reformulated his theory of schizophrenia, but he did not.

Discussion

Freud's theory of schizophrenia is here conceived as a body of knowledge that Freud contributed to the understanding of the various aspects of the clinical phenomena designated as schizophrenia. As I have indicated, this body of knowledge accrued in three phases during a period of some 40 years. Freud's theory, as it stood at the end of his life, may be stated thus: (1) Conflict is spoken of in structural terms, that is, as the result of tension between ego and id, superego, or reality. (2) The ego assumes greater importance in the production of schizophrenic phenomena, but this knowledge is restricted to a descriptive level. If, in conflict, ego is overcome by id (in combination with superego) and thus torn from reality, libidinal detachment occurs. In its relation to reality, the schizophrenic ego tends to use certain defense mechanisms—denial and splitting. (3) An application of the new theory of aggression is attempted; for instance, negativism or other hostile destructive acts are explained in terms of a combined process of defusion of instinctual drives and withdrawal of libido (but the experience of world destruction has not been revised in accordance with the new theory of aggression). (4) Otherwise, most of the 1911 theory is retained—e.g., withdrawal of libido from object representations and its investment in the ego[9] in the face of conflict; fixation at the autoerotic level; return to primary-process functioning as a result of regression; megalomania and hypochondriasis as a result of hypercathexis; delusions and hallucinations as attempts at recovery; and incapacity for transference[10] because of regression to the autoerotic level.

Because Freud's theory of schizophrenia is mostly derived from his 1911 theory, I shall, in what follows, give consideration to that theory. Although Freud confided to Abraham (H. Abraham and E. Freud, 1965) that he rarely had contact with schizophrenics, he must have had the opportunity to observe that the patient begins with an increased degree of bodily preoccupation, followed by panic, from which results what may be described as experiences of "the end of the world." Thereupon the patient breaks with reality and slips into catatonia. When he finally emerges from catatonia, he exhibits such symptoms as hallucinations, delusions, disturbed patterns of thinking, inappropriate emotional responses, enhanced unrealistic self-evaluation, etc. Moreover, his personality has often undergone a profound change. From these observational data, Freud decided that the symptom formation can best be characterized as occurring in two phases: the first phase from the intensification of conflict to breaking with reality or crystallization of catatonia, and the second phase from catatonia to the partial return to reality. That the "break with reality" was chosen as the demarcation point for the two phases was to account for the patient's personality change after the break with reality. On the other hand, Freud recognized that, as is also the case in neurosis, the clinically

---

[9] Hartmann (1950b, 1953) later considered that the libido is invested in the self rather than in the ego. This consideration led to a completely different theoretical framework (see Chapter 5.).

[10] Kohut (1971) takes up the whole issue of transference—whether its definition must be restricted to the transferring of an object relation and so by definition excludes the projection onto the analyst of experiences from preobjectal developmental stages, or whether these significant early experiences do appear in the therapeutic relationship and the definition should be widened to include them.

eye-catching psychotic symptoms are manifestations of a secondary order—secondary to the underlying conflict. In psychosis, the primary conflict lies between the patient's need to detach libidinal cathexis from the representation of people and his need to maintain that cathexis. When the primary conflict is intensified, the need to detach object libido is also intensified. While the libidinal detachment serves to set the stage for symptom formation, the crystallization and perpetuation of symptoms depend on the continuous struggle[11] between a need to detach and an attempt to reattach the object libido.

In order to encompass the two sets of data—namely, the formation of symptoms in two stages and the continual conflict over libidinal detachment and reattachment to the object—Freud formulated his 1911 theory. This theory clearly demonstrates the working of the mind of a genius, for in a most parsimonious way, through the two words "decathexis" and "recathexis," the mechanism in symptom formation was lucidly depicted. Furthermore, Freud took into consideration the genesis of schizophrenia by determining the fixation point of libidinal development. He seemed certain that his 1911 theory offered the basic outline of an insightful theory, with only the details to be filled in. Thus, as late as in 1938, despite added knowledge about the workings of the human mind, he did not modify the basic schema of his theory.

Unfortunately, his theory was often misunderstood. Because Freud used the terms "decathexis" (also called "detachment of libido" or "withdrawal of libidinal cathexis") and "recathexis" (also called "attempt at recovery" or "attempt at restitution") at times to denote two successive stages and at other times to denote two opposing forces of a conflict, two sets of conceptions evolved. Those who had only a cursory

---

[11] Of neurosis, Freud (1915c) said, "We are too apt to think that the conflict underlying a neurosis is brought to an end when the symptom has been formed. In reality the struggle can go on in many ways after this. Fresh instinctual components arise on both sides, and these prolong it. The symptom itself becomes an object of this struggle; certain trends anxious to preserve it conflict with others which strive to remove it and re-establish the *status quo ante*" (pp. 271-272).

understanding of Freud's views tended to understand his 1911 theory (decathexis-recathexis) either as portraying symptom formation in two stages, or as characterizing the continuous interplay of conflictual forces, but rarely as both.

Those who understand the 1911 theory in terms of conflicts emphasize the following: (1) Clearly, Freud tried to explain schizophrenia in terms of regression and fixation, as he had explained neurosis. The difference between schizophrenia and neurosis lies in the depth of regression and the timing of the fixation point. (2) Freud (1924c) indicated that "neuroses and psychoses are not separated by a hard and fast line, any more than health and neurosis; and it was plausible to explain the mysterious psychotic phenomena by the discoveries achieved on the neuroses . . . a similar interplay of forces [in psychoses] as in the simple neuroses" (p. 204). (3) Freud had compared psychosis with dreaming and had called dreaming a mild form of psychosis.

Those who see the 1911 theory as delineating symptom formation in two stages tend to overlook the conflictual aspect.[12] According to them, conflict sets off the schizophrenic illness, but once established, schizophrenia simply proceeds from the decathexis phase to the recathexis phase without involving conflict. Some of the conceptual confusion was, however, initiated by Freud. To illustrate: (1) Although elsewhere in describing neurotic symptom formation Freud repeatedly pointed out the continuous struggle between the repressing force and the repressed striving, he neglected to give equal stress to the continuous struggle of the conflicting forces in the formation and perpetuation of the symptoms in schizophrenia.[13] Thus whenever he described "detachment of object libido" or "attempt at recovery" he gave the impression that the detachment of object libido is followed by the attempt at recovery, and that after the attempt at recovery everything becomes frozen; so it would seem that the symptoms do not

[12] Based on questions asked by those (e.g., psychiatric residents) with only a cursory knowledge of Freud's teaching.

[13] He did detail the conflict over homosexual strivings in paranoia.

result from the two processes continually opposing each other, but from the unfolding of each process. For instance, Freud described certain thought disorders as resulting from cathexis being brought back only to the word presentation and not to the thing presentation, whereas he probably meant to say that a continuing struggle between the opposing needs brings about a condition in which only the word presentation is cathected.

(2) Other symptoms, such as hallucinations and delusions, do indeed occur after the attempt at recovery, for through this attempt, conflicts with the object become heightened and only then do the symptoms result. The mechanisms involved in the precipitation of delusions,[14] hallucinations, etc., are complex; therefore a single attempt at recovery would not be sufficient to bring about these symptoms. Rather, it is the continuous attempt at *resolving* the *conflict* that does so. However, such a shorthand expression as an-attempt-at-recovery-brings-about-noisy-symptoms-of-delusion-and-hallucination does tend to lead readers away from thinking of two conflicting forces in a continuous struggle.

(3) Freud clearly indicated that frustration brings about the libidinal detachment, and then postulated that the detachment brings about the experience of catastrophe (or the experience of the end of the world), megalomania, and hypochondriasis. These formulae have the effect of leading people to think that with symptom formation, conflicts recede; in actuality the conflicts continue. Furthermore, the formula—megalomania or hypochondriasis resulting from hypercathexis—emphasizes economic factors at the expense of a more dynamic investigation of the conflicts involved.

Freud's 1911 theory is an incomplete one. It encompasses the genetic, economic, and dynamic points of view, but it fails to clarify the structural viewpoint. In 1911, hamstrung by a lack of knowledge about the structural concept, he could do no more than say:

[14] See Lichtenberg and Pao (1974). See also Freud's description in the Schreber case (1911).

We can no more dismiss the possibility that disturbances of the libido may react upon the ego-cathexes than we can overlook the converse possibility—namely, that a secondary or induced disturbance of the libidinal processes may result from abnormal changes in the ego. Indeed, it is probable that processes of this kind constitute the distinctive characteristic of psychoses [1911, p. 75].

Subsequently, as Freud focused his attention on the ego, he began to have many additional insights about the functioning of the human mind. He formulated the structural theory, the theory of anxiety and its relation to defenses, the concept of a hierarchy of danger situations, the concept of narcissism, and many others. In the meantime, in his theoretical conceptualization of schizophrenia, he stressed that the ego disturbance plays a determining role in symptom formation. Thus he said: "One would like to know in what circumstances and by what means the ego can succeed in emerging from such conflicts, which are certainly always present, without falling ill" (1924a, p. 152). And he added, "Neurosis and psychosis are evidently intimately related, but they must nevertheless differ in some decisive respect. That might well be the side taken by the ego in a conflict of this kind. In both cases the id would retain its characteristic of blind inflexibility" (1926b, pp. 204-205). Nevertheless, in his attempts to conceptualize the ego disturbance in schizophrenia, he swung back and forth between describing disturbances in certain ego functions and making broad generalizations about the ego's relations to other psychic structures. Then, toward the end of his life, Freud took up the issue of an "alteration of ego" (1937a) and the "State within a State" (1939), which concepts could potentially offer an explanation of the decisive differences between ego functioning in psychosis and in normality and neurosis. Regrettably, a fuller application of these promising ideas to psychosis was not made. Most unfortunate for us is that Freud never attempted to integrate his old and new ideas into a more complete theory of schizophrenia.

As a result, his followers have evolved several points of view. Some uphold the decathexis-recathexis concept, but with their own emendations. Others adhere to the general concepts of psychoanalysis but propose major modifications. Still others attempt altogether different reinterpretations, including deviations from basic psychoanalytic concepts. In the next chapters, I shall take up some of the contributions made by these followers.

CHAPTER 4

Fenichel's Restatement of Freud's Theory of Schizophrenia

Fenichel's chapter on schizophrenia in his venerable book, *The Psychoanalytic Theory of Neurosis* (1945), occupies an important position—partly because it encompasses a thorough, up-to-date review of the literature on schizophrenia before 1943, but more significantly because it attempts to revamp the whole body of Freud's theoretical conceptualization of schizophrenia consistently from the structural point of view. In restating Freud's earlier and later views in one conceptual framework, Fenichel did provide cohesion to Freud's theory of schizophrenia. Limited by the psychoanalytic knowledge available to him at the time, however, Fenichel could not rectify the deficiencies inherent in Freud's theory. Like Freud, he still held on to the concept of across-the-board regression and did not consider the role that aggression might play in schizophrenia.

Fenichel's View of Schizophrenia

Fenichel supported Freud's view that "the nucleus of schizophrenia is the patient's break with reality" (p. 439). Stressing the similarity between psychosis and neurosis, he pointed out that the precipitating factors in both are essentially the same (they begin with a revival and intensification of infantile sexual impulses), and that the difference between the two lies essentially in the depth of regression. Stressing the dissimilarity, he said: "Decisive for the difference between psychosis and neurosis is the way in which the patient defends himself against this reawakening of his infantile instinctual conflicts" (p. 442). Essentially, the schizophrenic patient uses the break with reality as "a very archaic mechanism of defense. . . . A tendency to apply this archaic mechanism of defense may be the essence of what is called narcissistic fixation" (p. 442).[1] By narcissistic fixation, Fenichel meant a fixation at the level of primary narcissism. At this level of development the ego and the id are not yet differentiated.

Thus Fenichel built his interpretation of schizophrenia around the concept of narcissistic fixation and regression to that fixation. With regard to the origin of the fixation, Fenichel said that because of the diversity of schizophrenic phenomena, a comprehensive explanation is impossible. He suggested that the use of schizoid mechanisms on a psychogenic basis can be distinguished from real schizophrenic processes. In the former category are cases in which psychic traumata and impediments cause a narcissistic fixation; in the latter category are cases in which unknown organic factors are decisive. Perhaps what Fenichel intended to say was exactly what Freud meant by "complemental series." The way he said it, however, was awkward; it leads one to think in terms of one group of schizophrenias as psychogenically determined and another as organically determined.

In the regression to the narcissistic level, "The ego returns to its original undifferentiated state; that is, it dissolves entirely or partly into the id, which has no knowledge of objects and reality" (p. 439). That is to say, when there is a regression to the narcissistic level of fixation, there is libidinal withdrawal from the object world, a regressive breakdown of the ego, an undoing of differentiations acquired through mental

---

[1] Fenichel seems rather tentative about his concept of "archaic defense." A similar, but more sophisticated, idea has been advanced by Mahler (1968) in the concept of the "maintenance mechanism." See also Chapter 11, below.

development (i.e., primitivization). For Fenichel, such phrases as "the schizophrenic has regressed to narcissism," "the schizophrenic has lost his object," "the schizophrenic has parted with reality," "the schizophrenic's ego has broken down" are merely different ways to describe the same phenomenon.

According to Fenichel, regression as a defense differs from other types of defense mechanisms. For once regression is resorted to, the ego is passively dragged back to the fixation point. In the use of any other type of defense mechanism, on the other hand, the ego always plays an active part. Thus for Fenichel, on the reawakening of infantile instinctual conflicts, once the schizophrenic patient resorts to regression he has no recourse but to reach for the fixation point. When that happens, the patient's ego dissolves into the id and there is a break with reality.

Considering the break with reality as the nucleus of schizophrenia, Fenichel stated that in every patient the schizophrenic process begins with regressive symptoms, which are followed by restitutional symptoms in the later phase of the illness. In cases where the order of symptoms is reversed, such as in some paranoid cases of very insidious onset, Fenichel assumed that "a preceding period of renunciation of the objective world has escaped attention" (p. 441).

Freud spoke of libidinal recathexis following decathexis. Fenichel spoke of restitution following regression. Freud did not say why recathexis must follow decathexis. Fenichel, on the other hand, offered tentative explanations. At one time he spoke of "the tendencies to restore what was lost through the pathogenic narcissism" (p. 425), implying that a void must be filled. At another point he said, "the ego, after having broken with reality, endeavors to create a new reality that will be more suitable" (p. 426), implying the function of a wish fulfillment. But, after considering that hallucinations and delusions are often associated with unpleasurable feelings, he became equivocal in his commitment to the idea of wish fulfillment. At still another time he said: "It is probable that the mental systems . . . become sensitive to stimuli from within whenever the acceptance of further external stimuli is blocked . . . in schizophrenia, [blocking is caused by] the pathogenic withdrawal of the object cathexes" (p. 426). Here he came close to anticipating the findings of current sensory deprivation research.

In speaking of regression and restitution, Fenichel supported Freud's conceptualization of symptom formation as occurring in two phases (decathexis and recathexis). Because schizophrenic symptoms are formed in two stages, Fenichel conveniently grouped schizophrenic symptoms under two headings: regressive and restitutive. Under the heading of regressive symptoms, he listed almost all the symptoms that Freud classified as caused by libidinal decathexis; under the heading of restitutive symptoms, he listed hallucinations and delusions, which Freud classified as following libidinal recathexis.

While he used most of Freud's explanations for symptom formation, Fenichel supplemented them with some of his own. He believed, as did Freud, that the feeling of the end of the world stemmed from libidinal withdrawal. He also attributed megalomania or delusions of grandeur to hypercathexis of the ego. However, Fenichel added, "a regression to narcissism is also a regression to the primal narcissistic omnipotence which makes its reappearance in the form of megalomania" (p. 420). While he considered hypochondriasis as due to hypercathexis of body parts, he added that in regression, the body ego (i.e., the nucleus of the ego) is reexperienced. He also believed that the opposite of hypercathexis of the body part may occur: The lack of sensation results from the countercathexis against unpleasant feelings that arise from hypercathexis.

Fenichel explained other symptoms, such as peculiarities of schizophrenic thought, delusions, and hallucinations, in almost exactly the same way Freud did.

Following Freud, Fenichel spoke of regression in global terms. To elaborate his ideas about across-the-board regressions, Fenichel explained hebephrenia as a pure form of regression to an intrauterine or vegetative existence of pas-

sive receptivity, and the automatic obedience of catatonic patients as a regressive phenomenon corresponding to the
imitative fascination of the infant. (These explanations seem
awkward.)

Like Freud, Fenichel tended to disregard the importance
of the aggressive drive in the development of schizophrenia.
He hardly ever discussed destructive impulses in connection
with symptom formation. After describing a hebephrenic patient's regression to an infantile existence with predominant
features of passive receptivity, he did say, "Occasional explosive outbreaks of excessive, destructive rage occur; the destructive impulses have previously been warded off by a
'peaceful' acquiescence" (p. 423); he also said, "A mutism may
not only express the fact that the patient has no longer any
interest in the objective world but may also contain a certain
amount of hostile antagonism. In the symptom of negativism,
resentment against the external world finds open expression"
(p. 418). But in neither case did he follow the observation
with a comprehensive treatment of the topic.

Although Fenichel tried to interpret schizophrenia in terms
of the structural theory, his over-all conceptualization of
schizophrenia closely follows Freud's. In only one respect did
Fenichel make a drastic departure from Freud's theory, that
is, with regard to the schizophrenic patient's capacity for
transference and the possibility of his benefiting from psychoanalysis. Having learned about the treatment experiences
and results of analysts who had done pioneer work with schizophrenic patients, Fenichel expressed the belief that some
schizophrenics are capable of transference and that "an analytic effect on schizophrenia is possible because the regression
to narcissism is never a complete one" (p. 447).

Discussion

In his formulation, Fenichel made it clear that whatever
the cause of the narcissistic fixation and of the revival and

intensification of the infantile instinctual conflicts, the ego holds the central position in the symptom formation. Conflicts arouse anxiety, and as anxiety mounts, the ego regresses to narcissistic fixation. In so doing, the ego may itself become totally or almost totally dissolved into the id. Along with ego regression and ego dissolution, certain symptoms make their appearance. Then, for various reasons, the ego re-emerges (or perhaps it was not altogether lost in the beginning), and this may be followed by re-emergence of other symptoms.

In the conceptualization of symptom formation in two stages, Freud spoke of libidinal detachment from (decathexis) and libidinal reattachment to (recathexis) object representations. Although his theory implied that an agency (the ego in the structural sense) must be doing the detaching and reattaching, Freud emphasized the resultant phenomena rather than the agency that gives rise to them. In Fenichel's restatement the emphasis is clearly very different: It is the ego that plays a significant role in bringing about decathexis or recathexis.

It was perhaps because of his wish to emphasize the ego's role in symptom formation that Fenichel used the terms regression and restitution to denote the two phases in symptom formation, rather than the terms decathexis and recathexis; at the time Fenichel wrote his book, cathexis was strongly associated with the notion of libidinal investment. There is, however, another possibility: Fenichel's choice of the term regression might have been determined by the possibility of placing neurosis and psychosis on one continuum. Let us consider the following statement:

> Freud succeeded in bringing schizophrenic mechanisms into consonance with his theory of neurotic symptom formation by grouping all the phenomena around the basic concept of regression. With such a grouping, no judgment was given as to the somatogenic or psychogenic origin of this regression. In different cases, the regression may have different causes and a different range, but it always has the same great depth. It reaches back to much earlier times than does any regression in neu-

roses, specifically, to the time when the ego first came into being
[p. 415].

From this, it seems that in Fenichel's view the term regression not only depicts the phenomena of reaching back, but also puts neurosis and psychosis on a continuum. However, Fenichel also thought schizophrenia could be "organic" and is fundamentally different from neurosis (p. 442).

Fenichel's choice of the term regression to denote the first phase is not ideal. In fact, the term "disorganization" might be preferable. For Fenichel, regression was an abbreviation for narcissistic regression, which described the return to the narcissistic fixation or the dissolution of the ego. In the proper context, his use of the term regressive could in no way cause any misunderstanding. Yet when he said that all symptoms that occur during the first phase are regressive, he led us to think that all symptoms that occur during the second phase are not regressive. That is certainly not true, for all restitutional symptoms are regressive in nature as well as in content.

The substitution of regression-restitution for decathexis-recathexis has both advantages and disadvantages. Regression-restitution depicts the ego's disorganization and reorganization (in terms of either function or content) more clearly than does decathexis-recathexis. But regression-restitution does not convey the idea of opposition so much as the idea of two consecutive processes. Thus, decathexis-recathexis better suggests the patient's continuous struggle with object relations. When we consider terminology, it is evident that words can never fully describe the phenomenon—that is often the reason why schizophrenic patients are reluctant or unwilling to describe their experiences.[2]

2 See Winnicott (1963); Burnham (1955).

CHAPTER 5

Hartmann's Application of Ego Psychology to Schizophrenia

In this chapter my purpose is not to consider Hartmann's contributions to psychoanalysis;[1] my discussion is confined to his contribution to the understanding of schizophrenia. It should be said at the outset that Hartmann wrote only one short paper on the subject. Yet what is contained in that paper makes up for many of the deficiencies inherent in Freud's theory of schizophrenia (and also in Fenichel's restatement of it).

Hartmann's Interpretation of Schizophrenia

In "The Metapsychology of Schizophrenia," Hartmann (1953) applied ego psychology[2] to the interpretation of schizophrenia. His central thesis is stated as follows:

> What Freud actually thought was that this conflict with reality, and the ensuing break with reality, could be traced either to features of reality itself or to increased pressure of the instinctual drives. . . . I would like to consider here a third factor . . . which will emphasize more strongly the role of the ego

[1] For appreciations of their scope and merit, see Eissler and Eissler (1964), Rangell (1965), Loewenstein (1966), and Schafer (1970).

[2] Hartmann explicated his ego psychology in the monograph *Ego Psychology and the Problem of Adaptation* (1939), the many papers collected in *Essays on Ego Psychology* (1964), and his works in collaboration with Kris and Loewenstein (1964).

in the process. Increased pressure on the ego by the drives may of course be, and often is, due to a real strengthening of the id forces. But there is another possibility that, for whatever reasons, the ego's role as a mediator between the drives and reality is impaired: either the defensive countercathexis of the ego, or those ego functions that maintain the contact with reality, may be incompletely developed or weakened [p. 184].

Out of a consideration of this "third factor," Hartmann delineated and clarified the following concepts:

1. Schizophrenic symptoms represent a selective regression of certain ego functions: Following Freud's later conceptualization, Hartmann (Hartmann et al., 1946; Hartmann, 1950b) defined the ego in terms of its functions. The development of each ego function is phase specific. Such ego functions as objectivation, reality testing, intentionality, attention, anticipation, organization of affects, and use of language do not make their appearance all at one time. Even a single ego function may develop in stages. For instance, the ego function of self-object differentiation requires that the child first have made a distinction between his activity and the object toward which his activity is directed. Only then can he distinguish the inner perception from the external reality.

Since the development of each ego function is phase specific, Hartmann suggested that a traumatic experience sustained during the maturational-developmental course may have less effect on the development of those ego functions that have already been established for some time than on those that are just being established. In accordance with this view, those ego functions, the development of which was more adversely affected, are more likely to be reflected in the symptoms.

Hartmann implied that, once it has appeared or has adequately developed, an ego function may follow one of several courses. (a) It may further differentiate or evolve into more complex forms. For instance, language originally serves an expressive function; later it acquires a communicative function, and finally the propositional or representational function. In regression, the highly differentiated function is most vulnerable to dedifferentiation. Therefore the propositional or representational function of language, which develops last, is lost first. The propositional or representational function of language normally allows signs to be distinguished from what they signify. When the representational function is lost, sign and signified are no longer distinguished. "The keeping apart of [the signs and what they signify] belongs to that state and distribution of mental energy that we call the secondary process" (1953, p. 190). With the loss of secondary-process functioning, language is once again governed by the primary process. (b) Certain ego functions may develop outside the sphere of conflict, others in the midst of mild or severe conflict. In symptom formation, the more distant the ego function has been from the conflict, the more resistant it will be to regression. (c) Sometimes a given ego function rises above the conflict, changes its function, and attains the status of secondary autonomy. Such an ego function may then become highly resistant to regression.

In view of these considerations, it is understandable that, at the time of symptom formation, not all ego functions will be regressed to the same extent. Rather, there will be a high degree of selectiveness as to which will regress severely, which mildly, and which not at all. This selectiveness is what accounts for the wide variety of symptoms among schizophrenic patients.

2. Megalomania and hypochondriasis result from hypercathexis of self-representations and not from hypercathexis of ego functions. Because the term ego is now defined in terms of its function, Hartmann carefully distinguishes ego and self; earlier, Freud tended to use "ego" to mean both. Hartmann observes, "the opposite of object cathexis is not ego cathexis, but cathexis of one's own person, that is, self-cathexis; in speaking of self-cathexis we do not imply whether this cathexis is situated in the id, ego, or superego. . . . It therefore will be clarifying if we define narcissism as the libidinal cathexis not of the ego but of the self. (It might also be useful to apply

the term self-representation as opposed to object representation)" (1950b, p. 127). Hartmann points out that when one speaks of "ego" or "self," one is actually using two completely different sets of referents. One has id and superego in mind when speaking of ego, and objects in mind when speaking of self. In the former case, one is concerned with functions; in the latter, one is concerned with content. This distinction is of particular importance when we consider such symptoms as megalomania and hypochondriasis. According to Freud, megalomania results from the investment of libido in the ego (self) and withdrawal of libido from the object, and hypochondriasis results from the excess libido that cannot be used in the production of megalomania. In the case of megalomania, we may still argue that for Freud "ego" stands for both ego and self, and that Hartmann's clarification is welcome but not essential. (However, Hartmann's formulation does make it possible to describe hypercathexis in terms of various aspects of self-representations instead of simply megalomania of a monolithic order.) In the case of hypochondriasis, the matter is somewhat different. Fenichel had already attempted a modification of Freud's formulation by suggesting that hypochondriasis results from hypercathexis of body organs. Hartmann's contribution is another step forward, spelling out that hypochondriasis reflects hypercathexis of the representation of body organs or of the contents of the mind.

3. Aggressive drives play an important role in symptom formation. Another aspect of Hartmann's revision of Freud's theory of schizophrenia is related to his studies of aggression in the schizophrenic process. In previous chapters, I have mentioned that both Freud and Fenichel left aggression out of their theoretical formulations on schizophrenia. Earlier, Hartmann (1948; Hartmann et al., 1949) had established libido and aggression as two separate and independent instinctual drives of equal importance for the ego, and neutralization as a specific process that concerns itself with drive energies. To summarize his view: (a) Neutralization is a continuous process by which both libidinal and aggressive instinctual

energies are transformed, deinstinctualized, and placed in the service of the ego as neutralized energy (Hartmann, 1948; Hartmann et al., 1949). (b) Normally, the ego forms a reservoir from which the neutralized energy may be drawn to maintain various ego functions (Hartmann et al., 1949). (c) Because of neutralization or deinstinctualization, the object is not merely the target of drive discharge; consequently, a constant relation with the object of a more complex nature may be maintained (1953). (d) The energy used in counter-cathexis is derived from neutralized aggression (1950b, 1952, 1953). (e) Neutralization or deinstinctualization is an ego function. It may be defective to begin with, it may develop incompletely, or it may be lost; when it is lost, evidence of deneutralization or reinstinctualization may be manifest.

In "Contribution to the Metapsychology of Schizophrenia," Hartmann (1953) demonstrates that the role of aggression is as important as libidinal withdrawal in the schizophrenic process. Although he does not spell out that the end-of-the-world experience may be attributable to the projection of aggressive destructive fantasy, he prepares the way for us to think along that line. However, in that particular paper, with regard to the role of aggression, Hartmann is more concerned with the totality of the problem than with the reinterpretation of a few symptoms. He says: (a) The schizophrenic ego is defective in its capacity for neutralization. This defect may be inborn, that is, faulty by heredity or constitution—a primary ego apparatus defect. (b) Because of this inherent defect, the preschizophrenic ego cannot neutralize (or deinstinctualize) the object cathexis. As a result the object remains a constant target for instinctual discharge. Because of the lack of sufficient neuralized energy, the development of the object-directed ego function is interfered with. This further handicaps the development of a constant object relation. Repression as a defense mechanism is assumed to require a stable maintenance of countercathexis, the energy for which is derived from neutralized aggression. Since the preschizophrenic ego does not have sufficient neutralized energy to maintain the countercathexis, it apparently cannot make use of repression. Consequently, it has to resort to more primitive defense mechanisms, such as turning against one's own person, reversal into the opposite, projection, and detachment of libido. (c) In later life, when aggression is mobilized by a narcissistic injury, the preschizophrenic ego, incapable of neutralizing the aggression, is flooded with an unmanageable amount of unneutralized energy. As a result, the self-image may become hypercathected with unneutralized aggressive drives. The free aggression may also be discharged against the object or internalized and absorbed by the superego. The defensive system may be overrun as well as the various ego functions; regression and dedifferentiation may occur. Deneutralization or reinstinctualization results, thus setting up the vicious circle of precipitation and maintenance of various symptoms.

4. All ego functions are superordinated by the synthetic function of the ego. In "Contribution to the Metapsychology of Schizophrenia," however, Hartmann does not mention the synthetic function of the ego. This particular ego function (thoroughly discussed earlier, in 1939) seems to me to play a significant role in symptom formation (see Chapter 14).

5. The development of the ego is shaped by the earliest object relations. Placing emphasis on the structure and function of the ego, Hartmann would naturally be concerned with factors that influence the ego's development. Not discounting the defects in the primary autonomous ego apparatus, he concludes, "the formation of the ego, e.g., its cathexis with neutralized energy, seems to be dependent on, among other factors, the nature of the earliest object relations" (Hartmann et al., 1951, p. 94). The confirmation of this idea is to be found in Mahler's work (1968).

Discussion

In the elucidation of the decathexis-recathexis theory of schizophrenia, Freud implied that an agent (unidentified) brings about the symptoms—just as an agent is assumed to effect the compromise between the repressed and the repressing forces in neurosis. Thus, in a sense, when he emphasized the role of the ego in the schizophrenic process, Hartmann did no more than make explicit what was implied in Freud's theory of schizophrenia. But in so doing, Hartmann substantially modified Freud's theory. With the emphasis now shifted from libidinal fixation and regression to the structure, function, and development of the ego, a different, albeit better, explanation is possible for the lack of uniformity of schizophrenic symptoms that we witness in our clinical practice. When libidinal regression to the narcissistic stage of development was postulated as the cause of all symptoms, it was hard to imagine why there should be such a wide range of symptoms among schizophrenics. Since all schizophrenics were supposedly regressed to the same narcissistic level, why were there so many symptoms that did not quite fit in with the picture of the narcissistic developmental stage? To answer this question, supplementary qualifications must be resorted to—for instance, while the regression is always to the narcissistic level, the subsequent restitution is what creates the diversity of symptoms and unevenness of the levels of regression. This kind of strained qualifying statement, however, becomes unnecessary when we turn to Hartmann.

Hartmann's consideration of the role of the ego in the schizophrenic process goes beyond Fenichel's exposition of the ego's role in regression and restitutional symptoms. Although he spoke of ego regression, Fenichel actually trained his sights on libidinal regression. His "ego" was active only to the extent of activating the archaic defense of regression to narcissistic fixation. Once the archaic defense was reactivated, the ego seemed to subject itself passively to being brought back to the point of disintegration. In contrast, Hartmann's "ego" was consistently active in its role as a mediator between the id and the superego on the one hand and reality on the other. Moreover, unlike Fenichel, Hartmann spoke of ego and self as separate entities of the mind, thus clarifying many conceptual issues. According to Hartmann's way of conceptualizing, the occurrence of *each* symptom can be logically explained. The development of each ego function is phase specific. Traumatic experience during different developmental phases can produce very different effects on the development of various ego functions. Because of these different effects, there is no even or across-the-board dedifferentiation of all ego functions at the same time. Rather, in any given patient, certain ego functions become more primitivized than others.

In his study of Spinoza, Hampshire (1951) says that "to 'explain' means to show that one true proposition is the logically necessary consequence of some other; explanation essentially involves exhibiting necessary connexions, and 'necessary connexion' in this context means a strictly logical connexion to be discovered by logical analysis of the ideas involved" (p. 35). With Hampshire's definition in mind, we may conclude that, all things considered, Hartmann's revised theory truly explains the formation of each symptom.

Perhaps because the revised theory explains the formation of each symptom so well, Hartmann did not consider the drastic, total personality change often encountered in schizophrenic patients. Nor did he consider it necessary to delineate two phases of symptom formation in schizophrenia. Yet it is a fact that the sum total of the explanations for each symptom does not quite explain the drastic personality change that takes place. Nevertheless, in separating cathexis of function (ego) from cathexis of content (self), Hartmann did pave the way for a possible explanation of the drastic personality change (see Chapter 14).

Hartmann's contribution to the role of aggression is particularly valuable. Clinically, we are only too familiar with the important role aggression often plays in the initiation of symptoms (see Bak, 1954), with schizophrenic patients' very low tolerance for their aggressive feelings (e.g., they become disorganized when they entertain angry or aggressive thoughts, etc.), and with their strong tendency to hostile, aggressive, and violent action. Before Hartmann elevated the role of aggression in the ego to a level as important as the role of libido, these clinical phenomena could not be adequately explained (see Chapters 3 and 4).

In describing the ego's action on drives, Hartmann postulated the concepts of neutralization (deinstinctualization) and deneutralization (reinstinctualization). In applying these concepts to schizophrenia, Hartmann attempted the parsimonious hypothesis that the schizophrenic has a defect in the primary autonomous ego apparatus—a defect in the capacity to neutralize the instinctual drive. As a result, object relations and defenses are interfered with, thus giving rise to increased frustration, mobilization of aggression, incapacity for neutralization, etc., eventuating in symptom formation. Although the hypothesis seemingly brings together a rather complex set of observations, the postulation of such a defect is open to objection. This objection is not so much determined by the current debates over the theoretical validity of the concept of neutralization and/or psychic energy (see, for instance, Holt, 1967; Schafer, 1968, 1970; Applegarth, 1971). Rather, it is rooted in the fact that neutralization and psychic energy are merely theoretical constructs, and that to equate a theoretical construct with a biological defect is to confuse levels of abstraction. Moreover, when Hartmann took up the task of considering "a third factor" in the schizophrenic process, he opened up possibilities for explaining the wide range of combinations of schizophrenic symptoms that Freud's theory failed to explain. Along with these possibilities, we are hopeful that our psychological inquiry and psychological-mindedness may lead to a better therapeutic approach to the schizophrenic patient. Now, by assuming a specific defect in the primary autonomous ego apparatus, Hartmann seems to undo his earlier assumption of a developmental error stemming from a "traumatic" earliest object relation. In making this theoretical shift, Hartmann has in fact impressed upon us a therapeutic nihilism. Since there is no way to make up a biological defect by psychological means, psychotherapeutic endeavors with schizophrenic patients would be a waste of energy and time.

Hartmann never defined schizophrenia. It may be assumed that when he formulated the concept of a defect in the capacity for neutralization as a primary autonomous ego apparatus error, he had in mind the type of patients we designate as schizophrenic-III (and some that we classify as schizophrenic-II and -IV). If he had had in mind the patients classified as schizophrenic-I, he would probably have formulated a theory that gave as much attention to developmental defect as to biological error.

CHAPTER 6

Jacobson's Contributions to the Explanation of Schizophrenia

Jacobson has said, "although I have observed hospitalized schizophrenics in florid, acute, and chronic psychotic states and discussed treatment problems with their therapists, my own therapeutic experience has been limited to manic depressive and to ambulatory schizophrenics or patients during periods of remission from a psychotic episode" (1967, p. 51). In the preface to her book *Depression* (1971) she reiterated that her theoretical conclusions are based on work with borderline cases and ambulatory manic-depressive and schizophrenic patients (p. vii). Although deduced from work with less sick patients, her theoretical conclusions, particularly those related to self- and object representations, self, and identity, are highly relevant to the explanation of schizophrenic phenomena and should be incorporated into a theory of schizophrenia. I shall therefore elaborate on some of these theoretical conclusions.

Jacobson's Theoretical Conclusions

The Elaboration of the Concept of Self- and Object Representations

In his theory of schizophrenia, Freud focused his attention primarily on the decathexis and recathexis of object representations. When he spoke of megalomania as a hypercathexis

of the ego, he obviously had in mind the idea of a hypercathexis of self-representations. He did not, however, make the
idea explicit. When Hartmann made the distinction between
the self and the ego (1950b, 1953), he clearly delineated the
difference between hypercathexis of ego functions and hypercathexis of the self or self-representations. It was Jacobson
(1953), however, who demonstrated that "self-representation . . . is a concept . . . indispensable for the study of psychosis" (p. 54). She went on to trace the development of self-
and object representations:

> The nuclei of the early infantile self-images are our first body-
> images and sensations. Like the primitive object-images, our
> concept of the self is at first not a firm unit. It is fused and
> confused with the object-images and is composed of a constantly
> changing series of self-images, which reflect mainly the inces-
> sant fluctuations of our mental state. With advancing psycho-
> sexual and ego development and the maturation of reality test-
> ing, a more stable, uniform, and realistic concept of the self and
> a lasting, firm cathexis of the self-representations will normally
> be established [pp. 56-57].

Jacobson further considers that "Normally, the early infantile images of the self and of the love objects develop in
two directions. On the one hand, they grow into consolidated
realistic object- and self-representations, whose site is in the
system ego. On the other hand, they also form the core of the
superego and ego ideal" (p. 57). She observed that, in a potentially schizophrenic patient, development in the two directions cannot be easily delineated. The self- and object
representations do not consolidate along the realistic line in
the ego. In a potential schizophrenic the demarcation between
self- and object representations is only precariously maintained. The unstable self- and object representations tend to
split regressively into archaic self- and object images. The
fusion of these archaic self- and object images may then result
in what Jacobson calls a fusion of self- and object representations, or more simply, the loss of self-boundary (see Federn's
concept of ego boundaries in Chapter 10). In the meantime
the superego and ego ideal "will retain attributes of early

infantile object- and self-images, and they will be carriers of primitive infantile values" (p. 62). The superego will not be a firmly integrated system. "It will be personified, unstable in its functions, and will tend either to assume excessive control of the ego or to disintegrate, dissolve, and merge with object- and self-representations" (p. 62). The ego ideal will also not be sharply separated from the self- and object representations. The instability of the superego and ego ideal further subjects the preschizophrenic patient to frequent and intense instinctual and narcissistic conflicts.

Through the elaboration of the concept of self- and object representations, Jacobson offers new ways to explain certain commonly encountered schizophrenic symptoms. For instance, the schizophrenic's experience of "the end of the world," the loss of identity, and feelings of dying or being dead may be tied to the regressive fusion of self- and object representations and a general collapse of the psychic systems. (According to Freud, these schizophrenic symptoms are explained in terms of libidinal decathexis of object representations, and according to Hartmann they are probably explained in terms of disturbances in ego functions.) Jacobson also advances a new way to explain delusion formation: "Regressively revived, primitive object- and self-images, which have found their way to consciousness, will merge and join with remnants of realistic concepts to form new units. In this way, delusional object- and self-representations will be built up, in disregard of reality, and will be reprojected on the outside world" (pp. 64-65). (According to Freud's conceptualization, delusion results from libidinal recathexis of object representations, and according to Hartmann's formulation, delusion would be evidence of impaired reality testing. In Jacobson's formulation the impairment of reality testing occurs concomitantly with or after, but not before, delusion formation.)

The Development of the Self and Identity

Jacobson's interest in the treatment of psychotic and borderline patients has unavoidably led her to the observation that while a detailed study of defenses and resistance is sufficient in the treatment of neurosis, it is not enough in the treatment of psychotics or borderline patients. In psychosis, especially schizophrenia, the analysis of defense, resistance, and ego function must be supplemented and sometimes even superseded by consideration of the disturbance in the self and identity and the sense of the self and identity.[1] From the patient's point of view, to hold his "self" together may at times be far more important than to learn about certain resistances or defenses and dispense with them; and in treatment the therapist may simply have to go along with the patient. In Jacobson's systemic study of the normal development of the self and identity (1954c, 1964), she stresses that the development of the self and identity and of the sense of the self and identity is a continuous process. Beginning with the earliest transaction between the infant and his mother, the libidinal and aggressive cathexis of self- and object images and of self- and object representations spurs on the delineation of the concept of the self along with the sense of the self. In further interaction with the object world during subsequent developmental phases, the self becomes increasingly elaborated and consolidated. Jacobson's developmental description of how the self and identity (as well as the sense of the self and identity) are normally delineated and elaborated is important, for her description makes it possible for us to draw inferences about how the development of one's self and identity (and the sense of the self and identity) might be interfered with in a potentially schizophrenic patient, and why a schizophrenic patient would try to alter the outer reality at all costs in order to preserve a sense of self-sameness, even if it is a very precarious one.

---

[1] Jacobson (1964) considers that identity has two aspects, an objective and a subjective aspect. She calls the former "identity" and the latter the "sense of identity." Identity is characterized by the observable capacity to remain the same in the midst of change, whereas the sense of identity is the consciousness of such sameness.

The Detailed Study of the Break with Reality

Freud's decathexis-recathexis theory of schizophrenia is based on his stress on the schizophrenic's break with reality. I have pointed out that, implicitly, Freud used the break with reality as the criterion for the diagnosis of schizophrenia (Chapter 1). Fenichel even went as far as to say that in certain paranoid cases, where symptoms develop insidiously, there must also be a break with reality, but one that occurs imperceptibly. Through a detailed study of the break with reality, Jacobson noticed that

> certain types of psychotic patients will not immediately break with reality but will first attempt the opposite: they try to turn to and to employ the external world as an aid in their efforts to replenish their libidinal resources, to strengthen their weakening ego and superego, and to resolve their narcissistic and instinctual conflicts with which their defective ego cannot cope.... For this reason they may not only hold on, or even cling, to the external world, but try to change it, to create one that will suit their special needs, and to reject and deny those aspects that are of no use to them....
>
> Psychotics give up reality and replace it by a newly created fantasy reality only if reality fails to lend itself to their purposes and to help them in their conflict solution [1967, pp. 18-20].

In Chapter 2, I gave a clinical example of Bleuler's. He described a young girl who suddenly became very proficient in her intellectual work shortly before she broke down. Bleuler was not able to decide whether he should consider the change of personality before the psychotic break as a part of the illness. Many of us may share Bleuler's dilemma, but Jacobson's explanation, rooted in her astute clinical observations, shows beyond doubt that such a change in personality is the prodromal stage of the illness. If we follow Jacobson's thinking, we may learn to pay attention to such evidence of illness and try to help the patient at the earliest stage, when he can still be relatively easily reached through psychotherapy.

Clinical Illustration of Aggressive Drives in the
Eventualization of Schizophrenia

Although Hartmann had established earlier the importance of aggression in schizophrenia, he had discussed the
issue only in broad theoretical terms. Jacobson approached
the issue of aggression differently, using illustrative cases to
demonstrate just how schizophrenia eventuates through the
aggressive cathexis of self- and object representations.

Jacobson disagrees with Hartmann in certain respects. In
"Contribution to the Metapsychology of Schizophrenia," Hartmann (1953) postulated that the schizophrenic's ego lacks the
capacity to neutralize the instinctual drives. When there is
conflict, the aggressive drive is mobilized. Since the ego lacks
the ability for neutralization, its functions and defenses are
greatly handicapped; the result may be further deinstinctualization, further weakening of the ego, an increase in the
harshness of the superego, and subsequent symptom formation. In Jacobson's (1967) view, however, "deneutralization of
the sexual and aggressive drives cannot sufficiently account
for the intensity of the destructiveforces that we observe in
psychotics." She advocates "Freud's idea [that] fusion and defusion of drives has bearing on the . . . conflicts which play
such a prominent part in the psychotic's relations to the external world" (p. 11).[2]

Jacobson also seems to differ from Hartmann in explaining the ego's incapacity to deal with aggression. Hartmann
assumed that this incapacity is due to an error in the primary
autonomous ego apparatus. This inborn error adversely affects ego and superego development, predisposing the person
to a schizophrenic outbreak. Jacobson speaks of libidinal and

---

[2] Here my intention is only to state Jacobson's theoretical position, not to state
which of the two views are correct. Both are descriptive and not explanatory. In
advocating the viewpoint of defusion of drives, Jacobson emphasizes the intensity of
aggression in schizophrenics, often with little evidence of libido. Such phenomena
can, however, be considered from other points of view; for example, in a state of
panic, the patient's distorted perception and cognition may make him consider that
the object is extremely dangerous and must be destroyed.

aggressive cathexis of self- and object representations, and of how these cathexes affect the formation of ego and superego as well as self and identity. Libidinal and aggressive drives constantly interact at each phase of development before the outbreak of schizophrenia. Thus, even though Jacobson often openly stresses constitutional factors, her formulation still allows for the view that environment and constitution are linked as an etiological unity.

The Distinction between Mood and Affect

Jacobson (1971) defines affect and mood in the following way: Affect is directed at objects or is determined by specific objects in which the feelings are vested, whereas mood is not—even though a mood may start out as an object-directed affect. For instance, anger may turn into an angry mood as soon as it has ceased to relate only to a particular object or idea. The economic function of the mood is to help to bind affects. Once established, a mood tends to exert a continuous influence over a person's thought and behavior, even to the extent of temporarily impairing critical judgment and discrimination in regard to the self or the object world. Moods may produce "a primitive, 'subjective,' prejudicial or even illusional type of feeling, thinking, and behavior, which tends to resist reality testing. To the extent to which this reality testing can assert itself, the mood condition will subside" (p. 87). Jacobson therefore defines mood as "a particular state of mind" or "a temporary fixation of generalized discharge modifications." Moods allow a repetitive affective discharge[3] on a large number and variety of objects. "Even though moods do not preclude and may induce repeated, sudden, dramatic discharge reactions, such as outbursts of sobbing or laughter or anger" (p. 74), the gradual discharge process common to moods generally serves to protect the ego from the danger of

[3] The term "discharge" is often used to reflect the energy concept (see Jacobson, 1957). However, the term may be divested of energic connotations and be conceptualized as simply descriptive.

a too explosive, overwhelming discharge. In binding the affect, mood also serves the function of stabilizing, for longer or shorter periods, special concepts of the self and the world.

Jacobson conceives of superego formation as having

> a singular influence on the development of affect and mood control and thus of mood predisposition . . . as long as guilt feelings remain localized and refer to specific—conscious or unconscious—forbidden strivings . . . they serve as an effective warning and directive signal. . . . But defective superego structure or superego regression may lead to a permanent loss of the signal function of the superego, which is then replaced by a tendency either to conspicuous rapid or extreme pathological mood swings, or to a more or less fixated lowering or rising of the mood level [pp. 77-78].

Discussion

Jacobson impresses upon us that while the schizophrenic patient has difficulty in maintaining a satisfactory object relation, his most basic problem lies in his inability to sustain a more "realistic" type of self-representation and in turn to maintain the self or a sense of self. Furthermore, the concept of a collapse of psychic structure involves not only the collapse of the functions of the ego or superego, but also the disintegration of a more "realistic type of self- and object-representation and of the self and identity." Clinically, we know this is exactly the case.

Jacobson (1971) said that the schizophrenics' "outbursts of panic, their fantasies of *Weltuntergang* arising from an inner perception of their disintegration . . . of the breakdown of object relations and ego identifications, reverberate the processes of dissolution both of the object and of the self representations. Split up into archaic images, they cease to be entities" (p. 261). I believe, however, that some clarification is in order lest the cause-effect relationship between the panic and the refusion of the self-and object representations be misinterpreted. Phenomenologically, refusion of the self- and object representations may be observed in the following situations: (1) It often appears temporarily in borderline patients and sometimes even in neurotics during their analysis; (2) a total obliteration of self- and object representations may occur corresponding to and immediately following the so-called schizophrenic break with reality; and (3) it often reappears after the break with reality.

In the first instance, we are not speaking of schizophrenia. Temporary refusion is spontaneously rectified; its defensive nature is often demonstrable. The refusion, of course, corresponds to the experience of anxiety, but the patient would not report his subjective experience as reaching the degree of organismic panic, nor would any skillful observer. Only in the second and third instances are we concerned with schizophrenia.

In the second instance the refusion is often attended by the patient's subjective experience of organismic panic, which can also be documented by the observer through the patient's affectomotor behavior. In most patients, the terror continues for quite some time, until the self- and object representations are gradually reorganized into delusions, as described by Jacobson. This period corresponds to what I have characterized elsewhere as the acute phase of the illness (from the break with reality to the reorganization of the self). During this period, the intensity of the terror fluctuates. Corresponding to the fluctuations, fusion of self- and object representations appears and disappears. Although the fusion phenomenon is defensive, identification of the defensive quality is difficult. In the third instance (presumably the patient is well entrenched in the subacute phase or even the chronic phase), the refusion of self- and object representations occurs at a time of increased anxiety. But at such moments there is no detectable affectomotor behavior that we would characterize as organismic panic. The refusion can be observed as being used defensively, but it now assumes the quality of being used automatically and habitually so that it is difficult to get the patient to recognize its defensiveness.

From these three groups of refusion phenomena, we note that affectomotor behavior, which may be characterized as organismic panic, is observable only in the second instance. When organismic panic does occur, it seems to be intimately related to the collapse of psychic structure or the splitting up of the more realistic self- and object representations into archaic self- and object images. To be consistent with Freud's theory of anxiety, it may be suggested that the panic results in the collapse of psychic structure rather than the other way around. I shall return to this issue in Chapter 14.

Jacobson says that, at the outset of his illness, the schizophrenic patient may cling to reality, and relinquish it only when he finds that it fails to support him. The importance of this observation not only orients us to detect the earliest evidence of the illness and thereby give the patient the necessary help, it also offers us some understanding of hope, despair, and chronicity. Clinically, we have all observed that before breaking with reality the patient often struggled fervently to establish some sort of equilibrium through fighting with his parents; sexual escapades; use of marihuana, LSD, and other drugs; etc. During this long period of struggle, not only his ego capacity to master his conflicts but his will to master them are gradually undermined. Especially when the latter happens, there is a total collapse of ego capacity, increased anxiety, and disintegration of originally precariously maintained self- and object representations into the archaic self- and object images. It is then that grave symptoms, such as a break with reality, ensue. Thus, after the break with reality, we are often confronted not only with the patient's loss of more mature ego function and self-identity, but also with his extreme despair. And despair is a serious problem, as it accounts for many a patient's long hospitalization as well as for the revolving-door phenomenon. Nunberg (1925) believed that the patient has a will to recover; but while a will to recover can be taken for granted in the neurotic patient, it cannot in the schizophrenic patient. In the treatment of schizophrenics, the foremost task is usually to rekindle the will to recover or to master conflicts. This is not an easy task; yet, with sincerity and perseverance, many therapists (e.g., Fromm-Reichmann, Will, and Sechehaye) have proved that it is not impossible.

I believe that Jacobson's effort to distinguish moods (a slow, diffuse discharge onto many less personal objects) from affects (a possible quick discharge onto a definite object) has very great clinical usefulness, for through this distinction heretofore unintelligible phenomena may be explained. For instance, one patient became acutely ill in his early 20's and was admitted to a hospital where he soon became a management problem. Since he was very confused "and out of it," he had to be assisted at meals and with the simplest kind of hygiene. Yet he struck out at anyone who came near him. As he was big, muscular, and powerful, he soon established a reputation of being a holy terror. It often took four to six male aides to clean him. In the free drug era, the only way to deal with him was to leave him in a quiet room 24 hours a day. After eight or nine months without any sign of a letup, it was recommended that he be transferred to Chestnut Lodge. There, he attempted assault a couple of times, but rapidly calmed down. With the help of psychotherapy, his "confusion" increasingly cleared. Ultimately he left Chestnut Lodge very much improved.

How can we explain the sudden improvement of this patient's ego functions after the transfer from one hospital to another? Obviously, in the first hospital he became very angry. This affect soon turned into an angry *mood*. Thus he had perhaps succeeded in sparing the object against whom the anger was originally felt. Now, in an angry mood, he discharged anger of a toned-down degree at everyone who came close to him. But, in the process, he incurred angry feelings in others around him. Mutually irritating each other, neither the patient nor the staff could extricate themselves. After the transfer to Chestnut Lodge he was still in the same mood, but the nursing staff responded to him differently, that is, without irritation. The unperturbed staff allowed him to re-establish his rituals[4] to regulate the rate of discharge of aggressive impulses. Thus his mood was rapidly modified and, in time, his ego functioning and over-all behavior as well.

[4] With regard to rituals, see Chapter 17.

CHAPTER 7

Melanie Klein's "Paranoid-Schizoid Position" and Schizophrenia

In the late 1920's, from her work with young children, Melanie Klein began to draw theoretical conclusions that were often at variance with Freud's (see Klein, 1946, p. 2). For instance, she believed that the infant is born with a functioning ego, that he has a distinct awareness of sexual differences and a full faculty for complicated fantasying, that the Oedipus complex appears in the second half of the first year, that the superego is being formed at the first evidence of introjection, that the early superego is intimately associated with aggression, and so on (see Klein, 1932). Nevertheless, the formulation of the schizoid-paranoid and depressive positions and their respective anxieties in 1935 marked the beginning of an independent line of psychoanalytic theorizing often referred to as Kleinian theory.[1] In what follows, I shall not concern myself with the differences between the Kleinian theory and the mainstream of psychoanalytic thinking with respect to basic assumptions; these differences have been considered by others (e.g., Waelder, 1936; Glover, 1945; Bibring, 1947; Brierley, 1951; Zetzel, 1953, 1956a, 1956b; Joffe, 1969; Kernberg, 1969; Yorke, 1971; Gillespie, 1971; Whitehead, 1975) from various points of view. Instead, I shall confine my considerations to Klein's views on schizophrenia.

---

[1] This theory was further elaborated in her later writings (1957, 1975a, 1975b).

83

The Paranoid and the Depressive Positions

Klein postulated that in normal development the infant lives through two critical phases (or positions)—the paranoid-schizoid[2] and the depressive. The first lasts three or four months, the second two or three years. Three conditions must be fulfilled before the transition from the first phase to the second can occur. (1) The ego must advance in its capacity, from a partial to a whole object relation, that is, the baby perceives more and more of the whole person of the mother. (2) The baby must develop some realization of the disaster caused by his own sadism; this propels the ego toward reparative activities and guilt feelings. (3) The baby must have greatly overcome his early paranoid-schizoid anxieties through good relations with the mother.

The Paranoid-Schizoid Position

Klein was among the few analysts who not only endorsed Freud's postulation of the death instinct,[3] but also made elaborate use of it in formulating her theories. She said, "The threat of annihilation by the death instinct within . . . is the primordial anxiety, and it is the ego which, in the service of the life instinct—possibly even called into operation by the life instinct—deflects to some extent that threat outwards" (1975b, p. 190).

Klein assumed that the ego is not differentiated from the id (Freud, 1923) or from the id-ego undifferentiated matrix (Hartmann, 1939). Rather, "it exists from the beginning of post-natal life, though in a rudimentary form and largely lacking coherence. Already at the earliest stage it performs a number of important functions . . . which derive from the imperative need to deal with the struggle between life and death instincts" (1975b, pp. 190-191). Introjection, projection,

---

[2] Klein's original term was "paranoid" position. Under the influence of Fairbairn, the term was later changed to "paranoid-schizoid" (1946).

[3] Klein first incorporated Freud's death instinct into her theory in 1933 (p. 269).

and splitting are among the earliest ego activities. The infant experiences the breast, the prototypical object, as either "good" or "bad" depending on its actual experience of the breast as either gratifying or frustrating. Through introjection, the good and bad breast become internalized. But the good and bad qualities of the breast are greatly influenced by the projection of the life and death instincts. While the projection of the former may give good qualities to the breast, the projection of the latter turns the breast into a dangerous persecutor who will devour the infant, scoop out the inside of its body, cut it into pieces, poison it—in short, destroy it (1975b, p. 69). Such a bad breast, when introjected, becomes an internalized persecutor. Surrounded by external and internal persecutors, the infant experiences the kind of anxiety that, in content, resembles the experience of psychosis in adults; hence the earliest phase of life is designated as the paranoid-schizoid position.

The fear of persecution in the paranoid-schizoid position forces the ego to adopt certain defense mechanisms. "Outstanding among these defenses are the mechanisms of splitting internal and external objects, emotions and the ego" (1975b, p. 22). The splitting of the ego begins with the natural alternating tendency of the rudimentary ego toward integration and toward disintegration. In its effort to disperse fear of persecution, the ego may turn a natural tendency into a defensive device; that is, in order to defend itself, the ego may simply disintegrate. This falling to pieces is a primitive process and is likely to be closely linked with the mechanism of disintegration in schizophrenia. The splitting of the breast into bits results from the projection of oral aggression. "In states of frustration and anxiety the oral-sadistic and cannibalistic desires are reinforced, and then the infant feels that he has taken in the nipple and the breast *in bits*. Therefore in addition to the divorce between a good and a bad breast in the young infant's phantasy, the frustrating breast—attacked in oral-sadistic phantasies—is felt to be in fragments" (1975b, p. 5). Moreover, during those moments of frustration and anxiety the infant may not be able to maintain the division of the good and the bad breast; he then begins to experience the good breast too as in pieces.

Klein believed that the splitting of the ego and the splitting of objects are closely linked: ". . . the ego is incapable of splitting the object—internal and external—without a corresponding splitting taking place within the ego . . . the more sadism prevails in the process of incorporating the object, and the more the object is felt to be in pieces, the more the ego is in danger of being split in relation to the internalized object fragments" (1975b, p. 6).

When instinctual development leads to the confluence of oral, urethral, and anal desires, both libidinal and aggressive, the fantasied onslaughts on the mother follow two main lines.

> One is the predominantly oral impulse to suck dry, bite up, scoop out and rob the mother's body of its good contents. . . . The other line of attack derives from the anal and urethral impulses and implies expelling dangerous substances (excrements) out of the self and into the mother. Together with these harmful excrements, expelled in hatred, split-off parts of the ego are also projected on to the mother. . . . In so far as the mother comes to contain the bad parts of the self, she is not felt to be a separate individual but is felt to be *the* bad self [1975b, p. 8].

To this particular form of identification, which occurs frequently during the early development phase of life, Klein gave the name "projective identification." Projective identification forms the basis of paranoid-persecutory anxieties. For instance, the fantasy of forcefully entering the object may stir up the fear of being controlled and persecuted inside it. By reintrojecting the forcefully entered object, the person's feelings of inner persecution are intensified because the reintrojected object contains the dangerous aspects of the self to begin with. What is expelled and projected, however, is not limited to the bad parts of the self. The good parts of the self too may be expelled and projected into the object. Under unfavorable conditions, the result can be an overstrong dependence on external representatives of one's own good parts or a weakened capacity for object love because the object is predominantly loved as a representation of the self.

Even in the most normal circumstances, the schizoid-paranoid position is fraught with anxiety, and the threat of annihilation from the death instinct impels the infant to resort to all available defenses. Ordinarily the good ministrations of the mother help establish the good internal object, reducing the need for and the fantasies of annihilation. But in the absence of such a mother, the ego is constantly beset with anxiety. Splitting, and therefore disintegration, may occur too often and go on for too long. This may lead to fixation in the schizoid-paranoid position.

The Depressive Position

In the third or fourth month, the depressive position comes to the fore. It is the central position of the child's development, for his "satisfactory relation to people depends upon his having succeeded in his struggles against the chaos inside him (the depressive position) and having securely established his 'good' internal objects. . . . the introjection of the whole loved object gives rise to concern and sorrow lest that object should be destroyed (by the 'bad' objects and the id), and . . . these distressed feelings and fears, in addition to the paranoid set of fears and defences, constitute the depressive position" (1975a, p. 348). When the depressive position arises, the ego is forced to develop new methods of defense, among them idealization and denial. In idealization a splitting of objects into good and bad is followed by an exaggeration of the good aspect of the object as a safeguard against the fear of the persecutory object. A related process is "the flight to the idealized object," through which persecutory fear is avoided by seeking refuge from the idealized unassimilated internal object. Under unfavorable conditions, this can lead to feeling totally dependent on the internal object. In denial, which is best exemplified by hallucinatory gratification, the persecutory object is first kept apart from the idealized object, and then its very existence is omnipotently denied and annihilated. In the omnipotent denial of the existence of the bad object, a part of the ego from which the feelings toward the object emanate is denied and annihilated as well. Thus in the denial of reality, not only is a part of the ego denied, but the object relation is denied as well.

During the depressive position, the ego must work through the depressive anxiety. A failure to do so results in a fixation at the depressive position, which may pave the way for manic-depressive illness in later life.

Some fluctuation between the paranoid-schizoid and the depressive positions always occurs. When confronted with the mourning process that has to be worked through in the depressive position, the child re-experiences his early anxieties again and again. If the persecutory fears remain strong, the ego will not be able to work through the depressive position. This incapacity may force it to regress and become fixated to the earlier position, creating the basis for various forms of schizophrenia in later life.

The Paranoid-Schizoid Position in Schizophrenia

According to the above formulation, the death instinct is primarily responsible for producing the paranoid-schizoid anxiety, which in turn spurs on the various ego activities. The libidinal activities are completely dwarfed in the process. On the basis of this theoretical framework, Klein (1946) believed that the potential schizophrenic is endowed with strong sadistic impulses and with an ego that has a low tolerance for anxiety. Consequently, he is prone to intense schizoid-paranoid anxiety and is likely to use schizoid mechanisms, especially splitting and projective identification. The ego is then unable to work through the depressive anxiety during the depressive position, and the result is a developmental fixation at the paranoid-schizoid position.

Schizophrenic illness represents a falling back onto the fixation point, with a re-experiencing of the paranoid-schizoid anxiety and a deployment of the schizoid mechanisms. Schizophrenic symptoms such as thought disorders, emotional aberrance, and disturbances in object relations are all described as resulting from the schizoid mechanisms. For example (Klein, 1975b), ". . . impairment of logical thinking . . . amounts to thoughts and associations being cut off from one another and situations being split off from one another; in fact, the ego is . . . split" (p. 14). And "splitting . . . brings about a dispersal of anxiety and a cutting off of emotions. . . . The sufferings of the schizophrenic are . . . not fully appreciated, because he appears to be devoid of emotions" (p. 144). And

> the schizophrenic feels that . . . he cannot rely on an external and internal good object, nor can he rely on his own self. This factor is bound up with loneliness. . . . The sense of being surrounded by a hostile world, which is characteristic of the paranoid aspect of schizophrenic illness . . . vitally influences his feelings of loneliness. . . . Another factor which contributes to the loneliness of the schizophrenic is confusion. This is the result of . . . the fragmentation of the ego, and the excessive use of projective identification, so that he constantly feels himself not only to be in bits, but to be mixed up with other people [pp. 303-304].

Discussion

Klein's contribution may be looked at from two points of view—the theoretical and the therapeutic. According to Klein, schizophrenic illness represents a regression to the paranoid-schizoid position. Thus regressed, the patient experiences fear of persecution and reactivates primitive mechanisms to cope with his anxiety. As for the paranoid-schizoid position, it is postulated as a developmental phase and is organized primarily around the death instinct. Theoretically, this formulation is inadequate. First, to postulate schizophrenia as a wholesale regression to an earlier fixation point is awkward. The pitfall of such a hypothesis has been discussed elsewhere (see Chapter 4). It will be remembered that Fenichel analogously described schizophrenic illness as a regression to a narcissistic level of development. There is no question that during the illness the patient is regressed, in some respects to a very early stage of development. But his regression is never even. While many of his later-developed ego functions have disappeared, some of them can remain intact. The primitive needs appear to dominate most of the time, but more mature needs may occasionally be evident. Second, the symptom formation in schizophrenia is quite complicated. It does not seem possible to explain all symptomatic manifestations in terms of introjection, projection, splitting, and projective identification alone—just as not all symptoms can be explained away, for instance, in terms of the loss of inner and outer ego boundaries (see Chapter 10). Third, in Klein's description the fixation at the paranoid-schizoid position is brought about through the interaction between the infant's projection of his libido and death instinct on the one hand and his introjection of the nurturing person on the other. Yet on closer scrutiny, the determining factor of this fixation is really the constitutional strength of the infant's death instinct and his capacity to tolerate the paranoid-schizoid anxiety. According to this formulation, the maternal person can do good only in the sense of providing good experience, and from this good experience the infant is then enabled to establish a good introject to offset his bad affects and the internalized bad objects. But clinical observations bear out that this is not always the case. Often, for instance, an extremely pathological environment (which can be the mother herself) can also make a normal infant schizophrenic.

From the therapeutic point of view, Klein's contribution is enormous. Since the late 1920's, psychoanalysts have been greatly interested in psychosis. But the general tendency was to apply psychoanalytic concepts to the understanding of psychosis, rather than to use psychoanalytic knowledge to treat psychotic patients. Klein did more than anyone else in Europe to encourage analysts to treat psychotic patients. By linking the paranoid-schizoid position and the depressive position to schizophrenic and manic-depressive illness respectively, Klein provided the basis for a psychoanalytic approach to psychotic patients.

Klein's concepts of schizoid mechanisms are useful in the treatment of schizophrenic patients. The concept of projective identification, which Klein (1975b) conceived of as "the prototype of aggressive object relations" (p. 18), especially illuminates many interactions between patient and therapist.

To conceptualize the paranoid-schizoid position as related primarily to the ego's handling of the death instinct, the Kleinian theory necessarily calls for treatment of the patient's most primitive conflict[4] in order to deal with his death instinct. Thus, contrary to Federn, who tried to maintain a positive transference in therapy by not dealing with aggression, Klein advocated taking up the negative transference whenever it made its appearance—even very early in treatment. The task of calling the patient's attention to his sadistic impulses is not an easy one. Ill-handled, it may make the patient feel accused of being irreparably bad and, in turn, further shatter his already damaged self-esteem. Klein, however, succeeded in developing a special technique by means of which the patient is made aware of his sadism but at the same time assured of a sense of relatedness. In Segal's words (1964b), "we do not interpret to him mechanisms, we interpret and help him to relive the phantasies contained in the mechanisms" (p. 192).

Klein's contributions have been amply elaborated by her followers (see, e.g., Segal, 1950, 1954, 1956, 1964a, 1964b, 1972; Bion, 1956, 1957, 1959, 1968a; Rosenfeld, 1965, 1972). They deserve to be studied, especially by those who are interested in the treatment of schizophrenia.

---

[4] Others (e.g., Sechehaye, 1951; Rosen, 1953) have also attempted to reach their patients by immediately focusing on the most primitive conflicts.

CHAPTER 8

Fairbairn's "Object-Relations" Theory of Schizophrenia

In the early 1940's, from his work with patients suffering from "schizoid conditions," Fairbairn began to formulate his "object-relations" theory. His work was eventually published in book form (1952), with a preface by Ernest Jones, who stated succinctly:

> Instead of starting, as Freud did, from stimulation of the nervous system proceeding from excitation of various erotogenous zones and internal tension arising from gonadic activity, Dr. Fairbairn starts at the centre of the personality, the ego, and depicts its strivings and difficulties in its endeavour to reach an object where it may find support. Dr. Fairbairn . . . has worked out [the] implications [of his theme] both biologically in regard to the problems of instinct and psychologically in the baffling interchange of external and internal objects. All this constitutes a fresh approach in psycho-analysis which should lead to much fruitful discussion [1952, p. v].

Although Fairbairn was greatly influenced by Klein, his theoretical framework differs from hers in many respects. Moreover, unlike Klein, who claimed to adhere to Freud's basic views, Fairbairn aimed constantly at revisions. In his writing, such titles or subtitles as "Revision of libidinal theory," "Revision of the theory of repression," etc., repeatedly occur. Owing to the fact that Fairbairn used the same words Freud and Klein used but actually assigned special meanings to them, the reader may often find it difficult to understand Fairbairn unless he takes the whole theory into consideration.

92

The "Object-Relations" Theory

Like Klein, Fairbairn regarded the ego as present at birth. This view differs from Freud's and Hartmann's. Freud postulated that the ego is a structure that differentiates from the id; Hartmann assumed that ego and id derive from an undifferentiated matrix.

Fundamental to Fairbairn's conceptualization is that the libido is essentially object-seeking and not pleasure-seeking: ". . . impulse-tension in the ego must be regarded as inherently oriented towards objects in the outer reality" (p. 167). He therefore proposed a revision of the libido theory, suggesting that (a) erotogenic zones are not primary determinants of libidinal aims, but channels mediating the primary object-seeking aims of the ego; (b) what Abraham described as "phases," with the exception of his "oral phases," are really techniques used by the ego to regulate relations with internalized objects; (c) the psychopathological conditions Abraham ascribed to fixation at specific phases are, with the exception of schizophrenia, depressive—really conditions associated with the use of specific techniques; (d) the libidinal developmental phases should be replaced by three stages of ego development: infantile dependent, transitional, and mature dependent.

According to Fairbairn, the infantile dependent stage is divided into two substages, the schizoid and the depressive positions, which correspond to Abraham's early and late oral phases. During the early oral stage, the child's great need is to obtain conclusive assurance that his parents genuinely love him as a person and in turn genuinely accept his love. Frustration of this need results in the basic conflict in the form of the alternative "to suck or not to suck," or "to love or not to love." Since "to love or not to love" is the central conflict of schizophrenics, Fairbairn preferred to call the early oral stage the "schizoid position," which corresponds to Klein's paranoid position. In the late oral stage, aggression becomes more differentiated. Frustration of needs leads to depressive conflicts in the form of the alternative "to suck or to bite," or "to love or to hate." Likewise, since "to love or to hate" is central to the conflict of depressives, Fairbairn called the late oral stage the "depressive position," which corresponds to Klein's depressive position.

For Fairbairn, schizophrenia and depression represent fixations at the stage of infantile dependence. Because of the devastating nature of the schizoid and the depressive conflicts, which are associated with the feelings of futility and depression, respectively, the person will defend against their emergence. Thus, during the transitional stage of development, the child, in his attempt to deal with the schizoid and the depressive conflicts, may employ obsessional, phobic, hysterical, and paranoid techniques.[1] In other words, obsessional, phobic, hysterical, and paranoid symptoms are seen as merely reflections of the operation of four specific techniques adopted during the transitional stage. That is why schizophrenic and depressed patients exhibit obsessional, phobic, hysterical, and paranoid symptoms.

The infant's first libidinal object is the maternal breast, which is soon extended to the person of the mother. As long as the infant experiences gratification, it does not need to do anything specific. But as soon as it experiences frustration by the object, it splits the mother into satisfying and unsatisfying aspects. (Thus far, Fairbairn's formulation strongly resembles Klein's, but the similarity ends here.) The frustrating mother presents the infant with a devastating dilemma. He feels rejected and unloved. If he expresses aggression, he is threatened with the loss of his good object. If he expresses his libidinal need, he is risking the discharge of his love into an emotional vacuum, which is equivalent to the loss of his libido

---

[1] In the obsessional state, both the accepted and the rejected objects are treated as internal. (Hence the conflict presents itself as one between expulsion and retention of the contents.) In the phobic state, both the accepted and the rejected objects are treated as external. (Hence the conflict can be formulated as one between flight toward the object and flight from the object.) In the hysterical state, the accepted object is externalized, whereas in the paranoid state the rejected object is externalized (1952, p. 45).

(which in turn is equivalent to the loss of his own goodness), and he is threatened with the loss of the ego structure which constitutes his self. In this dilemma, the infant concludes[2] that since he is impotent to control the bad mother in outer reality, he had better transfer the traumatic factor in the situation to the field of inner reality, within which he can feel situations are more under his control. This means that he internalizes his mother as a bad object. (While Klein assumed that internalization is the result of a natural process, Fairbairn postulated a specific motivation for internalization. And while Klein considered that internalization involves both good and bad objects, Fairbairn believed that, in the beginning, only the bad object is internalized.)

The bad object is one that combines allurement with frustration. After internalization, these two aspects are retained. Thus there are two internalized bad objects: the needed and exciting internal object, and the frustrating or rejecting internal object. Because the two create internal conflict, the child makes use of the simplest and most available defense, i.e., repression.[3] Fairbairn said, "repression represents a defensive reaction on the part of the ego, not primarily against intolerably unpleasant memories (as in Freud's earlier view), or against intolerably guilty impulses (as in Freud's later view), but against internalized objects which appear intolerably bad to the ego" (p. 164). In the process of repressing, the ego develops "pseudopodia" by means of which it still maintains libidinal attachments to the internalized objects that are undergoing repression. But when the repression is complete, the ego's attachment to the internalized object is lost. As a result, the original ego is split into three, namely, a central ego and two subsidiary egos. The central ego is the constricted version of the original ego, which remains partly

---

[2] Fairbairn's description implies that the infant is capable of making decisions. Such an assumption is, of course, highly questionable.

[3] In describing repression as the "simplest and most available" (p. 65) defense, Fairbairn seems to be going against the prevalent belief that there are many more primitive defense mechanisms (see Klein, 1935; A. Freud, 1936).

conscious and partly unconscious and continues to cope with external and internal reality. Both the subsidiary egos, which correspond to the libidinal ego (linked with the exciting object) and the internal saboteur (linked with the rejecting object), are repressed and unconscious. The central ego and the two split-off subsidiary egos (with their attached internalized objects) constitute what is called basic endopsychic structure. Lest there be confusion between his own concept of basic endopsychic structure and Freud's constructs of id-ego-superego, Fairbairn asserted that "the central ego corresponds to Freud's 'ego,' the libidinal ego to Freud's 'id,' and the internal saboteur to Freud's 'super-ego.' Nevertheless, underlying this correspondence there is a profound difference of conception" (p. 148).

Fairbairn conceptualized the superego as a structure of later development than the ego; it is composed of internalized *good* objects and may serve as a "moral defense." Before the superego is established, the child can only become "unconditionally" bad when he identifies with or has a relation with the internalized bad object. After the superego is established, the child has the option of becoming "conditionally" good or bad.

> In so far as the child leans towards his internalized bad objects, he becomes conditionally [i.e., morally] bad vis-à-vis his internalized good object [i.e., his superego]; and in so far as he resists the appeal of his internalized bad objects, he becomes conditionally [i.e., morally] good vis-à-vis his superego. It is obviously preferable to be conditionally good than conditionally bad; but, in default of conditional goodness, it is preferable to be conditionally bad than unconditionally bad [p. 66].

Although according to Fairbairn aggression is an important dynamic factor in producing disturbed object relations, he considered it a reaction to frustration. Contrary to Klein's assumption that the infant has to project his death instinct in order to survive, Fairbairn asserted that the infant does not direct aggression toward his libidinal object in the absence of some kind of frustration. In the face of frustration, when aggression cannot be discharged against the frustrating mother, it is used as the dynamic of repression[4] as well as of ego splitting. If excess aggression is not used up in repression and splitting, it is taken over by the internal saboteur. (In Freud's conceptualization, the excess aggression is absorbed by the superego.)

Fairbairn assumed that the frustrated child seeks to circumvent the danger of expressing both libidinal and aggressive affects toward the object by using a maximum of aggression to subdue a maximum of libidinal need. Since excessive amounts of aggression and libido are taken over by the internal saboteur and the libidinal ego respectively, the child's technique of using aggression to subdue libidinal need thus resolves itself into an attack by the internal saboteur on the libidinal ego and the exciting object.

Application of Fairbairn's Theory to Schizophrenia

From a clinical point of view, Fairbairn considered that schizophrenia proper is on a continuum with a group of other clinical phenomena (e.g., the schizoid type of psychopathic personality, the schizoid character, the transient schizoid episode), which he called collectively "schizoid conditions." These conditions are fixated in the schizoid position.

To Fairbairn, aggression is a reaction to frustration. In schizophrenia, the infant-child has presumably had more experience with frustration. The repeated experience of frustration leads to a fixation in the schizoid position and to a crystallization of the conflict, to love or not to love. On the other hand, fixated in the schizoid position, the child can only experience being unconditionally bad (the superego as a moral defense is developed later). Without the protection of the superego, the conflict continues, worsens, and eventually leads to an inability to direct libido to the external object; the even-

---

[4] This postulation resembles Hartmann's view (Hartmann et al., 1949) that the aggressive instinctual drive is responsible for the countercathexis.

tual outcome is a feeling of futility. Repression and splitting of the ego are used to defend against this feeling. Later, during the transitional period, the ego uses obsessional, phobic, hysterical, or paranoid techniques. In the meantime, because of his feeling of futility, the patient may even come to regard his love as destructive:

> ... if it seems a terrible thing for an individual to destroy his object by hate, it seems a much more terrible thing for him to destroy his object by love. It is the great tragedy of the schizoid individual that his love seems to destroy; and it is because his love seems so destructive that he experiences such difficulty in directing libido toward objects in outer reality. He becomes afraid to love; and therefore he erects barriers between his objects and himself [p. 50].

Fairbairn obviously treated the withdrawal of libido as most pathognomonic of schizophrenia. It may be carried to any lengths. It may reach a point where all emotional and physical contacts with other persons are renounced; it may even reach a point where all libidinal links with outer reality are surrendered, all interest in the world around fades, and everything becomes meaningless. Libido may be withdrawn from the realm of the conscious into the realm of unconscious, or, in extreme cases, even from the unconscious parts of the ego. In the latter case, what is left on the surface is the picture of what Kraepelin described as dementia praecox.

Fairbairn assumed that withdrawal of libido and repression may be related to each other: "... massive withdrawal of libido has the significance of a desperate effort on the part of an ego ... to avoid all emotional relationships with the external objects by repression of the basic libidinal tendencies" (p. 52). When all emotional relation with the external object is removed, the external object world is lost. In the process, the ego is lost as well: "... in renouncing libido the ego renounces the very form of energy which holds it together and the ego thus becomes lost. Loss of the ego is the ultimate psychopathological disaster which the schizoid individual is constantly struggling, with more or with less success, to avert by exploiting all available techniques for the control of his libido" (p. 52).

When libido is withdrawn from the outer objects, it is directed toward internalized objects. The excessive libidinization of internalized objects results in secondary narcissism. According to Fairbairn, "primary narcissism [is] defined as a state of identification with the object [and] secondary narcissism a state of identification with an object which is internalized" (p. 48). A sense of superiority is characteristic of secondary narcissism. It is based on an orientation toward internalized objects. However, in relation to objects in outer reality, the schizoid person's basic attitude is essentially one of inferiority.

Fairbairn stressed that aggression is not as much an issue in schizophrenia as it is in manic-depressive psychosis. While in the schizophrenic the basic issue is to love or not to love, in the manic-depressive it is to love or to hate. The aggressive and violent behavior of the schizophrenic is presumably the reflection of frustration.

Discussion

In what follows I shall not discuss Fairbairn's object-relations theory in detail. I agree with Jones that Fairbairn's is a "fresh approach in psychoanalysis" and that his ideas are "extremely stimulating to thought."

Concerning his views on schizophrenia, it must be said that, for the most part, Fairbairn talked broadly about "schizoid conditions." His comments directly related to schizophrenia are few. According to Fairbairn, a potentially schizophrenic infant encounters frustrations, introjects the bad objects, develops an ego split, and wrestles with the problem of to love or not to love.[5] In the presence of this conflict, the infant soon acquires a sense of futility against which he defends. Because

---

[5] The conflict over loving and not loving is comparable to Freud's formulation of decathexis-recathexis (see Chapter 3).

of the fixation in the schizoid position, and because of the presence of a sense of futility, the potential schizophrenic eventually withdraws libido from external objects. The extent of the libidinal withdrawal varies: Schizophrenia represents an extreme degree of withdrawal. In speaking of withdrawal of libido, Fairbairn gave the impression of speaking of the same process described by Freud. In a way, he was, but the meaning he assigned to "libido" is different from the one Freud assigned to the term. To Fairbairn, "libido is the fundamental 'life-energy' and sexual and aggressive energy are specialized aspects of it" (Guntrip, 1968, p. 422).

When Fairbairn talked about fixation in the schizoid position that eventually leads to schizophrenia, he was merely trying to describe the psychopathogenesis of schizophrenia. He was not at all concerned with how various symptoms of schizophrenia occur. His consideration of the phenomenon that "the world of internalized objects is always liable to encroach upon the world of external objects" (p. 50) is limited to phenomenal description; he offers no explanation for symptom formation or chronicity.

Although Fairbairn did consider aggression as a dynamic factor in the formation of the basic endopsychic structure, he underplayed the role of aggression in schizophrenia. This position is diametrically opposed to that of Klein, who stressed the need for constantly dealing with the patient's aggression (and not love) in therapy. It is of great interest that despite their differences in theoretical orientation and therapeutic approach, both Fairbairn and Klein were able to claim success with their patients.

All things considered, Fairbairn's view of schizophrenia is inadequate to explain all aspects of schizophrenic phenomena. Yet many of his clinical observations are extremely valuable. For instance, he observed that schizophrenics cannot allow themselves to love. Clinically, this observation can be readily confirmed. Schizophrenics feel acutely that their love for others can only bring rejection, narcissistic hurt, and therefore disaster to their own self-valuation. Thus they tend to maintain distance from others and not get involved with them. Or, if they find themselves involved, they withdraw immediately. They appear aloof, independent, and diffident. Their fear of involvement is often described as fear of loss of self-identity or of self-boundary, fear of the merging of self- and object representations—in Fairbairn's terms, fear of the loss of libido or of the ego (Fairbairn never used the term "self"). Fairbairn further suggested that schizophrenics also feel that their love is destructive to the object. Such feelings are, however, comparatively less ascertainable.

Fairbairn observed that feelings of futility are prevalent among patients with schizoid conditions, just as feelings of depression are predominant among depressive patients. This observation is invaluable, regardless of theoretical considerations. It does not really matter whether the feeling of futility results from the inability to resolve the conflict whether to love or not to love or whether it stimulates the use of various defensive techniques. What matters is that schizophrenic patients do experience feelings of futility, and in therapy those feelings must be dealt with squarely. So very often the patient feels that it is useless for him to try to invest libido in the object. It is this attitude that leads the schizophrenic to let his life rot away, sitting on a bench in a corner of a hospital ward.

CHAPTER 9

Schizophrenia in the Light of Sullivan's Interpersonal Theory

In his presidential address at the 28th International Psycho-Analytical Congress of the International Psycho-Analytical Association, Rangell (1974) spoke about "splits in analysis" and various "alternative systems." He said,

> But whatever their points of difference, in all cases the alternative systems utilize the mechanism of *pars pro toto*—and their followers prefer the part to the whole. . . . Gestalt therapy picks our 'whole' concept (while leaving out its inner parts!) . . . Horney pick[s] the environment, Sullivan the interpersonal, Rado adaptation, transactional analysts only aspects of the transference, etc. None of these are wrong, but all of them are incomplete. Sullivan's interpersonal as later Fairbairn's object relations have a place and need to be squarely in the middle of it all—but never alone or separate. I never forget 'object relations' in clinical work or analytic thinking. No analyst can [p. 6].

This statement places Sullivan's contributions in proper perspective.

Sullivan's emphasis on interpersonal relations was perhaps determined by his concentrated study of patients who were afflicted with schizophrenia, just as Fairbairn's emphasis on object relations was based on his clinical observations primarily of patients with schizoid conditions. It is a moot question to what degree Sullivan would have singled out interpersonal relations if he had been exposed exclusively to neurotic patients. After all, in the treatment of schizophrenic patients, the therapist must often concern himself only with the patient's manifestly studiable relations with others for a long time before he can help him resolve his basic conflicts.

It has been suggested that Sullivan's personal experience, especially during late adolescence, was the source of a special capacity to understand the schizophrenic experience. (Farber [1977] has said that Sullivan's own personality make-up necessitated his paying particular attention to interpersonal relations.) His early papers (1924a, 1924b, 1925, 1926, 1927, 1929, 1931), in which he made phenomenological recordings of schizophrenics' experiences with a minimal amount of theorizing, are still important to students of schizophrenia. Beginning in 1931, however, he attempted a comprehensive theoretical formulation of personality development (1972). He discarded the instinct theory (as Fairbairn did in the 1940's) and coined new terms to describe Freudian concepts—especially those explained in "The Ego and the Id" (1923) and "Inhibitions, Symptoms and Anxiety" (1926a). Sullivan's subsequent conceptualization of schizophrenia is phrased in the language of his interpersonal theory.

Interpersonal Theory

Interpersonal theory concerns itself with processes that involve or go on among people. It stresses that "the personality can never be isolated from the complex of interpersonal relations in which the person lives and has his being" (1940, p. 4). Although Sullivan began to formulate interpersonal theory in the early 30's,[1] his *Conceptions of Modern Psychia-*

[1] Before the posthumous publication of his book, *Personal Psychopathology* (1972), it was difficult to determine when Sullivan's break with classical psychoanalysis occurred. This book indicates that it took place in the years 1929 to 1932.

try, delivered in 1939 and published in 1940, seems to mark the birth of the theory. Sullivan subsequently elaborated and refined his conceptions in a series of lectures given at the Washington School of Psychiatry and at Chestnut Lodge. The 1946-1947 series at the former and the 1943 series at the latter were published posthumously (1953, 1956).

Basic to Sullivan's theory is the distinction between what is biological and what is cultural. He wrote, "The most general basis on which interpersonal phenomena, interpersonal acts, may be classified, is one which separates the sought end states into the group which we call satisfaction and those which we call security or the maintenance of security" (1940, p. 6). "Satisfactions" are closely related to the body organization of man; the pursuit of "security" pertains more closely to man's cultural equipment. When the satisfaction of physical needs is deferred to the point where they become very powerful, "fear" appears, whereas *"anxiety*[2] is called out [in the infant] by emotional disturbances of certain types in the significant person—that is, the person with whom the infant is doing something" (1953, p. 9). The nature of the situation in which fear appears is usually definable, whereas the nature of situations that provoke anxiety is never completely grasped. "It is quite clear that since anxiety in the mother makes the infant anxious, we cannot expect the infant to understand very much about what caused anxiety" (1953, p. 190).

According to the intensity of anxiety in his interpersonal relations, the infant soon comes to appreciate three distinctly different experiences: "good-me," "bad-me," and "not-me."[3] The good-me experience is relatively free of anxiety. The bad-

[2] He said, "there is no difference between anxiety and fear so far as the vague mental states of the infant are concerned" (1953, p. 9). Nevertheless, from the theoretical viewpoint, he differentiated fear and anxiety and reserved anxiety for interpersonal use only. In common psychoanalytic parlance the term anxiety reflects, in the beginning, a bodily reaction to the frustration of biological needs; in the course of object relations, the experience of anxiety becomes related to object loss, loss of the object's love, and fear of castration.

[3] In the literature, not-me usually refers to what stands in opposition to "me" (e.g., Jacobson, 1964). Sullivan's not-me implies a loss-of-me experience.

me experience refers to an increased degree of anxiety. The not-me experience comes from the expression of extreme anxiety; it is attended by uncanny emotions usually described as awe, dread, loathing, or terror. Because of its unpleasant nature, the not-me experience is one that "we know about only through certain very special circumstances . . . [it] is most conspicuously encountered by most of us in an occasional dream while we are asleep; but it is very emphatically encountered by people who are having a severe schizophrenic episode" (1953, pp. 162-163).

The essential desirability of the good-me or the essential undesirability of the not-me leads to the organization in the infant of "what might be said to be a dynamism directed at how to live with this significant other person" (1953, p. 165). Sullivan called this organization the "self-dynamism"[4] or "self-system." "The self-system is derived wholly from the interpersonal aspects of the necessary environment of the human being; it is organized because of the extremely unpalatable, extremely uncomfortable experience of anxiety; and it is organized in such a way as to avoid or minimize existent or foreseen anxiety" (1953, p. 190). By definition, the self-system undergoes reorganization in accordance with the needs of each developmental phase, to assure smooth functioning that not only works negatively toward maintaining security (i.e., minimal anxiety), but also works toward assuring the maximal satisfaction of needs.

To safeguard the function of the self-system, that is, to ensure minimal anxiety as well as maximal satisfaction, various strategies or "security operations" will be devised, including selective inattention, substitution, sublimation, projection, regression (disintegration), etc.[5] Like the self-system, security operations will undergo phase-specific restructurings during the various developmental stages. For instance,

---

[4] He uses the term dynamism to denote the ever-changing quality. The self-dynamism is described as crystallizing at the time when the infant acquires language.

[5] "Security operations" seem to refer to activities that in psychoanalytic language are called defense mechanisms.

selective inattention[6] may be elaborated into dissociation, substitution into obsessive dynamisms, and projection into paranoid dynamisms.

The security operation of dissociation is particularly related to keeping the not-me experience out of the self-system. Through dissociation, the not-me experience and the attendant uncanny emotions are kept from being experienced except when one is asleep. As a security device, "dissociation isn't a matter of keeping a sleeping dog under an anesthetic. It works by a continuous alertness or vigilance of awareness, with certain supplementary processes which prevent one's ever discovering the usually quite clear evidences that part of one's living is done without any awareness" (1953, p. 318).

The excessive use of dissociation leads to limitations and peculiarities of the self-dynamism. "Needless to say, limitations and peculiarities of the self-[dynamism] may interfere with the pursuit of biologically necessary satisfactions. When this happens, the person is to that extent mentally ill. Similarly, they may interfere with security, and to that extent also the person is mentally ill" (1940, p. 10).

Schizophrenia in the Light of Interpersonal Theory

With the salient points of interpersonal theory outlined, I shall now attempt to show how Sullivan integrated it with his conceptualization of schizophrenia. He assumed that the mothering person of the future schizophrenic is more anxiety-ridden than the average mother. Her anxiety is so intense that it imparts an excessive amount of not-me experience to the child, and consequently a special vulnerability to not-me

---

[6] "Both repression and suppression, as I understand them, refer to processes which are at least alleged to apply to motives; and when I talk about selective inattention I am not talking about motives at all. I am talking about things which you notice but never attend to" (Sullivan, 1956, pp. 63-64). By "motives" he probably meant instincts. Yet "not attending to" involves both intentionality and motivation. In the concept of "selective inattention," however, he touches on perception-cognition and its potential for being caught in conflicts.

experience. At the time speech is acquired, the self-system becomes crystallized. As soon as it does, it operates to ward off the not-me experience, resulting in an excessive use of the specific security operation of dissociation. In the course of personality development (which, according to Sullivan's terminology, proceeds from infantile to childhood, to juvenile, to preadolescence and adolescence), the self-dynamism is greatly compromised. Then, during the adolescent period, the powerful lust dynamism interferes with the function of the self-system. Thereupon the dissociative process fails. As the not-me experience returns, there is established "a state which is so completely disorganizing that it may be called, with certain reservations, panic" (1953, p. 326). During the panic state, the foundation of the structure of one's beliefs and convictions about the guarantees and securities and dependable properties of the universe in which one is living disappears. Thereafter

> the personality . . . has moved from what was actually its developmental level into a state which we call the schizophrenic way of life. In the schizophrenic state, very early types of referential process occur within clear awareness, to the profound mystification of the person concerned. And since many of these referential processes are literally historically identical with the composition of the not-me components in personality, their presence is attended by uncanny emotions, sometimes dreadfully strong [1953, p. 327].

One of the strong uncanny emotions experienced is terror.[7] Terror may be conceptualized as "an almost unceasing fear of becoming an exceedingly unpleasant form of nothingness by collapse of [the self-system]" (1956, p. 318). To avoid this fear, the patient feels an urgency to get away from an extremely menacing real situation: ". . . but there is no way to [determine] what it is that is menacing. . . . his urgency has such a sort of totality that good clear thinking cannot be done

---

[7] According to Sullivan, terror is different from panic. Panic is a momentary experience, whereas terror may be lasting.

about it, for it is more real than thought" (1956, p. 317).[8]
Because of this "urgency," the patient is very often driven
toward "blind frantic activities which can be very destructive
to oneself or others" (1953, p. 327). When the patient becomes
dimly aware that the frantic activity does not help to solve
his problem, particularly the threat of recurrent terror, he
ties up all his skeletal muscles and becomes catatonic. In catatonia, beneath the immobility, the self-system maintains its
functioning capacity. "Even if the [self-system] is not effective
in achieving security, the schizophrenic still has a [self-system]
as shown if he falls into the paranoid (or hebephrenic) type
of maladjustment" (1956, p. 318).

Although in his early papers Sullivan mentioned the
schizophrenic patient's violent acts against the physician and
other members of the treatment team, he addressed the issue
only from the management point of view. He suggested that
the physician must take into consideration the patient's distorted perceptual-cognitive process, that he must attempt to
understand his patient, and that he must not counter the
violence with violence. In the process of refining his theory
of anxiety, he offered an explanation of the origin of the patient's violence in the concept of "malevolent transformation":

> A child may discover that manifesting the need for tenderness
> toward the potent figures around him leads frequently to his
> being disadvantaged, being made anxious, being made fun of,
> and so on, so that, according to the locution used, he is hurt, or
> in some cases he may be literally hurt. Under those circum-
> stances, the developmental course changes to the point that the
> perceived need for tenderness brings a foresight of anxiety or
> pain. The child learns that it is highly disadvantageous to show
> any need for tender cooperation from the authoritative figures
> around him, in which case he shows something else; and that

---

[8] "I suppose that if we had two or three of our most gifted schizophrenics here
now, and I should turn to them and ask, 'What is this urgency for?' one of them
might say, 'Well, we are really a little interested in getting back to being human
beings. It seems quite imperative. I guess that must be what you are talking about.'
In other words, the urgency is to get together again, to have the world remain, you
might say, at peace" (Sullivan, 1956, p. 320). An application of this urgency has been
provided in Burnham's (1973) study of Strindberg.

something else is the basic malevolent attitude, the attitude that one really lives among enemies [1953, p. 214].

Earlier, Sullivan said that the schizophrenic patient's thoughts and language are autistic, and that in the treatment of these patients the therapist must be aware that they may use common words but assign completely different meaning to them. Now, Sullivan postulated three modes of experience: (a) Prototaxic experience, which refers to a momentary experience an infant must have, and in which his knowledge of past-present-future is dim and not differentiated; (2) parataxic experience, wherein the older infant not only knows of past-present-future, but is able to make connections of momentary experience—although these connections are not reflected on and may not follow logical steps; (3) syntaxic experience, the experience of older children in which the personal meaning of the experience is validated by that of others around him. The occurrence of the three modes of experience follows a developmental sequence. In schizophrenia, either the sequential development of the three modes of experience is blocked or there is a regressive reappearance of earlier modes.

At first Sullivan did not postulate the whys and hows of hallucination in schizophrenia. After he formulated the concept of self-system, he suggested that although oral dynamisms and lust dynamisms have the mouth and the genitals take part in the zonal interaction, the self-system "may not have any particular zones of interaction, any particular physiological apparatus, behind it; but it literally uses all zones of interaction and all physiological apparatus which is integrative and meaningful from the interpersonal standpoint" (1953, p. 164). Developmentally, the self-system as a dynamism occurs much later than the oral dynamism and the lust dynamism. In schizophrenia, therefore, when regression sets in, the function of the self-system is weakened. As a consequence, "there will be the phenomena which arise from autonomous function of some zone of interaction, often the auditory apparatus" (1940, pp. 67-68).

As early as 1924, Sullivan thought that schizophrenia might be conceived of as a disorder of the mind in which "there is a great eruption of primitive functions [and] in which the total experience of the individual is reorganized" (1962, p. 12), and that psychotherapeutic effort may bring about a "better" form of reorganization. As far he was concerned, schizophrenia is "conservative." "Even in the group who came out of their psychosis with a decidedly paranoid adjustment to reality, there had been a change from an obviously ineffectual adaptation to one in which the social contacts of the individual caused him much less profound discomfort; emotional introversion and brooding gave way to the less individually destructive projection of discomfort and hate" (1962, p. 14). This ultraoptimistic viewpoint surpassed even that of Bleuler, who had, 15 years earlier, stressed that not all schizophrenics are headed for dementia and that many of them do recover (even though the recovery may not be total, i.e., not *restitutio ad integrum*). Sullivan was, of course, speaking of what we have described as schizophrenic-I patients (and perhaps also some schizophrenic-II patients). These were the types of patients admitted to his special research ward at Sheppard and Enoch Pratt Hospital. For this group of patients, he advocated psychotherapy as well as sociomilieu therapy. With regard to psychotherapy, he stressed the role of the therapist as a participant observer.

Although he viewed schizophrenia as a process for reintegrating the unacceptable experience (the not-me experience), he did not think that the reintegration had to be accompanied by insight:

> The degree of "insight" which the patient brings from his psychosis is quite generally accepted as having an important relation to the stability of recovery. Insight, however, is never perfect, and there are a large proportion of recovered or arrested schizophrenics who have achieved a reasonably unified personality, fairly adapted to the social integration, without any ability for the conscious formulation and expression which we generally seek as evidence of insight [1962, p. 15].

Regarding most schizophrenic-III and some schizophrenic-II patients, he said,

> there are some people who, rather astonishingly early, perhaps at the age of 14, 15, or 16, get more interested in philosophizing about good and evil, the nature of God and the Universe, and one thing and another, than in how to make the grade in school social affairs. Gradually they become more and more preposterously unrealistic in the statements they make about the nature of God, good, and so on, and less and less interested in their appearance and their activities—in fact, in living. . . . I believe that these people suffer some kind of organic deterioration. . . . I have not been able to find anything except the grossest appearances which seem to have anything to do with what I know to be schizophrenia. . . . I am quite willing to think that here we may have an hereditarily determined deterioration [1956, pp. 309-310].

Discussion

Psychoanalysis established the first conception of reality relations in terms of the secondary process and in relation to danger situations, but did not generalize it into a concept of adaptation until 1937. Thus the theory of object relations remained outside the scope of psychoanalytic ego psychology, and the psychosocial implications of reality and object relations remained unexplained theoretically. In the late 30's this gap in psychoanalytic theory apparently became so conspicuous that several simultaneous attempts to bridge it were made. Some of these attempts (Erikson, Hartmann, Kris, and Loewenstein) showed a clear awareness of the foundations which existed in psychoanalysis for a theory of reality relationships in general, and interpersonal (psychosocial) relationships in particular. They also took into account the incipient theory of the ego's autonomous roots, development, and functions implied in Freud's ego psychology. [Other] attempts (Horney, Kardiner, Sullivan, etc.) . . . showed no such awareness [Rapaport, 1959, p. 11].

It seems that the sharply contrasted attitudes Sullivan showed to the schizophrenic-I patient on the one hand and the schizophrenic-III patient on the other could have been anticipated as soon as he formulated his interpersonal theory of anxiety. According to this theory, the genesis of schizophrenia can be traced to an early mother-infant relationship in which the infant is a passive, unfortunate victim. This formulation does not take into account the decisive role of the ego's autonomous roots in the etiology of schizophrenia. Obviously, neither the constitutional nor the environment factor is the sole cause of schizophrenia. Rather, the interaction of these factors may give rise to a range of basic experiential disturbances, with schizophrenic-I patients at one end of the range and schizophrenic-III patients at the other. For schizophrenic-III patients, the effect of therapeutic intervention can be seen only after a long time, whereas with schizophrenic-I patients it can be seen very quickly.

In terms of symptom formation, according to the interpersonal theory of schizophrenia, the break with reality is followed by a collapse of the patient's self-system. But the self-system continues to operate; the result is hebephrenic or paranoid symptoms.[9] In this particular aspect, the interpersonal theory of schizophrenia affirms Freud's conceptualization of symptom formation in two phases. Because of Sullivan's unique experience with schizophrenics, this affirmation is extremely valuable.

Sullivan's conceptualization is similar to Fairbairn's in that the not-me experience (which is essentially affective) of the former and the feeling of futility of the latter are presumed to be dissociated or repressed in order to prevent the schizophrenic illness from becoming clinically manifest. In both theories affect is assigned the central role in making the self-system or the ego work. Such an assumption obviously becomes necessary when one discards instinct theory.

A concept that Sullivan made use of in his interpersonal theory was the feeling of security. Regardless of its origin from the theoretical point of view, the concept is a useful one.

---

[9] Cf. Fenichel's formulation of symptom formation (Chapter 4). Except for the difference in language, Sullivan's and Fenichel's formulations are strikingly similar.

It has been explored by Sandler (1960) in the treatment of neurosis, and it is especially useful in the treatment of schizophrenia. Too often, the schizophrenic sacrifices instinctual gratification for the sake of the feeling of security (Sullivan) or for the sake of maintaining the background feeling of safety (Sandler).

With respect to the treatment of schizophrenia, Sullivan's emphasis was on the study of interpersonal relations with current significant others in terms of the past. This approach can be a useful orientation, at least in the beginning of treatment, as it encourages the patient to look outward. The study of conflicts, on the other hand, inevitably invites the patient to look inward.

CHAPTER 10

The Place of Federn's Ego Psychology in a Contemporary Theory of Schizophrenia

Federn's terms "ego feelings," "ego boundaries," and "ego states" derive from his pioneering attempts to apply psychoanalytic insights to the treatment of psychotic patients. These terms have such great descriptive power that they have remained in common usage in psychoanalysis, while the theoretical edifice Federn built has remained on the periphery of psychoanalytic thinking. Federn derived his "ego psychology" from his observations of the dream and his work with psychotics. In this chapter I shall review Federn's conceptualizations primarily to determine their present relevance for interpreting schizophrenic phenomena.

In what follows, I shall first define Federn's concepts of "ego feelings," "ego boundary," and "ego state," then review his application of these concepts to the understanding of schizophrenia, and, finally, evaluate the place of his contribution in a contemporary theory of schizophrenia.

This chapter is based on a paper of the same title published in the *International Review of Psycho-Analysis*, 2:467-480, 1975.

Definitions of Federn's Basic Terms

Federn's conceptualization, as Bergmann (1963) has pointed out, originated in phenomenological psychiatry and was greatly influenced by the work of Husserl, Jaspers, and Schilder.[1] To describe the phenomenological concept in psychoanalytic terminology, it was only natural that Federn should assign new meanings to many familiar psychoanalytic terms. As a result, Federn's writings are obscure and difficult to understand.[2] I shall therefore try to clarify some of his basic terms.

Ego Psychology

Federn's ego psychology is very different from Hartmann's. To Hartmann, the ego is defined in terms of its function. As an organization, it stands in contradistinction to other substructures of the personality—namely, the id and the superego. It is also specifically distinguished from the self. To Federn, the ego is conceived "not as merely the sum of all the functions, but as the cathexis which unites the aggregate into a new mental entity" (1949a, p. 185), or,

> the ego ... includes the subjective psychic experience of these functions with a characteristic sensation. This self-experience is a permanent ... entity, which is not an abstraction but a reality. It is an entity which stands in relation to the continuity of the person in respect to time, space and causality. It can be recognized objectively and is constantly felt and perceived subjectively [1932, p. 61].

As a subject, the ego stands for "I," and as an object, the ego stands for "self."

---

[1] Ernest Federn of Vienna, Austria (personal communication, 1976), however, has informed me that "P. Federn was not influenced by Husserl, Jaspers, or Schilder, but by Hans Driesch, and much in agreement with Berze as far as schizophrenia was concerned."

[2] Some of Federn's concepts have been clarified by Grauer (1957), Weiss (1952, 1960), and Bergmann (1963).

In his editorial note to "On Narcissism" (Freud, 1914b), Strachey (1957) said,

the meaning which Freud attached to 'das Ich' (almost invariably translated by 'the ego' in this edition) underwent a gradual modification. At first he used the term without any great precision, as we might speak of 'the self'; but in his latest writings he gave it a very much more definite and narrow meaning. The present paper occupies a transitional point in this development [p. 71].

Federn's "ego," then, takes off [3] from the concept of the ego as Freud used it in "On Narcissism" (1914b), whereas Hartmann's "ego" is conceptualized in terms of its functions, in accordance with Freud's later formulation in "The Ego and the Id" (1923).

In concerning himself with the delineation of id, ego, and superego in terms of their functions and their interrelatedness, Hartmann found it necessary to trace the origin of the ego and to conceptualize the undifferentiated matrix from which the ego and the id are differentiated. On the other hand, while he accepted that self-awareness or ego feelings reflect the functioning of the ego, he did not dwell on the nature and meaning of self-awareness or ego feelings. In Federn's ego psychology, the phenomenological or experiential self-awareness or ego feeling is central. Although he spoke of the ego as "not merely the sum of all [its] functions," Federn never concerned himself with the nature of these functions. In fact, Federn never assimilated Freud's later structural theory:[4] For instance, he conceived of the superego not as one of the three structures of the personality, but as a special ego state.

Thus, although they used the same terms, Federn and Hartmann were addressing themselves to very different is-

---

[3] Federn stressed the phenomenological, or subjective-descriptive, aspect far more than Freud did.

[4] Yet, in contrast to the trend of his time, Federn wholeheartedly accepted Freud's death instinct—calling it "mortido"—even though, as Jacobson (1954a) has pointed out, he said little about its role in schizophrenia.

sues. More recently, in defining ego and self in terms of "experience-distant" and "experience-near" levels of abstraction, Kohut (1971) seems to have raised the possibility of a theory that might include both Federn's and Hartmann's ego psychologies.

Ego Feeling

Federn (1932) observed that "we possess . . . an enduring *feeling* and knowledge that our ego is continuous and persistent, despite interruptions by sleep or unconsciousness" (p. 61; my italics). Federn introduced the term ego feeling to stress that "the ego's experience includes a sensory element" (p. 62). From the very outset, Freud had made it quite clear that ideation and affect are intimately related, that we cannot consider one without the other, and that only for the sake of brevity would we speak only of ideation (or only of affect). But in the early and middle 1920's, when Federn called attention to the importance of feeling tones, the emphasis in the psychoanalytic literature was on the ideational side. It was the general practice for the writer to confine himself to a description of the ideational content and for the reader on his own to infer, from that content, the affective component. This phenomenon was a reflection of the treatment of neurosis. Usually, the neurotic patient's feelings can be deduced from a report of his coherent verbalized productions. To overstress feelings seems redundant. In the case of schizophrenia, however, where the patient's cognitive process is severely disturbed, it is not easy at all, as Federn had obviously noticed, to infer the patient's feelings from his verbalizations. In such circumstances it is imperative for the therapist not to assume that in understanding the patient's ideation he knows what to do with his patient; he must also carefully survey his patient's affective state before he can make any appropriate intervention. Perhaps because of this discovery, and because he made it at a time when the ideational side was stressed, Federn not only felt the need to refer to the

affective component, but also felt compelled to overemphasize the "importance of ego feelings in contrast to ego images . . . [and] to ignore the intimate connection between
cognitive and emotional self-awareness" (Jacobson, 1954a, p.
521).

From an experiential point of view, Federn (1926) distinguishes three kinds of ego feelings: somatic (body), psychic
(mental), and superego. He indicates that in "normal" circumstances body ego and psychic ego feelings cannot be distinguished; they are experienced as one. In dreams, however,
these two ego feelings may be experienced as separate. For
instance, the dreamer who moves about without being encum-
bered by gravity exemplifies the awakening of the mental ego
feeling without the body ego feeling. A similar separation
may also occur in the process of falling asleep or waking up,
and in such pathological states as depersonalization, derealization (which Federn calls estrangement), and schizophrenia. We are greatly indebted to Federn's clinical observational
astuteness, which enabled him to distinguish between the
mental and body ego feelings at a phenomenological or de-
scriptive-experiential level. This early observation of Federn's (and of Isakower and others) is a useful contribution to
our knowledge of altered states of consciousness in which
body experience is dissociated from self-observation.[5] As for
superego feeling, it has never been adequately defined—it is
in fact one of those expressions that make Federn's exposi-
tions obscure. He said that superego feeling is experienced in
certain conflictual states, such as melancholia; we may take
him to mean that superego feeling reflects the feeling tone or
tension between the ego and the superego. But that may not
be the meaning Federn attached to the term, for he did not

---

[5] Arlow (1966) states, "Depersonalization and derealization may be understood
as representing a dissociation of the function of immediate experiencing from the
function of self-observation" (p. 456); and, "in depersonalization, self-awareness is
heightened and the sense of participation in action is minimized and alienated" (p.
463). I (1969a) have observed that, in the syndrome of delicate cutting, "the reverse
was true, i.e., the sense of immediate experiencing was highly invested, whereas
self-awareness was obliterated" (p. 199).

subscribe to the structural theory and spoke of superego feeling as one particular form of mental ego feeling.[6]

Most of the time, Federn defined ego feeling as "the totality of feeling which one has of one's own living person" (1932, p. 62). It is what allows the person to experience himself as a subject in contradistinction to the outer world and also to experience himself as an object among all representations of objects. It is because of ego feeling that the person experiences the present as existing between past and future; without ego feeling he would experience the present not as anchored in a continuum but as something new and strange. Thus defined, ego feeling seems to approximate what we would now call a sense of self or a sense of identity.[7] But Federn occasionally assigned other meanings to ego feeling. For instance, when he said, "the total subjective experience of one's ego orientation toward an act is qualified by the feeling that is present at that time" (1932, p. 62), he seems to have been referring to what is today called "mood" (see Jacobson, 1957; Weinshel, 1970). And when he said, "I was justified in introducing the term ego feeling (*Ichgefühl*)" (Federn, 1929, p. 290) and then, in a footnote, expressed his agreement with Freud's (1917) usage of *Ichgefühl*, he seems to have been extending his definition of ego feeling to include self-esteem as well. Judging from his various definitions of ego feeling, Federn appears to have been exploring many important problems that still confront us—problems like "sense of self," "sense of identity," "mood," and "self-esteem." Moreover, he seems also to have been reaching toward what Sandler (1960) later conceptualized as a background affective state of safety.[8]

[6] Ernest Federn (personal communication, 1976) has informed me that "Federn says clearly that superego is another ego state.... The ego is a state cathected by instinctual drives ... while the superego as an ego state is cathected with parental and social representations or ... is of a later and essentially social origin. This is another of the complications in Federn's conceptions that he mixes freely biological, social and phenomenological concepts."

[7] A "sense of self" and a "sense of identity" are, strictly speaking, different from "self" and "identity." See Jacobson (1954c, 1964), Erikson (1959, 1968), and Lichtenstein (1961, 1963).

[8] According to Sandler (1960), "this feeling of safety is more than a simple absence of discomfort or anxiety, [it is] a very definite feeling quality within the ego; ... we

Ego Boundary

First introduced by Tausk (1919), the term ego boundary was given new meanings by Federn. Tausk used the term negatively. By "loss of ego boundary," he meant the clinical phenomenon Bleuler (1911) called "merging of self into others." Federn, on the other hand, used the concept of ego boundary more positively. For Federn, the ego boundary "sharply distinguishes everything that belongs to the ego in an actual moment of life from all the other mental elements and complexes not actually included in the ego" (1949b, p. 22). Or, defined in terms of ego feeling, the ego boundary is the periphery of the ego feeling; it reflects "How far the ego [feeling] extends or more correctly, the point beyond which the ego [feeling] does not extend" (1936, p. 331).

Federn established the concept of two ego boundaries: outer and inner. The outer ego boundary separates the ego from the external world; the inner boundary separates conscious from unconscious. It is difficult to determine when Federn conceived of the inner ego boundary. It is evident, however, that in his earlier writings the ego boundary refers to the outer ego boundary only, and it is also evident that he studied the outer ego boundary much more carefully. While theoretical concepts attached to the outer ego boundary are very much rooted in clinical phenomenological and experiential observations, the concepts related to the inner ego boundary are principally theoretical.

The outer ego boundary separates the ego from the external world. At the phenomenological-experiential level, Federn observed that the outer ego boundary is never static—it changes constantly. It may not correspond to the person's actual boundary. It expands and shrinks to where one's ego feeling is. Thus, when driving a car, one's ego boundary may

---

can further regard much of ordinary everyday behaviour as being a means of maintaining a minimum level of safety-feeling; and . . . much normal behaviour as well as many clinical phenomena (such as certain types of psychotic behaviour and the addictions) can be more fully understood in terms of the ego's attempts to *preserve* this level of safety" (p. 352).

be at the fenders of the car; when addressing a group, it may embrace the audience, etc.[9] From this observation Federn (1929) theorized that in every psychic act which is fully experienced there is a merging of the libido of the ego boundary with the libido of the object representation. This view could be taken to mean that even in a "normal" object relation there is a merging of the two persons' ego boundaries. Of this, Jacobson says, "Federn's [view seems] . . . likely to create confusion. . . . This view would characterize any object relation, even a normal one, in terms of narcissistic identification" (1954a, p. 521).

At any rate, Federn held on to the concept of merging and believed that in each such merging there is a transient expansion of the ego boundary. The repeated expansion and subsequent adjustment of the ego boundary leads to the establishment of numerous ego boundaries that reflect "the narcissistic cathexis with ego feeling of many representations of the external world" (1929, p. 302). In the course of development, each of the numerous early ego boundaries may be given up and may again be newly invested. But none of them will be totally lost. If they are never "lost," what happens to them? To this question, Federn's answer was that each ego boundary is "repressed," kept in the unconscious, and that "the entire world of primary narcissism remains extant, as dreams and psychosis reveal" (1929, p. 302).

Federn saw the outer boundary as in constant negotiation with one's experience of the environment. This process makes it possible for the person to sense thought as occurring within the mental and physical ego boundary and to sense as "real" what lies outside it. Consequently, the outer ego boundary is conceived as the ego's "sense organ."[10] This sense organ, once

[9] It is this ever-changing quality of the outer ego boundary that made Weiss (1952) characterize Federn's view as the "dynamic" concept of ego boundary (p. 12).

[10] The concept of the outer ego boundary as the ego's "sense organ" is perhaps derived from Freud's concept of "consciousness as a 'sense organ' of the ego." Although Freud offered this concept as early as 1900, he did not elaborate on it for some 25 years. In "The Question of Lay Analysis," he wrote: "The ego, as you will

developed, automatically determines what is "real" and what is "unreal."[11] "The discrimination between the data which are felt as pertaining to the ego and those which are *felt* as belonging to the non-ego is a matter of particular sensation, of the sense of reality, and does not rest on the functioning of reality testing" (Weiss, 1952, p. 7).

The inner ego boundary. As I mentioned above, Federn postulated that (outer) ego boundaries are subject to repression, and, once repressed, are kept in the unconscious. Along this line of reasoning, he suggested that what separates the conscious from the unconscious is the inner ego boundary. Thus the ego is assumed to have definite confines: It is set off from the outside world by the outer ego boundary and from the unconscious by the inner ego boundary. The outer ego boundary is assigned the function of "sensing" reality, and the inner ego boundary is assigned the function of maintaining repression. If the outer ego boundary becomes weakened or lost, in whatever circumstances, the external objects, however distinctly perceived, are sensed as strange, unfamiliar, lifeless, or even unreal. Similarly, if the inner ego boundary is weakened or lost, as in psychosis or in dreams, the unconscious content, including the repressed outer ego boundaries, will return, and the person starts hallucinating or dreaming.

Federn's concept of inner ego boundary was not altogether new, although the term was. It corresponds to Freud's (1900) concept of "censorships" between the unconscious and preconscious and conscious. By giving censorship a new name, Federn brought order and coherence to his theoretical edifice;

---

remember, is the external, peripheral layer of the id. Now, we believe that on the outermost surface of this ego there is a special agency directed immediately to the external world, a system, an organ, through the excitation of which alone the phenomenon that we call consciousness comes about. This organ can be equally well excited from outside—thus receiving (with the help of the sense-organs) the stimuli from the external world—and from inside—thus becoming aware, first, of the sensations in the id, and then also of the processes in the ego" (1926b, p. 198).

[11] This view of Federn's anticipates Frosch's (1966) more recent conception of "reality constancy."

he could now explain schizophrenia in terms of loss of the two ego boundaries. I shall return to this matter shortly.

It must be noted that, in the current literature, the term ego boundary refers to the boundary between the ego and the outer world.[12] If the term is limited to this narrower usage—as Tausk originally intended—and if we adopt Hartmann's distinction between the self and the ego, we may prefer to speak of self-boundary rather than of ego boundary.[13]

Ego States

Federn defined ego state as what corresponds to a specific ego boundary with specific content, including mnemic images and associated affective experience. "The specific contents which are at any given time included within the ego boundary determine the specific ego state. Different ego boundaries are correlated with different ego states" (Weiss, 1952, p. 14). The term ego state is obviously used to lay special emphasis on the content, an emphasis that the term ego boundary cannot convey. It is because of this difference in emphasis that much of what has been said before in terms of ego boundary must now be restated in terms of ego states. Previously, Federn said that in object relations, the ego boundary expands and shrinks, and thus numerous ego boundaries are established. Now we must say that in object relations numerous ego states are established. Temporally speaking, some ego states are archaic and some are current.

After introducing the concept of ego states, Federn offered new ways to define a fixation point and regression to that point. If an established ego state is repeatedly cathected, it becomes the dominant ego state. When such an ego state is repressed, a fixation point is established. Regression to the

---

[12] Although Federn used the concept of loss of the inner boundary to explain the occurrence of hallucinations in schizophrenia, the concept was not widely adopted. That is understandable, for "loss of inner ego boundary gives rise to hallucinations" is a descriptive statement, not quite a theoretical explanation.

[13] Or, in Jacobson's terms, "Federn's ego boundaries are to be viewed as boundaries between . . . self-representations and object representations" (1954a, p. 520).

fixation point is marked by the revival of that particular ego state.

Ego Cathexis

Drive investment in the ego is called ego cathexis.[14] Although Federn wholeheartedly accepted Freud's death instinct, by and large, he treated ego cathexis as the equivalent of libidinal cathexis of the ego. Only rarely did he speak of ego cathexis as a compound of libido and mortido (1949c, p. 227). As I pointed out earlier, Federn's ego psychology is built on ego feeling, from which he derived the concepts of ego boundary and ego state. Ego feeling is a phenomenological observation. To correlate this observation with psychoanalytic theory, Federn conceptualized ego feeling as a reflection of ego cathexis. Thus ego feeling is intact when the ego is cathected, and ego feeling is lost when the ego loses its cathexis.

Federn's Conceptualization of Schizophrenia

Federn was among the first psychoanalysts to treat schizophrenics. He disagreed with Freud about the schizophrenic's incapacity for transference and inability to make use of psychoanalytic treatment. He therefore formulated his own conceptualization of schizophrenia.

The Genesis of Schizophrenia

According to Schwing (1940), who wrote about her experience with psychotics under Federn's guidance, psychosis results from unsatisfactory child-parent relations. Federn was

---

[14] Federn described four types of ego cathexis: (1) Active ego cathexis, which is experienced in the ego's planning, thinking, acting, and, in its most elementary form, in the phenomenon of attention. (2) Passive ego cathexis, which determines the need for stimuli. (3) Reflexive cathexis, which is manifested in self-love or self-hate. (4) Medial (objectless) ego cathexis, which is best illustrated by such expressions as "I grow," "I thrive," "I live," "I prosper," "I develop."

less explicit, as he was more concerned with a theoretical conceptualization. He postulated that object relations establish numerous ego states. Archaic as some of these ego states may be, they will persist, though in a dormant state, under repression.

> The narcissistic cathexes with ego feeling of many representations of the external world persist, they change and develop, they are given up and again are newly invested. Most deeply hidden . . . the entire world of primary narcissism remains extant, as dream and psychosis reveal; the primary narcissistic ego . . . is repressed and becomes unconscious in its totality [Federn, 1929, p. 302].

As described above, an ego state, after repeated cathecting, may become a fixation point, and regression to the fixation point revives that specific ego state. Accordingly, a personality is conceived as integrated when some later-developed, mature ego states retain their strong cathexis and are able to keep very early ego states repressed. In contrast to the integrated personality, the schizophrenic personality is unable to maintain the strong cathexis of mature ego states that keeps archaic primary narcissistic ego states repressed.

In this connection I shall briefly comment on Federn's concept of ego state. What Federn meant by ego state can perhaps be stated differently as follows: (1) Our experiences result from our bodily sensations and our interaction with the object. They include registry of instinctual gratification or frustration, registry of percepts and affects, registry of interaction between the self and the object offering pleasure and displeasure, and registry of the concept of an idealized object giving approval or disapproval. (2) Regardless of whether they acquire conscious representation, all our experiences, including the earliest ones, tend to persist in our minds (except for those that are modified in a "sequence of reorganization"). (3) Those persistent early experiences may not exert any influence over our daily lives; yet at times they may. (4) When they exert no influence, they are described as being repressed. (5) These repressed experiences may be derepressed or reactivated and thereby re-exert influence over our daily lives.

Assuming that this summary of Federn's view is correct, we are led to the following considerations. First, from the structural point of view, we envision that none of the persistent early experiences (or primitive ego states) can be a single experience. In its simplest form, each experience would represent the coupling of drive and ego defenses (and often a link to superego prohibition as well). Thus each experience (or ego state) should be more than an ego state.[15] Second, Federn assigned very special meanings to repression and derepression. As Brenner (1957) showed, Freud made numerous modifications in the concept of repression over the years: His early definition of repression reflects his thinking in terms of the topographic model; his later definition is in accord with the structural theory. On the surface, Federn's use of repression seems to follow Freud's early conception. But actually it does not. Federn said that, once repressed, an archaic ego state is not only kept out of consciousness but is also prevented from influencing one's daily life; only when it is derepressed can an archaic ego state exert its influence. (Derepression may or may not imply that the ego state is made conscious.) This formulation, in which the concept of the dynamic unconscious seems to be absent, does not represent Freud's early or late view. In a way, Federn could have made things much simpler by avoiding the terms repression and derepression, and speaking instead of cathecting and decathecting certain ego states. Third, when an archaic ego state is reactivated, the person presumably reverts to the original ego state. But clinically that cannot be the case. When a schizophrenic patient is in a panic, he may feel that the past is recurring in the present (and as a result, he may feel more panic); but his perception of the here-and-now adds new elements to the panic. Thus the panic of the present strongly

---

[15] In the literature, ego state tends to be used as an equivalent to affective state or as a state of altered consciousness (Ennis, 1971). The conceptual confusion caused by assigning different meanings to the same term must some day be straightened out.

resembles but is never exactly the same as that of the past. In other words, one does not really relive the original ego state. It is possible that Federn had this point in mind when he postulated that ego states of different developmental levels can coexist; but he did not elucidate this matter.

Incidentally, Federn called schizophrenia a "disease of the ego" (1949d, p. 241). By this term he meant that the ego is fixated at and tends toward regression to archaic ego states, and is therefore incapable of maintaining the later ego states that are necessary to uphold a mature, integrated, nonschizophrenic personality. In the concept of disease of the ego,[16] a stimulus that would bring about a loss of ego cathexis would set the stage for a return to the fixation point. Federn did say that the loss of ego cathexis "is sometimes explained by accumulated emotional strain" (1949c, p. 228). But we wish he had said more about how the accumulated emotional strain brings about the loss of ego cathexis.[17]

Symptom Formation

Federn saw schizophrenia as the result of a diminution or loss of ego cathexis. When the ego cathexis is diminished or lost, both the outer and inner ego boundaries are weakened or lost. The dividing line between ego and non-ego then becomes blurred, and there is a return of the repressed. As a result, reality is falsified, and conceptual or abstract thinking is interfered with. In the process, delusions, hallucinations, and thought disorder become manifest. About delusion, Federn said,

the generally accepted theory[18] is that this symptom is based

[16] Federn also used the expression "defeat of ego" without giving any explanation of it.

[17] A comment of Schwing's (1940), if it is representative of Federn's view, may clarify the issue somewhat. She wrote: "These primal conflicts are always most intimately connected with the mother. Since the life of the patient has always led him to new difficulties instead of a working through, that is, a dissolution of the primal conflicts, many fail in life and escape by regressing deeper and deeper until they have regained the period before these conflicts existed" (p. 49).

[18] Obviously referring to Freud's (1924a, 1924b) papers.

on the loss of reality. My own observations contradict this theory insofar as every schizophrenia case begins not with the *loss* of external reality, but with the *creation* of conceptions of false reality. These observations can be verified by anyone who studies the minutiae of any schizophrenic patient's earliest symptoms [1949a, p. 187; my italics].[19]

Earlier, he had also said,

by intensive investigation of the observable changes in object conception, I became convinced that reality is not given up by the ego, but that it becomes impossible for the ego to maintain knowledge of reality because of the establishment of a false conception of reality which is stronger than any remembrance of the healthy concepts [1943, p. 162].

To Federn, hallucination results from derepression of the primary narcissistic ego state. Thought disorders, too, result from this derepression. The inability to think abstractly and conceptually is due to

the inverse process by which the special residue of the specific ego states and the surroundings in which the original experience first occurred return in their entirety to the memory. Thus, for the schizophrenic, it is no longer possible to think generally of the table; he always thinks of a specific table [1949a, p. 198].

According to Federn, a loss of ego cathexis also brings about regression in order to preserve the remaining ego cathexis. In schizophrenia there is noticeable regression to the primary narcissistic ego state.[20] However, the mature ego state and the archaic ego state at times coexist; it is because of this coexistence that a schizophrenic patient is able to adjust to the real world while simultaneously having hallucinations and delusions.

---

[19] Federn postulated two ego boundaries. When the inner ego boundary is lost, the consequent return of repressed ego states will falsify reality. But when the outer ego boundary is lost, and ego and non-ego can no longer be distinguished, perception of reality becomes blurred. The two positions are not irreconcilable, but Federn never made that clear.

[20] Federn makes no direct connection between regression to the primary narcissistic ego state and the loss of ego boundaries. There is no direct cause-effect relation between the depth of regression and the loss of ego boundaries. His emphasis is on loss of ego cathexis, which brings about both.

Since Federn's view of schizophrenic symptom formation is so very different from Freud's, it seems useful to compare the two. According to Freud,

> we can distinguish three groups of phenomena in the clinical picture: (1) those representing what remains of a normal state or of neurosis (residual phenomena); (2) those representing the morbid process (detachment of libido from its objects and, further, megalomania, hypochondria, affective disturbance and every kind of regression); (3) those representing restoration, in which the libido is once more attached to objects, after the manner of a hysteria (in dementia praecox or paraphrenia proper), or of an obsessional neurosis (in paranoia) [1914b, p. 86].

According to Federn, the detachment of the object libido is not primary; it is secondary to the loss of ego cathexis. Megalomania and hypochondriasis reflect a deficiency in ego cathexis, not a hypercathexis of the ego. Delusions and hallucinations result from the loss of ego boundaries, which is secondary to the loss of ego cathexis, and are not at all related to a libidinal recathexis of previously abandoned objects. To elaborate:

1. The most basic difference between the views of Freud and Federn concerns whether the primary disturbance is of ego libido or of object libido. Freud focused on the patient's conflict, whereas Federn focused on the aftereffect of that conflict. Focusing on the conflict, Freud noted the patient's simultaneous wishes to decathect and recathect the object, and he concluded that the primary disturbance lies in the object cathexis. Focusing on the aftereffect of the conflict, Federn noted that the patient was no longer able to distinguish ego from non-ego or to maintain his integrated personality and repress his early ego states. Since Federn believed that these phenomena result from a loss of ego boundaries and that the intactness of ego boundaries is related to the intactness of ego cathexis, he postulated that the primary disturbance lies in the ego cathexis. We conclude that Freud and Federn constructed different theories because they looked at the problem from very different points of view. From the clinical point of view we witness, as did Freud, that a disturbance of object

libido *is* what sets the stage for a disturbance of ego cathexis. However, while disturbed object relations may set off a disturbance of ego cathexis, a disturbed ego cathexis in turn aggravates the disturbance of object cathexis.

2. Freud explained both megalomania and hypochondriasis as a hypercathexis of the ego with the libido withdrawn from objects. It must be admitted that this explanation is the most awkward and mechanical part of his explanation of schizophrenic phenomena. It is therefore not surprising that Federn did not subscribe to it. Unfortunately, Federn did not offer an alternative explanation of megalomania or hypochondriasis. In the case of megalomania, we may assume that he would have treated it as a form of delusion and have explained it as he would delusions. As for hypochondriasis, he did say that it is related to depersonalization (1949d, p. 243), but did not elaborate on what he meant by that. Perhaps he meant that both involved body ego feelings.

3. Federn believed that delusion follows falsification of reality, whereas Freud[21] postulated that delusion is connected with libidinal recathexis of the object (which follows decathexis or loss of reality). Again, Federn's and Freud's different theories can be traced to their different starting points. Federn was concerned with the gradual development of delusional ideas; Freud was concerned with the sudden reorganization of delusional ideas following the catastrophic experience.[22] Federn was perfectly right in that the gradual formation of a delusional system can be readily traced to

[21] Freud realized the incompleteness of his earlier formulation, later introducing the idea that delusion is preformed (1922) and also the idea of "a State within a State: an inaccessible party" (1939). But, regrettably, he did not weave all these ideas together into a whole.

[22] As a symptom, the catastrophic experience is an intriguing phenomenon. Freud was correct in attempting to explain it. But his explanation (decathexis) was inadequate, as he had not yet envisioned the important role played by aggression and defensive operations against aggression. Federn, on the other hand, never openly addressed the issue of the catastrophic experience. From his general theoretical position, we might assume that he would have attributed the suddenness of the symptom to a *sudden* loss of ego cathexis. To explain the catastrophic experience, however, we must take the aggressive drive into account. Federn, as Jacobson (1954a) and Bergmann (1963) observed, simply did not pay attention to it.

thought displacement. Freud had in fact said the same thing. For instance, in the Schreber case (1911) he remarked that paranoia[23] employs the obsessional defensive operation of using one set of thoughts to replace another.

4. To Federn, hallucination could be explained in terms of derepression, in which process the primitive ego state becomes reactivated. This is essentially Freud's explanation of hallucinations in his dream study. Freud, on the other hand, believed that any theoretical formulation about schizophrenia must take into account the catastrophic experience. He therefore asserted that hallucinations that appear to follow the catastrophic experience must be interpreted in terms of restitution—thereby abandoning his own earlier theory that hallucination is a regressive return to early ego functioning.[24] Unfortunately, neither Freud nor Federn offered any explanation of why there should be a predominance of auditory hallucinations in schizophrenia.

5. Federn contradicted Freud's view that the thought disorder is consequent to (a) decathexis and (b) recathexis of word presentation but not of thing presentation (Freud, 1915b, p. 222). Here again Freud seems to have been deeply preoccupied with the catastrophic experience. Thus, even though he compared schizophrenia with dream states, he had to resort to the theory of recathexis. Federn, on the other hand, stayed with Freud's earlier thinking. Although he spoke in terms of regression to early ego states, he retained Freud's basic idea of regression from secondary-process functioning to primary-process functioning.

To conclude, Freud thought that schizophrenia and paranoia should be treated as two distinct clinical entities and that a separate theory should be formulated for each. For

[23] For over 10 years Freud attempted to establish the term "paraphrenia," to which both paranoia and schizophrenia would belong.

[24] We assume that a theory of hallucination that is solely regressive or solely restitutive is inadequate; the two aspects must be integrated. Hallucinations, like any other experience, must be constituted of and determined by what is in the past as well as what is in the present. The concept of restitution, which implies the creation of something new, surpasses a pure theory of regression, which does not take sufficient account of the importance of current experiences.

Freud, what characterizes schizophrenia is the catastrophic experience, whereas what characterizes paranoia is the commitment to false beliefs. His theory of schizophrenia therefore focused on the catastrophic experience. Because of that emphasis, and because of his orientation toward human conflict, he decided, in applying the libido theory to schizophrenic phenomena, on the decathexis-recathexis theory; grandiosity and hypochondriasis he explained in terms of a hypercathexis of the ego with the libido withdrawn from objects, and delusions, hallucinations, and thought disorders in terms of libidinal recathexis. Federn, on the other hand, saw schizophrenia and paranoia more as being on a continuum; he paid very little attention to the catastrophic experience. Because of his general inclination toward phenomenology, he formulated a theory that lays less emphasis on conflict. Consequently, his theory became descriptive of the aftereffects of the conflict. Since Freud's and Federn's theories focus on different aspects of schizophrenic phenomena, they complement each other. Since neither theory is complete, however, the combined value of the two is still limited.

Treatment

Federn said, "my work [with psychosis] dates back to the first decade of the century" (1943, p. 123). From this work he found that schizophrenics are capable of establishing transference and that they can be analyzed. He did not define, as Kohut (1971) has done, the quality of transference schizophrenic patients are capable of establishing. But he did caution that "the transference of psychotics is quite unstable and does not warrant use of the same psychoanalytical method employed with neurotic patients" (1943, p. 119). For "in neurosis, we want to lift repression; in psychosis, we want to create re-repression"[25] (p. 136). He recommended the estab-

[25] The issue is not "to create re-repression." Kohut has said of the analysis of narcissistic personality disturbance that the essential part of working through "does not concern the overcoming of ego and superego resistances against the undoing of

lishment and maintenance of a positive transference and the interruption of treatment when the transference becomes negative. To win and maintain a positive transference, he advocated physical gratification of the patient's oral need, such as bringing him chocolates. He said, "in all cases which I treated with good results, I followed the rules dictated by the libidinous condition of the psychosis and not those dictated by the claim for analytical thoroughness" (p. 132). He protected his patients from undue anxiety and taught them how to improve their capacity for "attentive thinking." He made sure that his patients had a good night's sleep, instructed them not to become overtired physically or intellectually (including giving up life goals, e.g., higher education), and forbade them to indulge in sexual activities. Although he spoke of analysis of inner and outer conflicts, he gave no illustrations of how he did it. He gave the impression that his analysis would not go beyond an understanding of the patient's use of specific defenses in stressful situations.

He further observed that a requisite for successful treatment is that the patient be given support beyond the analytic hours. He preferred to treat the patient in his home environment. Keeping the patient at home, in his view, protected the patient not only from exposure to excessive separation anxiety (by removing him from his family and placing him in an utterly strange environment), but also from becoming fixated in chronicity in a regimented institutional setting. To treat the patient at home he found that he needed a skillful assistant in the person of a nurse or even the patient's close relatives (usually not the spouse) who could win the patient's positive transference. The outcome of the treatment, he noted, also depends largely on the patient's family environment. "If the patient is disliked by the rest of the family, the treatment is hampered" (1943, p. 120). He therefore recommended "talks"

---

repressions . . . but the ego's reaction to the loss of the narcissistically experienced object" (1971, p. 95). This statement also applies to schizophrenic patients who can be analyzed.

(presumably of a therapeutic nature) with the family members as essential to the patient's treatment.

Discussion

As outlined above, Federn's contributions to a theory of schizophrenia can be divided into etiology, symptom formation, and treatment. In terms of etiology, he attempted to build a theory around the concept of ego state. Phenomenologically, he noticed that the schizophrenic patient exhibits infantile behavior. He assumed that such behavior is the result of regression to a fixation point or the reliving of an archaic ego state. According to present-day standards, this simple formulation, though correct, is inadequate (see Chapter 14). Although Federn's theory implies that an early narcissistic fixation is caused by a skewed mother-infant relation, it offers no clarification of the nature of that disturbed relation, as, for example, Mahler's symbiotic theory does (see Chapter 11).

The best-remembered of Federn's contributions is his theory of symptom formation. It is remembered because it is simple. It leads the reader to believe that by focusing on ego cathexis and ego boundaries, or better yet, loss of ego cathexis and loss of ego boundaries, all schizophrenic symptoms can be explained. Thus, despite the fact that his over-all theoretical edifice remains on the periphery of psychoanalytic thinking, Federn's formulation is remembered and cited —sometimes even without a full appreciation of his theoretical position. Federn's theory of symptom formation in schizophrenic states is that, if ego cathexis is lost, ego boundaries will be lost. Consequently, the repressed returns and reality is obscured. As a result, delusions, hallucinations, and thought disorder make their appearance.

The first half of Federn's theory is that the loss of both outer and inner ego boundaries leads to all the symptoms. This part of the theory, at best, is no more than a descriptive statement; it offers no explanation. Besides, as I mentioned earlier, the concepts of inner ego boundary and of derepression are problematic. Furthermore, by assigning special meanings to existing terms, Federn created extreme conceptual confusion. The second half of Federn's theory is that the loss of both ego boundaries results from the loss of ego cathexis. "The loss of ego cathexis" is an abbreviated statement of "the loss of ego's capacity to retain a strong cathexis of certain mature ego states that are necessary for a well-integrated personality." Here Federn's conception seems to foreshadow the modern structural concept of ego fragmentation or Kohut's (1971) concept of fragmentation of the self.

But Federn did not have a modern structural concept in mind. His ego cathexis is basically id oriented. He said that ego cathexis is a compound of libido and mortido. Now matters get complicated. By loss of ego cathexis, did Federn mean loss of libidinal cathexis only? Mortido only? Or both? If only libidinal cathexis is lost, why should that be? Federn never made that clear. When he endorsed Freud's death instinct, did he do so because two instincts make better sense philosophically or because he thought that aggression might play a role in symptom formation in schizophrenia? At one point Federn took up the difference between depersonalization and estrangement on the one hand and schizophrenia on the other. He said that in depersonalization, "probably . . . the loss is more specific in that *only* the libido component is deficient" (1949d, p. 241; my italics). But he never followed up this assertion. On another occasion, Federn suggested that the ego boundary of manic-depressives becomes cathected with mortido, and that is why such patients are often plagued by self-destructiveness. Can we infer that Federn saw the destructive behavior of schizophrenic patients in a similar way? Unfortunately he offered no clarification.

Concerning treatment, Federn was ahead of his time in having discovered, in the 1910's, that schizophrenic patients can be analyzed, that they need support beyond the analytic sessions, that they are best treated in the home environment, and that the family members should be "treated" as well. Currently these basic principles are still upheld. In psychoanalytic treatment proper, Federn recommended the establishment of a positive transference and the interruption of treatment when the transference became negative. This advice is no longer considered sound even though, for the treatment to be successful, the negative transference should be neither untimely nor so extreme that it cannot be handled. Federn modified psychoanalytic procedure in order to avoid undue regression. He never specified how much regression is undue for a given schizophrenic patient in treatment. Federn advised that cautious steps be taken to protect patients from experiencing severe anxiety. But much of his advice seems unwarranted, as it amounts to suppressing the patient's potential.

Instead of being satisfied with his hard-earned insight into the appropriate therapy for schizophrenics, Federn decided to provide a theory for his treatment program. Thus he said that all his therapeutic effort was directed to reducing the loss of ego cathexis. Limiting emotional or intellectual strains and claims on the patient, and recommending that the patient avoid sleeplessness, physical and mental exhaustion, and frequent sexual activity, were all for the purpose of conserving ego cathexis (1949a, p. 195). He had now created utter confusion. Is not "ego cathexis" a theoretical construct? Does ego cathexis become reified as Federn used it?

We may conclude that Federn's phenomenological observations and his theoretical formulations must be evaluated separately. While he demonstrated penetrating clinical-observational acumen, he showed, in the area of theoretical formulation, a lack of skill in making systematic presentations, a tendency to treat descriptions as explanations, and at times an overzealousness in trying to fit things into his theoretical framework that did not fit. Both Grauer (1957) and Bergmann (1963) argued that Federn was greatly handicapped in expressing his ideas clearly because of his loyalty to Freud and his persistence in using Freud's terms while attaching somewhat different meanings to them. But as regards Federn's effort to provide theoretical underpinnings for his therapeutic program, this argument does not quite stand up. Jacobson said, "We realize with some astonishment that two or even three decades ago Federn studied normal and pathological processes in the ego upon which psychoanalytic research in general has begun to focus only within recent years" (1954a, p. 519). Another 25 years have elapsed since Jacobson made her statement. Today we may not have to read Federn to understand many important psychological issues. Nevertheless, because his pioneering study of ego feelings foreshadowed our current effort to understand sense of self, sense of identity, mood, background feeling of safety, etc., because his exploratory work on the (outer) ego boundary lent understanding to our current knowledge of narcissistic object relations, reality constancy, etc., and because his formulation of a deficient-ego-cathexis theory of schizophrenia anticipated the current deficiency theory of schizophrenia (in contradistinction to the conflict theory; see Wexler, 1971; London, 1973), we may still greatly benefit from reading Federn's attempts of half a century ago to solve problems that are still very much with us.

PART III

Toward a Comprehensive Psychoanalytic Theory of Schizophrenia

A.

General Considerations

CHAPTER 11

The Relation of Infantile Experience to the Etiology of Schizophrenia

During the years I have devoted to the treatment of schizophrenic patients, I have been preoccupied with the causes of schizophrenia, hoping to establish a rational therapeutic approach in both the area of work and the depth of exploration of the schizophrenic process.

Basic to all considerations of etiology has been the nature-nurture question. When "nature" is hypothesized as the primary cause of schizophrenia, something "inside" the person is believed to unfold gradually; the "outside" (environment) is considered incidental. When "nurture" is hypothesized as the primary cause, the person is thought of as being traumatized by something "outside" him, the "inside" (heredity-constitution) playing an insignificant role. The knowledge accumulated in the last few decades from early developmental studies of normal and deviant infants[1] strongly suggests that neither nature nor nurture alone can lead to schizophrenia. Rather, the interaction of the two in the very early phase of the infant's life results in certain experiences that later evolve into the multifarious symptoms of the schizophrenic illness.

[1] For instance, the work of Benjamin, Brody, Ekstein, Escalona, Fries, Furer, Greenacre, Mahler, Provence, Spitz, Winnicott, and Wolff.

143

In the following discussion these experiences will be referred to as *basic experiential disturbances.*

An etiological explanation of schizophrenia in terms of basic experiential disturbances is grounded in child developmental studies, and has practical value to those who are concerned with the prevention of schizophrenia and the treatment of schizophrenic patients. In the last half century, able clinicians like Sullivan, Fromm-Reichmann, Will, Searles, Melanie Klein and her associates, and many others have demonstrated that schizophrenic patients are responsive to treatment. Bellak (1958, 1974) is especially insistent that once a schizophrenic, *not* always a schizophrenic. These authors imply that in the course of further interaction with the environment, the schizophrenic's basic experiential disturbances may be worsened or ameliorated. Likewise, during treatment, the schizophrenic acquires new experiences that may ameliorate or exacerbate his illness. Indeed, in certain schizophrenic patients a complete remission can occur.

In this chapter I shall briefly consider the evidence for nature or for nurture alone as the primary cause of schizophrenia, and then argue that nature and nurture interact in the shaping of the basic experiential disturbances that prepare the way for the later development of schizophrenia.

Nature as the Primary Etiological Factor

Kety (1976) writes,

More compelling evidence has come from studies of the incidence of schizophrenia in the monozygotic and dizygotic twins of schizophrenics. . . . the results of studies of schizophrenic twins over the past 50 years [reveal that] with remarkable consistency, the concordance rate in dizygotic twins is similar to that in siblings, whereas in monozygotic twins it may be two to six times as high [p. 15].

About the results of the now renowned studies of Danish adoptees, Kety writes, "there is a concentration [of schizophrenia-spectrum disorders] in the biologic relatives of index cases in contrast to the persons who are not genetically related to a schizophrenic. . . . the prevalence in those genetically related to the schizophrenic index cases is 13.9 per cent, compared with 2.7 per cent in their adoptive relatives" (p. 25). From the evidence of a high concentration of schizophrenic disorders among the biological paternal half-siblings of index cases (with whom the adopted schizophrenics shared neither prenatal nor postnatal environments), Kety concludes that statistical evidence speaks strongly for the operation of genetic factors in the transmission of schizophrenia.

Compelling as this evidence may be, studies have been conducted that have failed to support the strong statistical correlation. For example, the Genain quadruplets (Rosenthal, 1963), although similarly endowed genetically and brought up in the same household, were born with different degrees of adaptive capacity, and consequently received different kinds of ministration and care. Rosenthal concluded that differences in parental responses were correlated with varying degrees of schizophrenic symptoms among the quads. While it does not discount the genetic theory, the quadruplet study does indicate that early experience is an important factor in the schizophrenic process. Perhaps Kety had this and similar studies in mind when he wrote, "None of the findings summarized preclude the importance of environmental factors in the etiology of schizophrenia; in fact, the concordance of considerably less than 100 per cent [roughly 50 per cent] in monozygotic twins argues cogently that other than genetic factors are implicated"[2] (1976, p. 32). And elsewhere he wrote,

> These data do not imply, nor do I believe, that genetic factors and the biological processes involved in their expression are the only important influences in the etiology and pathogenesis of schizophrenia. . . . Environmental factors have always been an

[2] Since in the Danish adoptee studies acute schizophrenic reaction is practically undiagnosed among the relatives of index cases, Kety (1976) suggests that "there are at least two forms of schizophrenia, one of which has a strong genetic basis that is weak or absent in the other" (p. 28).

important part of medical models of illness, and, in the case of disorders of thought, mood, and behavior, one recognizes the operation of psychological processes and social influences that cannot be described or examined in physicochemical terms [1974, pp. 961-962].

At present, the data from genetic studies do not establish the mode of transmission of the genetic factors. According to Rosenthal (1963), a small group of genetic researchers strongly emphasize the genetic contribution and de-emphasize the role of the environment. They present a monogenic-biochemical theory of schizophrenia as a specific inherited disease. This theory is considered confirmed by evidence that the incidence of schizophrenia is similar in widely differing cultures. These researchers hypothesize that a single specific mutant gene produces a specific but yet unknown metabolic error, which is clinically manifested in a schizophrenic illness. Thus the cure for schizophrenia lies in the discovery of an agent or agents that can correct the metabolic error. And they advocate an intensive search for biochemical abnormalities that would unmask the assumed error. Thus far, the results have been disappointing. In a comprehensive survey of biochemical investigations carried out from 1960 to 1970, Wyatt et al. (1971) concluded that "to date, no biochemical abnormalities have been consistently and exclusively associated with schizophrenia" (p. 44).

Many geneticists, however, offer formulations that may be called diathesis-stress theories (Rosenthal, 1963). According to them, schizophrenia per se is not inherited; rather, a *predisposition* to schizophrenia is transmitted genetically. Whether a single gene is responsible or whether the illness may derive from a range of genotypes is not usually clarified. A specific biochemical defect may or may not be proposed. Given the nonspecific predisposition, the schizophrenic illness is, however, believed to be triggered by an environmental "stimulus" that is described as "stressful." Supporting this viewpoint, Rolf and Harig (1974) write that

vulnerability to mental disorder (and, to a much lesser extent, vulnerability to some form of schizophrenic disorder), can be transmitted genetically. The exact mode of genetic transmission is unknown. . . . However, there is also a growing consensus among behavior geneticists that sufficient environmental stress must be present before the psychopathological tendency will be expressed in the behavior of a vulnerable individual [p. 539].

Nurture as the Primary Etiological Factor

In the treatment of some severely ill hospitalized schizo-phrenic patients, Fromm-Reichmann (1948) noticed that their mothers showed certain characteristics that interfered with their offspring's recovery. She postulated that these mothers might even have contributed to the severity of their off-spring's illness in the first place. For descriptive purposes, she introduced the term "schizophrenogenic mother." Soon the use of this term became overextended; it took on meanings that its originator could not have intended. For instance, the term was assumed to mean that schizophrenia is primarily produced by the mothering person. Once that assumption was taken seriously, many important observational data were similarly misconstrued. Thus Wynne and Singer's invaluable observations (1963a, 1963b) on the transmission of thought disorders from mothers to their offspring were taken as evi-dence that nurture is the primary etiological factor. Simi-larly, when Lidz et al. (1965) devoted particular attention to the character of the fathers of schizophrenics, those who be-lieved that mothers were being unfairly blamed breathed a sigh of relief. And when Stierlin (1973) beautifully demon-strated the various transactional modes (binding, delegating, and expelling) between adolescent patients and their family units, his studies were seen as additional evidence that pa-tients were victimized by a traumatizing environment.

All the above-mentioned studies, as well as many others (e.g., Shapiro et al., 1974), have illuminated the "predica-ment" of patients in their relations to their parents or the whole family unit. With this knowledge we are better able to treat these afflicted patients. But the predicament tells only about things at the present time. It would be a genetic fallacy, in Hartmann's term, to assume that the patient's current predicament is the primary cause of his illness. Still, many (e.g., Laing, 1964, 1967) have gone so far as to theorize that the environment must be blamed and that the patients have simply been victimized.

There is no question that the environment, like the constitution, contributes significantly to the production of schizophrenic illness. But the mode in which each makes its contribution requires careful scrutiny. In the following, I propose to examine the environment and its interaction with the constitution in terms of *experience.*

The Infant's Experience of the Environment

The human infant is rather helpless, and his well-being depends on the ministrations and care of the mothering person. A young professional woman had her first child, a son. After four weeks of breast feeding, she placed him on the bottle. Originally he had been a placid and happy baby, but now he cried. The mother, who decided that the child did not respond properly to the "change" and that she should not "give in" to his whims, chose to ignore the crying, but held him for long periods of time in order to quiet him. When her own mother suggested the possibility of colic, as the baby tended to cry more after each feeding, this young woman became even more fervent and stubborn in trying to "teach" the infant a good lesson. Not until a couple of months later did she tell the pediatrician about the baby's crying. Then it was discovered that the baby was indeed allergic to the formula. After the formula was changed, the baby calmed down considerably. But by now he was no longer placid and happy as he had originally been; he was anxious-looking, whined a lot, and was very irritable when he came in contact with any human being. In this particular example, the baby was born with an allergy that, when he was free of its symptoms, did not interfere with his being happy and contented. But, because of his mother's own emotional problems, his allergy forced him to live through a period of high tension, the result of which was a drastic affective-behavioral change in him.

Such an example demonstrates the unique role the mothering person occupies in the infant's life and environment. It is therefore not surprising that, even though in general we conceive of the environment as consisting of a host of animate and inanimate objects, we tend to single out the mothering person[3] and treat her as the principal representative of the infant's total environment.

From the very beginning of his life the infant must interact with the mother. Recent observational and experimental work shows that each neonate has its specific set of stable neurophysiological givens (see Lustman, 1956; Birns, 1965). In the mother-infant interaction, the infant's "givens" influence the mother as much as the mother influences the infant. For instance, the availability of the feeding mother is the stimulus for the functioning of the neonate's rooting reflex; the manifestations of the individual infant's rooting reflex in turn elicits specific responses from the mother, such as the positioning of her breast or the bottle, so as to maximize their mutual gratification. However, the mutual influencing process is not a balanced one. Mahler (1975) says:

> From the beginning the child molds and unfolds in the matrix of the mother-infant dual unit. Whatever adaptations the mother may make to the child, and whether she is sensitive and empathic or not, it is our strong conviction that the child's fresh and pliable adaptive capacity, and his need for adaptation (in order to gain satisfaction), is far greater than that of the mother, whose personality, with all its patterns of character and defense,

[3] Even the influence of the father on the infant is less direct. The colicky baby's father, a professional himself and a very passive person, chose to leave everything to his wife, although he was rather uneasy about his son's obvious suffering. Such a father may, in the long run, contribute to the infant's pathology, but his influence over the infant is nonetheless indirect.

is firmly and often rigidly set. . . . The infant takes shape in harmony and counterpoint to the mother's ways and style—whether she herself provides a healthy or a pathological object for such adaptation [p. 5].

In the case of the colicky baby, the lack of balance in the mother-infant mutual influencing process is obvious. But, as feeble as his influencing capacity was in comparison to his mother's, he did in the end change her through persistent protest. Leaving aside what effect this unpleasant experience at the dawn of the symbiotic phase might have on this particular baby, it seems clear that henceforth his interaction with his mother (or her substitute) would be somehow shaped by this experience. From now on, he would very likely emit distress signals at the slightest evidence of an unpleasant experience remotely resembling the one he had had. As a result, his mother might soon see him as a cranky, fussy, irritable baby, toward whom she might develop negative feelings. Without some sort of intervention, this mother-infant pair could easily perpetuate a kind of interaction that could lead to future pathological formations in the child.

In considering the etiology of neurosis, Freud proposed that "disposition and experience are here linked up in an indissoluble aetiological unity" (1914a, p. 18). To him, neither nature (hereditary-constitutional disposition) nor nurture (environmentally incurred traumata) was the cause of neurosis, but rather the "indissoluble unity" of the two factors. The indissoluble unity can be arranged in a "complemental series." At one end of the series are persons with severe inherited constitutional defects, who would probably succumb to mental illness no matter how ideal the early environment. At the other end are persons who might have escaped mental illness if the early environment had been less traumatic. Between these two extremes fall cases in which a greater or lesser amount of constitutional defect is combined with a greater or lesser amount of early traumatic experience.

In this connection we are also reminded of Piaget's work. In his studies of cognitive development, Piaget noted that cognition is structured in an invariant sequence of stages and that at each stage cognitive function reconstructs the interaction between the child and the environment in such a way as to produce the next stage. Each stage is a necessary step for the achievements of the next, more complex, stage. On the basis of this concept, Escalona (1965) asserts that neither disposition nor environment *directly* affects the over-all course of development or any specific aspect of personality organization. Rather, the organismic state (i.e., the biological-physiological total) of the infant *and* the immediate environment interact to yield "concrete experience."[4] The existing "concrete experience" may then be further influenced by the environment to give rise to a new "concrete experience." In the end, it is the sequence of concrete experiences that determines the developmental outcome.[5]

Basic Experiential Disturbances in Schizophrenia

In the conceptualization of schizophrenia as resulting from the continuous interaction of a sequence of concrete experiences with the environment, it is assumed that the experiences during the earliest phase of life are of extreme importance. As early as 1911 Freud recognized this fact and proposed that the schizophrenic is fixated at the autoerotic level. Melanie Klein and Fairbairn, in postulating the schizoid-paranoid position, not only stressed the importance of the earliest experiences of life, but described how pathogenic experiences are precipitated.

Mahler too, in her theory of infantile psychosis, has emphasized the importance of early pathogenic experiences. Ac-

---

[4] In regard to "concrete experience," Escalona (1965) says, "perhaps symbiotic experience would have been a better term, except that I am applying the model to infancy and early childhood, and the experience takes place on a sensori-motor level not necessarily accompanied by symbiotic experience" (p. 805).

[5] We envision that, in the beginning, organizing a new concrete experience is a relatively simple process. As time goes on, however, the process can become increasingly complex because of fantasies and efforts to realize them.

cording to Mahler (1968), infants who develop infantile psychosis (i.e., autistic or symbiotic syndromes) have lacked the experience of mother-infant "mutual cuing." Cuing is disturbed when the infant's responsiveness is impaired by a constitutional defect or when the mother is incapable of empathizing with her infant. A lack of mutual cuing results in a variety of disturbing experiences. These experiential disturbances may be of such magnitude that, in combination, they become central in the later development of schizophrenia. Though they crystallize at a very early phase in the life of the potential schizophrenic, they do not necessarily occur at one time. Some occur earlier than others. But, once established, each will find its own relatively independent (clearly demarcated) expression in the final clinical picture of schizophrenia. It must be stressed that these disturbances are not themselves schizophrenic symptoms; they only serve as the core of future symptoms. They are organized in a sequence of stages before they lead to symptoms. Not every disturbance need be present in every schizophrenic patient: Some occur in some patients, others in other patients. This fact may account for the various combinations of clinical symptoms seen in schizophrenic patients.

Some of the major, basic experiential disturbances that may potentiate the development of schizophrenia occur in the spheres of object relatedness, libido-aggression balance, anxiety potential, maintenance mechanisms, perceptual and affective functions, and body self-images.

Object Relatedness

Mahler postulates that in normal development the infant proceeds from the autistic to the symbiotic phase. A satisfactory symbiotic experience with the mothering person is a prerequisite for the infant's gradual differentiation and separation from his mother. The first step in the development from the autistic to the symbiotic phase is the cathexis of the "mothering principle." "The term 'mothering principle' [is] to stand for the perception of, and seeming acceptance of, the relieving ministrations coming from the human partner which, though vague and unspecific, are pleasurable need satisfactions from the mother" (1968, p. 43).[6] These pleasurable satisfactions are contingent on mutual cuing. Without mutual cuing and its consequent pleasurable satisfactions, the infant cannot adequately cathect the mothering person or the mothering principle. A failure to establish such a cathexis eventually leads to an inability to use and subsequently to internalize the mother as one who facilitates the maintenance of homeostasis. This inability constitutes what Mahler calls the "core problem" or "core deficiency" of the psychotic infant. Because of this core problem the infant cannot enter, or, after entry, cannot leave the delusional twilight state of a "mother-infant symbiotic common orbit." The repercussions of this can readily be observed in the therapeutic situation in the form of the patient's noninvolvement with the therapist or his everlasting effort to actualize a fantasy of merging with the therapist.

The lack of mutual cuing results in the baby's experiencing what I shall call pain-in-being-held and pain-in-being-laid-down. This experience is independent of his capacity to use the mothering principle, and may subsequently be manifested in schizophrenics in the form of a desire-to-move-toward and a simultaneous desire-to-move-away-from the object. This ambitendency in object relatedness is clearly embodied in Freud's decathexis-recathexis theory of schizophrenia. Fromm-Reichmann's (1950) statement that schizophrenics want to relate to others but are afraid to do so, and Burnham et al.'s (1969) description of the schizophrenic's tendency toward a need-fear dilemma also seem to be formulations of this ambitendency.

Libido-Aggression Balance

When Freud changed the emphasis of his theory from drives to a balanced view of the executive functioning of ego

[6] The infant's ability to be aware of the "mothering principle" occurs at a very early point in his development, long before he is able to differentiate self and nonself.

and drives, he also modified his concept of instinct. Instinct remained biologically rooted, but was conceptualized in psychological terms as a function of the mind. Schur (1966) was making this point when he wrote that what can be considered a biological need must become a psychological wish before it can be called a mental entity. Hartmann's concept of an id-ego matrix also makes this point, although it remains so closely tied to Freud's biological thinking that it is equivocal in this respect (Schafer, 1970).

Loewald (1971) has attempted a further freeing of instinctual drive from unchangeable biological givens, writing that "what is naïvely called objects plays an essential part in the constitution of the subject, including the organization of instincts as psychic phenomena and of the subject's developing 'object relations'; and what is naïvely called subject plays an essential part in the organization of objects (not merely of object representations)" (p. 117). According to Loewald, "the neonate's incoherent urges, thrashings, and reflex activities" are not to be considered as instinctual, but "become coordinated and organized into instincts and assume aims and direction by activities and responses coming from the environment. . . . 'mnemic images' are thus created, which are not additions to but constituents of instincts" (p. 120).

Observation has borne out that some experiences are likely to allow the child the fullest range of libidinal potential whereas others offer the fullest range of aggressive potential. Early in the autistic phase, maternal ministrations help the infant "to differentiate between a 'pleasurable'/'good' quality and 'painful'/'bad' quality of experience" (Mahler, 1975, p. 43). When mutual cuing is inadequate, the infant becomes accustomed to the painful/bad quality rather than the pleasurable/good quality of experience. Such experience is likely to influence his libido-aggression balance so that the fullest development of libidinal potential is suppressed and the fullest development of aggressive potential is facilitated. In schizophrenia, this basic disturbance of the libido-aggression balance is reflected in the clinical symptoms that led Klein (1946),

Hartmann (1953), Bak (1954), Bion (1956), Searles (1965), and others to stress the patient's aggressiveness, and Federn (1952) and Fairbairn (1952) to stress the patient's lack of libidinal capacity. It is reflected in what Sullivan described as a "malignant transformation"; that is, when tender feelings are called for, the patient becomes hostile and assaultive.

Predisposition to Panic

Mahler says that "children who cannot utilize the mothering principle . . . show *panic* at any perception of actual separateness" (1975, p. 7; italics mine). By the choice of the term panic, Mahler emphasizes the extreme intensity of anxiety as well as the ego tendency toward disorganization and regression at the moment of panic. Since a schizophrenic patient may start his life with a lack of mutual cuing, he may develop a predisposition to panic. He does not know what "ordinary" anxiety is like; instead, he experiences "organismic panic." By organismic panic I refer not only to the panicky, ego-disorganizing properties of the experience, but also to the ego's lack of capacity to regulate and modulate the disorganizing affect. Like an infant in "organismic distress" (Greenacre, 1941; Mahler, 1968), a schizophrenic patient in organismic panic is utterly helpless. He cannot master his disorganization without outside help.

The tendency toward organismic panic is not necessarily the sequel to, but may be the cause of, an absence or inadequacy of symbiotic relatedness. For instance, a disturbed fetal life[7] could pave the way for a predisposition to panic. From her therapeutic experience with schizophrenic and severe borderline patients, Greenacre (1941) postulated that a set of reflex reactions occurring in fetal life may represent a

---

[7] According to Montagu, "the prevalent notion that the fetus is thoroughly insulated from the influences of the environment is utterly without foundation. The truth being that the organism within the womb is vastly more sensitive to environmental influences than is the maternal organism, that conditions which are symptomless in the pregnant woman and leave her unaffected may seriously injure the child in her womb" (1962, p. 500).

"preanxiety" reaction. Although these reflex preanxiety reactions are devoid of psychic content, they may become assimilated into the person's make-up so that they are almost, if
not entirely, indistinguishable from inherited constitutional
factors. The specific make-up consists of "a genuine physiological sensitivity, a kind of increased indelibility of reaction
to experience which heightens the anxiety potential and gives
greater resonance to the anxieties of later life" (p. 54).

Sullivan's observation (1962) that anxiety is contagious is
also useful here. Just as ordinary infant reactivity can stimulate an anxious response in the mother, so will the mothering person's anxiety significantly accentuate a pre-existing
"predisposition to anxiety" in the baby. Once such a cycle
begins, the mother must cope with such fantasies as that her
infant will not thrive and will reveal her incapacity as a
mother. She may then approach the infant with so much anxiety of her own, or so great a readiness to be smotheringly
over-protective, that establishing an infant-mother symbiotic
relatedness may in turn aggravate her concern and pain. Further, it may later cause her to deny all awareness of the problems of this early interaction and lead her, as Hill (1955)
noted, to describe this early interaction as idyllic.

Maintenance Mechanisms

According to Mahler (1968), if the infant is unable to cathect the mothering principle and is consequently unable to use
the mother to establish affective-tension homeostasis, he may
establish homeostasis by resorting to "maintenance mechanisms." These mechanisms, including deanimation, devitalization, dedifferentiation, fusion of self-object boundary, and
drive defusion, are often reactivated in children who suffer
from autistic or symbiotic psychoses. Mahler distinguishes
maintenance mechanisms from object relations as well as from
ordinary defense mechanisms. The maintenance mechanisms
operate to maintain an archaic contact with a primitive global

"environment" or a primitively differentiated object. They are neither adaptive mechanisms for the development of object relations nor defense mechanisms (e.g., introjection, projection, denial, splitting) for the regulation of drive discharge in response to an internally structured conflict. Mahler's concept of maintenance mechanisms is extremely important for an understanding of clinical manifestations of adult schizophrenia as well as childhood psychosis. The patient's relations with the nonhuman environment, his identification with inanimate objects, and his experience of others as inanimate objects, so richly documented by Searles (1960, 1965), are manifestations of reactivated maintenance mechanisms.

A temporary erasure of self- and/or object representations —clinically resembling repression of a profound order —may also be included among the maintenance mechanisms. An erasure of self- and/or object representations does not involve boundaries and therefore differs from a fusion of self- and object representations. When the self- or the object representation is erased, it temporarily ceases to exist. This phenomenon is commonly manifested by schizophrenic patients in what is clinically described as "absence" or "blocking." In his conception of "decathexis of object representation" as the primary deficiency of schizophrenia, London (1973) appears to address the maintenance mechanism of erasure of self and/or object representations.

Perceptual and Affective Responses

The perception of schizophrenic patients is said to differ from that of normal people, and theories (e.g., minimal brain damage) have been advanced that the ultimate source of schizophrenia is to be found in inborn perceptual defects. On the other hand, it is quite possible that perceptual problems arise from a disturbed mother-infant symbiotic relationship. Mahler (1975) notes that during the autistic and early symbiotic phases there is a "shift of predominantly proprioceptive-enteroceptive cathexis toward sensoriperceptive cathexis of the periphery" (p. 46). In unfavorable circumstances the shift is obstructed or disordered, and as a result perception is used in the service of the id and to repudiate reality (Hartmann et al., 1946, p. 14).

Disordered affective responses are common in schizophrenics. Many patients are described as having shallow to flat emotions, others as being unable to show gradations of affective responses. Strictly speaking, these phenomena are not "postpsychotic" manifestations. Careful scrutiny may reveal that they have existed in these patients from very early life and are analogous to what Eissler (1953b) calls basic defects. Recent studies tend to support the view that while the capacity for emotions is a natural endowment, the ability to discriminate different shades of emotions belongs to the ego and must be acquired gradually (see Brenner, 1974; Mahler, 1975). It is therefore not surprising that an early disturbed symbiotic relationship could indeed pave the way to depriving the patient of the natural but time-consuming unfolding process of discrimination and the proper experiencing of the various emotions.

The serious difficulty schizophrenic patients have in communicating may likewise have an early origin. Winnicott's description of not communicating and non-communicating is worthy of consideration. He (1963) suggests that an "environment mother" and an "object mother" can be distinguished. The infant experiences the environment mother subjectively, the object mother objectively. The environment mother is first experienced and then "created and recreated"; she resides inside the infant. The object mother is originally "repudiated"; she is external to the infant. The infant's relations to the two mothers are therefore different. Because the environment mother is subjectively experienced, explicit communication with her is unnecessary. Because the object mother is objectively perceived, communication must be explicit. In the latter case a disorder may be reflected in a simple not communicating or in an active or reactive noncommunicating. In active noncommunicating the infant fails to communicate with the object mother while it continues to relate to and communicate with the environment mother. The potentially schizophrenic infant may tend to become (defensively at first and perhaps autonomously later on) bound primarily to subjective experience and to diminish communication with the objects in the objectively perceived world. Clinically, the phenomenon of the-patient-is-now-with-me-and-he-has-now-disappeared-from-me is readily observable. In severer cases the patient seems to be sealed off by an impenetrable wall; in milder cases the patient seems to make strenuous efforts to guard against any exposure of his inner, private, and secret life.[8]

Schizophrenic thought disorder is usually conceived as a regression from secondary-process to primary-process mental functioning. Though that may be the case, more often than not the thought disorder originates in maldevelopment, not in regression. The form and style of our thoughts are learned. If, in early life, the potential schizophrenic adopted reactive noncommunicating (Winnicott), he must develop his own dereistic or autistic mode of thinking. In the case of the Genain quadruplets (Rosenthal, 1963), the isolation of the family from friends and relatives not only augmented the autistic use of language among the family members, but also reinforced the quadruplet's identification with the parental mode of disordered thinking.

Body Self-Images and the Sense of Self-Cohesion

"Self" must be distinguished from "ego" (Hartmann, 1950b, 1953). The earliest self consists of a series of dimly registered sensations of alternating body tension and pleasure. There is

---

[8] Writing about treatment, Fromm-Reichmann constantly demonstrated her effort and skill in getting patients to share their "secrets" with her. It must be noted that she was not interested in the content (if there was any) of the patient's "secret," but in helping the patient to diminish his disturbance in communication with objectively perceived objects, so that those needs and desires that must largely be fulfilled by others could be given a chance of fulfillment.

no sense of continuity; temporal cohesion or continuity develops later. Kohut (1971) postulates that a firm sense of self-cohesion is established alongside the establishment of the superego (pp. 41-42). In tracing the development of the sense of self-cohesion Lichtenberg (1975) distinguishes three components. In the order of their development, they are body self-images, the self-image in relation to objects seen as distinctly separate, and images of the grandiose self associated with the idealized self-object. In the autistic-symbiotic phases, the body experiences are registered as body self-images. If the infant living through these phases lacks mutual cuing with the mother, or if the quality of the experience is predominantly painful/bad, he will register a series of disturbed body self-images. Such disturbed body images may not only interfere with the eventual development of a sense of self-cohesion, they may also form the nuclei of the distorted self-images manifested in schizophrenic patients[9] (see Schilder, 1935; Searles, 1965). These distorted self-images are not merely postpsychotic manifestations. In the form of hypochondriacal complaints or depersonalization, such distorted images can often be traced to the very early developmental stages of the patient's life.

I have described a group of basic experiential disturbances that may aggravate one another so as to distort the development of each of the affected areas of the mind. For instance, a libido-aggression imbalance or a disturbed perceptual registration may tend to intensify an exaggerated predisposition to panic; repeatedly experienced panic may interfere with the development of the sense of self-cohesion; inadequate affective responses may heighten aggression. As each disturbance is intensified, schizophrenia may eventuate.

Each basic experiential disturbance may be conceived as organized in successive stages in the context of experience-environment interactions. In each stage of organization there

---

[9] Lichtenberg (1978) has demonstrated that the early body self-images are closely linked to the development of the ego function of reality testing.

is always the possibility that the basic disturbance will be further consolidated on the one hand or undone on the other. Thus we not only have hope but rational explanations for the possibility of modifying any or all of the basic disturbances after they have crystallized. On the assumption that these disturbances are modifiable, Mahler has advocated a therapeutic "corrective symbiotic experience" for those afflicted with childhood schizophrenia. For the same reason many analysts in the 1940's and thereafter in the United States and abroad recommended intensive psychoanalytic psychotherapy for adult schizophrenics.

But to what degree can the basic experiential disturbances be modified? For practical purposes we must recognize that in schizophrenics these disturbances are not uniform but vary within a certain range. At one extreme are infants with defective constitutional equipment who develop basic experiential disturbances in an average expectable environment. At the other extreme are infants who develop basic disturbances when their mothers, though quite "normal" by any standard, are temporarily under extreme stress. The basic disturbances of the first group of patients may be less amenable to later modification than those of the second group. In our therapeutic work with schizophrenic patients, the range of basic disturbances warrants our close attention and examination, and may determine the areas in which we wish to work and the depth of exploration we undertake.

CHAPTER 12

The Pathway to Schizophrenia

In Chapter 11, I described a gamut of basic experiential disturbances that may occur in the infancy of the potential schizophrenic. Between these basic experiential disturbances and the eventual crystallization of the schizophrenic illness, a series of very complex and involved processes takes place. From the clinical point of view it is therefore never possible to speak with certainty of a linear connection between the basic disturbances as the starting point and the schizophrenic illness as the end point. The cause-effect connection between them is at best inferential. However, Mahler's penetrating study of infantile psychosis has yielded convincing evidence of a close relationship between basic experiential disturbances during infancy and adult schizophrenia.[1]

To scrutinize the relationship between basic experiential disturbances and adult schizophrenia I shall give the "history" of a case of schizophrenia from the beginning of the patient's life to the outbreak of her psychosis. I have chosen to describe this particular patient because in psychoanalytic psychotherapy she was able—after she had recovered from a long illness—to reconstruct her memories and fantasies from early childhood. Her reconstructive work gives a glimpse of a possible link between the earliest traumatic experiences and her defective adaptive capacity. Because of the initial

[1] Mahler (1968) has said that her symbiotic theory of infantile psychosis may serve as an explanation of the etiology of schizophrenia, beginning at any age (p. 32).

162

experiences, her adaptive capacity eroded in each subsequent life crisis, resulting in the crystallization of schizophrenic illness.

The Patient

The patient is Tina J. Her history had two sources: the patient's mother and the patient herself (her father had recently died of a heart attack). The mother, who was mourning the loss of her husband, was very self-blaming and felt somehow responsible for her daughter's illness. She was, however, unspecific about just how she might have been responsible. Besides, she gave the impression that the patient was a "happy baby" and had a "usual childhood." She dated the onset of the patient's problem to her marriage, at which time Tina, aged 23, was a struggling young actress. The marriage seemed to transform Tina completely. Overnight, she became increasingly and steadily disorganized, irrational, and irascible. In the next several years things went from bad to worse, until she lost contact completely. At the time of her admission to Chestnut Lodge at the age of 29, Tina was unable to give a coherent and relevant account of herself. On recovery, some 10 years later, Tina, who by now had been influenced by her therapeutic work, tended to consider herself as having been "sick all her life."

Heredity

No close relatives on either side of the family were said to have suffered from any mental illness that required institutional care. (The parental personalities will be considered below.)

Comments: This kind of information does not represent the true state of affairs. But at present there is no reliable measure for determining the hereditary predisposition to schizophrenic illness.

The Family

Tina's father died of a heart attack shortly after she was admitted to a psychiatric hospital. He had left his poverty-stricken family after graduating from high school. Ashamed of his background, he severed his relations with his family and never wanted to talk about them. Ever since Tina was a child, he had had an alcohol problem, and was hospitalized several times for detoxification. Nevertheless, he managed to keep his bureaucratic job. Tina's mother, though frail-looking and suffering from numerous psychosomatic illnesses, was apparently in good health. She was the youngest of three children, and had lost her own father in childhood. She had been very dependent on her "powerful" mother. She had wanted to be an actress but felt too shy to be one. She had worked as a secretary before she was married.

The parent's marriage was described as an unhappy one from the outset, for reasons not specified. The wife's persistent nagging and the husband's alcohol problem were said to have contributed to the difficulties of their later life. Tina described her father as basically a warm person with a good heart, who would have given her anything he had. (She was referring to receiving subsistence from him during her brief marriage and thereafter.) She recalled that she and her father were very close until she was 5½. As for her mother, Tina could not describe her in objective terms; all her memories about her mother were unpleasant. Shortly before she broke with reality, Tina had felt strong hatred toward her mother and had even entertained the idea of killing her. On recovery, she was still very much troubled by her mother's invasiveness. According to other sources, during Tina's childhood her mother had given Tina suppositories when she herself was constipated. When Tina showed improvement in therapy, her mother was openly jealous. She started to find fault with the hospital and the patient's therapy; for example, she tried to convince the therapist that in order to help Tina he should read certain religious pamphlets.

Tina had one younger sister, nine years her junior, who was described as relatively healthy and of whom Tina was intensely jealous. Tina's maternal grandmother, who played a very important role in Tina's early life, was described as having been a very powerful woman. Widowed early, she traveled around the country, reading poetry to groups. She was said to have wanted to be an actress.

Comments: Tina's mother had in fact been characterized as a typical "schizophrenogenic mother" (Tietze, 1959). The hospital staff had perceived her as narcissistic, self-centered, and markedly oriented to getting attention from others (hypochondriasis and self-pity). She seemed to be quite fearful of closeness. In relation to Tina, she was perceived as possessive and incapable of keeping a distinct boundary between Tina and herself (e.g., she tried to enter therapy with Tina's therapist). She was much concerned with Tina's immediate physical well-being, rather than with her severe emotional problems. She was supersensitive to and hypercritical of Tina's negative qualities. She was certainly very ready and able to get Tina into "double bind" predicaments (Bateson et al., 1956). According to the conceptualizations of Wynne and Ryckoff (1958), Lidz et al. (1965), Stierlin (1973), and others, Tina's family could be described as schizophrenogenic.[2] There was the mother who was insecure, domineering, and proud of her heritage, and the father who was insecure, passive, and ashamed of his background. In their early years together she often became sick and returned to her own mother for consolation. In the course of time she became healthier and stronger, and the father began to drown his defeat and loss of pride in alcohol. Initially, because of her illnesses, etc., she was a neglectful mother to Tina. Later, as she grew stronger, she tried to make up. She created a special tie between herself

---

[2] Hilde Bruch (personal communication, 1976) has told me that, according to her observations, some "schizophrenogenic" parents are perfectly "normal" by conventional standards. They are, however, basically narcissistic, able to give generous support to their children only when they feel narcissistically gratified by their childrens' talents, achievements, etc.

and Tina, and it was this tie that led to a schizophrenogenic family atmosphere for Tina. Hill (1955) made the empirical observation that a schizophrenic is created in three generations, beginning with the grandmother. Tina's grandmother, perhaps, filled the bill. The grandmother, who died in her mid-80's, had exerted a strong influence on the life of her youngest daughter (Tina's mother).

Pregnancy

The parents were of the same age. They married in their middle 20's. Tina was born in the second year of their marriage. The mother was said to have a violent temper and crippling migraine headaches. But there was no clear-cut information about the marital adjustment in the first couple of years. According to the record, the mother was frightened by the pregnancy, which was not planned, and was very nervous throughout it. The mother's fantasies about the pregnancy were unknown.

Comments: This historical information offers no direct proof of anything. What can be inferred is that the mother's affective tension state must have had some effect on the fetus. That such a state causes "preanxiety," which in turn aggravates the patient's "predisposition to anxiety" (Greenacre, 1941), cannot be proved. Still, the hypothesis is highly plausible. Moreover, if the mother was troubled during the pregnancy, it is unlikely that she would be a relaxed mother during the first few months of the infant's life.

Birth and the Symbiotic Phase

Tina's labor was prolonged because of a breech presentation. The mother was said to have been so weakened that she was in bed for months afterwards. Because of her mother's condition, Tina's care was entrusted to a maid, about whom little was known. The mother breast fed Tina for two or three weeks. Why she switched to the bottle was not clear. As the story went, the mother was so anxious about looking after the baby that she read books all the time, and the books she read instructed her "*not* to give too much attention to the infant."

Comments: This information was provided by the mother and could be considered factual and reliable. Mahler (1975) has impressed on us the importance of mutual cuing between mother and infant in the earliest phase of life. Without mutual cuing, the infant cannot establish a satisfactory relation with the mother and subsequently cannot internalize the representation of the mothering person as one who facilitates the maintenance of his homeostasis. Because of this defect, the child will maintain a tendency constantly to seek to establish a symbiotic relationship. This tendency to regress to the symbiotic stage of development will immensely complicate his future life and will set the stage for the eventual development of schizophrenic illness. In the case of Tina, for a number of reasons the establishment of mutual cuing was probably difficult. On the one hand, the prolonged labor not only weakened the mother (already torn by conflicts) physically, it must also have reduced her motivation to care for a totally helpless infant. On the other hand, Tina's traumatic birth could have left some hemorrhagic spots (temporary as they may have been) in her brain that could in turn have made her irritable, cranky, or not "normal" in other ways. The process of mutual cuing could have been disrupted by these factors in combination with others. Such a disruption may have been reflected in the mother's conscious desire to "reach" the infant through books: Unconsciously she sought to relieve her guilt by selecting books that justified her neglect of the infant.

The nature of the mothering that Tina might have gotten from the maid and the father was not clear. The maid was undoubtedly less conflicted and therefore less anxious in handling the baby; yet it may be supposed that she might not have been able to feel very much empathy with an irritable and less than normal baby. As for the father, he was not described as having had much to do with the care of either of his children during their infancy. All in all, Tina seems to

have been the kind of baby who could not have had a satisfactory symbiotic relationship, the lack of which results in
various basic experiential disturbances (see Chapter 11). As
will be shown later, Tina's most agonizing disturbances seem
to have lain in the areas of object relations, libido-aggression
imbalance, and a tendency to experience organismic panic.

The Separation-Individuation Phase

During this period, the father was assigned to several foreign countries whose languages the mother could not speak,
and the mother was described as having angry outbursts and
headaches. Because of her physical condition she often took
Tina and returned to the United States to live with her own
mother for long periods of time. At times she left Tina with
the grandmother and, alone, joined her husband. The mother
did not clearly remember the landmarks of Tina's development, but believed that when Tina became upset she screamed.
At such times she often lost control of her urine. This tendency lasted until Tina was three or four or five. She particularly remembered one instance that occurred when Tina was
14 months old. Tina wet her pants; the mother changed her;
Tina immediately wet them again, and they had quite a fight.
(During her psychosis incontinence was quite a problem.) One
of Tina's screen memories was of standing at the door crying
and screaming for the maid, who had disappeared. According
to Tina, this incident occurred when she was 14 months old.
But whether the mother's and Tina's memories referred to a
single event could not be determined. All in all, the mother
considered that Tina was a happy toddler, and Tina described
her life during this period as pleasant, especially when she
was at her grandmother's.

Comments: According to Mahler (1968), a satisfactory
symbiotic relation is the prerequisite for the infant's gradual
differentiation and separation from its mother, and without
such a satisfactory relation the infant will experience separation anxiety as separation panic. In the case of Tina, she

probably did not have a satisfactory symbiotic relation with her mother or any mothering person. If this lack caused Tina problems in respect to separation and individuation, these problems were further compounded by the instability of her life situation during the next few years. Her reactions to the frequent separations from her parents, her maid, her grand-mother, though not noticed as such by her mother, were per-haps summarized in Tina's own screen memory. This memory suggests that Tina lost emotional control (she cried and screamed) when she lost the maid. If the mother's memory of Tina's loss of sphincter control referred to the same event, then we can appreciate why, later on during her psychosis, Tina reacted so strongly to physical or emotional losses. On such occasions she not only became incontinent but also screamed at the top of her lungs and struck out at others. Tina's subsequent struggle with her mother could have heightened her anal conflicts (during her psychosis she spent a great deal of time smearing and playing with feces), as well as her conflicts over aggression.

Hill (1955) observed that mothers of schizophrenics usu-ally report the patient's childhood in most idyllic terms. This is understandable, as we all tend to repress memories charged with strong emotions. Thus, aside from the single memory of the fight about the changing of pants, Tina's mother could remember hardly anything. Consequently, there is virtually no information from which to determine Tina's separation-individuation patterns or to trace the developmental lines (A. Freud, 1965b), the formation of self, and the ego-id-superego functioning unity. Tina's own description of this period as satisfactory was perhaps determined not by her memory but by what her mother told her.

Mahler (1975) has observed that object constancy is estab-lished at the end of the separation-individuation phase, when the child is able to tolerate the coexistence of libidinal and aggressive cathexes of the same object. In the potentially schizophrenic child, this experience could be interfered with, for instance, because of a libido-aggression imbalance, so that later on it may become lost for a longer or shorter period. In the case of Tina, the regressive loss of object constancy was most evident during the first few months after she became an outpatient. Then, in stressful situations, for instance, on reunion with the therapist after his vacation, she repressed her anger at him but exhibited extreme anxiety and agitation. She called him at home in the evenings and on many occasions said, "I am afraid to hang up [the phone] . . . my own magics [obviously referring to her earlier modes of defenses] do not work any more . . . I need to hear your voice. . . ." Obviously, when Tina felt ambivalent toward her therapist she could no longer experience him as an internalized constant object. She needed his voice to establish a tie with him.

The Oedipal Phase

There were no reliable direct observations from this period. Tina reported that before the age of 5½, when her mother had headaches and took to her bed, she often climbed onto her father's lap and he cuddled her. She also reported that her mother had impressed on her such memories as the following: The mother, who was so very anxious, had often given Tina suppositories when she herself was constipated. The mother had rescued Tina (aged 4) from being cruelly whipped with a belt by her father.

Comments: Since the cumulative trauma (Khan, 1963) of schizophrenics is of pregenital origin, their oedipal experiences are consequently de-emphasized. It seems that, except for persons suffering from extreme autism, all living beings, schizophrenics included, have experienced greater or lesser degrees of self-object differentiation. Jacobson (1964) observed that

> The distinction between objects can probably proceed more rapidly and consistently than the distinction between self and objects, because perception of the external world is easier than self perception and, besides, because the child normally has less

instinctual motivation for a fusion between different objects than for a re-merging with his mother. In fact, the child's insatiable instinctual appetites stimulate his ability to discriminate between persons who may offer him supplementary gratifications and those who bar his way to need fulfillment. In any case, the beginning constitution of boundaries between images of different objects ushers in the development of specific and different relations to his various love objects. Concomitantly the child's first envy and rivalry conflicts take shape [p. 60].

This is to say that very early in life a potential schizophrenic may have some knowledge of different objects and may even develop some capacity for triadic as well as dyadic relations.[3] Equipped with these capacities, he would enter the oedipal phase with feelings of possessing the object of the opposite sex and being in rivalry with the object of the same sex similar in every respect to those of a more normal child. The difference would lie in the way in which each would integrate the new experience. The more normal child will integrate the new experience at the genital level, whereas the potentially schizophrenic child will use the new experience to rehash the earlier mode of experience: He will try to use the oedipal object to repeat his symbiotic experience. Thus, at the taste of oedipal triumph, he will not feel guilty and experience castration fear; rather, he will feel panic at being re-engulfed. Likewise, the major force determining the dissolution of the Oedipus complex is not the fear of castration but the fear of re-engulfment. In the case of Tina, a schizophrenic-II patient, we note that she established a quasi-oedipal relation with her father; she remembered being cuddled by him when her mother was bedridden with a headache, and entertained the feeling of having possessed him. But because of her fixation at the symbiotic level, her notion of competition and her fantasy of triumph seem to be strikingly different from those

[3] Abelin (1975) has observed that toward the end of the practicing period, at about 18 months, the toddler enters a "triangulation proper" relation with his parents.

related to real oedipal struggles. Later in treatment, when Tina flirted with and then repelled the therapist, she seemed to be repeating a conflict over establishing a symbiotic reunion rather than a conflict over genital strivings for the father.

The whipping episode, which represented the mother's teaching that all men are cruel and mean because they are "babies" and weak, was also later incorporated into the pattern of her dealings with men. The pattern was that, in distress internally, she longed to be cuddled by a male and would reach out for him. If her relation with the man turned out to be more than a brief encounter, a sadomasochistic mode of interaction was established between them. Thus in treatment, just as she had viewed her father, Tina viewed her therapist in two ways: either as a cruel and merciless torturer—in response to his whipping she could only shout at the top of her lungs—or as a weak and alcoholic "baby" about whom she had no feelings but contempt.

This longing for and reaching out to someone of the opposite sex is a defensive flight. Tracing the developmental history of patients who resort to such flight, I have said that

> [the] mother is usually not the only caretaker. When she is totally flustered and is unable to console the infant, someone else might step in and take over. In this changing of hands, the infant learns gradually to expect that "if I don't get what I need from my mother, I may get it from someone else." Thus, the "splitting" may extend from an experience of viewing the same mother as being "good" or "bad," to an experience of separating "good" and "bad" feelings between the representation of two separate persons. When this happens, fantasies of a flight from the "bad" person to a "good" person will follow [Pao, 1973, p. 333].

Still later, during the practicing period, the child may learn to make an actual flight rather than resort solely to a fantasized flight. The case of Tina suggests that the consolidation of this defensive flight to a new object of the opposite sex occurs during the oedipal phase.

Latency

When Tina was 5½, her father changed jobs, and the family no longer had to move from city to city or country to country. As far as Tina was concerned, the stability of family life was superficial. For her father, it seemed to her, was drunk most of the time (in her memory, when he was not drunk he was reading the newspaper), and her mother suffered frequent headaches and depression. Consequently, Tina was often sent to stay with her aunt, who lived in the same city, or to her grandmother, who lived 100 miles away. At 5½, Tina started grade school in the United States. She recalled that she was very scared about starting school and had to be accompanied to school by her parents. A little later, she remembered that she was laughed at because she could print but could not write. She always felt terribly inferior to other children. Constantly worried about one thing or another, she was a very poor student. She had many colds and sore throats, which necessitated her staying home. Her mother was good to her when she was sick. Tina recalled that she was a malingerer and postponed going back to school.

During these years her happiest times were during the summers she spent at her grandmother's; her worst times occurred when her parents fought. She described frightful arguments and vicious fights between them, during which her mother took out knives and threw things. Distressed by these fights, she usually called up her grandmother and received an invitation to spend some time with her. She never told her grandmother what she had witnessed. At 8, Tina's mother became pregnant for the second time; this pregnancy was planned. When Tina was 9 her sister was born. According to the mother, "Tina's nose was out of joint when her sister was born and has been out of joint ever since." But the mother could not give examples to substantiate her point. The sister was bottle fed. Tina recalled that she was extremely envious and jealous of her sister. When her mother took the two girls out for a walk, passers-by would look at the little sister and tell the mother that she had a daughter prettier than Shirley Temple. On these occasions and many others, Tina hated her sister and entertained such horrible thoughts as drowning her or pushing her out of a window. Also at the age of 9, Tina started dancing lessons. When she was told she had the potential to be a good dancer, she began to dream of herself as Shirley Temple.

Comments: Because of the mother's amnesia, she remembered and described Tina's early years as idyllic. Consequently, we did not get a clear picture of what Tina was actually like before she was 5 years old. Thereafter, this deficiency seemed to be somewhat made up by Tina's own memory. According to Tina, her impression of her father underwent a definite change before and after she was 5 or 5½—before that, he was very cuddly and available, but afterward he was distant and unreachable. This change was perhaps related to "the dissolution of the Oedipus complex" (Freud, 1924d), although as I mentioned above the force that determines this mode of dissolution is more related to fear of re-engulfment than to guilt feelings. Whatever conflictual feelings are stirred up by the desire to possess and to compete seem to be finally settled by declaring that the object is contemptible and unavailable.

Tina's own memories also allowed us to appreciate that her school phobia could have been a manifestation of her striving for a symbiotic union with her mother. Her frequent illnesses could have been an identification with her mother, and the secondary gain derived from them perhaps a presage of her long psychotic illness. Her own experience of early deprivation might have exaggerated her envy and jealousy of her sister, etc. The passers-by's comments about Shirley Temple, and her grandmother's and mother's frustrated wishes to be an actress, could have inspired her dream of becoming an actress. At a time when she felt displaced at home and was derided at school, her self-esteem was at a low ebb. The discovery of her talent for dancing could have been a piece of good fortune. Even if it reinforced her exhibitionistic tendency, it at least temporarily stopped a further decline of self-esteem, and perhaps enabled her to set aside her conflicts in the next 10+ years while she unfalteringly channeled her energy toward fulfilling the dream of becoming an actress or a performer.

The discord between the parents became increasingly obvious. Although the father was described as cruel and mean, the mother was actually the one who took up a knife and threw things. The discrepancies between what she was told and what she had seen must have caused great confusion in Tina. Since neither parent was able to help her rectify the confusion, she reached out to her grandmother by calling her frequently. Unfortunately, she could not articulate her confusion lest she antagonize her mother. Tina was like most schizophrenics in her inordinate fear of catastrophic retaliation should she evoke rage in her mother and consequent appearance of extremely loyalty to her. Tina's inability to articulate her confusion is typical of schizophrenics, who have somehow learned not to ask for help when help is needed.

With the passing of the oedipal phase, the superego structure is gradually consolidated. In the case of Tina, her superego formation, influenced by her identification with her mother and by her disturbed early experiences (which affected, for instance, the libido-aggression balance), would probably show a heightened severity and harshness and a parallel reduction of its beneficent supporting quality. According to Kohut (1971), a sense of self-cohesion is normally safeguarded by the formation of the superego. In Tina's case, a pathological superego formation could have increased her vulnerability to a loss of self-cohesion.

During the transition from the oedipal phase to latency, libido is transferred from the parental figures to peers, teachers, etc. Hampered by her early relations with her parents (and others), Tina did not successfully carry out this transfer; she was an "outsider" to her classmates. Latency does not diminish drive intensity. As Fenichel (1945) observed, "During the latency period, the instinctual demands themselves have not changed much; but the ego has" (p. 110). After the development of the ego's capacity for symbolization, for instance, dreams and fantasies are used as pathways for drive discharge. In the case of Tina, those discharge pathways seem to have been used to excess (especially after the birth of her sister). As a result, she was too absorbed to cope with the real objects in her life or to do well in her school work.

Preadolescence

At 11, Tina was reported to have had no close friends; she was characterized as a loner and a dreamer. She collected photos of movie stars and busied herself with arranging and rearranging them on the wall in her bedroom. She often talked to herself, especially at bed time. At 12, Tina had a nightmare, the content of which was not recoverable, following which she was very much afraid to close her eyes; in fact she stayed awake many a night until the fear of the nightmare was replaced by a concern about insomnia. Menarche took place at 13. Somewhere around this time she began to "date" (whatever that meant)—obviously, she needed company and sought company not among girls but among boys.

Comments: A. Freud (1965b) has observed that

at the transition point from latency to preadolescence . . . changes in the quality as well as quantity of the drives and the increase in several primitive pregenital trends (especially oral and anal) cause a severe loss of social adaptation, of sublimations and, in general, of personality gains which have been achieved during the latency period. The impression of health and rationality disappears again and the preadolescent seems to be less mature, less normal, and often appears to have delinquent leanings [p. 163].

The regression activated by the pubertal change of drive pattern is supposed to be in the service of progressive development (Blos, 1962). Because of cumulative trauma in the earlier phases of life, this regression can bring about ego fragmentation and the dissolution of self-cohesion. If this is the case, the person (a schizophrenic-III) may at this juncture succumb to psychosis. Tina did not—even though she had enough symptoms to cause serious concern (e.g., she had increasing difficulty in peer relations, was increasingly isolated, and clung desperately to her fantasy world). Things might have been different if her parents had noticed her distress. But they were too busy fighting with each other to give her any help. That was unfortunate; for, after a period of receiving no help from them, Tina seems to have turned more toward solving her problems on her own—whether she could do so or not. Thus, failing to master the revived conflicts that caused the nightmare, Tina sought help from nobody, eventually acquiring a lifelong intractable insomnia. Tina's nightmare or night terror (although the content of the nightmare was unknown, it was probably related to unneutralized aggression) had the quality of a "diminutive psychosis" (Sullivan, 1962; Mack, 1970), with marked amnesia for it and a lingering effect of loss of reality testing (she obviously believed that the content of the nightmare would return if she closed her eyes). Dating boys after the nightmare did not appear to be a normal unfolding of "removal of objects" (A. Katan, 1951); rather, it had a defensive quality—the defensive use of a phase-specific tendency by the preadolescent girl "to push hetereosexual wishes or fantasies into the foreground, while regressive tendencies assert themselves, peripherally and secretively" (Blos, 1970, p. 27).

Adolescence

From the ninth grade on, she seemed to become more self-engrossed. Her memories were all about herself. She recalled that she became increasingly popular with boys. She also recalled admiring her own naked body, inspecting herself without clothes on before a mirror for hours at a stretch. She daydreamed of herself as being the most beautiful and most admired star. She experimented with sexual relations, although she never enjoyed them for a minute. As she gave the boys what they wanted, she was nicknamed the "mother of sex."

The parents had always fought viciously for diverse reasons. But by now, Tina was often the cause of their fights. If the father insisted that Tina should return home earlier from dates, the mother would come to Tina's rescue. If the mother forbade Tina to go out with certain fast boys, the father was ready to contradict her. During one summer vacation, the father decided that idleness was the source of Tina's trouble with boys and that she should get a job. Instantly, the mother felt that to make Tina get up too early every morning could hurt her health (Tina regularly returned home from dates during the wee hours of the morning), and after five days told Tina to stop going to work. As this was going on, Tina grew to feel responsible for her parents' unhappiness and tried to avoid seeing them so as not to be reminded of her guilty feelings. Thus the time of her return home at night became increasingly unpredictable. She neglected her studies and almost failed to graduate from high school. After graduation she now, a bit over 18, went to a distant, small, all-girl college to study dancing and acting. At college, she felt lost. Before a year was up she dropped out and returned home. For the next two years she continued to spend a great deal of her time with boys, although she took dance and voice lessons. At 21, she worked in a summer theater. Although she was extremely anxious, she was nevertheless assigned a few secondary roles, and was said to have done a decent job.

Comments: Following the nightmare, which could have been equivalent to a brief psychosis, Tina appears to have become more regressed and narcissistically self-engrossed on the one hand, and more driven to acquire companionship with the other sex on the other hand. Regressed and self-engrossed, she studied herself before a mirror and daydreamed of becoming a star without putting in any effort to become one. In the process, her sense of reality became increasingly compromised. This gradual erosion of reality sense is what Federn spoke of as the slow displacement of contact with reality. But slow erosion is not the only way in which reality is lost. Some years later, when Tina became catatonic, she lost her remaining tenuous contact with reality rather abruptly. As for the driven quality of her seeking the companionship of members of the other sex, it was defensive in nature. By this act she was at least temporarily distracted from her inner emotional tumult. However, in order to assure the companionship of young men, she had to do what they wanted her to do, although she did not really enjoy it. The promiscuity must have been out of keeping with her general views. By getting into the middle of her parents' struggle she seems to have been both asking for external censure and, in an "ambivalent" way, calling their attention to her desperate need for help. But they were too involved in their own squabbles to be aware of her needs and distress.

Her dropping out of college was not unexpected. Not only was she already on a regressive course, but separation from her parents' home was in itself stressful. Many schizophrenic patients become crippled at this juncture. But Tina did not. Perhaps her fantasy of becoming a star in the future kept her from falling apart. The same force perhaps helped her to live through the next two years at home, where she resumed the chaotic style of life she had lived before she entered college. Working at the summer theatre was, in a way, approaching the fulfillment of her dream, and must therefore have aroused great anxiety. The anxiety was further compounded by the experience of separation from her family. Thus it is not surprising that she soon made the defensive flight to an object of the opposite sex and, so to speak, fell in love.

One of the major phase-specific tasks of the adolescent period, especially during its late part, is the consolidation of identity. In the case of Tina, the early fantasy or delusion[4] of becoming the greatest star in the future seems to have superseded the normal identity crisis (Erikson, 1959) as well as the subsequent consolidation of an identity suitable to adult

---

[4] For a differentiation of the two, see Lichtenberg and Pao (1974).

living. The phase-specific task was totally bypassed and replaced by the hardening of a delusional system that became
manifest when the psychosis occurred. In this sense, the fantasy of being a star is what Freud (1922, 1939) meant when
he said that delusion is preformed.

Engagement and Marriage

Shortly after she arrived at the summer theatre, she met
her future husband, a young actor who was also struggling
for recognition. She described him as attractive because of his
independence, his austerity, his aloneness, and his quality of
being diffident and very shy. They fell in love with each other
at first sight. When the summer was over, he was to follow
the troupe to other cities, while she had decided to further
her study of voice in preparation for her future on Broadway.
In the midst of saying goodbye, they became engaged. During
the next two years they met infrequently. Almost immediately after they married, the young couple began to have
problems. He preferred to travel from city to city as long as
he could get roles, whereas she preferred to stay in the big
city. He did not mind playing secondary roles, whereas she
dreamed of being the leading lady and did not mind continuing her study with renowned teachers in the hope of an important assignment in the future. When he got roles she
viewed him as a better professional and became violently jealous of and hateful to him. He expected her to take care of
household chores while he worked, but she did not know how.
He was jealous when he saw her flirting with other men,
whereas she felt he should not interfere with her pleasure.

As the struggle between them grew in intensity, she turned
into a screaming, insomniac child. She would then sleep from
dawn until noon and go to dancing class in the late afternoon.
When she returned home her husband would have dinner
ready. Later, as she dreaded going to bed, she would make
scenes by belittling herself or accusing her husband of interest in other women. They fought (as her parents did), but they

made up (which her parents could not do); and the same drama would repeat itself the next night. For the 3½ years they lived together he was said to have been so troubled by her that he was emotionally unable to work, whereas she continued to prepare herself for a big role by taking voice and dancing lessons. Since neither of them worked, they were helped out by her family. Finally, her husband left her. The separation was followed by a divorce a couple of years later. The marriage was childless. During the marriage the patient was frigid, as she had always been.

Comments: Originally, falling in love perhaps represented no more than a defensive flight on Tina's part, to deal with her anxiety at being drawn closer to the fulfillment of her fantasy and her separation panic at being away from home. The engagement, which occurred in the midst of saying good-bye, was probably also her effort to deal with separation panic. Whatever romantic fantasy she might have attached to the prolonged engagement, during which she and her fiancé met infrequently, it was brought to an end when they got married. The husband, basically her narcissistic self, now demanded that she should stop dreaming and face the exigencies of life squarely, at least sometimes. He proposed that they build their success by working in the theatre, and not by waiting around to be discovered. Although he yearned for success, he was eager to earn a living by joining the road company. Furthermore, he pressed her to pay attention to the household chores; she must give up the immediate adoration of men (if she was to get admiration as an actress she had to earn it now on the stage), etc. The fights between them not only mobilized aggression, they also reminded her of her parents' married life. She became increasingly distressed and unable to cope. Regressively, she identified with her mother, becoming vicious and hypercritical on the one hand but helpless and hypochondriacal on the other. But this solution only made the situation worse. She regressed further. When the insomnia reappeared, she was on the verge of a psychosis. Yet, by ritualistically maintaining her life as a student, taking dancing lessons and preparing herself to be a great star, she managed to hang on for 3½ years. Her whole life was a fantasy—a long-standing fantasy to recapture the love and attention she wanted, but did not get, from her mother. The fantasy promised that she would one day replace her sister and be the star and the center of her mother's attention. The fantasy had the effect of recapturing the past, promising a future, and it therefore imparted special meaning to her present life. Real life, which her husband was interested in, in fact threatened the lifesaving fantasy she had harbored since preadolescence. Thus, when it came to the point of choosing between the fantasy and her husband, Tina chose to cling to her fantasy.

The Downhill Slide

Following the separation from her husband, Tina felt somewhat relieved. She even contemplated going to work. But each time she prepared herself for an audition, she invariably had some sort of mishap—a sprain, torn muscles, even fractures. She continued to depend on her family for financial support. More and more often, her mother came from another state to visit her, witnessing a continuous downhill drift to a grave disorganization. Under family pressure, as well as from an inner need, Tina finally started individual treatment with a woman therapist. As soon as the treatment began, Tina became involved with a young man. The formation of a triangular relationship gave Tina a certain sense of security. Thus, in the early months of her relation with this boyfriend, she was gratified sexually for the first time in her life. But soon the interaction between her and her boyfriend made it necessary for the treatment to focus constantly on their interpersonal crises. When the boyfriend was not thinking about marriage, Tina wanted it. When he wanted it, Tina backed out. When both finally came around, they couldn't decide whether they should have children. Tina began to see double and became whining and helpless. When he threatened to leave her, she went into a near-catatonic state in which she could neither think nor move, although she preserved her contact with reality. At this point the therapist recommended hospitalization. Driving back with her mother to their home state, they stopped at a motel. Because of a sudden impulse to kill her mother, Tina secluded herself in the bathroom for a whole night.

Comments: The loss of the husband seems to have had a profound effect on Tina. For the first time since her work in the summer theatre, she even entertained the idea of finding herself a job. Did the idea of going to work result from an increase in energy, energy freed by getting rid of the envied competitor? (With the husband gone, she did not have to compare herself with him unfavorably all the time.) Did it represent an identification with the lost husband who had advocated work? Did it reflect an impairment of the ego's capacity to discern the importance of maintaining her fantasy as a fantasy at all costs, as in the past? The mishaps that occurred when she was preparing for auditions indicate that she was working out in a very tense body state. Now she began treatment; it was unclear why a woman analyst was chosen. At this point, there was presumably no indication that hospitalization might be necessary. But her immediate creation of a triangular relationship involving her therapist, her boyfriend, and herself was an ominous sign that an ego disorganization was imminent. The triangularization was obviously a distancing maneuver (to create a distance between herself and the therapist) and a desperate struggle against the symbiotic pull. While the establishment of the triangle might be a life and death matter for Tina, it undermined her treatment altogether. In such circumstances, the therapist must proceed with caution, to get across to the patient that what requires scrutiny in the treatment is the patient's relation with the therapist.

The Total Break with Reality

Tina was hospitalized. Because she exhibited catatonia-like symptoms (with her sense of reality preserved), ECT was recommended. When it was declined, she was transferred to another hospital. Shortly thereafter her father died of a heart attack. On learning this news, Tina said, "I killed him." Instead of mourning the loss (she was not capable of mourning it until many years after treatment), she began to show fragmentation of thought processes (according to the observation of the attending psychiatrist). After two more transfers she was admitted to Chestnut Lodge. In the meantime, her boyfriend kept making demands on her to hurry up and make a decision about their future. Failing to get a response from her, he finally wrote and told her that he was engaged to another girl. At that point, she became catatonic.

Comments: It was obvious that, even without the recent cluster of losses (loss of therapist, loss of father, loss of her boyfriend, losses in connection with changing hospitals three times), Tina was heading toward a grave disorganization. Ever since her middle teens there had been evidence of a gradual but steady impairment of ego functioning capacity in the face of various phases of psychological development, which necessarily brought about "social disarticulations" (Burnham et al., 1969). By clinging to the fantasy of becoming a star in the future, she had, however, managed to hang onto reality—even though the tie was becoming increasingly weakened. The recent losses were the last straw, bringing about a total break with reality.

Tina's effort to develop the fantasy and to live it out corresponds to Jacobson's (1967) statement: ". . . certain types of psychotic patients will not immediately break with reality but will first attempt the opposite . . . they may not only hold on, or even cling, to the external world, but try to change it, to create one that will suit their special needs . . . Psychotics give up reality . . . only if reality fails to lend itself to their purposes and to help them in their conflict solution" (pp. 18-20).

It is generally considered that heightened conflict over aggression, with a parallel increase of deneutralized aggression (Hartmann, 1953), brings about "schizophrenia as a defense" (Bak, 1954). At first glance, that seems to have been the case with Tina. The bickering between her and her husband marked the beginning of her downfall. The aggression associated with the loss of her husband and then her woman therapist fostered further regression, whereupon she failed to assess the strength of her aggressive impulses. Consequently, she had to stay in the bathroom all night lest she actually kill her mother. By the time she received the news of her father's death, she was so flooded with aggression that she was only too ready to blame herself for his death, just as she had assumed the responsibility for her parents' fights and unhappiness. Abandonment by her boyfriend further mobilized her aggression, overbalancing her ego capacity altogether. The schizophrenic break was then erected as a defense.

The validity of this formulation is strengthened when one takes into consideration the aggressive behavior that schizophrenic patients exhibit in the course of their illness. On closer scrutiny, however, it appears that even though conflict over aggression indeed plays a very prominent role, it is but one of many factors that set the schizophrenic illness in motion. In the case of Tina, for instance, there was evidence that from her latency onward she experienced separation anxiety to an extreme degree; her object relations were very strained, her capacity to get her needs fulfilled by others was poor, her narcissistic self was overstimulated, her self-image was totally based on fantasy and was not in tune with reality, her emotions were dominated by envy, jealousy, and hatred, her harsh superego encouraged her tendency to self-blaming, and so on. Only in combination with these sundry factors would conflicts over aggression become enlarged in the course of time.

Discussion

This case presentation was based on data obtained through the patient's reconstruction of her past in the course of treatment. However accurate the reconstruction is, it is not the same as if the illness were actually traced, through direct observation, from the earliest experience until the final break with reality. But, for now, the latter approach seems out of the question.

We postulate that a lack of mutual cuing between Tina and her mothering person before and during the symbiotic period resulted in various basic experiential disturbances that aggravated one another, leading eventually to a total break with reality. In the review of Tina's history, we noticed that some disturbances were manifest before her psychosis and others only during her psychosis. For instance, throughout her life there were repeated experiences of separation panic. This interacted with disturbances in object relations and resulted in her tendency toward symbiotic union with others on the one hand and her fear of being close to others on the other hand. Her libido-aggression balance was greatly tilted in the direction of aggression; her libidinal capacity seems to have been dwarfed. As the course of her treatment showed, she was most aggressive, hostile, and assaultive when she felt tender and loving.

During her psychosis, we witnessed the reactivation of maintenance mechanisms—deanimation, devitalization, obliteration of self-object boundary, erasure of self- and object representations (e.g., not being able to mourn the death of her father). We also noticed her inappropriate affect, communication problems, reactivation of primary-process functioning, etc. (We could not be certain whether there was a perceptual disorder since her verbalization was quite inadequate to demonstrate it.) Her sense of self was unquestionably fragmented during catatonia. Her body self-image was not only distorted but became a dominant component of her self-representation. Even before she became overtly psychotic, she was very much caught up with her body, her strength, her headaches, etc. When she was floridly psychotic, she spent at least 90 percent of her waking time obsessing about "the slab in her mind," the food she ingested, her discharges, etc.

From the diagnostic point of view, at the time of admission

Tina fell into the category of schizophrenia II. All her disturbed behavior seemed to have come on during her middle adolescent years. Without knowing her systematized fantasy-delusions, it was, however, at first difficult to imagine what had kept her from becoming psychotic earlier. This fantasy-delusion is an interesting phenomenon. The good experience (according to her memory) with her grandmother, aunt, and father must have, to some degree, undone her early traumatic experience. But the undoing was not complete. Thus during the latency period all sorts of difficulties had already made their appearance (school phobia, isolation in school, etc.). The birth of her young sister when she was 9 further taxed Tina's already enfeebled ego capacity. By an excessive and defensive use of a phase-specific capacity for fantasy, she somehow succeeded in building a systematized fantasy or predelusion of going-to-be-a-star-in-the-future. The fantasy-delusion turned out to be of extreme importance to her. Although it curtailed her growth, it staved off distressing and disappointing affects and protected her from a quicker, earlier disorganization. In the end, however, the fantasy-delusion exacted its toll. Later, her need to cling tenaciously to the fantasy-delusion greatly prolonged her treatment. Even after she was no longer psychotic, for two to three years she organized her day around taking dancing lessons (now more as a ritual and less as a defense). She consumed so much energy in this way that she had none left for other activities that, from the bystander's point of view, could have been more enjoyable or more rewarding.

In early psychiatric textbooks, paranoia and paranoid schizophrenia were treated as two separate clinical entities. From what we learn from Tina, we may assume that in paranoia, the patient's cognitive capacity is not only minimally affected but usable to organize the fantasy-delusion. By means of the fantasy-delusion the patient is able to "suppress" the overt manifestations of the impairment of other ego functions.

Tina's memory of good experiences with her father could also have determined her future use of defensive flight, during stressful moments, to a male person. The value of this defense is rather two-edged. While it obviously mitigated anxiety or panic at the time of its reactivation, it created situations in which she could no longer maintain her "distance" from others. When the "distance" was removed, her conflicts over close relationships were revived. Anxiety then became intensified, and symptoms resulted.

CHAPTER 13

An Excursion to the Recent Debate on Conflict versus Deficiency

Arlow and Brenner's paper, "The Psychopathology of the Psychoses: A Proposed Revision" (1969), prepared for the 26th International Psycho-Analytical Congress in Rome, seems to have brought into focus a needed "debate" (Gillespie, 1970) on two issues: first, whether schizophrenic symptoms can be better explained in terms of Freud's 1911 theory or in terms of a theory based on his post-1926 theoretical conceptualization; and second, whether schizophrenic manifestations result from conflict or deficiency. By and large, the 1911 theory is associated with the deficiency hypothesis, and the later conceptualization is linked with the conflict hypothesis.

The debate on how schizophrenic symptoms can best be conceptualized theoretically is not an idle one. It is profoundly imbued with the philosophy of treatment. Because of my primary concern with the philosophy of treatment, I shall scrutinize the several viewpoints espoused by the participants in the debate.

The Substance of the Debate

Arlow and Brenner's Rome Congress paper is, in fact, a restatement of a view they had expressed earlier (1964). In essence, they believe that Freud's 1911 theory, which explains schizophrenic symptoms in terms of decathexis, hypercathexis, and recathexis, should be laid to rest. As an alternative, they propose to apply "to the psychoses Freud's later views of mental functioning as conceptualized in the structural theory . . . [and] to apply to the formation of symptoms in the psychoses the same principles which Freud applied after 1926 to the formation of symptoms in the neuroses" (1969, p. 10). They stress that neurosis and psychosis are on one continuum, and that neurotic and psychotic symptoms should be and can be explained by one theory. The differences between neurosis and psychosis are "of degree, not of kind," quantitative rather than qualitative. And the most characteristic differences are: (1) In psychosis, instinctual regression is more pronounced than in neurosis. (2) In psychosis, conflicts over aggressive impulses are more intense and more frequent. Disruption of the patient's relations with external objects often results from his need to protect them from his own aggression. (3) In psychosis, disturbances of ego and superego functioning are much more severe than in neurosis. Such disturbances may result from faulty endowment, maldevelopment, or regressive deterioration as a consequence of conflict.

According to the revised theory, the ego plays the central role in the psychopathology of psychosis, and symptom formation is conceptualized in terms of conflict, anxiety, and defenses. That is, conflicts lead to danger situations and to anxiety; in anxiety the schizophrenic's ego reactivates various defense mechanisms and brings about a "regressive alteration in ego function"; and the disturbed ego functioning results in symptoms. Applying the conflict-anxiety-defense hypothesis (instead of the decathexis-hypercathexis-recathexis hypothesis), Arlow and Brenner suggest that the catastrophic experience or the end-of-the-world experience can be explained in terms of projection of aggression; the grandiose delusion of being a savior in terms of reparative efforts following destructive fantasies; and hallucinations and other systematized delusions in terms of disturbed reality testing. Arlow and Brenner consider the decathexis of internal object representations as a defense, a protective measure the patient makes use of, for instance, to safeguard the object from his own aggressive impulses. They also believe that object representations are not lost in schizophrenia and that schizophrenics are capable of developing transference. Consequently, some schizophrenics can benefit from psychoanalytic interpretation of conflict and resistance.

At the Congress, Blau, Wexler, Greenson, and others voiced their disagreement with Arlow and Brenner's proposal from the floor (Gillespie, 1970). They argued that psychosis and neurosis are essentially different, for only in psychosis do we witness the loss of internal object representations. They endorsed Freud's decathexis-recathexis theory because it depicts so well this loss of object representations and the subsequent phase of restitution. They believed that it would be a mistake to abandon the decathexis-recathexis theory.

In a subsequent paper entitled "Schizophrenia: Conflict and Deficiency," Wexler (1971) elaborated the views he had expressed at the Congress. He compiled a long list of schizophrenic manifestations, including the external appearance of self-engrossment, a malignant "loss of distance," dereistic or autistic thinking, a deficiency in personal or sexual identity, and an inability to use the psychoanalytic type of treatment. He observed that none of the listed manifestations can be very well explained by a theoretical model of conflict-anxiety-loss of ego function and symptom formation. He further observed that these manifestations reflect the combination of two processes, namely, a "loss of more complex . . . object-representations involving both ego and superego" and "a variety of . . . restitutional efforts." In view of these observations he concluded that Freud's decathexis-recathexis theory must be retained. Wexler further expressed the opinion that in hallucination and delusion formation the loss of reality testing is not primary, as Arlow and Brenner suggest; rather, it is secondary to the loss of object representations. "Memory traces

are the road map to assessment of the external world" (p. 94).[1]
Since memory traces are intimately related to object representations, the loss of them results secondarily in the loss of
various ego functions (i.e., the reality-testing function) that
are essential for assessing the external world. Using the loss
of object representations as the criterion, Wexler believes that
psychosis and neurosis differ qualitatively rather than quantitatively. Because the loss of object representations is characteristic of schizophrenics, schizophrenia may be conceived
as a deficiency disorder. Neurotics, in contrast, do not lose
object representations, and neurosis may therefore be conceived of as a conflict disorder. Because schizophrenia is a
deficiency disorder, its treatment should be fundamentally
different from the treatment of neurosis. Essentially, the primary effort in the treatment of schizophrenic patients should
be to rebuild the structure that has been lost rather than to
interpret conflicts.

In his "critical summary" of the main theme of the Congress, Bak (1970) pointed out that Arlow and Brenner seemed
not to have taken into account the following: (1) Decathexis
of object representations does not preclude transference, for
decathexis may not involve all object representations. Besides, transference manifestations are often in the stream of
restitution. (2) Decathexis of object representations can indeed be seen as a schizophrenic defense, but in schizophrenics
the cathexis of object representations is originally defective.
(3) The unusually strong aggressive conflict in schizophrenia
is the consequence of excessive libidinal decathexis: "Simply,
the libidinal decathexis of object-representations opens the
way to their destruction by aggressive cathexis" (p. 259).[2]

---

[1] Wexler also said, "even more important is the inevitable consequence that self
representations must also disappear progressively since these are so intimately linked
with object representations" (p. 94). But he did not elaborate on this loss of self-
representation.

[2] I believe that this statement is correct only when we consider "decathexis" as
a phase in the two-phase theory of symptom formation and, following that phase,
changes in the ego, superego, and self result in a marked shift in the patient's
attitude toward his aggressive conflict. Otherwise the idea appears very mechanical
and insufficiently dynamic.

(4) It is possible that the sequence of conflict-anxiety-defense-alteration of ego functioning runs in the opposite direction; that is, "changes in the ego are primary (thought disorder, reduced neutralization, etc.) and make overt hitherto latent conflicts secondarily" (p. 259). (5) There may be a difference between schizophrenic and neurotic anxiety. Schizophrenic anxiety is a reaction to the danger of damage to ego functions or to the dissolution of the self. (6) Schizophrenics have the same conflicts as normal or neurotic persons. The difference lies in the schizophrenic's incapacity to deal with these conflicts in any other way but by archaic modes of defense. "The ego's incapacity . . . is due to the schizophrenic process, which for the time being defies definition" (p. 259).

In "The Psychopathology of Psychoses: A Reply to Arlow and Brenner," Freeman (1970) also expressed the opinion that Arlow and Brenner's revised theory does not explain all the psychotic manifestations as adequately as does Freud's classical theory. In Freeman's view, the revised theory gives "full weight to the dynamic factors which set the scene for the appearance of the symptoms, but the economic aspects are dismissed as being contradicted by the observable phenomena" (p. 407). This, Freeman says, is unfortunate, for "by the exclusion of the economic standpoint much is left unexplained when the full range of psychotic phenomena are taken into account" (p. 407). Moreover, in the postulate that conflict over aggressive impulses is the cause of symptom formation in schizophrenia, the revised theory seemed to Freeman to overemphasize content. According to Freeman,

> it is not the content of the drive-representation which creates the danger situation and the anxiety but the intensity which the drive has developed. . . . When drive-representations reach that degree of intensity which leads to a danger situation the first line of defence is repression . . . The withdrawal of cathexis from object- and drive-representations as postulated in the classical theory of psychosis is the initial phase of repression [p. 411].

In respect to whether object representations are lost in schizophrenia, Freeman wrote, "The object-representations may be present as mental structures but they are inadequately cathected. There is no constancy of object-cathexis" (p. 411). Like Wexler and Bak, Freeman disputed that delusions and hallucinations originate in faulty reality testing. After object representations are decathected,

> The ego no longer operates under the influence of the secondary process. . . . Once thinking, remembering and perceiving fall under the influence of the primary process the perception and judgment of the real world are governed by the tendencies to displacement, condensation and hallucination. The capacity to discriminate between psychical and external reality is abolished and reality-testing lost. . . . The considerations taken up here suggest that the defect in reality-testing which occurs in psychosis is a consequence rather than the cause of the processes which lead to hallucinations and delusions [p. 413].

Freeman argued against ascribing to the ego the central role in symptom formation, saying that because in psychosis the cathexis changes from bound to mobile, "Every aspect of mental functioning is disordered. . . . This adds weight to the view that a general disorganization has affected the whole of the mental apparatus rather than a defect involving one specific part—the ego" (p. 414). Freeman further pointed out that psychosis is not a homogeneous entity. The illustrative cases cited by Arlow and Brenner were not very sick. It is doubtful that the conclusions Arlow and Brenner drew from the study of these not-very-sick patients could serve as a comprehensive explanation of all schizophrenias. Freeman suggested that, taking all schizophrenias into consideration, "The classical theory still comes nearest to . . . ideal" (p. 414).

In "An Essay on Psychoanalytic Theory: Two Theories of Schizophrenia," London (1973) argued that the classical theory can be separated into two incompatible theories—the unitary theory and the specific theory. In the unitary theory, schizophrenic behaviors are considered to be unconsciously purposeful responses to intrapsychic conflicts. In the specific theory schizophrenic behaviors are considered as reflecting unique psychological deficiency states that result from a "decathexis" of object representations. In London's view, even though Freud strongly favored the unitary theory, "at this point in the development of psychoanalysis, pursuit of a unified and cohesive psychoanalytic theory is an unwise research strategy" (p. 177). To facilitate the conceptualization of the specific theory, London proposed the following definitions: "The definition of instinctual drives should be limited to mental representations, derived from the internalization of tension and need states, which serve as intrapsychic motivating forces" (p. 190). "Mental representation refers to the mental organization of memory traces; memory traces deriving from experiences involving internal and external stimulation and the responses of the stimulated subject" (p. 180). Mental object representation "refers to a complex representation of experiences with emotionally significant persons such as to provide an integration of the drives, perceptions, affects, related memories, and fantasy elaborations of such experiences" (p. 181). Decathexis of object representations should therefore be conceptualized as "a disturbance in the capacity to organize memory traces into mental object representations and to sustain mental object representations.... [This disturbance] is rooted in developmental factors which are subordinate to the development of instinctual drives, is linked biologically to withdrawal responses, and is regulated by the unpleasure principle" (p. 182). In accordance with these definitions, London concluded that "the Specific Theory is focused on a deficiency in mental representations.... [It] is consistent with all of the serious aetiological hypotheses concerning schizophrenia, be they nature or nurture, physiological or cultural" (p. 190).

At its fall meeting in 1972, the American Psychoanalytic Association presented a panel on schizophrenia. Two of the papers presented are particularly relevant to our concern. In "The Influence of Theoretical Models on the Treatment of Schizophrenia," Philip Holzman (Panel, 1974), as the representative of a group of six from Chicago, presented a "systemic approach" to treatment. But basically, Holzman said,

> The Chicago group's view coincides with that of N. London (1973) and those members of the Los Angeles group who regard schizophrenic symptoms as having a coherence that reflects a deficit in internal organization which manifests itself in a sense of some "internal catastrophe." This sense of "inner disaster" is thus regarded as an outcome, not of conflict, as in neurosis, but of a deficiency in important psychological functions. Neurosis and schizophrenia are thus not to be conceived as a continuum [p. 189].

In "Defense and Deficit Models: Their Influence on Therapy," Gerald Aronson (Panel, 1974) presented three viewpoints of a study group of six from the Los Angeles area. (1) Those who view schizophrenia as a deficiency disease include Wexler and Greenson. Their main viewpoint has been stated by Wexler (1971) in the paper quoted earlier. (2) Those who support the conflict concept share the views of Arlow and Brenner already cited. (3) The third view, which is influenced by the work of Mahler and others and which conforms more to Aronson's own view, suggests that at crucial times of infancy, genetically prepared tendencies are activated to internalize whatever is provided by the environment (mother) in the way of devices to regulate, modulate, soothe, and cope with anxieties and distress arising from various sources within the child. Through internalization, a function of the protective object is taken over by an internal structure. Later in life, at times of stress, the psyche turns toward the set of structures that has been prepared early in the separation-individuation phases. In the case of schizophrenia, the mother either fails to provide buffering of any major kind or provides "regulatory" functions of a grossly confused, destructive, or highly erotized order. The deficient or disturbed regulatory functions then become internalized and are built into internal structures. Later on, at times of stress

> the schizophrenic patient attempts to reverse the fateful appeal to the deficient "regulatory" structures by propitiation, placatory behavior, defensive autonomy, restitution of less inimical

images, memories, and percepts. These restorative maneuvers, however, only create more anxiety, leading to a further decathexis of the mental representations of any helpful reality and the repeated hypercathexis of the pathogenic substitutes of regulatory devices. And so the clinical picture demonstrates variable features within glacial fixity [p. 187].

It follows from the above conception that the schizophrenic patient is not empty of memories and object representations, on the contrary, "these elements are securely bound in an ego which suspiciously or confusedly scrutinizes all experiences in conformity with them. An ego organization exists which is possessed of extraordinary sturdiness—predictable and adamant, rather than disorganized and chaotic" (p. 186).

Discussion

The impression I get from the debate is that most of those who took issue with Arlow and Brenner preferred the classical theory to the revised theory. Their preference was determined by certain clinical phenomena that they characterize as decathexis or loss of object representations. Although decathexis can be conceived of as a defense (e.g., Bak and Freeman), it is to them more than a defense. In what way is decathexis more than a defense? From Wexler's list of schizophrenic manifestations, I infer that what is considered more than a defense implies a drastic personality change. It may be asked, can this drastic personality change be explained in terms of "alteration of ego (and superego) functioning" (Arlow and Brenner's position)? Most of those involved in the debate did not ask or answer this question. Again by inference, I conclude that they would probably answer the question negatively. If the answer is "no," what alternative do we have? I imagine that we might have to fall back on the concept of recathexis. How can recathexis be initiated? Do we have to think in terms of ego activities? Are we then going around in a circle?

Going over the debate, I also find conceptual confusion about certain issues. In the following, I shall only mention a few.

Internal Catastrophe

By an "internal catastrophe" Freud referred to a specific phenomenon that the patient may or may not subjectively feel as an experience of the end of the world, but that is objectively observed as attended by visible paniclike experiences. But of more significance is that this panic is followed by a loss of earlier levels of ego functioning and earlier personality organization. After an "internal catastrophe," the patient appears regressed, primitive, and childlike; his relations with current significant others are radically changed (e.g., he ceases to be a dutiful son to his mother, he does not seem to recognize her, he assaults her or makes open sexual advances toward her). The panic, the loss of earlier levels of ego functioning and earlier personality organization (or in Freud's term, the loss of object representations), all occur together, in a flash. This sequence of events was Freud's criterion for the diagnosis of schizophrenia (see Chapter 1). With this diagnostic criterion, Freud formulated a two-stage theory (decathexis-recathexis) to describe the formation of symptoms in schizophrenia (see Chapter 3).

As far as we can tell, Arlow and Brenner do not define "internal catastrophe" in the same way. First of all, they seem not to consider it a regular occurrence in schizophrenia, and consequently would perhaps not use it as the diagnostic criterion. Second, they seem not to conceive of an "internal catastrophe" as a cluster of experiences inseparably knitted together. In their theoretical framework, the end-of-the-world experience and the subsequent personality change seem to require relatively unrelated explanations. Thus the end-of-the-world experience is explained in terms of projection of destructive impulses, whereas the changes in personality are explained in terms of a regressive alteration of ego functions.

It does not really matter what criterion one uses for the diagnosis of schizophrenia. Nor does it matter whether a theory of schizophrenia treats an "internal catastrophe" as a single symptom or as a cluster of symptoms. But it does matter whether the theory adequately explains the clinical manifestations. According to Arlow and Brenner's formulation, heightened aggression[3] brings about conflict, anxiety, and, finally, the defense mechanism of projection. The result is the end-of-the-world delusion. Or heightened anxiety interferes with reality testing and other ego functions, and the result is hallucinations and delusions. These formulations seem quite adequate. But to explain the relatively sudden and possibly permanent personality alteration in terms of a regressive alteration of ego and superego functioning goes too far. For the alteration of ego functioning explains certain aspects of the patient's behavior, but not quite the total personality change. After the personality alteration, the patient retains only a trace of his old self. He may still be witty, cunning, shrewd, as he used to be, but over-all he is not the same person. He may be described as regressed. But the regression is not a wholesome one to a primitive developmental level, as postulated by Freud and Fenichel, nor does it seem to affect selected ego functions, as postulated by Hartmann.

On the other hand, as I see it, Freud's classical theory does depict the dissolution of self and its reorganization, even though it does not quite adequately explain other clinical manifestations without the benefit of later theoretical conceptualizations. Freud's theory is not a complete one (see Chapter 3). Perhaps that is why Freeman wrote that "The classical theory still comes *nearest* to . . . ideal" (italics mine).

Faulty Reality Testing

Is faulty reality testing the result of or the cause of the processes that lead to delusion and hallucination? According

---

[3] Freeman argued that Arlow and Brenner neglect the economic viewpoint. That does not seem to be the case.

to Arlow and Brenner, faulty reality testing is the cause. Bak, Freeman, and Wexler, on the other hand, believe that it is the result. In the debate, reality testing seems to have been conceptualized as fully developed and in good order until the moment of dysfunction. Clinically, as well as theoretically, that cannot be the case. Schizophrenia as a process begins very early in the patient's life. Consequently, such ego functions as reality testing must become increasingly disturbed for a very long time before crippling symptoms finally break through. (See the case illustration in Chapter 12.) Federn specifically made that point as early as the 1930's.

The debate also gives the impression that reality testing functions up to the moment of dysfunction, but stops functioning after that moment. Clinically, we note that the loss of the capacity for reality testing—or in Robbins and Sadow's term, reality processing[4]—is not an either/or matter: It fluctuates from moment to moment. For example, after a period of acute disorganization and confusion, a young schizophrenic-IV woman, whom I shall call Ellen, appeared clinically to be more together. To her therapist, she had been exhibiting a one-moment-close-and-another-moment-distant emotional tie. During one Monday session, following a weekend interruption, she rushed to his side, sat on the floor near him, looked at him warmly, genuinely, and adoringly, and said, "It is good to see you, Doctor X." The therapist responded in kind, although not in expressive language. Ellen remained on the floor for a while, then slowly and thoughtfully stood up and paced the floor a bit. Then she suddenly turned toward the therapist, looking icy cold and distant, and announced in a harsh and demanding tone, "I don't even know you. Who are you?" After a pause, she said in a more suspicious tone, "Can you show me your driver's license?" (From previous experience, I understood her to be asking me, "Are you a doctor? Show me your license.") Then she retreated to the farthest corner of the room and tried to open the locked screen on a window by trying to insert a crayon (which was lying around)

---

[4] Robbins and Sadow (1974) define reality testing as the separation of what is inside from what is outside, and reality processing as a more complicated process.

into the keyhole. For a moment she was totally engrossed in her act. A moment later, she turned to the therapist and asked, "Can I get out of the window?" He now responded, "You were sitting very near me. Then you must have had some thoughts and feelings[5] which frightened you. You moved far away from me and even wanted to get away from me through the window. I wish you could talk with me about those thoughts which had frightened you." She seemed to listen, as she looked straight in his direction, but she said nothing. When he finished, she started pacing back and forth, but drawing closer to him. Before long she stopped quite near him and said, "I was always . . . and never like this before. I want to go home to my husband. No, to my mother's home." Thus, as well as she could, she articulated her need to withdraw (as well as her conflict about which home to go back to).

This vignette is cited to illustrate that the capacity for reality processing continuously fluctuates. The patient's capacity for reality processing was at its best at the beginning of the therapy session. Then her unrevealed fantasies (probably beyond her awareness) aroused anxiety in her. Her mounting anxiety impaired her reality processing. Thereupon she began to doubt the therapist's identity, tried to get away from him through a third-floor window, used a crayon as a key, etc. Later, when the anxiety (fear, guilt, or whatnot) was somewhat allayed by the therapist's comment (by either the content or the nonthreatening voice quality), her capacity for reality processing improved, whereupon she resumed the role of the patient and told the therapist about her fear or guilt at being too close to him and about her struggle between being a grown-up woman and being a little girl. (This knowledge of her conflicts had been recently conveyed by her through her idiosyncratic language.)

From the foregoing it seems that on the one hand, reality processing must gradually but steadily deteriorate before the crippling symptom breaks out. On the other hand, under close

---

[5] Because schizophrenics are easily overwhelmed by their feelings, I always try to elicit their thoughts rather than their feelings, especially during the early stage of treatment.

scrutiny the symptom formation closely follows the formula: heightened anxiety-impaired reality processing-symptom formation.

The above vignette illustrates yet another very important issue, which I shall refer to as the two realms of reality processing. When we say that Ellen's reality-processing function was impaired because she did not seem to realize that it was dangerous to climb out of a third-floor window or impossible to open a screened window without a proper key, we actually have in mind a reality that is external to the subject and identifiable by observers. But we must also consider the processing of inner reality. The processing of inner reality is not as readily perceptible as that of the external reality. Yet we are all aware of its existence. From very early in one's life external reality is defined by others, whereas inner reality is intimately bound up with one's primitive self-representations. In the processing of external reality, one relies on one's cognitive prowess and adapts (primarily unconsciously) one's views to what is defined by others. The processing of inner reality, on the other hand, is an affective process, relying on one's bodily sensations and emotions to determine whether to remain close to or deviate from the primitive self-concept.[6] Originally, one's primitive self-representations are a precipitate of one's interaction with others. But once formulated, the self-concept is regulated by one's own bodily sensations and emotions. A certain view of one's self must be upheld, for a marked deviation from it could bring about extremely disturbing body sensations and unpleasant emotions.

Normally, both realms of reality are processed. In the acute phase[7] of schizophrenia, both realms of reality processing are lost. Beginning with the subacute phase, the processing of inner reality is more or less restored, but the processing of external reality is not. To minimize unpleasant body sensations and emotions, the patient clings tenaciously to a self-concept that, in the eyes of others, is distinctly pathological.

---

[6] Lichtenberg (1978) has thoroughly explored the connection between body self and reality testing.

[7] For definitions of "acute," "subacute," and "chronic" phases, see Chapter 2.

As a result, the processing of external reality is greatly compromised. The above-described patient, Ellen, had not only denied that she was sick, despite all the external evidence pointing in that direction, but had also believed that she was in her middle teens before she was overwhelmed by conflicts. Thus she frequently perceived her meetings with her therapist as something other than therapeutic sessions. He could be one of her parents, her grandmother, one of her male school friends, but rarely himself. According to the role he was assigned, she would act like an obedient child, a flirt, and so forth, but not always like a patient in psychotherapy. In the therapeutic sessions, she could "hear" only what she wanted to hear. And what she wanted to hear were only those comments that fitted with her view of inner reality.

In treatment, during the subacute phase the therapist attempts to introduce new ideas to the patient in order to prevent his pathological self-concept from becoming a closed system. Whenever the therapist introduces a new idea, the patient will process his inner reality to determine whether that idea can coexist with or be incorporated into his self-view, or must be rejected outright. It is to this scanning that our psychotherapeutic effort with schizophrenic patients must be directed, so that the new ideas introduced to the patient will never be more disagreeable to him than he can tolerate. Otherwise, the "mutual cuing" between patient and therapist will be disrupted and a therapeutic stalemate will inevitably follow. During the chronic phase, the patient's pathological self-concept is a more or less closed system: Any modification of it requires Herculean effort without any assurance of success. And this self-concept will seriously interfere with the processing of external reality.

Conflict versus Deficiency[8]

Arlow and Brenner proposed to explain symptom forma-

[8] Long before the current debate, Hill (1955) was also concerned with the conflict versus deficiency controversy, saying that there are two views to explain schizophrenic manifestations: "[One view] gives the patient's ego credit for the ability to

tion in terms of the model of conflict-anxiety-defense-symptoms. They did, however, allow for the possibility of a certain inherent incapacity of the ego to cope with conflict. This incapacity includes Hartmann's primary autonomous ego defects. Thus, although they stressed conflicts, they did not preclude deficiency. Those who argued against Arlow and Brenner's formulation, however, seem to have had in mind a different definition of deficiency. For instance, Wexler spoke of the disintegration of both ego and superego functions. Freeman spoke of a disorganization involving the whole mental apparatus. London spoke of a disturbance of the capacity to organize memory traces into mental representations and to sustain the mental representations. All of them seem to have been more concerned with the patient's incapacity to carry on his life after a certain critical moment than with whether the ego is deficient in its capacity to cope with conflicts before that critical moment (as Arlow and Brenner were).

I believe that it is imperative to distinguish the two types of deficiency: One is the deficiency that existed before the internal catastrophe, and the other is the deficiency that comes into existence after the internal catastrophe. To facilitate the discussion, I shall call the former the genetic (developmental) deficiency and the latter the functional deficiency. In speaking of genetic (developmental) deficiency, we must specify whether it originates from a hereditary, inborn defect of the primary autonomous ego apparatus, environmental traumata, or what. In speaking of functional deficiency, we must specify whether it is in the realm of object relations, in communication, in the capacity to neutralize aggressive impulses, in the application of will power, and so on. Simply to say that a patient is suffering from a "deficiency disorder" is not

---

defend itself by denial and retreat, to endeavor to save itself by sacrificing much of its integrity. The latter view is that the ego of such a patient is lacking in drive, in force, in cohesiveness and is actually a victim of the assault from the unconscious. I think that patients exist to justify either one of these views but that most patients can be seen as involved to some extent in both the voluntary and involuntary regressions" (p. 50).

enough, for the term does not make clear what is deficient, when the deficiency begins, etc. And without such specificities, the patient will not be properly understood.

As I understand it, the postulation of a psychic deficiency in schizophrenics is essential from the therapeutic point of view. Therapeutically speaking, if the conflict hypothesis should prevail, the treatment of schizophrenia could follow the analytic model, which consists of free association and the interpretation of defense and resistance. That such a therapeutic approach can be disastrous was pointed out by many (e.g., Federn) who, from the beginning of the psychoanalytic movement, tried to treat schizophrenic patients with psychotherapy. But to say that interpretations of defense and resistance can never be used with a schizophrenic is fallacious. Bion, Fromm-Reichmann,[9] Hill, Rosenfeld, Searles, Sechehaye, Sullivan, Will, to name only a few, have clearly demonstrated the efficacy of such interpretations. In Chapter 2, I proposed a new classification of schizophrenia into I, II, III, and IV. By and large, the genetic (developmental) deficiency is mild in schizophrenia I, more severe in schizophrenia II, and still more severe in schizophrenia III. After the internal catastrophe, any patient (regardless of whether he was originally a schizophrenic-I, -II, or -III) may exhibit a profound functional deficiency. However, because his genetic deficiency is mild, a schizophrenic-I patient may overcome his functional deficiency and return to his prepsychotic adjustment, whereas a schizophrenic-III patient, burdened by a greater genetic deficiency, may never be able to overcome it. Thus, in treatment, we expect to give more interpretations (after a period of waiting) to schizophrenic-I and -II patients than to schizophrenic-III patients.

I have also proposed that, after the internal catastrophe, the illness may be classified into acute, subacute, and chronic phases. (Schizophrenic-I patients, if properly treated, are unlikely to enter the chronic phase, whereas almost all schizo-

[9] See also *I Never Promised You a Rose Garden*, by Hannah Green (1964).

phrenic-III patients do so.) During the acute phase the patient is so overwhelmed by panic that it would be meaningless for us to consider what conflicts he may be experiencing at a given moment. He needs relief from the panic, and we should help him to achieve it. However, beginning with the subacute phase (and throughout the chronic phase), it becomes obvious that the patient is not free from conflict, nor from anxiety (or panic). Facing the conflict and anxiety, he still uses defenses, or adopts the compromise solution of symptom formation. (Although it was not his intention to illustrate this particular point, Freeman gave numerous examples of it in his "Reply to Arlow and Brenner.") In the above illustrative case, during the therapeutic session Ellen certainly showed her struggle with conflicts, and during each therapy session resorted to a compromise solution to mitigate her anxiety. In treating patients like Ellen we must, of course, be aware of their genetic and functional deficiencies. But it is difficult to imagine how we could be of any use to them if we do not deal with conflicts.

Conflicts over Aggression

Arlow and Brenner said that in psychosis, conflicts over aggression are intense and frequent, and that disruption of the patient's relations with external objects often results from his need to protect the objects from his own aggression. Bak said that the unusually strong aggressive conflict in schizophrenia follows excessive libidinal decathexis. Freeman said that in postulating the conflict over aggression as the cause of schizophrenic symptoms, Arlow and Brenner seem to have overstressed the content. What does all this add up to?

It is my observation that the schizophrenic patient's most basic conflict is his wish to be simultaneously close to and distant from others. To escape his conflict he devises and perfects "distancing maneuvers." He maintains a certain distance from other persons—neither too close nor too far away. The result is a life of frustration. The mobilization of aggression seems only secondary to the frustration. Clinically, however, the patient's conflict over aggression is at times intense and on the surface—especially when the distance between himself and others is rearranged. This rearrangement is primarily in the patient's own interest, and does not usually reflect his wish to protect other persons.

There is no question that many a catastrophic experience is brought about by a sudden surge of aggression: That is, the aggression sets the stage for the appearance of symptoms. But conflict over aggression is not the only factor that can initiate symptoms. Any conflict that precipitates intense anxiety or panic can do so. Following the catastrophic experience, the patient will first have to "put himself together" (i.e., re-establish a sense of self-continuity) and then rearrange the distance between himself and others. During the period when the sense of self-continuity is fluid and unstable, the rearrangement of distance is not an easy job. At such times the patient may be especially hostile—he may be assaultive, for instance. Perhaps that is what Bak describes as decathexis (as one of two stages of symptom formation) preceding conflict over aggression.

With the above issues clarified, I believe we may find the answers to such questions as whether neurosis and psychosis are qualitatively or quantitatively different, whether schizophrenic patients retain object representations, and whether they can form a transference and benefit from psychoanalytically oriented psychotherapy.

In the treatment of a schizophrenic patient, we must be alert to the fact that his capacity for communication varies from moment to moment, and we must constantly monitor that capacity to make our communications meaningful to him. To do so, we must be attuned to both his conflict and his deficiency. If we set aside his conflict, we will be relying solely on the "corrective emotional experience" type of therapy—which can easily deprive the patient of an opportunity for a better life. If we ignore his deficiency, we may be talking over his head and may end up feeling frustrated because he does not respond. I have suggested that when to be more attuned to conflict and when more to deficiency depends on whether the patient is a schizophrenic-I, -II, -III, or -IV, as well as on whether he is in the acute, subacute, or chronic phase of his illness.

CHAPTER 14

Symptom Formation
in Schizophrenia

To explain the psychopathology of schizophrenia adequately we must, I believe, integrate Freud's earlier conception (the classical theory) and his later views as elaborated by Hartmann and others (the revised theory). (See Chapter 13.) I shall now attempt such an integration.

In my view, to explain symptom formation in schizophrenia, it is essential to conceptualize the ego and the self as discrete psychic entities (see Hartmann, Jacobson, Kohut). Both the ego and the self contribute to the clinical picture, as I shall describe.

Ego Function and Symptom Formation

From the very beginning, Freud regarded conflict as the cause of neurosis, and believed that neurotic symptoms arise from a compromise between the repressed and the repressing agent. Once formed, the symptoms have to be maintained. What maintains them is the continuous interaction of the repressed and the repressing agent. Later, when he formulated the structural theory, the ego was assigned the role of instigating the compromise. When in conflict with id, superego, and/or reality, the ego brings about the symptoms in order to restore some degree of harmony. But now the symptoms are maintained not only by the interaction of the repressed and the repressing agent, but also by the agent that demands repression—the superego. Freud also observed that symptoms satisfy previously unsatisfied wishes, although to an attenuated degree and at a regressed level. In this sense, symptoms and regression are intimately associated. But regression is not conceptualized as the *cause* of symptoms. The literature on schizophrenia, however, tends to confuse the relation between symptoms and regression. Reviewing this literature, we are repeatedly led to believe that regression actively brings about symptoms.

Freud himself is perhaps responsible for the impression that regression causes schizophrenic symptoms. In 1911, he noted that after a period of panic the schizophrenic patient shows markedly disturbed object relations and a fundamental personality change. As he tried to integrate this important observation into the libido theory, he came up with the two-stage decathexis-recathexis theory. By neglecting to describe the role of the "ego"[1] in the formation of schizophrenic symptoms and by repeatedly emphasizing schizophrenia as regression to the autoerotic stage Freud (1911) conveyed the idea (which he could not have intended) that conflicts initiate regression and regression then causes various symptoms, such as the end-of-the-world delusion, the loss of reality, hypochondriasis, and megalomania.[2] The lack of detail about the ego's role in forming symptoms also made Freud's theory a static one (see Chapter 3).

Fenichel did not improve Freud's explanation. He wrote, "Freud succeeded in bringing schizophrenic mechanisms into consonance with his theory of neurotic symptom formation by grouping all the phenomena around the basic concept of regression. With such a grouping, no judgment was given as to the somatogenic or psychogenic origin of this regression" (1945, p. 415). After saying that in schizophrenia the regres-

---

[1] Although the "ego" in the structural sense was not formulated at that time, a dormant structural concept always existed.

[2] Freud did, however, describe the role of the ego in more detail in the formation of delusions and hallucinations.

sion reaches back to the time when the ego was not differentiated from objects, Fenichel proceeded: "Therefore, the following formulae mean one and the same thing, only varying in point of view: the schizophrenic has regressed to narcissism; the schizophrenic has lost his objects; the schizophrenic has parted with reality; the schizophrenic's ego has broken down" (p. 415).[3] By stressing these formulae without an accompanying consideration of the ego's role in symptom formation, Fenichel in effect led us to become further entrenched in a regression-centered theory of schizophrenia.

Hartmann (1953) explored "the ego's role as a mediator between the drives and reality" (p. 184) in the genesis of schizophrenia. By concluding that "either the defensive counter-cathexes of the ego, or those ego functions that maintain the contact with reality, may be incompletely developed or weakened" (p. 184), he so modified the "regression theory" that it is no longer necessary to conceive a wholesale regression to autoerotism. For as various ego defenses and ego functions may develop unevenly, so may they regress unevenly. In his exposition of ego psychology, Hartmann (1939) was particularly concerned with the integrative function of the ego. In his paper on schizophrenia (1953), however, he was more interested in the vicissitudes of aggression in the genesis of schizophrenia and in how an impairment of instinctual deneutralization may be related to a defect in the primary autonomous ego apparatus. Consequently, he left inexplicit whether schizophrenic symptoms are still to be explained in terms of a regression theory or, as is implied in his more

---

[3] In this passage, Fenichel did not distinguish between ego and self. Moreover, in speaking of the "formulae" as meaning "one and the same thing, only varying in point of view," he was probably following Freud's (1900) view that topographical, temporal, and formal regressions are "one at bottom and occur together as a rule; for what is older in time is more primitive in form and in psychical topography lies nearer to the perceptual end" (p. 548). In Freud's (1900) classification of regression, topographical regression refers to the backward movement that leads to the representations of thoughts in sensory form, as in dreams; temporal (or developmental) regression refers to the harking back of the libido to earlier stages of development; and formal regression refers to the return to the original primitive methods of psychic expression.

contemporary theory, in terms of a disturbance in the integrative function of the ego.

My own experience in the long-term intensive treatment of schizophrenics has led me to conclude that the regression theory does not explain the observational data, whereas Hartmann's concept of the vicissitudes of the "integrative function of the ego" does. In the discussion to follow, I shall use the latter concept in my interpretation of schizophrenic symptom formation. In order to approach a theory of schizophrenia in the light of the observational data, I shall begin with a clinical vignette.

John was the first-born of a professional family. His only brother, five years younger, was free of psychological problems. During the summer when John was 14, his father decided to "cure John's immaturity" by sending him to a foreign country to live with an old friend of the father's. As John spoke no foreign language, the only person with whom he could communicate for the next two months was his father's friend, but the latter was so busy that he was seldom around. At the end of the summer, when John returned to the United States, he was not necessarily more mature, but he was different. Henceforth he appeared detached, and was very much a loner in and out of school. He maintained average grades, and on graduation from high school was admitted to a small college some distance from home. While at college, he rarely wrote or phoned his family. There was a gradual decline in his school work.

At the end of his freshman year, John returned home for the summer. At home he sat around and did nothing. He seemed to be self-absorbed and daydreaming. Urged by his parents, he very reluctantly arranged to drive to the beach with two of his high school friends for a day. On the way to the beach, while driving over a suspension bridge, John became very much frightened. On the return trip, while going back over the bridge, he was even more frightened, at one point begging his companions to stop the car right in the middle of the bridge, amidst heavy traffic. When he finally arrived home, he was dazed, and his parents said that he was never again himself.

Although John returned to college in the fall, he was unable to remain there. After a year of moping around at home feeling depressed, he was finally taken to a psychiatrist, who found him superficially held "together" by numerous phobias and obsessive-compulsive behaviors. The treatment was of a supportive nature and lasted for over two years. In treatment, he was "cooperative" but was not "psychological enough." By the time treatment was discontinued, John had mobilized himself enough to work and establish an apartment away from his parents' home. For the next 15 years he worked at various odd jobs, such as stock boy at a supermarket and carpenter's assistant. During these years he visited his parents rarely and had no close companions of either sex. He did offer his services freely to older women living in his apartment building, and occasionally visited bars where there were "go-go" girls.

In general, his life was quite peaceful until one day, at a bar, a go-go girl came to sit with him after her sexually provocative performance. In the past he had had fantasies of asking girls to come sit and have a drink with him. This time the girl had come of her own accord, without an invitation. He became bewildered and felt sick. That night, after arriving home, his thoughts began to race. He decided that this girl liked him and that she had not come for money but for sex. Throughout a sleepless night and the next day, he felt a compulsion to go to the same bar to look for the girl, but refrained from doing so. By early evening he felt he could no longer stay home. He took his car and drove aimlessly on the highway. He heard God's voice telling him to "take the power," and he began to ask God to give him specific instructions. At that moment a car passed by; he took this fact to mean that he should follow that car. When, after miles and miles of driving, the other car made a turn, John was unable to maneuver the same turn and went into a ditch.

When the police found him at the scene of the accident

some time later, he was catatonic, and they took him to a state hospital. During this hospitalization he neglected his physical appearance, had to be led about, and was spoon-fed. He continued to hear God's voice ordering him to "take the power," and on one occasion challenged the most muscular man on the ward to a fight. He lost his glasses and decided that another patient, who wore the same kind of glasses, had stolen his. This patient, by wearing John's glasses, was now able to read his mind. John therefore made a strenuous effort to avoid this patient. Three weeks later, with the aid of medication, his reality orientation improved considerably.

At this time he was transferred to Chestnut Lodge. Medication was discontinued,[4] and thereafter he responded well to psychotherapy. During the first several months of treatment he gave the above account of what had happened to him, but insisted that his nightmarish ordeal was the result of his food being poisoned.

In presenting this case I have concentrated primarily on regression and symptom formation, and have ignored the predisposing constitutional and developmental factors.[5] Before the catatonic episode following the incident with the go-go girl, John had undergone at least two drastic personality changes, the first in the foreign country and the second on the suspension bridge.[6] Because John could remember about the recent catatonic episode, I shall discuss that experience. Before that experience, John seems to have settled for a life in which his ego functioned best by denying, suppressing, or controlling his libidinal and aggressive impulses. During this long period his sense of self relied on his view of himself as

[4] Almost all new admissions to Chestnut Lodge are taken off medication. In John's case, medications were never needed again during his treatment.

[5] For instance, John's mother did not wish to nurse him but did so because her husband believed that mother's milk is best for the baby. The mother described John as a difficult baby whereas his brother was not. John was always "immature" for his age; this immaturity led his father to send him to a foreign country, etc. For further consideration of the interaction of constitutional and environmental factors that eventuates in schizophrenia, see Chapters 11 and 12.

[6] These two personality changes can also be explained in terms of five steps in the process of symptom formation (see below).

being separate and independent, and of being active and able to control a situation. Although this life was not a satisfactory one (when John looked back at it after three years of treatment), it was relatively stable and anxiety-free, and John seems to have tried hard to maintain it.

The equilibrium of this 15-year period was upset when the girl came to his table. Her performance had been provocative and John was sexually stimulated. He was a bit under the influence of alcohol and had dared to allow himself to have anticipatory wishes about sexual satisfaction with the girl. In the past, he had handled the oedipal conflicts by limiting his activities to fantasy and avoiding actual contact. Now that delicate balance was upset. His impulses were so strong that he feared he would be overwhelmed by them, and be unable to restrain his behavior in the routinized fashion he had used for years. In addition, he severely condemned himself for having such strong impulses.[7] But John's tension was not limited to tension between the macrostructures. He was also subjected to a forced alteration of his sense of self when he lost his familiar apartness and aloofness and his sense of being actively able to control the situation in the bar. The active self who invited a girl (his previous fantasy) was suddenly replaced by a passive self who might be engulfed by her excitement; an in-control self who made approaches (in fantasy) and who was proud of being able to restrain himself (in reality) became in his anxious view a self who was going to be controlled by another person; altogether, a sane self with manly wishes and "solid restraints" had turned into a self exposed to "crazy ideas" of a passive relationship with a dangerous phallic Medusa.

The go-go girl incident reactivated John's oedipal conflicts and forced an alteration in his sense of self. In this situation he experienced extreme anxiety and a disturbance of the ca-

[7] In the course of treatment, evidence accrued that an early shift in the libido-aggression balance had resulted in accentuated aggressive urges, arrested and deviant ego development, and an unbalanced loving-critical functioning of the superego.

pacity to coordinate his perceptual-cognitive-motor processes so severe that it amounted to a "paralysis of the integrative function of the ego."[8] There followed a structural (or formal) regression in which the more advanced ego functions and ego defenses were supplemented by more primitive ones. Now, acting without reasoning, he drove aimlessly along the highway. Operational forms of secondary-process functioning yielded to more primitive forms of secondary-process functioning.[9] Condensation, displacement, and symbolization became predominant. Now the car became a symbol of power; his fear of body immobility was displaced to his car, while the other car stood for the girl. Chasing turned passive back into active. In the meantime, through the reactivation of the narcissistic configuration, the lost power of the self was restored through an idealized all-powerful self-object,[10] God. Being active by chasing the other car and feeling powerful through his relation with the idealized all-powerful self-object, God, John succeeded in restoring his familiar sense of self and thus in retaining his "sanity" until his car went into the ditch. At that point he was brought face to face with his conflicts about being actively in control. A new wave of anxiety caused another round of temporary paralysis of ego functions, followed by the reactivation of even more primitive ego functions and defenses in the clinical picture of catatonia.

Five Steps by the Ego in Symptom Formation

Through scrutiny of the observational data in this case, we can distinguish five steps in the formation of the symptom. (1) The incident with the girl in the bar aroused John's con-

[8] I believe this term is more descriptive than "ego fragmentation," "ego dedifferentiation," and other such terms, which are more descriptive of the aftereffect of the described phenomenon.

[9] Sandler (1976) has pointed out that what we ordinarily speak of as regression from secondary-process functioning to primary-process functioning is actually a regression from operational forms of secondary-process functioning to more primitive forms of secondary-process functioning.

[10] Kohut (1971) introduced the term "self-object" to describe those "objects which are themselves experienced as part of the self" (p. xiv).

flicts about erotic and aggressive impulses. (2) The experience of these conflicts aroused extreme anxiety, or what I prefer to call "organismic panic." (3) Under the sway of organismic panic, the integrative function of the ego was temporarily paralyzed, and all other ego functions were temporarily suspended. (4) The integrative function of the ego soon recovered and proceeded to order and modulate the mental content so as to find the "best possible solution." (5) The symptom crystallized in the wake of the best possible solution. A similar sequence occurred when the car went into the ditch. Here the intensity of the anxiety and the subsequent disorganization were even greater, and the resulting symptoms more pathological.

The above observations point to anxiety, or organismic panic, as the initiator of symptoms. Regression accompanies symptoms, it does not cause them. In the illustrative case, the anxiety-provoking incident was discrete and readily identifiable, the anxiety reaction intense and dramatic. I have found that in patients whose symptoms seem to have come on very gradually the same five steps are identifiable if, in the course of treatment, the onset of symptoms is reconstructed. Furthermore, in such cases the five steps can be discerned *in situ* in the therapeutic setting.

Conflict

Anna Freud (1973) has taught us to distinguish between "genetic" deficiency and conflict, and has suggested that the two conditions may require different treatment. That conflicts play a role in symptom formation in schizophrenics does not imply that we can ignore genetic deficiency (see Chapter 13). Freud (1911) laid equal stress on conflict and deficiency. "We can no more dismiss the possibility that disturbances of the libido may react upon the ego-cathexes than we can overlook the converse possibility—namely, that a secondary or induced disturbance of the libidinal processes may result from abnormal changes in the ego" (p. 75). Advances in psychoanalysis have not contradicted Freud's basic views. They have, however, deepened our understanding of the conflicts and of the nature of deficiency in schizophrenia.

In the literature, the initiation of schizophrenic symptoms is usually ascribed to conflicts over aggression (e.g., Klein, 1946; Hartmann, 1953; Bak, 1954; Bion, 1957), although it has also been attributed to libidinal conflicts (e.g., Fairbairn, 1952). I selected the case of John particularly to show that the conflicts do not have to be over aggression. The content of John's conflicts, as stirred up by the go-go girl, was complex. It contained both libidinal and aggressive components, and in respect to libidinal components, it ranged from the oral to the oedipal level of development.

I want to stress that schizophrenics are burdened by the same kinds of conflicts as are other human beings, and that symptoms are determined not by the content of the conflicts but by how the schizophrenic ego responds to those conflicts (whatever the content). Schizophrenics can, like other human beings, keep their conflicts in a dormant state by means of defense mechanisms, which are, however, commonly quite primitive in nature (denial, introjection, fusion, etc.). But when conflicts are reactivated, schizophrenics do not experience anxiety as it is familiar to the average human being; they experience organismic panic.

Organismic Panic

The term "organismic panic" describes the extreme anxiety the schizophrenic experiences in severe conflictual states. During "organismic panic," "normal" ego-functioning capacity is thrown completely out of kilter. Without the help of an empathic person in his environment, the schizophrenic cannot restabilize ego-functioning capacity.

The term "organismic panic" is modeled on Mahler's use of the term, "organismic distress" (1968).[11] By organismic dis-

---

[11] Mahler's use of the term "organismic distress" derives from Greenacre (1941). In the original version of this chapter, written in 1974, I used the term "organismic panic." Mahler also used the term "organismic panic" in her most recent book (1975),

tress Mahler refers to the physiological state of high tension that an infant experiences in the earliest phase of his life. At that time the infant cannot relieve the tension on his own, but is utterly dependent on the mothering partner's empathic understanding and ministrations. The parallel between the infant's need for the mothering partner's empathic understanding and ministrations and the schizophrenic's need for an empathic person in his environment is but one reason for my proposing the term organismic panic. More important, the origin of organismic panic can in fact be traced to the experience of too great and chronic organismic distress during the earliest phase of the schizophrenic's life.

In Chapter 11 I stated that constitutional and environmental factors interact and result in a sequence of concrete experiences. In schizophrenia, due either to defective biological givens or to traumatic environmental forces (or some combination of the two), the mother and infant fail to establish mutual cuing. As a result, maternal empathic understanding and ministrations are from the very beginning neither adequate nor timely. The infant is often left in a state of organismic distress. The somatic memory traces of organismic distress would be reflected in the "predisposition to anxiety" (Greenacre, 1941). The memory traces of too great and chronic organismic distress would lead to a greater predisposition to anxiety. In potentially schizophrenic persons, the predisposition to anxiety may be so heightened that each time he should experience anxiety he experiences panic instead.

In "Inhibition, Symptoms and Anxiety" (1926a), Freud distinguished between automatic anxiety and signal anxiety. The former denotes the ego's experience of helplessness in the face of an accumulation of excitation (external or internal)

---

and traced its origin to a lag in emotional readiness to function separately from the mother concomitant with a maturational spurt of locomotor and other autonomous ego functions (p. 10). As early as 1952, however, she introduced a similar concept without the benefit of the term.

that cannot be dealt with, whereas the latter denotes the ego's experience at the threat of a traumatic situation. Although in his earlier formulation Freud spoke of anxiety as on the border between the physiological and psychological realms, he now postulated a concept of anxiety in more psychological terms. According to the new concept, anxiety presupposes the existence of the ego—"the ego is the seat of anxiety." The term organismic distress, as used by Greenacre and Mahler, emphasizes more the physiological than the psychological aspect of the matter, whereas the term "organismic panic" refers to psychological experience—the experience of the ego, even though the ego has developed defectively. Conceptually, organismic panic and automatic or traumatic anxiety may be similar. Yet the term organismic panic offers the possibility of linking the early experience of organismic distress to the later ego-disorganizing experience of panic, which the term automatic anxiety does not.

As the result of a lack of mutual cuing, the infant is subjected to prolonged periods of intense organismic distress. Subsequently, certain basic experiential disturbances (see Chapter 12) will crystallize and in the course of time become the instigators of maladaptive behaviors, including a tendency to use maintenance mechanisms (Mahler, 1968), an impaired capacity for instinctual neutralization (Hartmann, 1953), an inability to internalize the maternal capacity to master anxiety (Hendrick, 1938), an inability to maintain a solid sense of "reality constancy" (Frosch, 1966), an inability to blend and integrate archaic and mature affective and cognitive functioning (Hartmann, 1939, 1956), etc. Burdened by these basic disturbances, the potential schizophrenic fails to establish satisfactory relations with others. His dissatisfaction tends to heighten his aggressive urges. These heightened aggressive urges, accompanied by a sense of an incapacity to control them, makes him consider any close relation with others as a potential source of panic. Because he is vulnerable to experiencing an ordinary anxiety situation as one of organismic panic and because the panic is perceived as a matter of life and death (Kafka, 1971), the potential schizophrenic is constantly (though unconsciously) on guard; the outcome of his guardedness is the adaptive attitude of moving simultaneously toward and away from any significant object. He erects defenses (usually the primitive ones) that restrict his responsiveness to new situations and give rise to stereotyped unrewarding reactions. His chances for libidinal gratification are thus restricted, and his need for "symbiotic help toward the maintenance of his homeostasis" (Mahler, 1968) is intensified. He responds to people less as well-differentiated separate individuals and more as idealized, omnipotent self-objects from whom he hopes to gain symbiotic nurturing. There is a gradual, almost imperceptible, widening of the gap between the developmental and the chronological age.

Acute Paralysis of the Integrative Function of the Ego during Organismic Panic

As the gap between the developmental and the chronological age widens, the potential schizophrenic finds it more and more necessary to deploy a defense against an anticipated experience of organismic panic. Then, one day, because of an extreme stimulus or because of increased deterioration of the ego's capacity to defend, he actually experiences organismic panic. The concept of organismic panic involves an intertwining of an affective response and an inadequately developed ego that gives rise to such a response. Organismic panic is a relatively brief, often recurrent, affective experience; it must *not* be reified into a structured state. Unlike more modulated affects, organismic panic is attended by a shocklike reaction in which the ego's integrative function is temporarily paralyzed. After a brief suspension, this function "recovers"—that is, it once again establishes and maintains psychic equilibrium. As it recovers, regression in perceptual-cognitive-motor processes makes its appearance.[12] Along with the reactivation

[12] According to Laplanche and Pontalis (1973), "The concept of regression is a predominantly descriptive one" (p. 388). Why regression occurs is difficult to explain.

of more primitive structures and defense mechanisms, self-experience will also be regressed.

The shocklike paralysis[13] of the ego's integrative function is followed by a drastic change in the person's personality. Before the "shock," he was by no means free of symptoms. In responding to anticipated or "signal" organismic panic, he resorted to various primitive ego functions and defenses and showed definite ego restrictions. But, on the whole, he could pass as "normal." Following the paralytic shock, in addition to the loss of all "normal" ego functions and defenses, he becomes a completely different person, with all sorts of psychotic manifestations. Freud, very much aware of this shocklike experience, introduced the term "internal catastrophe." In the meantime, because of the drastic change in personality following the internal catastrophe, Freud formulated the biphasic decathexis-recathexis theory (see Chapters 3 and 13).

Fitting Together and the Best Possible Solution

In speaking of symptoms as a compromise, Freud had already recognized the capacity of the "ego" to achieve such a compromise. Nunberg's (1929) "synthetic function of the ego" is a conceptualization of that capacity. Hartmann (1939) expanded Nunberg's conceptualization by including an adaptational viewpoint, describing that capacity in such terms as "the organizing function of the ego," "the integrative function of the ego," or "fitting together," in addition to "the synthetic function of the ego."

Attempts at explaining "why" inevitably lead to a description of "how." A plausible answer to the "how" is: "So far, I have been successful in staving off organismic panic. But now my familiar way (which was a more mature way) does not work. I must search for 'new' ways. Since no real 'new' ways are instantly available, I'll go back to the 'older' way which did work for me once upon a time." See also the group of papers by Frosch (1967) and others.

[13] I use the term "shocklike paralysis" because it seems befitting to a language that could perhaps describe the ego functioning. "Internal catastrophe," "loss of object representation," "disturbance in the organization of mental object representations" (London), and other terms have been used to describe the same clinical picture. But none of these terms immediately evokes a linkage to ego functioning.

Hartmann (1939) wrote, "The relationship of the individual to his environment is 'disrupted' from moment to moment and must again and again be returned to an equilibrium. The 'equilibrium' is not necessarily normal; it may be pathological" (p. 38). He adds, however, that

> Our knowledge of the mental apparatus enables us to discern, besides the equilibrium between individual and environment, two other relatively well-defined states of equilibrium. These, the equilibrium of instinctual drives (vital equilibrium) and the equilibrium of mental institutions (structural equilibrium), are dependent on each other and on the first-mentioned equilibrium. . . . Actually, however, we must add a fourth equilibrium . . . [which] is between the synthetic function and the rest of the ego [p. 39].

Thus "fitting together" involves all the equilibria and the discovery of the best possible solution in any given circumstance. Since "adaptation and fitting together . . . are interdependent" (p. 40), the best possible solution achieved must suit the inner as well as the outer reality.

Sandler and Joffe (1969) and Lichtenberg and Slap (1971, 1972) have described the relationship between the best possible solution and the feeling state. Sandler and Joffe defined "adaptation" more broadly. In their view, "adaptation to the external world is only one aspect of adaptation. . . . Other aspects of adaptation have also to be included—to inner drives and wishes, as well as those internal standards which have arisen during the course of development and which we normally refer to as 'superego' " (p. 80). Subscribing to this broadened view of "adaptation," they believe that "a neurotic or psychotic state can be considered to be the 'best' solution which the [psychic] apparatus can find in the given circumstances and with the resources at its disposal" (p. 81). They suggest that

> the apparatus responds to only one ultimate "master" which determines the course of psychic adaptation, to only one basic regulatory principle. This is its own awareness of (and the consequent "demand for work" imposed by) changes in the con-

> scious or unconscious feeling state. Adaptation to reality (and
> the "reality principle") can be regarded as a normal but secon-
> dary consequence of the operation of the primary regulatory
> principle [p. 81].

They further suggest that "one type of feeling comes to play
a major role in the regulation of experience. . . . This is the
feeling of *safety*. . . . The gaining of pleasure will, as the suffering of our neurotic patients testifies, be sacrificed in the
interests of maintaining or attaining a minimum level of safety
feeling" (p. 84).

Lichtenberg and Slap (1971, 1972) focus on the "defensive
organization" of the ego; they describe affect as what sets off
"the defense organization to order, to modulate, to modify or
to channel the mental content" so as to effect the best solution
at a given time. The ego makes use of perceptual-cognitive
devices for adaptive as well as defensive purposes. With repeated use, these devices establish themselves as defense
mechanisms. Since the perceptual-cognitive apparatus ma-
tures in accordance with a developmental timetable, the defense mechanisms develop only when the means they use are
cognitively or perceptually possible. Thus such mechanisms
as denial, introjection, and fusion are available as soon as the
psychic apparatus is capable of primitive regulation of percepts (denial), and of differentiating inner and outer (introjection and projection), self and non-self (fusion). Defenses
that deal with more subtle modifications of the contents of
awareness, such as repression, isolation, and intellectualization, require a far more sophisticated psychic apparatus (ego)
and so are found in the older child. Lichtenberg and Slap
suggest that the older defense mechanisms can be resorted to
at a later stage, during a search for the best possible solution.

In considering the order of appearance of various defense
mechanisms, Lichtenberg and Slap did not take psychotic persons into account. In the case of psychotic or potentially psychotic persons, the primitive defense mechanisms (denial,
introjection, projection, fusion) are preceded by what Mahler
has called maintenance mechanisms (deanimation, dediffer-

entiation, deneutralization, etc.). Thus psychotic patients, in regressively seeking the best possible solution, may resort to maintenance mechanisms in addition to denial, introjection, projection, and fusion.

Following the above authors, we may say that the potential schizophrenic, because of his vulnerability to organismic panic derived from early object relations, has a precarious sense of safety. The psychic apparatus is therefore constantly called on to direct its effort to maintaining that precarious feeling of safety. Later in life, whenever conflict is intense, and when organismic panic is experienced, the psychic apparatus is likely to shift to the use of older, previously highly practiced but now inhibited structures to come up with the best possible solution. Maintenance mechanisms and early defense mechanisms (e.g., denial, projection) will be substituted for the later type of defense mechanisms (e.g., repression). Archaic ego functions will also be substituted for the more mature ego functions—e.g., the substitution of the primitive form of secondary-process for the operative form of secondary-process functioning—resulting in a confusing sense of disorientation and a distorted reality sense. The composite picture described above constitutes what is ordinarily designated as the symptomatology of schizophrenic illness.

Symptom Formation

Symptoms are therefore the best possible solution the person can come up with at a given moment. In this sense the symptoms of catatonic, paranoid, hebephrenic, or simple schizophrenia are each the best possible solutions attainable in the given circumstances. When and if the patient assumes the catatonic, paranoid, hebephrenic, or simple "posture" for a longer period of time, there is a general tendency in psychiatric practice to consider that posture as a diagnostic entity. In the course of long-term therapy with schizophrenic patients, however, we find that diagnostic entities are not permanent, as symptoms frequently change from paranoid to

hebephrenic to catatonic, and vice versa,[14] each change presumably representing the best adaptive solution at a given
moment. Nevertheless, each patient tends to assume a certain
posture. The tendency to assume a catatonic posture is somewhat determined by the patient's previous inclination to inhibit his aggressive actions lest they lead to the annihilation
of others; the tendency to assume a paranoid posture by the
patient's predilection to excessive projection of blame on others; the tendency to assume a hebephrenic posture by the
patient's predisposition to yield to an infantile existence, etc.

On assuming the catatonic, paranoid, or hebephrenic posture, the patient tends to use archaic defenses and ego functions. Still, to a limited degree, more mature structures and
functions are always present. The clinical manifestations of
this phenomenon prompted Freud to say: "Even in a state so
far removed from the reality of the external world . . . one
learns from patients after their recovery that at the time in
some corner of their mind (as they put it) there was a normal
person hidden, who, like a detached spectator, watched the
hubbub of illness go past him" (1938a, pp. 201-202). Similarly,
M. Katan (1954) and Bion (1957) recommend that, in treating
the schizophrenic, the therapist acknowledge the healthier
aspects of the patient's ego.

Self-Reorganization and Symptom Formation

I have described the role of the ego in the five steps of
symptom formation. I shall now take up the role of the self
in symptom formation. In the literature, the term "ego" often
refers to both ego and self. As Hartmann (1950b) pointed out,
in speaking of ego and self, two completely different sets of
referents are being used. When one speaks of the ego, one has
id and superego in mind. When one speaks of the self, one has
objects in mind. With this clarification by Hartmann, Jacob-

---

[14] Mahler (1968) has also indicated that her patients change from the autistic to
the symbiotic syndrome and vice versa in the course of intensive psychotherapy.

son (1954b, 1964, 1967, 1971) was subsequently able to elaborate her concepts of self- and object representations, self and identity. Jacobson (1953) observed that the concept of self-representation is "indispensable for the study of psychosis" (p. 54). I agree with her and would like to add that the concept of self is indispensable for the theoretical explanation of aspects of schizophrenia. I note with interest that it was in working with psychotics or potentially psychotic patients that Federn (1952) formulated his "ego psychology," which concerns itself with self-experience and the self (see Chapter 10). Similarly, Winnicott (1955), Jacobson (1964, 1967), and Kohut (1971) focused their studies on the self.

It is generally believed that the infant begins to be dimly aware of the distinction between self and non-self at about two or three months. But it is still undetermined when that distinction becomes crystallized into a definitive knowledge that guides the developing child's destiny.[15] When that crystallization occurs, however, definitive knowledge about oneself or the self may be thought of as reflecting (1) a sense of the immediate intrapsychic instinct-affect tension, (2) a sense of the interchange with current objects real or fantasied, and (3) a sense of continuity with the self and object in the whole of prior experience, conscious or unconscious. Each of these senses is a variable that changes from moment to moment. In "normal" circumstances, through the mediation of various ego functions, each variable is allowed to change within a very narrow range. As long as that is the case, one experiences a sense of self-sameness or self-continuity. Otherwise, a sense of self-discontinuity will result.

If self and ego are conceptualized as differing, the sequence of development of the ego (out of the id-ego matrix) and the maturation of each ego function seems to require a different genetic formulation from that of the unfolding of the early awareness of the self[16] (out of self and object interac-

---

[15] See Lichtenstein (1961) and Jacobson (1967).

[16] Lichtenberg (1975) has traced the development of the sense of self to three component groupings that become blended to give cohesion to the over-all experi-

tion) and the sense of self-continuity. The development of ego
functioning and the development of the sense of self-continuity greatly influence each other. On the one hand, the normal function of the ego safeguards self-continuity and permits
the assimilation of new experiences that enhance the expansion and development of the self. On the other hand, a sense
of self-discontinuity determines an excessive use of primitive
defense mechanisms such as fusion and denial; it impairs the
development of secondary-process functioning, etc. The sense
of self-continuity is itself an affective experience—formed out
of the basic sense of safety and combining increasingly differentiated emotions with a pleasure-unpleasure range typical of the individual. Once the sense of self-continuity has
been experienced, the affects associated with its maintenance
are the ones that guide and signal the ego to work for the
best possible solution so that a sense of self-continuity can be
guaranteed.

In the case of schizophrenia, either because of a defect in
the infant's primary autonomous ego apparatus, or because
of maternal emotional incapacity, mutual cuing between
mother and infant is greatly disrupted. Consequently, the infant is subjected to repeated experiences of organismic distress without relief, these resulting in a libido-aggression imbalance, a preponderance of organismic panic, and a developmental disturbance in both the formation of a sense of self-
continuity and ego functioning. In regard to the self, whenever it comes into being, each of three components (the sense
of intrapsychic instinct-affect tensions, the sense of the interchange with current objects, real or fantasied, and the sense
of continuity with the self and objects in the whole of prior
experience) will be subjected to a wide range of fluctuations.
That being the case, the ego's task is constantly to maintain

---

encing of the self. "Bodily self-images, self-images in relation with objects seen as
distinctly separate, and images of the grandiose self associated with idealized self-
objects become blended experientially into a sense of self that has the quality of
cohesion—of unity and continuity in time, space, and state" (p. 482).

a precarious sense of self-continuity; that is, to avert the experience of organismic panic. As a result, certain defense mechanisms (including maintenance mechanisms) are excessively resorted to and the maturation of certain ego functions is arrested. The outcome is what are described as ego distortions or ego deviations (Eissler, 1953b; Beres, 1956; Gitelson, 1957). As the disturbed ego functioning paves the way for adaptational failure, the immensely dreaded and heavily guarded-against experience of organismic panic occurs. Whenever organismic panic is felt, ego functioning is temporarily suspended and the sense of self becomes discontinuous.[17] It is difficult to determine whether the disturbance begins as an experiential sense of self-discontinuity, or as an impairment of ego functions and the whole structural support underlying self-experience, or, as seems most likely, the two processes occur simultaneously. In any case, disturbances in self-experience and in ego functioning have a reciprocal dysfunctional influence on each other.[18]

An absence of a sense of self-continuity is unbearable. In an ever-changing world, the self, as the philosopher Hampshire (1959) says, serves as the best referent. Thus, when ego functioning recovers, one of the first urgent tasks is to establish a new sense of self-continuity. In this task, the patient resorts to prior experience with objects with some sense of continuousness. Since much of the schizophrenic patient's prior

[17] A sense of self-discontinuity is often described as "fragmentation of the self." In the literature, fragmentation of the self is often considered as synonymous with loss of the self. Since regression has often been conceived as the core of the theory of schizophrenia, and since some confirmation has been obtained from child study that the sense of self developes gradually, a loss of self is assumed to be a regression to the time before the self was formed. Such an assumption does not, however, correspond to clinical observation. For instance, after recovery, several patients have told me that during those moments when their behavior could be characterized as manifesting fragmentation of the self, they had actually shifted very rapidly from one self to another (e.g., in the case of John, from an oedipal competitor to a relatively carefree happy boy playing with the neighborhood kids; from a jealous, hostile sibling to a protective older brother). Experientially, there was never an actual loss of self. What was lost was the sense of self-continuity.

[18] Conversely, in treatment for example, improvements in self-experience and in ego functioning could have a reciprocal positive effect on each other.

experience consists of fantasy, fantasy now forms the kernel of his new self. Clinically, the new self built on prior fantasy is called a delusion. The reorganized new self or the delusion requires time to become consolidated, as is evidenced by the fact that, except for a few paranoid patients who suddenly reach an "insight" and know full well who they are, most patients drift in and out of dreamlike states and simply do not have a sense of self-continuity for a long period of time. During this period the ego only partially succeeds in staving off organismic panic; the patient is still experiencing terror, and his ego functioning shows no sign of stabilizing. In the case of John, his new self was one of being influenced and poisoned, which delusional belief, as he later revealed in the course of treatment, originated in his fantasy of his smothering, nagging mother who insisted on maintaining a symbiotic tie with him.

At this point, I venture to characterize the acute phase of schizophrenic illness as one in which a new sense of self-continuity has not yet been established and the subacute phase as one in which a new self has been established (see Chapter 2). I consider this classification useful, not from a descriptive but from a therapeutic point of view. In my experience, the treatment of the schizophrenic patient during the acute phase differs significantly from his treatment during the subacute phase. During the acute phase, the patient continues to experience organismic panic. The treatment must relieve him of that experience. In the establishment of a new sense of self-continuity, a consistent and continuous interaction with another person is usually required. Even in so-called spontaneously recovered cases, the importance of an external object cannot be ignored (see Boverman, 1955).

During the subacute phase, when a new sense of self-continuity has to some degree been established (and panic has greatly subsided), the therapeutic task is to modify the pathological self. The new sense of self-continuity is derived from a completely new set of self- and object representations, and will tolerate a new and usually narrower range of instinct-affect tensions. In the case of John, for instance, after the trip to the foreign country, after the episode on the bridge, and after his experience with the go-go girl, there were marked changes in him. Each change resulted in a conceptualization of his self as younger than his chronological age, in a lowered tolerance of instinctual drives, in increased passivity, and in the idea of being the victim. Following the experience of organismic panic, the ego functions at a regressive level and activates more primitive defense mechanisms. But these regressive ego changes represent only one facet of the problem. The changes related to the new pathological self organized at a regressed level are what most directly confront the therapist. For, from the clinical point of view, the reorganized self is the more "permanent" aspect of the toll that schizophrenic processes exact. When the panic subsides, the patient quite often regains most of the "lost," more mature ego functions (e.g., attention, memory, preconscious automatisms) and defenses (e.g., isolation, repression, intellectualization), but he is no longer the same "person" as he was before his illness (e.g., John after the trip to the foreign country and after the bridge incident). When Bleuler (1911) said that "the schizophrenic does not permit a full 'restitutio ad integrum'" (p. 9), he seems to have been speaking of the effect of the pathological organization of the self. When Freud (1896b, 1937a) spoke of an "alteration of ego" he was, I believe, addressing himself to the pathological organization of the self as well. On the basis of my experience, I believe that the therapy of schizophrenic patients after the acute phase must be directed toward the undoing of a pathological organization of the self. Once the pathological "self" is organized, deviation from it causes such a loss of the sense of safety that the patient needs to cling tenaciously to it. There is no question that in therapy no task is more tedious than the undoing of a pathological organization of the self. Often a negative therapeutic reaction is simply a reflection of an overzealous therapeutic effort to force a premature divorce from the pathological self.

B.

*Notes on Certain
Symptomatic Manifestations*

CHAPTER 15

On Delusional Experiences of Schizophrenics

So far I have spoken of symptoms only in general terms. In this and the next four chapters, I shall discuss in detail the five most commonly encountered schizophrenic symptoms, namely, delusion, hallucination, aggression, peculiar language, and emotional experience. Psychoanalysts long ago shifted their interest from symptoms to the person behind the symptoms. But to dwell on symptoms like delusions and hallucinations is not "regressive." For in psychotherapeutic work with schizophrenics a knowledge of the rise and fall of these symptoms is often useful.

In this chapter, I shall discuss delusions. Delusion refers to the patient's "fixed, dominating or persistent false mental concept" (Frosch, 1967) that is not shared by others of his culture and time. The delusional patient displays an utter conviction in his delusional belief that cannot be swayed by logic or reasons. As long as the patient possesses the capacity for reality testing or reality processing, he tends to keep his delusions to himself; only when his reality-processing function is grossly impaired does he reveal them to others. From the revealed content, the delusions of schizophrenic patients are classified as delusional beliefs about (1) themselves (e.g., delusion of grandeur, delusion of inferiority, delusion of being inhuman, delusion of bodily changes); (2) the world around them (e.g., delusion of unreality, delusion of the end of the world); (3) the people with whom they relate (e.g., delusion of persecution, delusion of jealousy); and (4) other matters (e.g., delusion of nihilism, delusion of mysticism). Why certain patients develop certain delusions is an intriguing question. But, content aside, a delusion is a delusion. The formation of all delusions is governed by the general principle of symptom formation as described in Chapter 14. A delusion appears in the wake of organismic panic. If a delusion occurs more than once, its content will be essentially unchanged. It is for this reason that delusion appears to be preformed and not newly created. If delusion is really preformed, its fate in therapy requires scrutiny. In this chapter I shall elaborate on these various issues.

Delusion as One Element of the Best Possible Solution

I have distinguished five steps in the formation of symptoms in schizophrenia. (1) An event in life arouses repressed conflicts. (2) The return of the repressed conflicts results in organismic panic. (3) The panic causes a "shocklike" paralysis of the ego's integrative function and a loss of the sense of self-continuity. (4) On the recovery of the lost function, the ego now seeks the best possible solution. (5) The best possible solution is what is generally characterized as symptoms. It will include the re-establishment of a sense of self-continuity. A sense of self-continuity is indispensable for orientation in the ever-changing environment, especially for a schizophrenic patient who has just recovered from a sudden paralysis of the integrative function of the ego. Delusions, which are extensions of pre-existing fantasies, contribute immensely to the re-establishment of the badly needed sense of self-continuity.

On the basis of this formulation of symptom formation, a delusion is but one element of the patient's best possible solution. The patient may have other symptoms too, such as hallucinations, affective disturbances, and thought disorders. A delusion is a "retrospective falsification" of the infantile experience (Lewin, 1968, p. 389). Since the early experience of each patient is unique, it is not surprising that the content of each patient's delusion is also unique. Influenced by their personal and developmental histories, certain patients lean toward delusions of body changes, other patients lean toward delusions of persecution, etc.

If delusion formation is conceptualized in this way, separate theoretical formulae to explain delusions of different contents seem quite unnecessary. Following Freud (1911, 1914b, 1916-1917), however, we tend to conceptualize the end-of-the-world delusion as due to withdrawal of libido from object representations; the delusion of grandeur as due to investment in the ego of libido withdrawn from objects; the delusion of body changes (hypochondriasis) as due to the ego's incapacity to contain the excess amount of libido withdrawn from objects; and the delusion of persecution (or other kinds of delusions) as due to attempts to recathect objects with libido previously withdrawn from them.

In the best-possible-solution formulation, all delusions are in Freud's sense "restitutive" symptoms, in that they are clincially recognized as delusions following (a) the paralysis and (b) the recovery of the integrative function of the ego. During organismic panic, the momentary paralysis of ego function precludes any possibility of formulating a delusion. It may be said that the cognitive function, among other functions, must recover sufficiently for the patient to conceptualize the self and object relations in an organized system of delusions. It is quite possible that the first best possible solution does not sufficiently control the panic. In that case, a second or third best possible solution may be necessary. Clinically, we often observe that an earlier solution—a delusion of body changes, for instance—may have to be replaced by a later solution—a delusion of persecution—and so on. But this appearance of one delusion after another does not necessarily mean that one occurs during the phase of decathexis and another during the phase of recathexis, as Freud had suggested. Each new delusion is the best possible solution, and follows the restitution of temporarily paralyzed ego functions.

Of the various kinds of delusion, Freud conducted a most exhaustive study of the delusion of persecution. As early as in the 1890's, he observed that delusions of persecution result from the use of a specific defense mechanism, projection. By means of projection, an unacceptable idea is not only disowned but is attributed to another person (1894, 1896b). In 1908, he informed Jung and Ferenczi (see Strachey, 1958, p. 4) that delusions of persecution result from the projection of homosexual impulses. In 1911, in the Schreber case, he detailed how "I love him" is converted into "he hates me," and made the observation that the conversion takes place in two steps—the change from "I (a man) love him (a man)" to "I do not love him—I hate him" through the use of obsessional defense mechanisms (i.e., thought displacement),[1] and the change from "I do not love him—I hate him" into "he hates me" through the use of projection.[2] In "A Case of Paranoia" (1915c) he conceptualized the relation between paranoia and homosexuality in the context of narcissistic object choice and narcissistic fixation; that is, from a developmental point of view.[3] In "Jealousy, Paranoia and Homosexuality" (1922), he introduced the idea that delusions of persecution are not formed when the disease breaks out, but are actually preformed. The preformed delusion becomes evident because of an increased cathexis of it.[4] In "The Ego and the Id" (1923), he wrote,

In persecutory paranoia the patient fends off an excessively

[1] In his description of the formation of the delusion of "influencing machines," Tausk (1919) also gave a detailed account of thought displacement without making this idea explicit.

[2] It is interesting to note that projection is resorted to only when "I hate him" is changed into "he hates me."

[3] Freud also expressed a developmental viewpoint in "On narcissism: An introduction" (1914b), although he was dealing with a different subject. In that paper he introduced the concept of the ego ideal and proposed that the delusion of being watched, criticized, and persecuted might result from the evolution of conscience reproduced regressively.

[4] In 1939, Freud equated the preformed delusional idea with "a State within a State," "an inaccessible party" that is not adjusted to the demands of the real world and does not obey the laws of logical thinking.

strong homosexual attachment to some particular person in a special way; and as a result this person whom he loved most becomes a persecutor, against whom the patient directs an often dangerous aggressiveness. . . . There is another possible mechanism, however, which we have come to know of by analytic investigation of the processes concerned in the change in paranoia. An ambivalent attitude [toward the persecutor] is present from the outset and the transformation [from loving the persecutor to hating him] is effected by means of a reactive displacement of cathexis, energy being withdrawn from the erotic impulse and added to the hostile one [pp. 43-44].

It is of interest to note that although the homosexual theory was repeatedly upheld by others (e.g., Ferenczi, 1911; Brunswick, 1929; Lagache, 1950; Waelder, 1951; Fenichel, 1953), Freud's own views underwent constant revision and modification, and he began to stress the importance of the role played by aggression. In view of the concept of the best possible solution suggested above, we may see Schreber's paranoid feelings about Dr. Flechsig in another light. Schreber had obviously suffered an internal catastrophe. Subsequently, as he approached the subacute phase of his illness, he reoriented himself enough to recognize Dr. Flechsig as the person to whom he could look for the kind of help he needed. That is, he believed that Dr. Flechsig could relieve him of the organismic panic, since Dr. Flechsig had previously helped him when he had suffered the illness in a milder form. To Schreber, Dr. Flechsig was an idealized omnipotent parent figure who could perform miracles. When Dr. Flechsig failed this time to perform a miracle and relieve his agony, Schreber might have felt disappointed and even angry. Unable to tolerate his own anger, Schreber resorted to projecting his hostile impulses, and a delusion of persecution then crystallized.

When insertion of the penis into the anus is the content of delusion, the validity of the homosexual theory may still be open to question. It is quite possible that the mothering person frequently gave enemas to the patient during his infancy. Now psychotic and desperately expecting relief of pain from the idealized parent figure, at present the doctor, the patient might believe that his panic and agony would be relieved if the doctor would only put something in his anus.

I am not suggesting that the delusion of persecution is more attributable to aggressive impulses than to homosexual impulses. What I am stressing is that, in terms of Freud's later anxiety theory, homosexual impulses and aggressive impulses can equally be the factors that precipitate organismic panic, following which some patients develop a delusion of persecution as the best possible solution. The study of the rise and fall of a delusion of jealousy (Pao, 1969b) showed that this delusion can be brought forth when the patient's conflicts over aggression and narcissism, as well as homosexuality, are stirred up. *Undifferentiated self/obj*

Factors Influencing the Content of Delusion

The content of each patient's delusion is not a matter of chance. It is determined by his personal life experience. As Freud conceived it, delusion is a retrospective falsification of historical truth (1937b). Niederland's study (1974) of Schreber's father strongly suggests that Schreber could not have helped developing a delusion of persecution and of being "made" or influenced—if he developed a delusion at all. Take also, for example, Tina and John (see Chapters 12 and 14). It did not just happen that Tina had a delusion of being the greatest star in show business and built her expectations of others in accordance with that delusion; nor was it accidental that John should have developed delusions of receiving messages from God, of external dangers, of being poisoned, etc. Tina's delusion of being a star seems to have been inevitable. In John's case, as it turned out in the course of his treatment, he would have to express his passive wishes in delusions of being poisoned, being endangered, being influenced, etc., because of his long-standing struggle against a symbiotic tie with his mother, his belief that he was a damaged and incomplete person (castrated), and his fantasy of being rescued from his entanglement with his mother by his awe-inspiring and remote father.

Although the historical truth about the effect of early life experiences on the content of delusion cannot be ascertained, the connection between such faintly registered experiences and the content of delusion is beyond doubt. Lichtenberg and Pao (1974) suggested that "Influencing machines, images of fragmentation of body parts, etc., give evidence of the dehumanized aspects of the early experience of children for whom the maternal environment seemed mechanical and segmented; world destruction, atom bombs and similar imagery reveal the rage and turmoil registered from the infantile experience" (p. 277). From the psychoanalytic treatment of a patient with megalomanic delusions, Segal (1972) inferred that a "catastrophe   [in]the infantile situation in which the ego is flooded by destructive and self-destructive impulses threatening annihilation" (p. 401) resulted in a megalomanic delusional system.

It is because of the historical truth that the patient usually holds an absolute conviction about the validity of the content of his delusion. Frosch (1967) said,

> When we examine the delusional content, we are at times struck by the rather overt, relatively undistorted or poorly disguised real aspects traceable to childhood. A patient . . . had as a recurring feature of her delusions the feeling of being watched, and of being checked as to her goodness or badness, etc. She borrowed not only from a universal situation, from early superego development, but actually specific experiences to which she did not have to bring too many fantasies in order to justify her reactions   [p. 478].

Historical truth aside, the current situation too shapes the content of the delusion. In a six-year study of a case of pathological jealousy (Pao 1969b), I was able to observe the recurrence of the same delusion of jealousy in the patient in strikingly different psychologically stressful situations. It was

obvious, however, that although the delusion remained the-
matically the same, the details of the content did change. The
phenomenon of change of detail in delusional content can also
be documented by the following clinical observation. In the
course of her treatment, Tina (see Chapter 12) often shrieked
at the top of her lungs when she felt her needs were frustrated, asking others if they knew they had just insulted the
best actress on Broadway. On one such occasion, a manic patient shouted back at her and told her that she (the manic
patient) had never thought much of the Broadway actress. If
she (the manic patient) had a choice, she would rather be a
Hollywood star, who could make millions of dollars. As the
manic patient started to shout, Tina quieted down, but no one
expected the aftermath. Some time later, however, it became
apparent that Tina had modified the content of her delusion
so that she now demanded to be recognized and respected as
an Academy Award winner. Henceforth she was at times the
best on Broadway and at other times the best in Hollywood.
It was impossible to determine each time why she preferred
one or the other, but occasionally it was clear that the presence of the manic patient made Tina the best in Hollywood.
Thus it seems that, psychotic and nonfunctional though she
was, Tina's psychic apparatus was constantly shaping her
representational world, assuring her of a background of safety,
and finding the best possible solution at the given moment.
If a delusion of grandeur was to compensate for her battered
self-esteem, then she had to reformulate its content to fit the
demands of time and place (from the point of view of her
representational world), to assure herself a maximum degree
of self-esteem and self-importance.

To account for the changes in the content of the delusion,
it may then be said that a delusion is newly formed each
time,[5] but in its formation it makes use of material primarily
drawn from the patient's past. The past or the historical truth

[5] In his description of the patient's realistic perception of the therapist in delusional transference, Searles (1972) implicitly presented a view similar to the one
offered here.

determines the sameness of the content of a recurrent delusion.

Preformed Delusion and Persistent Fantasy

Lichtenberg and Pao (1974) surveyed the relations between delusion, fantasy, and desire, and noted that in the case of Mrs. B., a patient who repeatedly experienced manic episodes, her persistent fantasy during latency of being the Egyptian queen Cleopatra (a fantasy that was repeatedly acted out in childhood games with friends) formed the kernel of her delusion during *each* of her later psychotic manic periods. Thus it appears that the material of the past on which the delusion was built was the persistent fantasy.[6] Now the question: What is fantasy? What is the difference between a persistent fantasy and a delusion? Why should a delusion be built on a persistent fantasy?

In respect to the first two questions, I shall refer to some ideas that Lichtenberg and I (1974) formulated elsewhere. A fantasy and a delusion are easily distinguished. A fantasy is notably associated with pleasurable feelings (even if the content of the fantasy is of being beaten), whereas a delusion is invariably attended by unpleasurable feelings of different gradations, often in the nature of unnamed fears. Despite the pleasurable experience the person derives from his fantasy, he can easily stop fantasying, either by his own volition or by external force, without exhibiting any evidence of disturbance. On the other hand, as much as the patient describes his delusion as unpleasant, he clings to it with tenacity and desperation. When or if he is deprived of it, he may experience extreme anxiety and disorientation.

The difference between fantasy and delusion is not determined by the content but by the different functions they serve.

[6] In Tina, the core of her delusion of being the best of Hollywood and Broadway also appears to have been derived from a latency-period fantasy of being like Shirley Temple.

A fantasy functions to restore a momentary pleasure-pain imbalance, whereas a delusion is a desperate effort to re-establish a "background feeling of security" (Sandler, 1960). In the
case of pain-pleasure disequilibrium, there may be a selective
disturbance of ego functioning (e.g., the use of such defense
mechanisms as repression and isolation and the predominance of primary-process functioning), but there is no over-
all impairment of it or any loss of self-continuity. In the absence of a background feeling of safety, on the other hand,
not only is ego functioning grossly impaired, but the sense of
self is also fragmented.

Dynamically, both fantasy and delusion are organized
around wish (drive) configurations. Fantasy is organized
around specific wish configurations of a given developmental
period, even though the pregenital components are molded
into and under the sway of a postoedipal organization. To re-
establish the pain-pleasure equilibrium, fantasy is unfolded
"unhurriedly," and is often acted out with others who are
willing to play the complementary roles (see Sachs, 1942).
Fantasy can therefore serve an important adaptive function
in the sensorimotor manipulation of objects during exploratory play. Delusion, on the other hand, is organized around
more archaic wish configurations following a marked impairment of over-all ego functioning, and at a time when the person's basic sense of security is adversely affected and there is
a lack of self-continuity. Delusion can serve only a defensive
function.

The content of fantasy is determined by both current stress
and past experiences, including the earliest ones. It is a transient aspect of mental life. Normally, the constant shifting of
the pleasure-pain balance and the particular needs of a given
developmental phase render the content of fantasy fluid. If,
however (as in the case of Mrs. B. or Tina), a pleasure-pain
imbalance recurs during a particular developmental phase,
the same fantasy may be repeatedly organized. In the case of
a recurrent fantasy, it may assume the quality of "a State
within a State," which Freud (1939) calls "an inaccessible

party, with which co-operation is impossible, but which may succeed in overcoming what is known as the normal party and forcing it into its service. If this happens, it implies a domination by an internal psychical reality over the reality of the external world and the path to a psychosis lies open" (p. 76). In a sense, this recurrent, persistent fantasy may be described as a precursor of delusion.

A persistent fantasy or precursor of delusion has the potential to become the nucleus of a delusion. But it is not a delusion. It is only after an organismic panic that the self is reorganized. Since the persistent fantasy consists of a blending of regressed elements, and since it is readily available, it is chosen for the reorganization of the self and thus as the kernel of the delusion.

Delusion and the Sense of Self-Continuity

In Chapter 2 I suggested that the sense of self-continuity may be used as a criterion for dividing the course of schizophrenic illness into three phases: the acute phase, when there is an absence of a sense of self-continuity; the subacute phase, when a new sense of self-continuity is gradually re-established; and the chronic phase, when a sense of self-continuity is now firmly re-established and along with it a "new" self is organized. I further suggested that the distinction among the three phases is significant from the point of view of intensive psychotherapy, a matter I shall elaborate in the next section of this book. At present, I want only to stress that the patient's subjective experience of his delusion differs in these three phases.

In the acute phase the patient is overwhelmed by organismic panic and cannot distinguish what is inside him from what is outside of him. He exists in a dreamlike state. Self and object are not differentiated. He does not know that he is hallucinating or has a delusion. He *is* the delusion or hallucination.

In the latter part of the acute phase or the early part of the subacute phase, along with some lessening of organismic panic, a sense of self-continuity is being re-established. The patient begins to conceptualize a "new" self experientially speaking, or a delusional viewpoint observationally speaking. At times he senses that the "new" self is foreign and unfamiliar and is not his "old" self. He therefore asks himself or often asks his therapist such questions as "Who am I?" ("I" referring to the "new" self), "Where was he?" ("he" referring to the "old" self), and the like.

During the early subacute phase, the ego functions are still not stabilized. Whenever instinct-affect tension is heightened, the ego functions are inactivated, and the "new" self is in turn threatened. This necessitates a repeated falling back onto the preformed delusion. In the process, a delusional view about the self and the object world becomes fixated. Frosch (1967) says,

> The sense of conviction of the reality of a delusion may, therefore, also relate to the historic truth of certain ego states and functions which are regressively re-experienced during the psychosis. In other words, the sense of conviction of the reality of a delusion may be related not *only* to the historic truth of the content of the delusion, but to the regressive reappearance of a whole series of associated psychic phenomena coeval with past experiences [p. 480].

I believe that, in addition, the process of repeatedly falling back on the preformed delusion with concomitant success in re-establishing a sense of self-continuity must also contribute heavily to the conviction of the reality of the delusion.

When the delusion becomes fixated and is no longer easily changed, the patient has arrived at the chronic phase of his illness. By now, the ego functions are relatively stable and the experience of organismic panic has almost subsided. The patient appears relatively comfortable, for his delusional new self assures him of a "background of safety." He no longer asks "Who am I?," for he "knows" that his "new" delusional self is his self. Similarly, he no longer needs to lament, "Where was he?," for his "old" self is long buried and forgotten. The "old" self is, however, not lost; at times it may make an appearance. When that happens, the patient, who has become accustomed to the delusional "new" self, may consider the "old" self as unreal, foreign, and unacceptable. Take the case of Carrie, for instance. Since her psychotic break 10 years before, she had been in several hospitals and on a chronic ward in two of them. Now she presented a most bizarre appearance. She smeared the wrong part of her face with powder and rouge. Her clothes, though clean and new, were always in disarray. She walked with a peculiar shifting gait that attracted attention. When she talked, she grimaced and giggled so much that the listener would become completely distracted. She used neologisms, only occasionally making intelligible remarks. It was at this juncture that she was admitted to Chestnut Lodge. Eighteen months later, when her therapist went away for his second summer vacation, Carrie was seen by an interim therapist. One day she told the latter, in the midst of her disconnected speech, that one of the young girl patients living on her ward had attempted suicide the night before (by slashing her wrist) and then said that she would like to do the same thing. The interim therapist, not knowing enough about her to be certain of her true intentions, passed this information on to the administrator, who in turn restricted the patient to the ward for close observation. The next day, she was lucid throughout her therapy hour. She scolded the interim therapist for his lack of ability to understand her and held him responsible for the loss of privileges and freedom that she had enjoyed in the preceding months. In the course of that session it turned out that the regular therapist of the girl who had slashed her wrist was also on vacation, and that Carrie's talk about suicide was a symbolic way of expressing the fact that she missed her own regular therapist. The next day, the interim therapist, who had hoped the lucid conversation of the previous day would continue, was disappointed. For Carrie had lapsed back to her usual fragmented way of expressing herself. When asked about it, she denied completely what had happened the day before and would say only that "that was not me." This clinical vignette demonstrates that Carrie clung tenaciously to her delusional self in order to maintain a background feeling of security, but that in special life situations she could shift from one aspect of self-continuity to another.

A temporary shift from one aspect of self-continuity to another is not uncommon in the schizophrenic patient during the chronic phase. When such a patient becomes physically ill, there is usually a shift toward his body self, resulting in a temporary period of freedom from psychosis. When unexpectedly invited to dinner at Bleuler's house, a dilapidated long-hospitalized patient could behave "normally at the dinner table." Likewise, George and Gibson (1959) reported that a group of long-hospitalized male patients who behaved strangely on the ward began to behave very normally during a short sojourn at a resort town.

The occurrence of such shifts is usually related to the patient's early life experience. For instance, a patient who becomes free of psychotic symptoms when physically ill could have had a previous experience of illness when his mother and his doctor and his whole world were good and made sense, and for longer or shorter periods of time he was allowed to be relatively free of tension and to be himself. Bleuler's and George and Gibson's patients could have had previous experiences of the fatherly person stepping down from his lofty position and treating them as equals. In the case of Carrie, during her latency she was said to have talked in as scatter-brained a way as an aunt who had spent most of her life in a mental hospital, and was consequently called "crazy Carrie." Shortly before her psychosis, in her mid-teens, she became promiscuous. When her father tired to set limits for her, she had shouting matches with him. At such times she was said to "talk normally." Thus the one-hour sensible talk with the interim therapist reflected her early experience with her father when, in an effort to stabilize Carrie's situation, he had revealed his concern for her.

The Fate of Delusion in Treatment

In treatment, we are interested in what happens to delusion. Can it be corrected, resolved, or modified? Freud (1927b) said,

> In studying some cases of paranoia I was able to establish the fact that ideas of persecution are formed early and exist for a long time without any perceptible effect, until, as the result of some particular precipitating event, they receive sufficient amounts of cathexis to cause them to become dominant. The cure, too, of such paranoic attacks would lie not so much in a resolution and correction of the delusional ideas as in a withdrawal from them of the cathexis which has been lent to them [p. 165].

What Freud said applies to most patients during the chronic phase. About many a patient during the subacute phase, however, we need not hold such a pessimistic view.

In the treatment of a patient in the chronic phase, we do not expect a resolution or correction of delusional ideas. Rather, we aim gradually to increase the patient's capacity to tolerate instinct-affect tensions so that he can arrive at the best possible solution without resorting to extremely distorted views about the object world. In fact, we may choose not to deal strenuously with the patient's delusional view of himself. But in the treatment of a patient in the subacute phase, we may take the opposite approach. We may aim specifically at the resolution or correction of his delusional ideas about himself. Sometimes, in the pursuit of this goal, the patient may become "sick" all over again (e.g., he may resume the catatonic position). That should not alarm us. For, if handled well, such relapses may prove to be integrative, rather than a sealing-over process.

Moreover, it seems that in therapy delusional views about oneself and delusional views about the object can have very different fates. Delusional views about oneself are initially more closely linked to body sensations than delusional views about the object world. For instance, because of rage and turmoil registered in early infancy, a patient conceptualized himself as a "fire-spitting dragon," "dynamite," or a potential murderer. Later, whenever he was angered, he sensed his endangering potential. Unaccepting of his self-view, he began to turn things around, conceptualizing himself as endangered by others. Because of this developmental sequence, delusional views about the endangering quality of the self would be more difficult to resolve or correct than delusional views about the object world. In other words, in treatment the patient's delusion of being endangered by others can be corrected once he realizes that it results from the projection of his own murderous feelings. But additional months or years may be required before the patient can modify his self-concept of being a potential murderer.

In speaking of resolving, correcting, or modifying delusions, it has not been my intention to imply that in the treatment of a schizophrenic patient one is concerned with symptom removal; my intention was only to depict the vissicitudes of delusional ideas in treatment. In the tradition of Fromm-Reichmann (see 1950, 1959), I do believe that if we expect any results from our therapeutic efforts with our patients, we must learn to see the patient as a person who has problems in living rather than as a person with symptoms.

CHAPTER 16

On Hallucinatory Experiences
of Schizophrenics

When Lynn's therapist went away on a vacation, I agreed to
stand by. Her history revealed that in the course of 10 years
of a turbulent childless marriage, Lynn had become increasingly paranoid and finally ended in totally breaking with
reality. After many months of regressive disorganization,
violence, and being actively delusional and hallucinatory, she
responded to psychotherapy and showed slow but steady improvement. During her prolonged hospitalization, she absorbed the loss of her husband through divorce and the loss
of her mother through death. Eventually, she recovered from
her psychosis, moved out of the hospital, and made a good
extramural adjustment. She continued her treatment. In the
past few years, she had not needed an interim therapist. But
this year, shortly before her therapist's vacationtime, she was
found, during her routine annual physical, to have a nod-
ule—probably malignant—in her breast. She reacted to this
news with extreme agitation, feeling very much embittered
about her "bad breaks." It therefore became necessary to consider a stand-by therapist. Five days after her therapist's vacation began, she called me and asked for an appointment.
She sounded so anxious that I felt compelled to see her the
same day. When we met, she appeared very anxious, though
less so than she had been on the phone. She said she had
decided to see me because for three nights she had been distressed by a "voice." In the past, when she prepared to go to

bed, the voice would descend on her, but after she got into bed and fought with it for a while, she could usually dismiss it at will. This time, however, it persisted despite her wish to the contrary. The voice had kept her awake all night and had driven her to distraction. She went on to say that the voice told her that Bob (her ex-husband) was scheming something that could be harmful to her (nothing more definite than that). She added later that the voice came out of a corner of her bedroom, near the ceiling and at the farthest end from her bed (obviously the farthest distance away from herself in bed).

When I first heard of her chief complaint, I was distressed, feeling that I might be pushed into making a decision about rehospitalizing her: this woman living alone, and now beset by the return of her psychotic symptoms. But as she entered into a conversation with me, she made me feel increasingly at ease. For she was soon able to set aside her complaints about her voice, and went on to review our earlier acquaintance with each other (when she was hospitalized years before), how she had been getting along all these years, how she was distressed at the news of the possibility of a malignancy, and how she felt lonely, sad, and very mad that her therapist had gone away at this particular time. In the course of our conversation, her affect became more and more appropriate. Thus, toward the end of the session, I was quite comfortable in reaching an agreement with her that we would meet twice a week during her therapist's absence (she met with her own therapist four times a week).

When we met for the second time, she began the session again with a report on her voice. She said that after the last session with me the voice had suggested "sex therapy" to her, and that she had argued down that suggestion. She added that sex therapy meant finding herself a male companion. In the circumstances,[1] I responded that she must have felt lonely.

---

[1] The transference implication of the voice was obvious. For instance, voice one about her husband reflected her critical feelings toward her regular therapist, and voice two about sex therapy reflected her curbing of a wish to make a "flight to a new object" (see Pao, 1973a), in this case the interim therapist.

She agreed with me, and subsequently appeared very relaxed and became very chatty. In the rest of the session she told me that in her younger days she had had many male companions and was never lonely. She confided that she always seemed to have a special eye for unacceptable characters—this included her husband, who she believed had married her for her family's money. At the end of the interview she said wistfully and with some insight that her current distress about her physical condition, as well as her feelings about her therapist's vacation, could have made it impossible for her to dismiss the voice according to her will as she had done before.

During the next several sessions, she apprised me of her physical condition and was happy that the biopsy report was in fact negative. And she no longer mentioned the voice. Despite my curiosity, I did not dare ask any direct questions about the voice. However, in the limited time I had with her, I did succeed in learning (and I had obtained confirmation from her regular therapist) that the statement about her ex-husband scheming against her reminded her of her mother's warning against her ex-husband's interest in other women, and the statement about sex therapy reminded her of the arguments between her parents during her late teens (her mother frowned on her going out on dates, but her father encouraged her). I also learned that her voice nowadays made only brief comments. It was an on-again-off-again matter. The voice appeared when she was alone or when she felt alone in a crowd. It appeared quite often at bedtime. The voice was nondescript, genderless, and rarely identifiable, although very occasionally she did hear her regular therapist's voice giving her sensible advice. As for the content, it could be either cautionary or encouraging. Most of the time she had no control over its appearance,[2] but could usually dismiss it if she used her will power.

Some time later her regular therapist informed me that

---

[2] I did not inquire whether she ever had the "listening attitude" described by Arieti (1974, p. 574)—that is, the patient expects to listen to the "voice."

in earlier days the content of her voice's utterances had ranged from very critical-demeaning to very seductive-tempting. In the course of the years it had become less and less threatening and pestering, and now it ranged from mildly cautionary to warmly encouraging. The therapist also told me that in earlier days Lynn located the voices as arising from far away. Gradually she conceived them as arising from very close to her body. Still later she recognized them as existing within herself. And still later she treated her voices as her own thoughts. Corresponding to the time when it became her own thoughts, the voice disappeared. When she was anxious, however, the voice sometimes reappeared. Then it lost the quality of being her own thoughts, and could move out of her body boundary as well. Ever since she had owned up to the voice being her own thoughts, she had given the voice the nickname of "Junior."

Of course, Lynn's current voice is not the typical voice of schizophrenics who have not recovered from their illness or who have not benefited from psychotherapy. Like Lynn's earlier voice, the typical auditory hallucination of a schizophrenic involves a voice that is more harshly and demoralizingly critical of something the patient has done, or more dangerously and seductively persuasive for the patient to do something forbidden; it usually makes comments about the patient's behavior or talks about the patient in the third person. Sometimes several voices argue with each other about the patient, or the voice is experienced as the patient's own but is broadcast into the world by a hostile force. Lynn's current voice apparently retained only a trace of the general characteristics of the schizophrenic's auditory hallucination. Still, it can be used as a starting point in the consideration of certain aspects of schizophrenic hallucinatory experience.

Hallucination in schizophrenia is always accompanied by delusion (the reverse is not necessarily true). For the perception of an object with no reality cannot be maintained without a false conception and a persistent belief, unconquerable by reason, in something that has no existence in fact. To talk about hallucination without also speaking of delusion therefore seems impossible. It is only for convenience in exposition that I shall talk about hallucination in isolation.

Freud (1911) once postulated that schizophrenia and paranoia are to be distinguished as two separate diagnostic entities because they differ in libidinal fixation point and because the former uses the hysterical defensive technique of hallucination and the latter the obsessive defensive technique of delusion. Whether or not we intend to go so far in establishing two diagnostic entities, it is clear that the different infantile experiences of these two groups of patients do contribute to the difference in the final shaping of the symptoms. Certain early experiences would pave the way for a preponderance of delusional symptoms, and very different kinds of early experience may lead to a predominance of hallucination. Both groups of patients are very conflicted about their dependency needs, but they have developed quite different attitudes to deal with their conflicts. Patients who become predominantly delusional tend to act as if they are very independent, whereas those who acquire hallucinations in later life tend to become very passive, their hallucinations expressing the derivative of a wish to have their mothers as constant companions. It may be obvious that the "independence" of predominantly delusional patients is spurious. They attempt independence only through fantasy; they never do anything to actualize it. Moreover, in their backgrounds is usually some important person with whom the patients closely identify and who had strong paranoid tendencies of blaming others.

Hallucination during the Acute and Subacute Phases

Ordinarily, we speak of hallucination in schizophrenia as if it were a uniform experience throughout the different phases of the illness. In actuality that is not so. Hallucinatory experience during the acute phase is not the same as hallucinatory experience during the subacute (and chronic) phase.

The acute phase follows organismic panic. When organismic panic prevails, all ego functions come to a standstill. As the ego loses its ability to discriminate internal imagery from external perception, the patient is hallucinating, whether or not he is able to confirm it verbally. This hallucinatory experience is dreamlike. Only fragments of it may be recalled by the patient after his recovery. Take Tom's report, for example. While he was in a catatonic state, Tom had to spend part of his day in a quiet room because of his unpredictable assaultive behavior. While there he exhibited certain repeated behaviors. He would walk from one end of the room to the other for long stretches of time, with his arms stretched out and fisted hands facing downward. Or he would sit in one spot, holding a pillow on his lap and making pulling gestures alternately with his right and left hands. After he had sufficiently recovered, he volunteered one day that his experience during the most acute stage of his illness was like a dream to him, and that he could still "visualize" fragments of the dreamlike experience. He then mentioned that in walking with his arms outstretched he was actually plowing his orange grove, and that in the pulling motion he was making shoes for himself. He further volunteered that plowing his grove and making shoes were consistent with his wish to be self-sufficient and self-reliant. This wish had determined his stubborn refusal of food during that time.[3]

As the patient moves steadily toward the late acute phase

---

[3] Compare Tom's experience with Dr. LeFever's dreamlike experience under LSD (1961). While very much under the influence of the drug, LeFever saw a colleague coming into the room where he was. LeFever, who had had some altercation with this colleague on the previous day, instantly visualized himself and the colleague sitting like two Indians, smoking a peace pipe together, without consciousness of the recent altercation or a desire to make peace, as he himself was now in a disadvantaged position. From a lengthy review of sensory deprivation, Zuckerman (1969) concluded that hallucinations caused by sensory deprivation are "more similar to drug-induced hallucination than they are to psychotic hallucinations" (p. 121). By "psychotic hallucinations" he was probably referring to schizophrenic hallucinations of the subacute phase. My point is that hallucinatory experience during the acute phase of schizophrenic illness and drug-induced or sensory deprivation experiences resemble each other in that all are dreamlike. I shall not consider the differences among them, for that would take us too far afield.

or the subacute phase, he re-establishes and gradually con-
solidates his sense of self-continuity. In the process, he appears less and less to be in a dream state. It is then that his
behavior indicates that he is responding to an undetectable
stimulus, and it is only then that we refer to the patient as
hallucinating. At this stage, although other types of hallucinations are also reported by patients, auditory hallucination
is by far the most common. Its predominance may be due to
actual earlier experience, characterized by the mother's in-
cessant comments about the patient's behavior and her ex-
hortations about what to do and what not to do. On the other
hand, clinicians tend to misidentify hallucination in nonau-
ditory modalities as delusions. For instance, when a patient
says that he tied his socks on his ankles because he wanted
his feet to stay on the ground, the observer will usually conclude that the patient has a delusion of flying rather than a
proprioceptive hallucination of weightlessness. Similarly,
when a patient says that she is being raped every night, her
actual physical sensation will usually be discounted, and she
will simply be considered delusional. And when a patient suddenly becomes frightened during a therapeutic session, retreats from his therapist, slumps on the floor, curls up and
covers his eyes with his hand, the possibility of a visual hallucination will be overlooked unless the patient reports almost at the same time that he has perceived the therapist as
a devil wearing horns, or as some other kind of threatening
creature.

The Characteristics of Auditory Hallucination

Let us return to Lynn, the patient discussed at the beginning of this chapter. At the time she came to see me, (1) she
gave the impression that her hallucinatory experience was
primarily auditory. (2) She claimed she had very little control
over the appearance of the voice; but at less anxious moments,
she did control its disappearance. (3) She heard the voice

mostly at bedtime when she was presumably alone and was possibly lonely. (4) She experienced the voice as talking to her, and she herself as reacting to it passively. (5) She experienced the voice as nondescript and unidentifiable. At times she claimed the voice was related to herself and called it Junior; but Junior was still nondescript and unidentifiable. (6) According to her therapist, the content of the voice tended to be less devastating to Lynn as she got better. (It is unclear whether the content had actually changed or Lynn's tolerance had improved.) (7) Also according to her therapist, as Lynn improved clinically the voice moved from a faraway location to one adjacent to her body boundary, and finally to inside the boundary. Still later, it was linked with her own thoughts. But in times of distress, the sequence could be partially and at times totally reversed.

A voice is the best possible solution at a given time. In Lynn's case, her fear of and bitterness about having breast cancer, her feeling of being abandoned by her regular therapist, her inability to accept her own hostility toward him, etc., resulted in extreme anxiety. By resorting to the voice, all these emotions were overshadowed. In addition, she solved the problem of having been abandoned by her therapist by creating human companionship in the form of bringing back important persons of the past (e.g., mother, father, husband). To accomplish the latter, Lynn might be expected to create a voice that would be pleasant and comforting to her. Yet in fact she created a voice that was not only nondescript and unidentifiable but also contrary and unpleasant. Why should she do that?

Earlier, I mentioned that the identity of the voice was only thinly veiled. According to Lynn's associations, voice one stood unmistakably for the voice of her mother telling her that her ex-husband was no good, and voice two stood for the voice of her father encouraging her to go out on dates.[4] But although

---

[4] Modell (1958) has also demonstrated that the voice is usually easily identifiable as that of one of the parents.

the veil was thin, the voice was nevertheless disguised. I assume that the disguise was not incidental. Take, for example, the voice advising sex therapy, which Lynn had evidently heard many a time before. On this particular occasion, she heard it while conflicted in her feelings toward the interim therapist. Although we do not have definitive knowledge about the circumstances in which Lynn had heard this voice in the past, it is likely that she had been similarly conflicted in her feelings, except about someone else. Even though the "voice is a memory of the past" (Lewin, 1968, p. 389), the purpose of the voice is not to recall, but to conceptualize and resolve the conflicts of this moment—a process very similar to dreaming. And if the voice is used to reflect a conflict, it will best serve that purpose if it is devoid of any identifiable quality.

Lynn's basic attitude toward her mother is another factor that might account for the voice's being unidentifiable, as well as for its being more irritating than comforting. Lynn had never learned how to be unambivalently comforted. From very early in life, she was taught, for instance, that the gratification of hunger had to be accompanied by high physical tension. As a result, she learned that it was better not to expect much from her mother in the form of tenderness and care. But this fact did not preclude her longing for such care. Thus she turned things around and tried to "look after her mother" (Hill, 1955). She read her mother's mood and learned not to upset her at all costs. Now, therefore, in a time of need, however much Lynn longed to be comforted by her mother, she had to create a situation in which her mother comforted her, not with sweet words, but with critical, distressing remarks—a situation in which her mother's identity had to be disguised, because knowledge of her identity would compel Lynn to look after her. Making the voice unidentifiable may be very similar to the transformation of instinctual wishes into an influencing machine (Tausk, 1919).

In Lynn's case, her conflicts and her defenses placed the voice at the far corner of the room. (See also Havens, 1962.) Only when her anxiety subsided and her conflicts were again under control could she again admit the voice as her own thoughts. As Lynn moved her voice toward herself, she also became increasingly able to distinguish between her self and external reality. These are parallel processes corresponding to the subsidence of anxiety or the ego's capacity to tolerate anxiety. In Chapter 13, I commented on the processing of internal and external reality. It may be useful to distinguish between the sense of external reality and the processing of external reality. The sense of external reality concerns itself with the recognition of its existence; with this recognition, the psychic apparatus will take external reality into consideration when it is formulating its best possible solution. The processing of external reality goes beyond mere recognition; it also concerns itself with the interpretation of external reality in accordance with prevailing sociocultural modes. Following the organismic panic, both the sense of external reality and the processing of external reality are lost. But toward the end of the acute phase, the sense of external reality is invariably recovered before the processing of external reality. By then the patient often seems to be aware of external reality, but does not process it. Thus, for example, Lynn responded to the therapeutic session by changing voice one into voice two. All the same, she had to continue to project, to de-emotionalize, to make the voice nondescript, to keep it outside of herself, etc. Then, when she finally recovered the ability to process external reality, she could relinquish the mechanisms that placed the voice outside her boundary. Now, the voice not only moved increasingly back to within her body boundary, it became a part of her own thoughts.

According to Lynn, most of the time the voice simply descended on her. Perhaps that implies that sometimes she consciously brought it on herself. I believe that she could not have achieved such a feat during the acute phase, when organismic panic interfered with both her ego functions and her sense of self-continuity. Even in the middle and later parts of the subacute phase, Lynn's ability to control her voice at will was determined by the state of instinct-affect tension. For instance, when she experienced voice one or voice two, she was in great distress, and was obviously unable to stop the voice. But during less distressed moments she was able to control the voice.

It seems clear that the voice, with or without Lynn's conscious effort, served the function of doing away with the distressing thoughts that caused disruptive anxiety. P. H. Tolpin (1975) has described hallucination as "a signal wish fulfillment" regulated by the pleasure-unpleasure principle. In Lynn's case (as in all schizophrenics), the voice was also geared to restoring the background feeling of safety; it did more than eradicate pain and gain simple pleasure. However irritating the content of its utterances, the voice had the advantage of stirring up only absolutely predictable feelings, whereas without the voice, Lynn might open herself to complete uncertainty and unnamed panic.

Interestingly, Lynn's voice often occurred at bedtime. Furthermore, taking into consideration the voice's soothing effect, Lynn's use of hallucination was comparable to the infant's use of its transitional object. From this point of view we might conceive of Lynn's voice as a transitional object, though in doing so we may be overextending the term "object." Winnicott (1958) conceived of the transitional object as the infant's first possession, which is originally created by him and which stands "for the 'external' breast, but *indirectly* so, through standing for an 'internal' breast" (p. 240). It belongs to an intermediate area of inner and outer reality, and is controlled by neither. However, by means of this possession, the infant is able to soothe himself before going to sleep or in times of distress. Whether the first possession is a corner of a blanket or a toy, it is something concrete and identifiable by others. Lynn's voice did not have all the qualities of the transitional object described by Winnicott. Except to Lynn herself, the voice was neither concrete nor identifiable. Yet to her the voice was as real and concrete as a blanket or toy is to the infant. In addition, the voice resembled the transitional object in that the soothing function of the therapist's voice could be internalized or "go inside as a structure" (see M. Tolpin, 1971). Following this transmutative internalization, the external soothing voice will no longer be needed. By then, the patient may give up his voice altogether.

Some Therapeutic Considerations

The treatment of schizophrenic patients cannot rely on an understanding of the mechanism of the rise and fall of hallucinations. Sullivan and M. Klein, for instance, who played important roles in getting the treatment of schizophrenia under way in this country and in England, paid very little attention to such a mechanism. Yet a fuller knowledge of the whys and hows of hallucination may be helpful in the treatment of some cases.

Hallucinations in the acute and subacute phases must not be thought of in the same terms. In the acute phase, the primary concern in treatment is to stabilize ego function and consolidate a new sense of self-continuity. In this endeavor it is hoped that the patient can eliminate his dreamlike hallucinatory experience altogether and again begin to function like a "normal" person. Given this primary concern, it is seldom necessary to deal directly with the patient's hallucination.

Hallucination in the subacute phase is quite a different matter. By now, the terror has greatly subsided and the ego functions are stabilized. The patient has developed a new sense of self-continuity. If the hallucination has been retained, it is now mostly in the auditory sphere. In this phase the voice is experienced as ego dystonic. Yet the patient has a great need for it. The therapist's main concern is with the patient's over-all need; he does not have to be directly concerned with the voice. However, he may often use hallucination as a therapeutic aid. For instance, a young schizophrenic patient, Ron, who had been admitted to 14 hospitals in six years because of a history of assaultiveness, was seen in therapy in pack. For a while during the sessions he babbled constantly and showed no sign of relating to the therapist. At times he appeared to be simply making noises; at other times he seemed to be screaming at the therapist; at still other times he seemed to be talking to someone else who was not physically present in the room. After the patient had been seen in pack four times a week for about three months, there began to be brief—very brief—moments when the therapist felt his mind meet the patient's at a nonverbal level. At such times the therapist would make some remarks that he believed were appropriate. Usually the patient did not seem to heed these remarks. One day, following such a nonverbal mind-meeting moment, the patient started a conversation with an unseen person to whom he said something to the effect that he was all by himself. The therapist thereupon commented that the state of being all by himself must at times be very distressing. Acting as if he were unaware of the therapist's comment, the patient chimed in, "Three is company, two is a crowd." The therapist said he was glad to have learned about the patient's difficulty in coping with the two-person relationship, and expressed the hope that someday the patient would be able to solve such problems. The patient's response was seemingly irrelevant. Soon after, however, with increasing consistency, the patient began to call the therapist by a nickname. This example shows that after a brief moment of mind-meeting, Ron's fear of being close to or becoming merged with the therapist necessitated his populating the room with a hallucinated person. To this third person (the hallucinated one) the patient seemed to feel freer to speak of his fear. When the alert therapist understood the patient's communication, he was rewarded by a comment that further clarified the patient's fear of closeness to the therapist. This example and similar ones illustrate that in hallucinations the therapist may find understanding of the patient's conflicts and needs at a given moment. The hallucination is useful, and there is no need to be rid of it.

Toward the middle of the subacute phase or during the

chronic phase, the voice often serves the function of a transitional object. It is the therapist's task to help the patient recognize that his hallucinations represent exactly his own thoughts. This task must be undertaken with caution, for a premature effort to remove a hallucination that serves a protective function may stir up tremendous anxiety and cause a new disorganization of ego functioning. The therapist must not be tempted to act on the patient's urgent pleas to eradicate the ego-alien, ego-dystonic, and tormenting experiences. Frieda Fromm-Reichmann is said to have often told her patients that "you may keep your voice as long as you feel you need it," or "you will give it up when you are ready." In such statements she seems to have been trying to do several things at once. While acknowledging to the patient her awareness of his conscious desire to rid himself of an unpleasant, disconcerting, and often tormenting experience, she was letting him know that he also needed it. While encouraging the patient to accept something unpleasant, she was nevertheless reassuring him that he could see an end to the unwanted experience.

CHAPTER 17

The Schizophrenic's Use of Devices or Rituals Against His Aggression and Violence

I shall confine my consideration of the vast problem of aggression and violence in schizophrenics to a study of the vicissitudes of the defensive maneuvers that each patient has adopted to regulate the rate of discharge of his aggressive impulses and that, in the course of his developmental years, he has elaborated into rituals.

In the treatment of schizophrenics we do not aim directly at reducing the intensity of aggressive drives, which in schizophrenics are hypothesized as being constitutionally strong. Nor do we aim directly at making up the primary deficit in ego apparatus that involves neutralizing aggression. In general, it is more productive for us to refrain from thinking of the patient's aggression and difficulty in controlling it in terms of his constitutional endowment. In describing narcissistic rage, Kohut (1971) apparently had the same thing in mind. It does not really matter what the patient's original constitutional endowment was. The fact is that he reacts to certain situations with impetuous rage. This rage, which the patient must deal with in his treatment, has as much to do with his early life experience with the mothering person as with his original constitutional endowment. When we work with a schizophrenic we must aim at helping him, among other things, to achieve the following: On the one hand, we must help him to inhibit excessive discharge of aggression so that the therapeutic relationship with the therapist as well as with the ward staff can be maintained. Indeed, the patient's tendency to physical or verbal assault on others has often abruptly disrupted an otherwise promising therapeutic relationship. On the other hand, we must help the patient learn to discharge his aggression freely but properly, so that he can eventually become a more separated and individuated person. As we know, in his past experience with his mothering person, he was deprived of any opportunity for expressing aggression, and consequently his emotional growth was stunted.

To work toward this dual therapeutic goal is at times comparable to balancing on a tightrope. Often, we unwittingly achieve it by studying the "rituals" that the patient uses to regulate the discharge of his aggression. From this study, which is often carried on outside of consciousness, we form a vague knowledge about the patient. By applying this knowledge, we may at times succeed in encouraging him to deploy his "rituals" or drop them so that the therapeutic relationship can be comfortably maintained and the therapy profitably proceed.

What I have in mind is exemplified by the following experience of mine, years ago. Before his transfer to Chestnut Lodge, Bernard R., a young man of 27, had been admitted to several mental hospitals. The change of hospitals was invariably occasioned by his unprovoked assaults on nurses and other patients—in a couple of instances, the victims were moderately badly hurt. At Chestnut Lodge he seemed to be well oriented. But he developed a tightly-knit delusion—that he was better qualified than his uncle to run the latter's textile factory and the uncle, feeling threatened, had "framed" him as crazy and had him locked up in a mental hospital. I met with him four times a week. During each session he told me that he was not ill and pressured me to release him. When his wish was not honored, he would threaten to knock me flat. I felt he might mean it. He was tall and strong (he had lifted weights in high school) and I knew I was no match for him.

Emphatically and repeatedly I told him that it did not seem fair for a person of his size to tussle with me, who was much smaller than he was, and suggested that he talk about his feelings rather than act on them. I learned when to take him seriously if he asked to cut the hour short. I also learned to give different answers at different times to his monotonously repetitive questions. He was the only patient who had ever made me admit that I was a mouse. Yet at other times I needled him about his bullyishness and told him that he covered up his fears by being a bully, etc. Over-all he was, I think, rather kind to me. For despite his verbal threats and assaults[1] he never did hit me. My interaction with Bernard was not premeditated. I acted on the spot and on my "instincts." Yet if I had been able to make a more conscious effort to study his "rituals," I believe we could have been more relaxed when we were together.

What I refer to as "rituals" belong to what Hartmann calls "preconscious automatized patterns." Hartmann (1956) said,

> These [patterns] are, in a way, defensive maneuvers, but hardly always defense mechanisms, in the stricter sense in which we use the word as an analytic term. I think we should say that, in these phenomena, what is not conscious avoidance is very often, though by no means always, preconscious rather than unconscious; it is kept from consciousness by that censorship which, according to Freud, works between the conscious and the preconscious mind [p. 254].

Rituals for the Sake of Social Order

In the social setting, the use of rituals to regulate the rate of discharge of our aggressive impulses is essential. Other-

---

[1] Searles (1975b) has said, "I have [elsewhere] described the violence which is done to the therapist's cherished image of himself as a lovingly dedicated physician . . . , and wish to add here the recurrent impression I have had in recent years, that those patients who tend most violently to damage one's image of oneself—those patients who most successfully make one feel malevolent and subhuman—have no need to resort to physical violence toward one" (p. 36).

wise the social order would be demolished. Schizophrenic patients, despite their grave distress, still try their utmost to uphold the social code. Thus, most of the time, they use rituals to inhibit the discharge of their aggressive drives. But at other times, compelled by their internal needs, they tend to disregard rituals.

In our dealings with the schizophrenic patient, if we note that he resorts to various rituals to inhibit the discharge of aggression, we must respect his need for social order and must not attempt an untimely removal of his rituals. For an untimely removal—by which I mean wittingly or unwittingly denying the patient full use of his rituals—may bring about disaster. For instance, Bernard R., the patient mentioned earlier in this chapter, had adopted a ritual of rapidly pacing the floor when he became agitated. After some pacing he invariably ended up in front of the nursing office door, tapped on it, and asked for cigarettes. He did not need to be given a cigarette, but needed someone to talk to. Obviously, he was at the end of his ritual and was in a mood to be "friendly," or at least to be with people again. However, occasionally he did interrupt a meeting behind the door. Then some staff member would say to him in an impatient tone, "Bernard, wait." Quite predictably, within 15 minutes Bernard had broken some furniture or had challenged some staff member to a fight or, on rare occasions, actually struck out at someone.

The catatonic position a patient may assume is his ritual. It should not be removed prematurely. If it is, the patient may become lost. Up to this point, the patient has had a built-in inhibitory system to regulate the discharge of his aggression. Now that his regulatory system is impaired, external forces must be applied to inhibit the discharge of his aggression. But external force can never be ideal. Under external restraint, the patient's behavior will be highly unpredictable. He will then be given a bad name, such as "a real assaultive patient." Before long he is no longer a person but an object of fear or hate. He and the community can no longer tolerate each other, and together they will work toward excluding him. Schulz's first case study (Schulz and Kilgalen, 1969, pp. 14-60) illustrates the point. Schulz's patient and the staff of the first hospital were feeding each other so much fear, rage, and hate that the patient was literally tearing the place apart. Thereupon he had to be transferred to another hospital. In the second hospital (Chestnut Lodge) the patient was allowed to re-establish his rituals, whereupon he settled down in a short time (no drugs were used). From then on the therapeutic relationship was maintained with reasonable comfort, and the patient eventually recovered.

In an effort to conform to the social code, schizophrenic patients often avoid striking out at their therapists, toward whom they develop a parental transference. Instead, they take out their dissatisfaction about their therapists on ward staff or, rarely, on other patients. Gary, who had gone into a deep catatonic state six months earlier, was now gradually emerging from it. He was still residing in the quiet room, where his therapist visited him regularly for sessions. On a particular day, he and his therapist had neither a good nor a bad session. By the time the session was to end, Gary, who was not willing to end the hour, dashed to the door and tried to prevent the therapist from leaving. Startled by the swiftness and unexpectedness of Gary's act, the therapist spoke in a frightened and insistent tone, telling Gary to let him out and that they would meet again the next day. Thereupon Gary stepped aside and let the therapist out the door. In the past, as soon as the therapist walked out of Gary's room, he would close the door behind him, leaving Gary alone in his room. But on this day, Gary would not let the door be closed. As the ward staff converged, Gary assaulted one of them. The interesting aspect of the matter was that Gary could easily have assaulted his therapist who was still right in the middle of the scene, but he did not. The explanation for this phenomenon has been well described by Jacobson (1964):

> At first the child's acquisitive strivings are of course concentrated on his mother. But as soon as he discovers that he has rivals, he begins to displace the envious hostile impulses pro-

voked by his frustrations from the mother onto these rivals. Projecting his own instinctual desires onto them, the child now wants to acquire what they possess and apparently received from the mother [p. 61].

And she continued that this displacement facilitates "the gradual fusion of good and bad maternal images into a unified 'good' but also sometimes 'bad' mother, [and] assists the development of tension tolerance and of those feelings of pleasurable anticipation which introduce the category of time and secure the establishment of lasting emotional relations with the mother, i.e., of object constancy" (p. 63).

The Structure of the Rituals

The rituals the patient uses to regulate the discharge of aggression were originally formulated out of the interaction of his constitutional givens and environmental demands. Once formulated, however, the rituals do not directly reflect drive intensity or a constitutionally defective capacity for deaggressivization. The rituals assume a life of their own. The patient will use certain rituals, often quite predictably,[2] in the presence of certain persons (i.e., certain transference figures) in certain circumstances. For instance, the patient may appear to inhibit his aggression in the presence of a person who evokes a maternal transference, or if the maternal person behaves a certain way. It is this predictability that makes treatment of the patient possible. For otherwise, expecting an explosion at any minute, we could never feel composed enough even to sit through a single session with the patient in the same room, to say nothing of making verbal interventions for curative purposes.

Because rituals assume a life of their own, they must be studied not only as to when and why they occur but also in terms of their structure. I shall make my point by the follow-

---

[2] In the acute phase of schizophrenic illness, however, the patient's ego is simply not functioning so as to make his behavior predictable.

ing clinical vignette. The patient will be called Michael M. Within 48 hours after his admission, he established himself on the ward as a person to be feared. Michael was thin, lanky, of medium build, and not at all muscular. He was 26, and had spent most of the last eight years in mental hospitals. At these hospitals, he was described as uncooperative, despite heavy medication. He did hit out at people, but only very rarely. Now, at Chestnut Lodge, he was receiving no drugs. Most of the time he sat slouched in a chair next to the stereo set, which he had turned on to the top volume. Completely immersing himself in the rock-and-roll music, he closed his eyes and wore a blissful smile. But there were moments when he paced the floor incessantly. At such times he carried himself extremely erect, walking with such rhythm that he was like a policeman on the beat. He appeared aloof, far away, and impenetrable. His eyes looked very mean and menacing. He often muttered under his breath, one of which mutterings was made out to be "Jews are most horrible." Obviously it was during these rather infrequent moments that he was feared, as he was considered potentially violent.

There was as yet no way to determine whether it was something happening on the ward or something inside Michael's mind that periodically disrupted his blissful contentment and started him pacing. It could be assumed, however, that some internal or external stimulus precipitated sudden surges of aggression in him. If this assumption is correct (it probably is, since there was a sudden change in his facial expression from blissfulness to menacing), it is of great interest that Michael did not seek a direct pathway for the discharge of his aggression. Instead, he shut himself off from new stimuli by becoming self-engrossed, tensed up, pacing like a policeman on the beat, muttering angry words to himself, etc. In going through this gamut of behavior, he seems to have moderated the rate of discharge of his aggression to such an extent that there could be peaceful coexistence between him and the people around him.

In the hospital what Michael displayed was only the be-

havior I have called rituals. He could not show us his constitutionally high level of aggression or his constitutionally
defective ego apparatus for deaggressivizing aggression.
Therapeutically, we have to deal with his rituals—how to
help him enhance their use now so as to preserve the therapeutic relationship and how to help him relax their use later
for the sake of growth. To deal with his rituals we must have
an understanding of their structure. For this we have to rely
on the history his mother gave at the time of his admission,
as well as his own story as he told it to his therapist. Michael's
mother was of Jewish extraction, and had been sent to Auschwitz at the age of 13. She survived, after having witnessed
many interned persons being tortured and after having bid-
den farewell to many of her relatives, whom she never saw
again. She had very fair hair and skin and could easily pass
as a gentile; there was no doubt that her physical attributes
had had a lot to do with her survival. Toward the end of the
war, she left the camp and lived with a Gestapo officer. Later
she escaped to Africa and received training as a nurse. After
the war, she arrived in the United States when she was not
quite 20 years old. Soon she met Mr. M. and married him.
Unable to conceive, she decided on adoption. At her insistence, the couple went to Germany and adopted a gentile infant of German extraction. The adoption agency knew that
both Mr. and Mrs. M. were Jewish, but decided to let them
have the gentile baby anyway because Mrs. M. looked so very
much like the baby's biological mother.

Mrs. M. was very much attached to the baby and was most
eager to raise him as a perfect child. By perfect, she meant
that Michael would be pleasant, courteous, dutiful, and outstanding in his scholastic work. To her, he was her own child.
She never revealed his origin to him; he found it out at the
age of 15, even though he could have been told when he was
eight. At the time of his bar mitzvah, Michael's school work
declined. He managed to graduate from high school, however,
and entered a small college. While there, he began to exper-
iment with sex and drugs. Soon he was said to have flipped

his mind. He retreated to a dark room, smoked pot all day long, and appeared to have lost his zest for life. He was repeatedly admitted to mental hospitals and placed on antipsychotic drugs. In the course of eight years there had been no basic change in his behavior.

Mrs. M. was said to have been amnesic about her past until her son was first hospitalized. After having given a "history" to the doctor who took care of Michael, her lost memory returned. She was quite upset and began to consult a psychiatrist. From the latter we learned that Mrs. M. was haunted by her devastating experience at Auschwitz; that at times she perceived Michael as one of those feared and hated Germans; that she was proud of having been able to live congenially with Michael before his illness; and that ever since Michael's first hospitalization she had had premonitions, would become suddenly very concerned about him, and would call the hospital at odd times to check on his welfare.

It seems that although Mrs. M. had repressed her traumatic experience at Auschwitz, the repression was not entirely successful. Her adoption of a German baby was dictated by her repressed wish to master the trauma. By living with the German baby, she was assured that she could indeed live with Germans without undue fear. If this was the case, we can imagine what might have been the emotional exchange between her and her son, Michael. If Michael were to display any libidinal interest, Mrs. M. would relive her experience of feeling flattered, seductive, and assured of a chance to survive on the one hand, but also the experience of self-loathing for having betrayed her relatives and friends on the other, resulting in a push-and-pull, double-bind type of message to Michael. However, if Michael were to exhibit any sign of aggression, Mrs. M. would relive her experience that life was endangered by enemies and try everything possible to inhibit its discharge, culminating in what was considered as the training of a "perfect" child. Consequently, Micahel knew less about what to do with his libidinal feelings than about what to do with his aggression. When he felt libidinally inclined, he became confused. But when he felt aggressive, he understood that he had only one job to do, which was to inhibit discharge with all his might.

Perhaps every schizophrenic patient has been taught to inhibit the discharge of aggression. But each patient will resort to his own specific device or ritual. Michael's most prominent ritual was the behavior of a policeman on the beat. He was not yet in a position to study his fantasies in depth. Perhaps at the bottom of the policeman-on-the-beat ritual, Michael was living out his mother's wish—a Gestapo officer who, despite his hatred of Jews, would not inflict harm on them, and a Gestapo officer with whom she could live without undue fear. If our postulation is correct, we can be assured that Michael as the Gestapo on duty would not seek direct discharge of aggression against the staff who were perceived as the interned Jews. On the other hand, should the staff do something drastic to remove Michael's ritual—policeman or Gestapo on the beat—Michael might strike out as he did in previous hospitals.[3]

The Effect of Therapy on Rituals

Anna Freud (1972) has beautifully depicted how one's skill in discharging aggression advances in the course of maturation-development. Along with this advance one's rituals for inhibiting or regulating aggressive discharge need to be refined. The ritual originates as a device to regulate aggressive discharge. The adoption of this device is determined by the person's constitutional endowment and the demands of his environment. Subsequently, however, the content of the rituals becomes increasingly complicated because of the person's fantasies.[4] Since the fantasies are intended to reinforce the

[3] In the next two years Michael was never assaultive. In the meantime, his condition improved so drastically without drugs that he held a regular job on the hospital grounds.

[4] Here I use "fantasies" to include delusions. As for their difference, see Chapter 15.

inhibitory or regulatory effect, their contents may be of the most grotesque kind. An extreme example is a patient who assumed a catatonic posture in the belief that he would topple the whole world and kill off all mankind, including the most beloved one, if he made any voluntary movement at all. Thus, to prevent any possibility of discharge of his aggression, he froze every one of his striated muscles.

When the patient establishes a ritual, and elaborates fantasies attached to it, he tends to curtail all aggressive acts, regardless of whether they are of a self-assertive, self-preserving nature or involve hostile or murderous feelings. In the course of treatment, therefore, it is imperative that after due preparation the patient be helped to study the fantasies he uses to inhibit the discharge of aggression. Otherwise the curtailment of self-assertive acts will so restrict the separation-individuation process that he will be forever oriented toward an infantile symbiotic existence, lack instinctual gratification, and always be subject to relapses into schizophrenic illness.

In the case of Michael, the treatment was not advanced enough to demonstrate this point. I shall therefore introduce another clinical vignette for illustration. The patient will be called Matthew.

After becoming involved with a girl, Matthew became increasingly restless. As their relation evolved into a sadomasochistic one, Matthew ended in an acute confusional state for which he was hospitalized. In the hospital he was catatonic. When he gradually emerged from his confusion and catatonia, he reported how scary it was when he was psychotic, as he kept hearing reports (hallucinations) of the deaths of his parents and younger siblings; but he could do no more than report these hallucinations. Several months later, he repeatedly reported dreaming about human-eating dragons arising from Loch Ness. Initially he believed his fear was external to himself. Later he conceived the dragons as symbols of his own aggressive, murderous impulses. Beyond this recognition, he could do no more on this subject. Yet, this preliminary study of his aggressive fantasies transformed him in such a way that he was no longer apathetic and directionless.

For the next two years he was busy setting up an apartment, returning to college, etc., and did not seem to have time to be concerned about his aggressive fantasies. When he completed his college work, he suddenly felt lost. He could not decide whether to go on to postgraduate work or find himself a job. Thinking of postgraduate work, he could not decide what subject to study. Thinking of a job, he worried that he might get one in which his potentiality would be compromised. Under the stress, he envisaged the therapist as his mother, who in his opinion was never available to him when he was in need, and began to harbor hatred toward him.[5] Anticipating the therapist's vacation, he joined his family at their summer home. While there, he was further distressed by what he conceived of as his mother's lack of interest in him, and he became increasingly morose and withdrawn. During the first session after the therapist's vacation, Matthew talked about his reluctance to resume treatment. He was not able to talk more about his feelings in general or his feelings toward his therapist in particular. The next day, he reported dreadful memories of things he had done that, in his view, were intentionally murderous acts against his younger siblings. He asked to be hospitalized, for these thoughts had become unbearable and he did not know what he would do next (there were indications of self-destruction). In the hospital, even though he behaved in as confused a way as he had two and a half years before, he was quite able to talk about his fears. After a phase of rehashing his murderous wishes toward his siblings and a phase of extreme behavior toward the therapist, he calmed down. In the next several months he was gradually able to recognize how he made use of fantasies of having committed murderous acts against his siblings to dilute his rage toward the therapist, for the therapist-mother

---

[5] Hatred may be conceived as a ritual. By hating, one thinks of getting even in the future and no longer desires immediate discharge of aggression (see Pao, 1965).

must be spared and preserved from his destructiveness at all costs.[6] Following this recognition he could begin to sort out his feelings about his therapist and his mother. He came to realize that he could never reach out to his mother for she was either depressed or busy with something. To reach out to her was like reaching out to a stone wall. He recalled his envy for the neighborhood friends who had good mothers. He had often wished his mother would die so that he could be adopted by these good mothers. He noticed that he was always a follower and never seemed to have dared to want anything for himself. He felt that to reach out to get something for himself would somehow hurt his mother badly. Gradually, he recognized that his fear of hurting his mother originated in his own hatred for her. Before the recent psychotic reaction, when he could not make up his mind whether to go on to postgraduate work or find himself a job, he was concerned that someone would be hurt by his decision. Almost three years earlier, when he was attracted to the girl and wanted to marry her, he had also been frightened that someone would get hurt.

Six months after this review of his hatred, fears, and inhibitions he was able to decide that he would postpone his graduate study. He found a job to his liking and developed a steady friendship with a girl.

The Misuse of Rituals

By and large, the schizophrenic patient is more certain about how to deal with his aggression than about how to deal with his libidinal strivings. Thus, to avoid the confusion attendant on becoming libidinally attached to the object, the patient may resort to the rituals he uses to inhibit aggression. This is a common phenomenon, and has been pointed out by many clinicians. In the treatment of such a patient, it is often necessary to clarify for him what he is actually doing and for what purpose.

[6] This case further supports Jacobson's observations quoted earlier.

The patient will be called Theresa A. After leaving college in the second year, Theresa was soon found spending her time sitting in a field and watching the family horses romp around. Because of her oblivion to what was going on around her, she was hospitalized. In the hospital she liked to jerk her hand in such a way that her waist-long hair was thrown way up in the air and then gradually fell back in place—in very much the way of a horse's mane. Left alone, she often smiled and grimaced without cause. Although deeply engrossed in her own thoughts, she showed no definite evidence of hallucinations. When spoken to she was able to hold a rational conversation for a very brief time. But before long her thoughts became philosophical, abstract, and very confusing to the listener. Her lack of affect further complicated the situation. At the beginning of her treatment there were numerous occasions on which she suddenly felt hostile toward me. At such times she either talked more abstractly or clammed up. Physically she remained with me, but emotionally she was far, far away. Sometimes the reason for the hostility was determinable, at other times it was not. Two years later things had greatly improved, and she resorted less to her rituals of emotional withdrawal in the presence of her hostile feelings. Then we had the following therapeutic session, which threw some light on her misuse of the rituals she used to inhibit the discharge of aggression.

She arrived for her hour in what seemed to be a pleasant mood. In recent hours she had mentioned that she felt terribly guilty about wanting or asking for anything lest I, the therapist, be critical of her as her mother had been. On this particular day she made no reference to that issue, but started the hour by announcing that Virginia Woolf, Ruth Benedict, and other "lost" women were all alike. Without elaboration, she went on to talk about human nature, and inserted in her long, dragged-out dissertation the concepts (some of which I knew were not very correctly quoted) of many philosophers. By now I was quite lost. Gently, I asked her who the "lost women" were. She went on for a while, but whatever she said could not, from my point of view, be a definition of a "lost woman." She said, "You know. I know it but I can't make it clear to you. But you know." I asked her to be patient and to just tell me her thoughts. She tried again and said, "Like Henry James's sister, who left school, stayed home, never got married . . . never was quite like others . . . she wrote in her diary . . ." I then asked her what made her feel like talking about "lost women," Virginia Woolf, and Ruth Benedict at the same time. In her digressive talk, she finally made clear that she was reading an edited book comprising excerpts from the diaries of these persons. The question remained in my mind: Aside from having excerpts of diaries in the same book, what to her did these persons have in common, and what did she have in common with them? So I asked her. In her additional digressive talk, I heard her saying that Virginia Woolf and Ruth Benedict were very accomplished women, that Virginia Woolf believed she would be happy if she had children, that Ruth Benedict wished she could have a happier marriage, etc. At this point, I still had no definite idea of what she was talking about, so I simply summarized what she had said and asked her if she was saying that Virginia Woolf and Ruth Benedict could not have what they very much wanted to have. As I heard my own question, it suddenly occurred to me what the link might be. So I said, "There was a force or perhaps a voice in each of them which prevented them from getting what they wanted. There is this voice of your mother's in you, which you often attribute to me and which forbids you getting what you want too." Momentarily she was visibly pleased, and said very affirmatively, "Yes." When I was just about to pat myself on the back for a job well done, she continued with a definite change in her mood, "The picture on your wall, it is not properly hung." Before I could say anything she trailed off into unrelated issues.

Up to this point there had been a comradeship between us; it was now gone—as if she had deliberately cut it off. She was far away, cold, and perceptibly hostile. She seemed to have completely lost her capacity for understanding our communication. On the surface, "the voice of your mother" seemed to have upset the applecart, yet I had used the expression in previous sessions without stirring up undue emotional tumult.

In the beginning of the session, when she talked digressively, circumstantially, and sometimes even irrelevantly, I was not discouraged, for I distinctly felt a tenuous tie between us. But her abrupt dropping of the topic and her cutting me off at the crucial moment[7] were very hard to take. After I got hold of my own feelings, I told her what had happened. She was noncommittal. Thereafter, however, I was better able to discern how her demeanor changed whenever she and I shared a moment of what I would characterize as closeness. But it was still months before she was ready to acknowledge the use of her rituals to ward off her momentarily heightened libidinal attachment to me.

Theresa's way of breaking off closeness was of a mild type. Some patients, following such moments of closeness, even resort to physical violence.[8] In rare cases, the violence may be so damaging as to break up the therapeutic relationship. But most of the time the patient is hostilely attacking for a moment and then immediately trying to "make up." This latter type of interaction is what characterizes the typical schizophrenic patient's effort to move toward and away from the object at the same time.

[7] See also Bion (1959).

[8] Sullivan's description of "malignant transformation" is one example (1953, p. 214).

CHAPTER 18

The Schizophrenic's Use of Language

Psychotherapy is often described as the "talking cure." It is clear that the participants in psychotherapeutic work must talk to each other and that they must talk the same language. Unless the verbal exchange between them can be mutually understood, psychotherapeutic cure will probably be impeded. As Cameron (1944) has observed,

> Everyone who begins to work with schizophrenic persons finds himself involved sooner or later in a very baffling situation. Although both he and the patient seem to be talking about the same thing, they are repeatedly missing each other's points. . . . the schizophrenic seems to be arriving at interpretations which others cannot share, by logical methods that others cannot follow [p. 50].

The question may be raised: If the use of language by schizophrenics is so incomprehensible, can psychotherapy be helpful to them? As the work of Fromm-Reichmann, Will, Bion, Rosenfeld, and Searles (to name only a few) attests, idiosyncratic schizophrenic language does not seem to be, and in fact is definitely not, a deterrent to psychotherapy with schizophrenics.

By and large, two approaches to the schizophrenic's unique style of communication are expressed in the literature. Fromm-Reichmann (1950), for instance, believed that in treating a schizophrenic patient, the therapist should pay attention to the patient's problems in living rather than to his peculiar way of expressing himself. Bion (1956, 1959), Searles (1962), and others, however, seem to believe that psychotherapeutic work may be enhanced through an understanding of the schizophrenic's use of language. In my opinion, the two viewpoints are compatible and complementary. There is no doubt that if the therapist concerns himself mainly with the phenomenology of his schizophrenic patient's idiosyncratic use of language, he will not be able to see and help the patient as a person. But there is also no doubt that if the therapist knows the general style and purpose of the patient's language, he may be more useful to him in the treatment.

In the literature, due attention has been paid to the form of thought disorder in schizophrenia. For instance, Bleuler (1911) spoke of "autistic or dereistic thinking," Kasanin (1944) of "concrete thinking," Von Domarus (1951) of "paralogic thinking," Arieti (1974) of "paleologic thinking," Cameron (1944) of "overinclusiveness," Lidz (1973) of "egocentric overinclusiveness." Freud (1915a, 1915b) studied the form of the thoughts from the developmental point of view and concluded that schizophrenic thought disorder reflects a regression from secondary- to primary-process functioning. Searles (1962) observed that concrete thinking and abstract thinking occur in successive developmental stages, and that the proper use of abstract thinking depends on the intactness of ego boundaries. In schizophrenia, with the loss of ego boundary the proper use of abstract thinking is lost as well; the latter process he calls "desymbolization." Wynne and Singer's (1963a, 1963b) studies of the schizophrenic's acquisition of cognitive style from his mother and Lidz et al.'s (1965) study of the transmission of irrationality from the parental figures to the patient are extremely valuable contributions to an understanding of schizophrenic thought disorder.

In this chapter I shall confine myself to a few observations about the schizophrenic's use of language in the psychotherapeutic setting. It must be stressed that when we speak of the schizophrenic's use of language, we are actually referring to his communicative style during the subacute and chronic phases. During the acute phase, when the patient is in a more or less dreamlike state, he does not seem to have any control over how to *use* language. Furthermore, it is schizophrenic-III and -IV patients in whom the special schizophrenic language is almost always observable. In schizophrenic-I and -II patients, it may be only briefly observed in the early part of the subacute phase.

I shall begin my discussion with excerpts from therapeutic sessions with a schizophrenic-IV patient. I have drawn material from early sessions with the patient in order to present samples of the patient's language that had not yet been greatly influenced by therapy.

Clinical Material

I shall call the patient Ellen. Ellen was a married woman in her late 20's, the mother of a four-year-old daughter. Although there had been all the earmarks of an oncoming psychosis since she was in her mid-teens, Ellen did not become overtly psychotic until she was 20 and was contemplating marriage. From then on she had been in and out of psychiatric hospitals where her treatment consisted mainly of major tranquilizers and ECT. As her condition worsened in the course of time, she was referred to Chestnut Lodge. I first saw her on the second day after her admission, having in mind evaluating her and then obtaining a therapist for her. During the first 24 hours in the hospital, she was reported to have been assaultive and incontinent of urine. Our first meeting took place on the ward. She was a petite woman who did not live up to her fierce reputation. At the meeting with me, she was very polite and friendly. Before I had finished introducing myself to her, she said, "Won't you come in, won't you sit down," soon initiated a conversation about the weather, and asked me, "Do you want to have a cigarette?"—which she did not have. Although her speech was plain and very under-

standable, the content of it impressed me as incongruent with
the place and time. This fact, plus her vacuous look, her af-
fectless tone, and her play-acting of a gracious hostess, made
me feel that she had been sick too long for it to be worth my
while to spend an hour with her. Then I thought that in spite
of her vague and far-away look, she was still able to look into
my eyes and made an effort to relate to me. Besides, she was
not on medication, so her pathology was not covered up by
medication. (She had been repeatedly prescribed antipsychotic drugs, but on her own had repeatedly stopped using
them.) As soon as my thoughts turned toward her "assets," I
began to feel that I rather liked her and that she was quite
"reachable." Thereafter we had a good talk, during which I
discovered that she had very negative feelings about psychiatrists who, in her opinion, are specialists of electroshock
therapy. Furthermore, even though she had flatly denied her
illness and her need to be in a psychiatric hospital, she did
share with me her desire to "go backwards," which could be
decoded as meaning to leave her husband's home and go back
to live at her mother's. Momentarily she even agreed that
this desire to go backwards deserved to be looked into, but
she also expressed the thought that "it is too late" and "if I
started on this I'd never leave this place." In a case like this
it seems likely that my initial response to the patient reflected her own ambivalent feelings about becoming involved
with me, a relative stranger. Obviously, only after I had studied my own feelings could I try to understand the meaning
and purpose of her communications.

I have described Ellen's communications as if they were
easy to understand. In actuality, aside from the rigidly styl-
ized conversation in which she presented herself as a gracious
hostess, her speech was quite jumbled. That is why I used the
term "decoded." The exchange between Ellen and me about
psychiatrists, the "going backwards," etc., went something
like this: I asked her why she had to come to a psychiatric
hospital. She said, "I was confused." I tried to find out more
about that. She said, "I bought a horse. I spent too much

money." Before I said anything she continued, "Do you ride, I am pretty good at it." I told her that she wasn't quite answering me. She disregarded my statement and said, "Are you a psychiatrist? I don't care much about psychiatrists." I said that it was my understanding that she had seen quite a few psychiatrists before, that she could very well have formed some opinions about them, and that she was now trying to fit me into this category. She said, "You dress up nicely. I like your taste." I thanked her and asked what the previous psychiatrists had done to make her not care for them. After she paused for a long while (I was beginning to lose the thread of our conversation), she asked, "Do you give electroshock treatment?" I told her that I did not and said that I understood she had had many of them. She did not answer. I inquired about her feelings about ECT. Again after a long pause she said, "I don't remember. I think it was terrible." I reiterated that I did not give ECT, and added that from her past experience I could see how she would link psychiatrists and ECT and that she might not believe that I, being a psychiatrist, would not give ECT. She looked at me vaguely and did not say anything.

A little later, when I returned to the question of why she had to come to a psychiatric hospital now, she took a long glance at me and said, "You have some good things. I like your taste." I said she did seem to have an innate capacity to judge people, and I hoped she would decide to make use of me to look into the reasons that had led to her being hospitalized. At that she rose from her chair, paced the room, and ended a few feet away from me. Thoughtful but hesitant, she announced, "I want to go backwards." Immediately she started to pace again. Then, at quite a distance from me, she said, "If you are a gentleman, you should take me home." I said something to the effect that she was not very happy with her desire to go backwards, and that I might be of some use to her in the understanding of why she wanted to do so. Then I repeated aloud, but to myself, "What could she mean by 'going backwards'?" She gave me what were, I thought, rather irrelevant answers until she said, "You will take me to my mother's." I expressed my surprise that she was not asking me to help her return to her own home. As I listened to myself verbalizing my surprise, it suddenly occurred to me that that might be what she meant by going backwards. So I asked her if she considered that wanting to go to live at her mother's was going backwards. By now she had sat down again. I said that she had perhaps run into some difficulties at her own home, which in turn made her feel like taking a brief sojourn elsewhere. Her facial expression suddenly became very pained, and she said, "It is too late." I asked her what she meant; she did not answer. I then asked what difficulties she might have had with her husband to make her want to stay away from him for a while. She closed her eyes and was motionless for a few minutes. Then she seemed to want to say something but held herself back. After another pause she said, "Do I see you again?" in a tone that dismissed me on the one hand and asked me to come back on the other. I told her that that could be arranged. During the final few minutes of the interview she was reticent. After I left her I became curious about her invitation, and decided to take her on as my patient and to work with her in psychotherapy.

The above description of the communication between Ellen and me may suggest that I had a full understanding of what she had said. I did not. In fact, over 50 percent of the time I was completely baffled by the way she communicated. For instance, after a brief exchange about going to her mother's, she suddenly gave the impression of ordering me to leave. To salvage the situation, I started to say, "I sense that you wanted to send me away when we brought up . . ." (I meant to say "when we brought up the issue of going backwards and going to your mother's.") She interrupted me before I could finish the sentence, saying, "You didn't bring me up." For a minute I was forced to think in so many directions that I was temporarily speechless.

In each of her subsequent therapy sessions with me, Ellen

ritualistically started by asking, "Can I go home?" I was forced to give a variety of answers, ranging from telling her straightforwardly that she could not do so to assuring her that her problems were quite soluble and her return home could be anticipated. Regardless of what I said, she would pace and repeat the same question for the first 10 or 15 minutes (with long pauses in between); then she would give out what I conceive as information. For instance, she would say, sometimes rather nonchalantly but at other times rather emotionally, with tears in her eyes, "My husband was never around," or "My husband took away my child's affection from me," or "Order these men [nursing staff] to stay away from me—I never used to feel this way about men." After each such statement, she would pace more and become completely self-engrossed, would change the subject, or would suddenly become very nasty toward me. As much as I felt tantalized because she had stopped short of telling me more about herself, I could not do anything to change the situation. In subsequent weeks, however, she spontaneously added ideas to each statement. For instance, her husband watched TV all the time; he loved to spend his leisure time building cabinets or working in the garden; he never seemed to be aware of her presence; her children seemed to prefer to be with their father to being with her; those aides put poison in her food and had intended to excite her; etc.

Comprehension of Ellen's communication was further complicated because all her utterances were flat and emotionless. That does not mean, however, that she was unable to experience appropriate emotions. For instance, on one occasion I grew tired of listening to her barrage and said, "It's a good thing I'm thick-skinned. Otherwise it would be difficult for me to come back to see you every day after you have tried in so many ways to discourage me from coming, including striking out at me and calling me horrible names." Unexpectedly, she broke out laughing, and I could not help laughing with her.

A Motivational Account of Schizophrenic Communication

Once acquired, the capacity to use language greatly aids the child in getting others to gratify his needs and desires. The better he is in command of his language, the better he can make his needs known to others, and the more satisfaction he will derive from living. On this premise, he learns in the course of development how best to communicate his needs. In the case of Ellen, had she not learned this general principle of communication? Why did she not tell me freely and straightforwardly what was the matter with her life at home so as to make it easier for me to help her straighten out her problems there? Why did she make her language so incomprehensible that I had to spend most of my time and energy in simply figuring out what she meant?

Ellen's relatives and friends attested that she had talked "normally" before she became ill. They further attested that even in the past eight years, when Ellen was at her best she was able to talk very "normally." Does this mean that Ellen did learn the importance of clear communication, and that the unintelligibility of her language resulted from the exacerbation of her illness? I believe Ellen must have learned how important it is to make oneself clear to other persons. But to know the principle does not necessarily mean that she had learned the skill. I shall return to this point later. For now, let us consider what we mean when we say that her incomprehensible language resulted from the exacerbation of her illness.

I suggest that after the experience of extreme panic, Ellen was never again assured of a background feeling of safety. In the absence of this feeling, she could not, among other things, feel good about herself—good as a person worthy of respect and attention. (In a sense, a feeling of unworthiness was her prepsychotic self-concept; the psychosis simply made her more aware of her self-concept.) Feeling so unworthy, she experienced great anxiety in the company of other people, worrying constantly that they would find her loathsome and leave her.

To protect herself from being abandoned, she would try to establish only a tentative relationship, in which she could test the other person's intentions or interest while she herself felt free to move away from as well as toward the person. The aspect of her language[1] that gave others the impression of simultaneously revealing and hiding herself[2] exactly reflected her half-hearted commitment in her object relation. This type of object relation will obviously cause frustration in both parties, eventually resulting in a total physical or emotional withdrawal of one or the other. The prescription of ECT and of short-term treatment when long-term treatment was indicated were the manifestations of her previous therapists' withdrawal from her. I believe a patient can tolerate being given up by therapists only a few times; after that he will decide never to get involved with anyone again. By then, his chance of recovery is completely ruined.

Earlier I pointed out that, when the patient is very anxious, the processing of external reality tends to be overshadowed by the processing of inner reality (see Chapter 16). In Ellen's case, her level of anxiety was high to begin with. When she entered into a conversation, unless the topic was absolutely neutral (which could not always be the case), Ellen could not help feeling periodically overwhelmed by anxiety. (Her impaired capacity to discriminate her various emotions made her experience any emotion as anxiety.) During these moments she was not able to distinguish whether the anxiety was stimulated by the topic of the conversation or by the other person's purposeful intention to hurt her. In either case she came to perceive the other person as dangerous, and tried to get away from him or did her utmost to drive him away. She

---

[1] This type of language is incomprehensible. In making her communication incomprehensible, Ellen, like other schizophrenic patients, did not disturb sentence structure. She continued to use nouns and verbs properly in the forming of sentences, for instance. (I do not consider that uttering half a sentence is equivalent to distorting sentence structure). This phenomenon, I believe, supports Chomsky's (1965) view that as far as language is concerned, the expression of action is an irreducible anlage.

[2] See also Chapter 1 for examples of this type of communication.

might strike out. She might stop talking.[3] Or she would express her feelings in terms of images,[4] and her communication in general would become increasingly obscure, nebulous, vague, and incomprehensible.

So far I have considered Ellen's obscure language from the point of view of her need to hide herself, to test the other person, and to protect herself from being hurt by running from the other person. Yet, sitting before Ellen five times a week, 50 minutes each time, I came to realize that her language served another function besides self-protection; she also used it to vent her hostile feelings about me. For instance, during the therapeutic sessions, Ellen often returned to "how can I get out of the building," etc. Periodically I had the thought that she must suffer from poverty of thought (as described by Bleuler) until one day she prefaced the ritualized comment with, "Now, I must talk." Only then did I begin to catch on that her ritualized comment was only a thin veil for her hostility. Schizophrenic patients are extremely compliant to persons toward whom they develop a maternal transference. They continually try to give such motherlike persons whatever they want, regardless of their own feelings. (In the presence of the motherlike person, the patients probably do not consciously know how they feel.) Obviously, Ellen knew she was supposed to talk to a psychiatrist. She complied with what was expected of her. But, in complying, she felt so resentful that she produced nothing but ritualized comments.

Not clearly documented in the illustrative case of Ellen, although obvious in the long-term therapy of any schizophrenic, is the fact that what the patient does to the therapist, toward whom he has established a transference, exactly duplicates what his mother did to him. During his life with his mother he suffers severe conceptual confusion from her consistent blurring of her communications—saying what she did not mean, diffusing the meaning of what she did mean, substituting generalizations for specifics or vice versa, tangent-

---

[3] See Winnicott (1963) on not communicating and noncommunicating.
[4] See Palombo and Bruch (1964) on this topic.

ing off to a new but vaguely related topic, etc. This conceptual confusion threatens his sense of well-being and enhances the motivation to identify with her (see Anna Freud on identification with the aggressor). In the end, the patient has learned not only all the mother's communicative styles[5] but also when and how to use them to create maximum confusion in the other person.[6] In the therapeutic sessions the patient does expect something from the therapist, e.g., in the form of anxiety reduction, or special care and attention. When such expectations are not instantly fulfilled, the patient feels angry. Because of his inability to express his anger directly, he has to get back at the therapist in a subtle way, such as by confusing him.

The Formal Aspect of the Schizophrenic's Communication

So far I have considered the schizophrenic's use of unintelligible language from the point of view of the patient's motivation. Accordingly, his peculiar language is conceived as intentionally (though unconsciously) designed to establish a maximum sense of well-being, security, or love on the one hand and to vent hostility on the other. I have also mentioned that in the case of Ellen, the patient seemed to have control over what she did when she was only moderately anxious. Then she seemed to be carefully weighing and selecting her words or phrases. When her anxiety was extreme, however, e.g., after a few minutes of serious talk about her feelings toward her family members, she did not seem to have any control over the appearance of very gross language pathology. At such moments regression set in, and there was a shift from secondary-process to primary-process functioning.

---

[5] Wynne and Singer (1963a, 1963b), for instance, demonstrated that by studying the projective tests of parents they were able to distinguish those with schizophrenic offspring from normative controls with an extremely high degree of statistical significance, to match sets of parents with the proper schizophrenic offspring, and to predict the cognitive style that the patient would display on his tests.

[6] See Searles (1959) on "driving the other person crazy."

But schizophrenic thought disorder cannot quite be explained by the concept of regression from secondary-process to primary-process functioning. Take the following observation, for example. In the early phase of her treatment, Ellen and I met in one of the living rooms on the ward. Because of Ellen's tendency to walk out of the room in the middle of sessions, the entrance door of the room was bolted. The room was rather spacious and had several windows that were securely screened. During the first 8 or 10 minutes of each session, Ellen paced a great deal. As she paced, she often walked to one of the windows. She did not seem to be particularly interested in the scenery outside the window. Rather, she went through motions of trying to open the screen, which required a special key. For instance, on finding a piece of broken crayon on the floor, she picked it up, took it to the window, and attempted to open the screen with it. Failing in her effort, she paced more vigorously. Or she would tear off a piece of newspaper, roll it into a cylinder, and insert it in the keyhole. When her efforts proved futile she seemed upset, as she would pace faster. Either she would try some other article like a hairpin, paper clip, or pencil, if one happened to be available, or stop trying. Eventually she would turn to me, asking, "When can I go home?"; "Can you help me to go home?"; etc.

What I want to focus on is the way Ellen went about trying to open the screen.[7] During the act she was momentarily totally absorbed; she tore the newspaper to the proper size and adjusted the diameter of the rolled paper so as to make it fit into the keyhole. Only through trial and error did she succeed in arriving at the right size. When she used other material she was also careful in her selection of it and seemed to have a definite notion about what might serve as a substitute for a key. It seems clear to me that her trial and error and selection of articles involving critical judgment should not be conceived of as manifestations of primary-process functioning

---

[7] The symbolic meaning of the act is not considered here.

but as of secondary-process functioning. Now, if Ellen's trial and error and selection of articles are conceived of as secondary-process functioning, they are certainly not comparable in quality to the secondary-process functioning of a "normal" person of her age and perhaps not even to her own performance during her relatively better moments. Imagine the use of paper, crayons, and the like as substitutes for a key to open a window screen!

One way to conceptualize Ellen's behavior is that while there is a shift from secondary-process to primary-process functioning, there is also a regression in secondary-process functioning. For an understanding of regression of secondary-process functioning, Piaget's study of cognitive development is particularly useful. Piaget has divided cognitive development into four stages.

The first, covering the period from birth to about two years, is the sensorimotor stage. This is when the child learns to coordinate perceptual and motor functions and to build up certain elementary schemata for dealing with external objects. The parts of external objects are gradually built into wholes that are recognizable from different perspectives.

Next is the preoperational stage, which extends from the beginning of organized symbolic behavior—language in particular—until about 7-8 years. During this stage thinking is prelogical and intuitive. "When the child considers static situations, he is more likely to explain them in terms of the characteristics of their configurations at a given moment than in terms of the changes leading from one situation to another. When he does consider transformations, he assimilates them to his own actions and not as yet to reversible operations" (Inhelder and Piaget, 1958, p. 246). For instance, in the balance-scale problem, the child, using prelogical thinking, expects the scale to stay in position when he corrects a disequilibrium by hand. He may, from an intuitive feeling for symmetry, add weight on the side where it is lacking, but he may equally well add more on the overloaded side from a belief that more action leads automatically to success.

The third is the concrete operations stage, which extends from 7-8 to 11 years of age. In addition to a definite capacity for organizing integrated systems, classifying serial orders, correspondence, etc., there develops a tendency toward complete reversibility:

> ... from this point on static situations are subordinated to transformations in that every state is conceived of as the result of a transformation. For example, the subject regards each position of the balance-scale as the result of previous additions and subtractions of weight or of equalities and inequalities introduced between the weights on the two arms of the apparatus and between the distances from the center, etc. [Inhelder and Piaget, 1958, p. 248].

Yet the concrete operations consist of nothing more than a direct organization of immediately given data.

The fourth stage is characterized by formal thinking.

> The most distinctive property of formal thought is the reversal of direction between reality and possibility; instead of deriving a rudimentary type of theory from the empirical data as is done in concrete inferences, formal thought begins with a theoretical synthesis implying that certain relations are necessary and thus proceeds in the opposite direction. Hence, conclusions are rigorously deduced from premises whose truth status is regarded only as hypothetical at first; only later are they empirically verified. This type of thinking proceeds from what is possible to what is empirically real [Inhelder and Piaget, 1958, p. 251].

In accordance with Piaget's division of cognitive developmental stages, Ellen's performance in attempting to open the screens was comparable to that of a child during the preoperational or prelogical stage. Like the young children in Piaget's experiments, Ellen was able to stay with her project for a while and intuitively to pick up seemingly proper instruments (in terms of sizes and shapes that could fit into the keyhole). Yet she did not seem to have any idea how to assure herself of success or why she had failed. All in all, like a child during the preoperational stage, she had shown virtually no tendency to organize an integrated system, which a child during the concrete operations stage can do.

On the basis of Ellen's relatives' reports, we assume that Ellen had once been able to function at a higher level of cognitive development. But we do not know what level of development she had reached. My observation is that almost all schizophrenic patients had once reached the third stage of concrete operations, but that quite a few of them simply did not reach the fourth stage of formal thinking. That is because the stage of concrete operations occurs during latency, and the stage of formal thinking occurs during adolescence. Although latency is not really a stage of diminished drive activity (Sarnoff, 1976), it is a stage in which ego development permits discharge of energies in the form of studies, sports, fantasies, horseplay and teasing, etc. No matter how badly they were traumatized, most adult schizophrenics seem to have been clinically asymptomatic during latency. The absence of symptoms does not mean that an active process was not covertly operating, e.g., the person might have been overburdened by guilt feelings, unable to identify with his father, unable to enter peer relations comfortably, etc. (see Chapter 12). But it does mean that he successfully kept his conflicts in check—so successfully that he had enough energy left to develop some new skills, including the concrete operations type of thinking. With the beginning of puberty, some potential schizophrenics can master heightened instinctual drives and continue to develop cognitively, whereas others become overburdened by the new demands. Those in the latter group seem to have too little energy left for the development of formal thinking. Consequently, their cognitive development tends to be arrested at the stage of concrete operations.

From a therapeutic point of view, it is important to recognize regression on the one hand and arrest on the other. In regard to regression, it is obvious in therapy that practically, as well as theoretically, we cannot give abstract interpretations to a patient if he is not functioning at the stage of formal thinking. It is hardly conceivable that the patient can comprehend abstract interpretive comments if he is regressed and most of the time functioning at the preoperational stage. Nevertheless, inasmuch as there is always a healthy section of the patient functioning (M. Katan, 1954; Bion, 1956, 1959), we must constantly strive to make sure that our words do reach the patient. Beyond the patient's "resistance" to what we may say to him, there is always a high probability that when he is regressed to the preoperational stage he simply cannot be concerned with what is not within his immediate surroundings. Even if his regression does not go beyond the concrete level, he may still be unable to comprehend abstract ideas. In regard to arrest of cognitive development, the issue may not be of immediate psychotherapeutic relevance. But knowing the patient's highest level of cognitive development may be crucial in his long-term treatment. For instance, a patient who has attained the stage of formal thinking may be able to make use of modified psychoanalytic treatment within a year or two. But a patient whose development was completely arrested at the stage of concrete operations may need nonexploratory psychotherapy for a very long time; even then, it is questionable whether he will ever be able to make use of the psychoanalytic type of treatment. In other words, for a schizophrenic patient to benefit from modified psychoanalytic therapy, he must be able to think abstractly and make "*reality* secondary to possibility," in Piaget's term; that is, he must acquire the capacity for formal thinking. Thus, according to the classification I presented above (Chapter 2), many schizophrenic-I patients who have reached the level of formal thinking may indeed make use of psychoanalytic therapy. A few schizophrenic-II patients may be benefited by psychoanalytic therapy after long preparatory work, and practically no schizophrenic-III patients, whose cognitive development barely reached the concrete level, will be helped by psychoanalytic therapy. Unless the therapist appreciates these facts, he may soon find himself discouraged, and the patient in turn may feel so exasperated that his symptoms are aggravated.

CHAPTER 19

The Experience of Emotions in Schizophrenia

Elsewhere in this book, I have pointed out that from early on the potential schizophrenic takes pains to guard against strong feelings lest they lead to organismic distress. Consequently, he deploys layer after layer of defenses, resulting in what is conceived as ego distortion, ego deviation, or alteration of ego. This ego distortion eventually interferes with his adaptation to the object world and brings about psychosis. In this chapter, I shall try to show the effect of this protective effort on the patient's total experience of emotions. I shall begin with a clinical vignette.

Mrs. Nicole D. is now in her early 40's. At 18, in her first semester at college, she suffered her first breakdown, from which she spontaneously recovered after a year of rest at home. Although considered "recovered," she was not quite the same girl, and she continued to believe that certain delusions had been actual occurrences. For instance, she believed that in college she had gone out with and had been engaged to the son of the president of a company that was in competition with her father's. In fact, the young man had never laid eyes on her. At 21, she had a relapse while traveling with her sister in Europe. She again "recovered" in about a year without professional help. Although she was by now very odd, she did marry and bore two children. After marriage, she suffered frequent relapses. During these relapses, because her mother was no longer available to nurse her, she was sent to various hospitals. At each hospital, with the prescription of drugs, she was able to return home in a few months. From her point of view, her relapses were related to her husband's ill-treatment of her, and her going to hospitals was to get some perspective about what to do with her husband and her marriage.

When she entered our hospital this time, she was very flighty and disorganized. Although she angrily complained that her husband had been mean and overcritical, she denied that she was angry at him but considered it wise to go away from him to ponder over whether she should get a divorce. In the meantime, she dressed and behaved like a woman half her age, believing in and talking about being pursued by young male aides and young male patients. She developed a strong attachment to me. She arrived for her therapy sessions on time and showed reluctance to leave when the sessions ended. She shared her thoughts with me as best she could. Without the use of neuroleptic drugs she showed steady improvement. Four months after her admission, she was free from psychotic symptoms. But evidence of the chronicity of her illness still showed in her vacant and bland facial expression. As she emerged from her psychosis, she did not show any evidence of depression, although she seemed to lack interest and purpose. Her life style was extremely passive. She did only what was asked of her. Another four months later her interests seemed to expand; she dressed up stylishly and began to go off the grounds by herself to the hairdresser when arrangements were made for her, and to visit her family at their nearby summer home whenever her husband could arrange transportation. Then I took my month-long summer vacation, during which time she was seen by an interim therapist of her choice.

When I returned from vacation, I found that the clinical picture had changed. Although the weather was in the 90's, she wore an extra jacket. Her appearance was otherwise slovenly and unkempt. She now moved slowly and had little to say to me. Sitting before me, she stared into space and at times smiled to herself. I drew a complete blank when I tried to find out from her what had happened to her in the past four weeks. She did tell me that her smiling was related to her voices. She heard voices of her own children and her sister's. Sometimes she also saw them close by her. From the interim therapist I learned that for the first two weeks I was away she did quite well. Then suddenly she stopped going to the hairdresser and did not visit her family. Increasingly she seemed to withdraw into her shell, spending most of the day on the ward, often in bed. He attributed the change to two events: (1) Her husband's brother and his family, who had been living in Europe for the past five years, had returned to the United States for a visit, and (2) her therapist was on vacation. In other words, he believed that the change in her had been brought about by the experience of loss: the loss of her husband, as he became preoccupied with his brother's family's visit, and the loss of her therapist.

Once therapy was resumed, her reversion to her previous state was also dramatic. In the beginning she had little to say, and the hours were mainly silent. In the fourth session, she announced that she did not think she was going to get her hair done, but she would like to go home for the weekend. She did go home that weekend and returned feeling chipper. She said she was well-received by her family and was pleased to see her in-laws again in time to say good-bye to them. Two days later she said she felt like going to the hairdresser before going home for the weekend. Following the second good week-end visit at home, she reported that she had started reading newspapers and magazines again. She expressed a desire to make some friends in the hospital, but immediately contradicted herself by saying that she hoped to go home in a few months. For such a brief period of time, it did not seem worthwhile to get mixed up with people in the hospital. (This had not been her general attitude before my vacation.) Another four days later she announced, however, that she had joined the hospital drama group. In the meantime she stopped talking to voices and her facial expression became increasingly lively.

The above vignette raises many interesting issues, only a few of which I can touch on here.

Depressive Feeling and Depressive Illness

At present, the term depression is used to refer to both depressive feeling (the affective experience of despondency, sadness, worthlessness, and the like) and depressive illness (melancholia). In my studies on manic-depressive psychosis (Pao, 1968a, 1968b, 1971a, 1971b), I have noted that in order to clarify theoretical concepts, it is preferable to distinguish between depressive feelings and depressive illness. Depressive feeling refers to the *normal* human affective response to a loss. In rudimentary form, it registers on the mind very early in life. As a discrete affect, however, it may become more distinctly crystallized during the rapprochement phase (a more discrete experience of normal elation probably crystallizes earlier, during the practicing phase). Depressive illness refers to a *pathological* reaction to a loss. Conceived as a disease entity, depressive illness is arbitrarily defined in terms of such observable symptoms as gross appearance of sadness, retardation in motility and thought process, and tendencies toward self-depreciation, self-castigation, and self-destructiveness. Dynamically speaking, following the loss, the patient mobilizes various defenses so that thoughts specifically related to the loss are kept out of awareness. But while the content is split off, the depressive feeling is retained. Thus, in the clinical picture of depressive illness, two broad groups of symptoms can be distinguished: One group is connected with the depressive feeling, and the other is connected with defenses and the impairment of ego-superego functions. Owing to the presence of the second group of symptoms, the patient may look sad and even feel sad, but will give irrelevant reasons for his sadness.

In speaking of reaction to a loss, we cannot ignore the person who reacts to the loss. While every "normal" person will react to a loss with depressive feelings, only in certain cases will the interaction of constitutional and enviromental factors culminate in a depressive illness. When a depressive illness is precipitated, the clinical picture is still shaped by the person behind it. Thus, in the case of manic-depressives, despite the underlying clinical picture during the phase of melancholia (despondency, retardation, self-depreciation, etc.), the symptoms vary considerably from patient to patient.

Since a distinct depressive feeling crystallizes during the rapprochement period and the formulation of a depressive illness depends on a clearer id-ego-superego delineation, and since the schizophrenic diathesis occurs before or during the early symbiotic phase while the id and ego are still undifferentiated, the question arises: Does a schizophrenic patient experience depressive feeling and can he suffer from a depressive illness?

Clinical observation bears witness that all schizophrenics can experience depressive feeling. Bleuler (1911) said most emphatically: *". . . there can be no doubt at all that the psyche's capacity to produce affects has not disappeared in schizophrenia"* (p. 47). It does seem that the arrest of ego development can never be so severe that the potential schizophrenic does not acquire the capacity to differentiate such a fundamental human affect as depressive feeling. On the other hand, the arrest of ego development and the accompanying ego alteration can seriously interfere with the potential schizophrenic's capacity to tolerate conscious depressive feelings, so that he will mobilize various defenses to exclude depressive feelings from consciousness. (This effort to ward off affects will be redoubled following the break with reality.) Thus Nicole, although clinically low-keyed and showing disturbed ego functioning, was herself not conscious of her depressive feeling.

If we use the clinical picture of subjective despondency, retardation in motility and thought processes, self-depreciation, and self-destructiveness as criteria for the diagnosis of a depressive illness, then we would say that Nicole reacted strongly to a loss but, strictly speaking, her reaction was not exactly a depressive illness. Does that mean that schizophrenic patients are not capable of having depressive illness? Facts do not bear out such an assumption. Jacobson (1971), for instance, has painstakingly described depressive illness in schizophrenia and has outlined the descriptive, dynamic, and structural differences between depression in schizophrenia and in manic-depressive illness.

As I have described earlier (see Chapter 2), the term schizophrenia comprises four subgroups: schizophrenia I, II, III, and IV. A patient like Nicole (orginally a schizophrenic-II, now a schizophrenic-IV) showed her reaction to a loss in low-keyedness but was not aware of her sad feeling. The reactions of other patients to a loss can be quite different. Rhona (a schizophrenic-I), for instance, became overtly psychotic after being jilted by her boyfriend but also showed symptoms that led her referring physician to diagnose her as a schizophrenic, schizoaffective type. Virgil (a schizophrenic-III) at 13 began to withdraw from his peers and to spend most of the day with his cancer-striken grandfather watching TV. When the grandfather died some two years later, Virgil was very much affected. He stayed in a room with the shade down for three days and refused to attend the funeral. During this time everybody was too busy to pay any attention to how he felt or looked. When he emerged from his room, he looked disheveled and confused. At first he denied that his grandfather was dead and then claimed that his grandfather had been poisoned. By then, outwardly, he showed no signs of depressive feelings or a depressive illness.

From similar clinical observations, it seems possible to draw the following conclusions: The reaction to loss in a schizophrenic-I may resemble that of a manic-depressive, so that the reaction takes on the characteristics of a depressive illness; the reaction to loss in a schizophrenic-III bears no resemblance to a depressive illness; and the reaction of a schizophrenic-II lies in between. The wide range of clinical manifestations among the subgroups seems to reflect a different degree of maturation-development of the ego. The more advanced the ego, the more the patient will react to the loss in the form of a depressive illness.

At this point, I shall briefly review Resch's (1976) findings on babies separating from their mothers in the nursery setting. From the data accumulated by direct observation, Resch found that the separation reaction can be distinguished into five groups according to the age of the child.

1. Preconditions of separating. In the early months of the first year, separation is developmentally not at issue. The separation is not cognitively or emotionally registered or anticipated.

2. The emergence of behavior focused on the mother's departure. In the latter part of the first year, the baby clearly distinguishes the mother from the familiar caregiver and is also able to track the mother's movements to her disappearance. With the acquisition of this capacity, the infant now connects a specific affect, distress, with the mother's disappearance.

3. The emergence of variable distress behaviors. Beginning in the early part of the second year, two separate forms of distress are observed: immediate distress at the mother's departure (e.g., crying) and diffuse distress that continues after her departure (e.g., low-keyedness and disturbances in performance levels). The caregiver's intervention is immediately effective in ending vocal distress at the mother's departure, but her intervention in diffuse distress does not have the same effectiveness. In this stage, a shift is taking place from the perception of the mother's departure as an immediate event to the understanding that in her absence she exists in other space (unseen and not in the toddler's here and now) and through time.

4. The emergence of prolonged focal distress. Toward the end of the second year, the toddler rather suddenly, for a period of a few months, begins to have prolonged periods of difficulty in initially engaging in play or in engaging in grat-

ifying relations with other children and caregivers. Obviously, intense feelings can be experienced focally through time only when perceptual-cognitive development permits the toddler an increasingly differentiated understanding of the movements of persons outside immediately observable space and time.

5. The emergence of structured child-generated modulations of separation behavior. Around the beginning of the third year, dramatic developments in language, thoughts, symbol representations, and fantasy take place. In the separation situation, the toddler is able to use fantasies and play to generate devices to modulate his distress.

Resch's observations are of interest in the present context. Obviously, the more the child approaches the rapprochement stage, and the more his perceptual-cognitive-affective development advances, the more definite is prolonged focal distress (stage 4), which begins to resemble the adult's depressive illness. In the case of Rhona, her original ego distortion might have been mild enough to permit an almost "normal" perceptual-cognitive-affective development; later in life, therefore, her reaction to loss resembled the clinical picture of melancholia. In the case of Nicole, her original ego distortion was severe enough to interfere with a "normal" perceptual-cognitive-affective development. Her reaction to loss, therefore, resembled the child's reaction to separation at stage 3.

Postpsychotic Depression

The descriptive term "postpsychotic depression" refers to the manifestation of a depressive state in schizophrenic patients as they emerge from the acute confusional state. As reality orientation improves and psychotic symptoms recede, the patients now become despondent and hopeless. Although still beset by the same delusions (usually they no longer hallucinate) as they were during the psychotic confusion some time earlier, the patients appear to be inconsolably unhappy.

Not aware of reasons for their depression, they nevertheless behave in a way quite consistent with their characterology. They consider the depressive experience unpleasant and tend to externalize their misery. They blame the therapist for it, and in therapy, they castigate him mercilessly and constantly; if only the therapist had been smart, compassionate, and caring, he would have made everything right for the patient. Perhaps to get even with therapists, these patients often threaten to commit suicide. One of the characteristics of this postpsychotic depression is that the patient shows no evidence of physical retardation. For this reason his suicidal ideas can appear as a real threat. But as distressing as the postpsychotic depression is to both patient and therapist, it is as a rule self-limiting.

The postpsychotic depression denotes a specific category of depressive state that can usually be observed in schizophrenic-I and -II patients but is rarely observed in schizophrenic-III and -IV patients. Because of the underlying personality structure, the depressive state in schizophrenic-III and -IV patients bears very little resemblance to that observed in manic-depressives. In the case of Nicole, who illustrates the typical depressive state of a schizophrenic-IV, she had shown only lifelessness, an extreme degree of passivity, and a lack of interest in planning for her future; there was little evidence of depressive affect, motor retardation, or self-depreciating and self-destructive ideas.

If a depressive state represents the patient's reaction to a loss, what is it that the patient loses after emerging from the acute confusional state? One suggestion is that the patient suffered a loss *before* he became acutely confused. Because the loss was sudden (as far as the patient is concerned), he could not allow himself to experience it and instead became so overwhelmed by sadness and aggressiveness that he entered an acute confusional state. On recovery, which means after he had realigned his defensive organization, he was able to allow himself to experience something other than confusion; hence the depressive affect and depressive state. This conception is certainly plausible. Klein (1975b), in fact, said the same thing, although in a quite different theoretical conceptual framework. According to Klein's formulation, the patient has sufficiently worked through his paranoid-schizoid anxiety to face up to depressive anxiety (p. 264-267).

Another suggestion is that the loss is related to narcissism. On the one hand, the patient feels narcissistically hurt at having lost his ego mastery and becoming psychotic. On the other hand, psychosis represents to him, in a way, the fulfillment of a wish for a fantasied life and allows him to escape the exigencies and hardships of real life. As far as the patient is concerned, his psychotic world is free from the restraints the real world once placed on him. Being the creator of his own psychotic world, he has control over it. Except at the moment of breaking with reality, he actually has considerable power to moderate his panic, terror, and feeling of persecution.[1] Recovery therefore means a loss of this omnipotence as well as of a relatively idyllic world.[2] This formulation is perhaps supported by Mahler's observation that the exaggeration of the toddler's depressive feelings during the rapprochement stage is related to the loss of omnipotence (in addition to his advancing development and maturation).

In the case of Nicole, as she was recovering, she remarked in passing that she was not yet ready to consider what to do about her marriage. Did this remark mean that she was once again becoming aware that she still had to consider what to do with her husband, whom she had blamed for her upset? Did it mean that she was mourning the loss of the good husband (since she was not yet sure whether he wanted her), and that after having vented her rage (through leaving him and flirting with other men) she was more capable of mourning?

---

[1] After emerging from acute psychosis, some patients report that they had assumed many personages and identities in a short space of time in order to break off terrifying thoughts. This phenomenon clearly represents what Kohut has identified as a lack of self-cohesion (as experienced by the patient) or what Bleuler called emotional lability (as observed by the physician).

[2] Patients of mine often accuse me of having deprived them of their trustworthy delusional companions.

As she was recovering she also made passing remarks that expressed her envy of her older sister, as well as of her daughter, who was going through a "teen-age rebellion" that she herself had been too timid to engage in. Does this mean that her depressive state was related to the loss of her psychotic delusion of living out the teen-age rebellion she had been deprived of? Could it be that, in dropping her delusion she had surrendered her omnipotence, a surrender that evoked a mourning process in her? These possibilities aside, the depressive state did seem to serve another function, which, as I have discussed in my studies of manic-depressive states, is to cut down stimuli from without as well as from within (e.g., through poverty and monotony of thoughts, retardation in thoughts, slowness to appreciate outside stimuli). Thus protected, the patient might then allow herself exposure to issues that she had to face in order to make an assessment and find solutions.

Affective Indifference

The four A's of Bleuler's diagnostic criteria for schizophrenia are: associational disturbance, affective disturbance, ambitendency, and autism. Among the affective disturbances, Bleuler considered emotional indifference as most characteristic. In acute and early cases, where elation, depression, or emotional lability is in the forefront, emotional indifference may be masked, although careful scrutiny will disclose its presence. As the illness advances, indifference becomes increasingly manifest and establishes itself as one of the predominant features of the illness.

Primarily concerned with diagnosis, Bleuler studied the affective disturbance from the observer's point of view. He did not ask what the patient might be experiencing behind his outward indifference. In the therapeutic situation, it may be ascertained that behind the facade of emotional detachment the patient often feels *empty* or *dead*. In milder cases (e.g., schizophrenic-I patients), the observed emotional detachment may be translated into the subjective feeling of emptiness or deadness. In more severely ill patients (schizophrenic-II, -III, and -IV patients), an emotional void is what is usually reported. For example, Nicole exhibited low-keyed behavior but experienced nothing. Her lack of emotion was consistent, even outside the transference situation. For instance, on admission, she spoke unfavorably about her husband but subjectively experienced no anger at him. Some time before my vacation, she had developed enough trust in me to begin to report in the therapy sessions events that occurred in the course of each day. The content of her reports often evoked a wide range of emotions in me, but when I questioned her she invariably claimed that she did not feel anything. For instance, after a very upsetting night in the unit where she resided, in the next therapy session she described in minute detail, though expressionless throughout, how three other patients including her roommate had carried on all night—each in his or her way—and how the other patients in the unit could not sleep and were very unhappy. As I listened, I began to feel increasingly fretful. But when I asked if she was as unhappy or perhaps as angry as the others were, she insisted that she did not feel anything. Similarly, when her plans to spend her first weekend at home were disrupted when her husband was unexpectedly sent away on a business trip, the patient acknowledged no disappointment.

The objectively observable emotional indifference and the subjective experience of feeling empty, dead, or nothing are unquestionably used for defensive purposes. Bleuler (1911) seems to have been aware of this fact in his formulation of "affect-blocking" and the "splitting off" of affect in order to avoid certain complexes (p. 355). He also said that *there can be no doubt at all that the psyche's capacity to produce affects has not disappeared in schizophrenia.* Therefore, it should be no cause for surprise to find one or the other affect still well preserved even in the severe cases" (p. 47). That Bleuler should have alluded to the possibility of a defensive use of emotional indifference may be considered weighty proof of the validity of the defense concept. For at the time he was writing he did not have available Freud's new theory of anxiety, which was formulated some 15 years later. In describing a patient's recurrent feeling of deadness, Eissler (1953b) too concluded that in order to avoid objectionable and ego-dystonic affective experience, the patient used one emotion—a feeling of deadness—to defend against another emotion (p. 207).

The objectively observable emotional indifference and the subjective experience of feeling empty, dead, or nothing represent one aspect of the schizophrenic's best possible solution. Like everyone else, the schizophrenic must process instinctual-affective and environmental stimuli. In response to these stimuli he automatically conjures up various wishes, some of which inevitably lead to frustration, rage, murderous fantasies, persecutory fears, and organismic panic. Since organismic panic is an extremely ego-dystonic experience, the patient has to exert an all-out effort to avoid it. In the course of time, he comes to rely on indifference (or feeling empty, dead, or nothing) as the best possible solution. Through this solution, he succeeds in dampening the effect of internal or external stimuli as soon as they are registered.

In the acute phase of the illness, indifference as a protective device is not yet fully developed. At such times, therefore, the schizophrenic may still show discrete moods of elation or depression, or what is generally characterized as emotional lability. Chronicity often plays a significant role in the degree of indifference, as the passage of time permits consolidation of the defensive use of indifference. The degree of early ego distortion is also a factor that determines the extent of emotional indifference. Thus indifference is more pronounced in schizophrenic-III patients than in schizophrenic-I and -II patients.

PART IV

Psychoanalytic Psychotherapy of Schizophrenia

A.

General Considerations

CHAPTER 20

The Treatment of Schizophrenic Patients— An Overview

No two schizophrenic patients are alike. It is only for the sake of presentation that I shall speak of the "treatment of schizophrenic patients." In actual practice, we must carefully evaluate each patient to see whether he should be treated in the office or in a hospital. If office treatment is decided on, we must appraise the situation to see whether supportive or insightful psychotherapy should be recommended; if and when antipsychotic drugs should be prescribed; if adjunctive therapies (group therapy, family therapy, art therapy, etc.[1]) should be incorporated into the treatment program, etc. When hospitalization is indicated, we must decide whether the patient will benefit most from a brief, an intermediate, or a relatively long period of hospitalization, etc.

In treating a schizophrenic patient, my aim is to improve his self- and object-representational world. I consider psychoanalytically oriented intensive psychotherapy the most reliable means to the attainment of that aim. I would prescribe antipsychotic drugs and recommend hospitalization to facilitate psychotherapy, but I would never use them in place

---

[1] I do not include ECT, insulin, lobotomy, or any faddish procedures that contribute only to distracting the patient from making an effort to improve his self- and object-representational world.

of psychotherapy. Antipsychotic drugs, for instance, do remove florid symptoms (e.g., terror, confusion, hallucinations),
but they do not alter the patient's self- and object-representational world. Consequently, if used alone (without simultaneous intensive psychotherapy), antipsychotic drugs will
result in a temporary remission of symptoms, but the symptoms will usually return after a period of time. In fact, drug
therapy without adequate intensive psychotherapy may have
caused the "revolving door" phenomenon that in recent years
has been one of the most serious vexations in the administra-
tion of public mental hospitals.

The term "psychoanalytically oriented intensive psychotherapy" was introduced by Fromm-Reichmann (1950). In
principle, it intends to achieve what psychoanalysis
intends—that is, to enable the patient to study and resolve
his conflicts in developmental perspective and subsequently
to change his self- and/or object-representational world. But
in terms of technique the two forms of treatment are different.
Whereas psychoanalysis relies primarily on interpretation of
transference manifestations and requires the patient to lie on
the couch and free associate, psychoanalytically oriented intensive psychotherapy allows room for parameters (Eissler,
1953a). For instance, depending on the specific needs of the
patient, therapy may dispense with the couch, free association, and, if necessary, even transference interpretations during the early part of (though rarely during the whole course
of) treatment. Because of these modifications in technique,
psychoanalytically oriented intensive psychotherapy may be
called "modified psychoanalytic treatment." Such modified
psychoanalytic treatment is at times quite supportive, but it
is not the same as supportive psychotherapy. In ordinary
usage, supportive psychotherapy does not aim at the study
and resolution of conflicts.

My rationale for using modified psychoanalytic treatment
with schizophrenic patients derives from my theoretical understanding of these patients, which I have considered in Part
III of this book. To recapitulate, I conceive the psychodyn-

amics in schizophrenic patients to be as follows: Conflicts generate panic or terror, which on the one hand results in the readoption of primitive ego functions and the use of primitive defenses (which bring out the clinical picture of regression) and on the other hand causes the loss and re-establishment of the sense of self-cohesion (which brings forth the new, pathological self). Because the organization of the pathological self causes the terror to subside, the patient tends to cling tenaciously to that pathological self, which elaborates his skewed view not only of himself but also of the object world. This state then constitutes what is called incomplete recovery, or residual symptoms. In my experience, the patient's pathological views about self and object world can be modified only if he is helped gradually to resolve his conflicts via modified psychoanalytic treatment.

In Part I of this book I said that diagnosis is a necessary preliminary for sound therapeutic planning. As the criterion for making a diagnosis of schizophrenia, I have suggested using our empathic response to the patient in our interviews with him or her. But the empathic response must be only an initial step in the process of diagnosis; for a definitive diagnosis, the interviewer's subjective feelings need to be objectified through the study of the patient's developmental records as well as the history of his illness (see Chapter 1). The emphasis on the developmental record leads to a natural way of dividing schizophrenia into subgroups I, II, III, and IV (see Chapter 2). I have already mentioned that different subgroups call for different treatment plans. In this chapter I shall discuss in broad terms what treatment can be recommended for schizophrenics-I, -II, -III, and -IV.

In early infancy, schizophrenic patients developed an ultrasensitivity to not disturbing the tranquility of their mothering persons, and later on any significant persons in their lives. This tendency leads eventually not only to hiding from others but also to complete unawareness of their own internal distress. Thus, except for a small number of schizophrenic-I patients (rarely a schizophrenic-II) who at the inception of the illness actively seek help from others, schizophrenic patients are quite oblivious to their need for help. Or, if they are dimly aware of such a need, they try to hide it from others. Only when disturbing symptoms (irrationality, violence, bizarreness) later break out are they taken to a psychiatrist's office. Because of the tendency to hide internal distress from themselves and others, the less sick the patient, the noisier the symptoms. For example, the symptoms of schizophrenic-I patients are often very flamboyant (e.g., suicide attempts, brushes with the law, acute breaks with reality), whereas the symptoms of schizophrenic-III patients are relatively silent (e.g., gradual withdrawal, slow onset of thought disorder).

For the small number of schizophrenic-I patients who ask for help on their own, office treatment may suffice to help them to stave off psychotic breaks. With such a patient, after a relatively brief period of preparation, psychoanalytic treatment can quite often be considered. In the early phase of treatment, however, I introduce parameters. For instance, before I am sure that the patient can tolerate certain degrees of separation, I prefer to talk to him in a face-to-face position. I keep my interpretations at a level that seems not too abstract for the patient. As much as I try to think a step ahead of the patient, I am always a step behind him. I see to it that he understands whatever we talk about. If possible, I refrain from pointing out his pattern of interaction with me until we have had an opportunity to establish beyond doubt that that pattern is as active with others as it is with me. I try not to be too eager to "find out" material that would only gratify my intellectual curiosity. Sometimes I assume an active position (short of giving direct instructions) to change the direction of the patient's pursuit of a bad goal; I do not simply pray that he will try to "understand" before he takes action. For, in my view, while pursuit of a bad goal may mean a detour in the treatment of a neurotic patient, it may mean disaster for a schizophrenic-I patient.

Once I commit myself to working with a schizophrenic-I patient who has sought help on his own, in intensive psychoanalytically oriented psychotherapy in the office setting, and once I am certain that the patient can indeed work out his conflicts via this treatment modality, I am very cautious about prescribing psychotropic drugs, lithium, or other chemical compounds, efficacious though some of these drugs are in the removal of symptoms. Prescribing antipsychotic drugs to such a patient whenever symptoms arise may temporarily give him some relief but may inadvertently distract him from the goal of resolving his conflicts and make subsequent modification of his personality that much more difficult.

As I mentioned earlier, only a few schizophrenic patients seek treatment on their own. Most schizophrenic-I, -II, and -III patients have to be taken to see a psychiatrist because of their symptoms. While symptoms themselves may not reflect the severity of the illness, they do influence the immediate treatment planning; for instance, in the case of schizophrenic-I or -II patients who are taken to a psychiatrist because of very flamboyant symptoms. Confronted with a patient who has just attempted suicide or has just run afoul of the law, the psychiatrist cannot help making a treatment plan that does not consist of regular office visits—even though the patient now appears perfectly "rational" and promises not to repeat his action. Or if during the first interview the patient is very confused, actively hallucinating and delusional, or in an acute panic, the psychiatrist must contemplate admitting him to a hospital. That is to say, regardless of the severity of the illness, certain symptoms make the psychiatrist automatically decide that the patient should begin his treatment in a hospital.

Sometimes the symptoms of schizophrenic-I and -II patients are less severe than those mentioned above. The patient may only feel very anxious, frightened, or depressed, and very eager to have the symptoms removed rather than work out his problems. For such patients, modified psychoanalytic treatment is probably out of the question. In these circumstances the psychiatrist is faced with the issue of prescribing drugs, in the hope that some reduction of the patient's anxiety will enable him to work on his problems in the office setting. Drugs can be very useful in suppressing the symptoms of a schizophrenic-I or -II patient—especially if he shows a panic reaction. But since the suppression of symptoms may distract the patient from wanting to work out his problems, I , as the psychiatrist, would prefer admitting him to a hospital for observation before formulating a definitive plan. In my view, the whole future of the patient (in a sense, the prognosis of his illness) is determined at this very first contact with the psychiatrist.

Paradoxically, in his first meeting with schizophrenic-III patients, the psychiatrist may be in more doubt about the need for hospitalization. Because their symptoms are usually of the withdrawn and quiet type and because of their need to defer to authority, schizophrenic-III patients can often be treated in the office for quite some time, especially when they are kept on medication. In the long run, however, keeping such patients in office treatment is not practical. For as long as they form no relation with the therapist, no therapeutic result will occur. On the other hand, whenever their feelings about the therapist are positive, they instantly feel anxious and torn apart because of their loyalty to their mothers. At such times they probably intend to get away from the psychiatrist. They carry out this intention not by running away physically, but by becoming regressively withdrawn. Eventually, hospitalization may become inevitable. In my view, therefore, even if there is no urgent reason to hospitalize schizophrenic-III patients during the first meeting, the psychiatrist is wise to consider hospital care for them from the very start—as long as he hopes to help them eventually change their views about their self- and object representations.

When we consider hospitalizing a schizophrenic patient, we must consider what type of hospitalization will be most appropriate for him, that is, whether it should be brief, intermediate, or long-term. According to the usual classifications, brief hospitalization lasts 3 to 6 months, intermediate hospitalization, 6 to 12 months, and long-term hospitalization, over one year. In recent years, under the influence of third-party payment, there has been pressure to shorten the duration of hospitalization to as brief a period as possible, one insurer suggesting 18 days of inpatient care for schizophrenia. I do believe that hospitalization is an artificial setup and that no patient should be unnecessarily kept there; I also deplore the once prevalent practice of forgetting patients in state or other public institutions. But I also believe that if we use the hospital at all, we must use it so as to give the maximum benefit to each patient. It seems to me a great waste of effort to race against a statistical figure and have the patient discharged from the hospital in 18 days, only to pave the way for his return to the hospital 18 or more times later.

In my opinion, we should do away with the concept of brief, intermediate, and long-term hospitalization. The duration of hospitalization should always be open-ended, tailored to the need of the patient rather than to an arbitrarily decided-upon statistical figure. Our approach to hospitalization should be that it is first and last for the patient, and that he should stay as long as his condition requires it.

It is my observation that if, after his first hospitalization, a schizophrenic-I patient calms down on his own and remains symptom-free without medication for two or three months, if in the meantime he can talk comfortably about the events that led to the symptoms, and if he is well engaged in treatment and seems to be genuinely interested in the study of the conflicts that brought on the symptoms, then he can certainly be released from the hospital within six months. His hospitalization may be even shorter if he can continue to see the same psychiatrist he sees in the hospital. If, however, discharge is to be followed by a change of psychiatrists or a move to a new city, it may have to be slightly deferred. Regardless of a surface rationality, the schizophrenic patient is fearful of establishing relations with strangers. Thus, if he has to change psychiatrists, special preparatory work must be done with him, which requires time. When a schizophrenic-I patient must be prescribed drugs before he can become free of symptoms, his stay in the hospital is likely to be very much length-ened. The drug could be discontinued before his discharge, and if it is, the length of time needed to place him on and take him off the drug has to be added to the time in the hospital required for a schizophrenic-I patient who has not been prescribed drugs. For a schizophrenic-I patient who, let us assume, is similar to the above two but was not well pre-pared for modified psychoanalytic treatment, was probably released too early the first time he was hospitalized, and who has by now been in and out of hospitals three or four times in a period of one or two years, we must not think of his present hospitalization as if it were his first admission. We must take into account the protracted course his illness has taken, a factor that necessitates a longer stay in the hospital this time.

The recommendation for hospitalizing a schizophrenic-II patient may be very similar to that for a schizophrenic-I pa-tient, although a schizophrenic-II patient generally requires a longer period to become engaged in modified psychoanalytic treatment. In planning treatment for a schizophrenic-II pa-tient, it may also be necessary to study and improve his re-lations with family members.

With occasional exceptions, all schizophrenic-III patients, it seems to me, require hospitalization for a long time. Be-cause of the strength of their ties to family members (inter-nalized as well as realistic), they may be unable to establish a durable therapeutic relation unless they are removed from the family: Close proximity to the family would overwhelm them with feelings of betrayal of loyalty. In planning the treatment of a schizophrenic-III patient, family therapy must be kept in mind. Unless the family member to whom the pa-tient is tied shows genuine interest in modifying his or her relations with the patient, the therapeutic effort with the pa-tient can be a total waste.

As defined earlier, the schizophrenic-IV subgroup is a het-erogeneous one. The schizophrenic-IV patient was originally a schizophrenic-I, -II, or -III. The schizophrenic-IV may or may not have symptoms that disturb others. He may or may not be an inmate of a psychiatric hospital. But he is characteristically preoccupied with the here and now. His past memories are inaccessible or devoid of meaning, and he does not allow himself to think of the future. He lives an aimless life in order to maintain the status quo—which sometimes means maintaining various symptoms. To others, he is merely a shell of what he was before the onset of his illness. His intelligence, inventiveness, and resourcefulness are preserved intact, but he uses them only when necessary. For instance, a 40-year-old single woman, Melissa, who had spent the last 15 years in hospitals and had shown no improvement despite the efforts of a dozen competent therapists, phoned her current therapist in distress one Saturday evening. She had been informed of an impending visit from her mother, which ostensibly had something to do with dwindling financial resources and the possibility that the patient might be removed from the hospital. The therapist had gone out without switching on a phone-answering device, and the housekeeper, a Cambodian who spoke Cambodian, French, and only a smattering of English, answered the phone. In the ensuing conversation, partly in English and partly in French, Melissa succeeded in getting the housekeeper to take a complete message, which included Melissa's name, the fact that she was a hospital patient of the therapist's, her phone number, and the wish that the therapist call her back. This event surprised the therapist not only because the patient had succeeded in getting the Cambodian housekeeper to take a complete message, but also because in his three years of working with her he had never discovered that she could speak French.

Rarely does a schizophrenic-IV patient go to a psychiatrist on his own. Exceptions are those who were originally schizophrenic-I patients and who, following a social recovery, have developed a paranoid orientation toward the world. In the course of time, as they become increasingly decompensated they may seek treatment on their own. Not infrequently, they are even treated as office patients. For instance, a 45-year-old single woman, Louise, sought treatment on her own because she had recently felt that her colleagues carried on "double talks" to confuse her and that her best friend's husband had used her stereo system to control her thoughts. Her past history revealed that during her first year in college, she had been invited by a young man to visit his family for Thanksgiving. Believing that he was going to propose to her, she became extremely panicky and developed marked ideas of reference and hallucinations. She returned home to her paternal grandmother, who had brought her up since her infancy when her mother died. After staying home for two years, her health was restored by the grandmother (obviously she made a spontaneous recovery). She returned to finish college, went on to complete a postgraduate course, and later became quite successful professionally. Yet she led a lonely existence and was always considered a strange person. Beginning at around the age of 40, she became increasingly obsessed with the idea that she could no longer bear children. From that time on she heard and talked back to voices, and soon developed symptoms that brought her to the psychiatrist's office. By now she was no longer functioning adequately at her job. Although she was aware that something was not right and was able to establish some equilibrium through regular office visits, her capacity to use exploratory therapy was very much limited.

But the majority of schizophrenic-IV patients are perhaps hospitalized patients to begin with. In the last two decades, the use of antipsychotic drugs has greatly reduced the number of patients in public hospitals from coast to coast. However, most of the patients who had been released from public hospitals on medication retain the characteristics described above. Modified psychoanalytic treatment may be attempted with certain cases—especially with those who were originally schizophrenic-I or -II patients and especially with those who, so to speak, still have some fight left in them. The latter may not totally have lost hope. In a psychotic way, they have been ritualistically and unproductively fighting with the object world. If their "fight" can be rechanneled to activities which could lead to the gratification of their needs, they may be on the way to recovery. But, at any rate, when modified psychoanalytic treatment is attempted with such patients, its duration tends to be long, even if medication is used in conjunction with it.

In the treatment of a schizophrenic-IV patient, the therapist must recognize the "fragility" of the therapeutic alliance. After building up hopes and losing them many times before, the patient is now unwilling to "expect" anything from anybody. In the therapeutic relation, he allows himself to be only minimally related to his therapist. He withdraws from the relation at the slightest narcissistic hurt, and the therapist often has to redouble his effort to pull him out of his withdrawal. For example, Claudia[2] had been in five other hospitals in the last 15 years and had received many courses of ECT and ICT. At Chestnut Lodge she was seen regularly by a woman therapist. For over a year, although she attended her sessions regularly, Claudia had never talked to her therapist. Finally, the therapist managed to engage the patient in doing some knitting together. Very gradually they began to discuss the stitches. Several months later, the therapist got the patient interested in making a sweater for herself. There was unmistakable evidence of increased closeness between the two. Then the therapist fell ill and canceled several hours in succession without warning. When she returned to work the patient declined to go to her office. When the therapist went to the ward to explain the situation, the patient said to her, in all seriousness, "I don't even know you. I never saw you before." At the time the patient made the statement she could have been so angry with the therapist that she said what she said in order to hurt. But it is also possible that, at such a moment of extreme rage, the patient, in an effort to protect the therapist from her own murderous impulses, had

2 See Chapter 25 for details about this patient.

defensively altered her perception so as actually to view the therapist as not being the same person she had known. Regardless of the motive behind Claudia's statement, the statement itself could have had a very chilling effect on the therapist's feelings about the patient. Worse yet, after the therapist "digested" her own feelings, she did not succeed in re-engaging Claudia at the previous level of relatedness until several weeks later.

In regard to families of schizophrenic-IV patients, after having gone through a great deal in the past, they do not dwell on the patient's recovery any more; often they have forgotten all about him. Now the therapeutic team must do something to revive their interest in him. Without the family's explicit encouragement of the patient to leave sickness behind and eventually leave the hospital, there is usually little hope that he will do so.

It should be evident by now that as far as hospitalization is concerned, I am not speaking of isolating the patient because he is dangerous to himself or to others. Nor am I speaking of keeping the patient briefly in the hospital to get medication started—a procedure that has resulted in the "revolving door" phenomenon. Rather, I have in mind a "good-enough holding environment," to paraphrase Winnicott, in which the patient may either work out his conflicts and make up his deficiency, or get started toward those goals.

Of course, hospital treatment programs must be tailored to the needs of the individual patient, and will vary from case to case, and from schizophrenic-I to schizophrenic-IV; but certain general principles are applicable to all cases of all categories. Basically, the program must include (1) modified psychoanalytic treatment that helps toward the resolution of the patient's conflicts; 2) optimal living conditions that will be inducive to his overcoming his "deficiency" or arrest; and (3) facilities that help family members to understand the patient's conflict and "deficiencies" so that they will work on the side of, rather than against, his progress.

1. In regard to intensive psychotherapy, it differs according to whether the patient is seen before or after his break with reality. In intensive psychotherapy, the patient must not only look at his problem, but must first of all become involved with his therapist. While both requirements may produce tension, the latter has an especially high potential for triggering the patient's most basic conflict and eliciting panic in him. When that happens, the patient may, in order to assuage his panic, seek a "best possible solution" in the form of ending the treatment at one extreme or of regressively withdrawing at the other. (It is probable that schizophrenic-I and -II patients tend to resort to the former method, and schizophrenic-III patients to the latter.) It is therefore sometimes necessary, while allowing the patient to get used to the therapist, to make a special effort not to rush him into the study of his conflicts in depth. Or, if the therapist finds it possible to do a bit of exploration, he must constantly and alertly determine the patient's moment-to-moment tolerance for tension—and he must do so more in the treatment of a schizophrenic patient than in the treatment of a neurotic patient.

Even though they have not totally broken with reality, many schizophrenic patients (more schizophrenic-III patients than schizophrenic-I patients) exhibit an off-and-on contact with the therapist. When they are "off," they do not seem to understand what the therapist does and says to them. To avoid the "offs," the therapist must rely on his empathic understanding of his patient's need and respond accordingly. If he empathically senses that the patient wants him to be quiet, then he had better be quiet. If he empathically senses that the patient wants him to talk, then he had better talk. In the latter case the content of the talk may not be important, as long as it does not cause continuous tension in the patient. In some instances the patient may even benefit from the therapist's constant comments about his own life situation. (But this must not be construed as a technique to be adopted.) What seems to be momentarily important to the patient is simply the therapist's soothing voice.

By and large, there must be a meeting of minds between patient and therapist. The therapist's empathic response of either talking or being quiet is a way of meeting with the patient's mind that is comparable to the mutual cuing between mother and infant and is the most significant aspect of the therapy. But, in the long run, the silent meeting of minds must be augmented by verbalization (often the silent meeting is merely a preparation for the verbalized meeting). Often the patient alone accomplishes a "solution" of his problems; he becomes less anxious, free of symptoms, and achieves better ego functioning. At such times he passes as socially recovered. But, since the solution is reached alone, without the benefit of a meeting of minds with the therapist through verbalization, it tends to have a highly autistic quality; that is, it is achieved with a pathological formulation of the self- and object-representational world, such as was obvious in the Schreber case.

2. On the hospital ward, any given patient spends "23 hours" with nursing personnel and other patients. In the majority of cases, the patients understand one another and are sympathetic with one another. Only rarely do they fight with one another in earnest. If a patient is disturbed and distressed, he tends to take it out on the nursing personnel, from whom he has high expectations in terms of need satisfaction and empathic understanding. After a bad session with his therapist, for instance, the patient feels very perturbed. If a nurse asks him to go to the field for a ball game, he may feel so pressured that he will strike out at someone. Even though his unfortunate act is an on-the-spot, unpremeditated response, he may be tagged as an assaultive patient. Identified as such, he may even, after a while, believe himself to be one. He will thereupon be readier to hit out—eventually to find himself completely alienated. To avoid such unfortunate and dangerous situations, the nursing personnel must be trained to deal with the patient's behavior as well as with his motivation. When Sullivan had the special ward at Sheppard and Enoch Pratt Hospital in the 1930's, he himself trained his

nursing personnel. He spent a great deal of time with them, both on and off duty, discussing the meaning of the patient's behavior. This no doubt contributed to the high incidence (91 per cent) of "social recovery" of the patients admitted to his ward (the majority of them were, however, schizophrenic-I and -II patients).

To surround the patient with understanding nursing personnel is not enough, as it tends to infantilize him. Unless he has just recently experienced an internal catastrophe, he is in tune with reality a good deal of the time in the course of a day. He needs to be kept active physically and mentally. He must be encouraged to participate in activities—one-to-one with a staff member, or in a group with other patients. The decision about what sort of activity a given patient should participate in must be made in accordance with his need at a given point. For instance, a schizophrenic-III patient may not be psychologically ready for group activities, and to a schizophrenic-I patient a one-to-one activity, on top of his therapy relation, may be overburdening.

3. Being in a hospital means different things to different patients. For the majority, hospitalization means separation from their familiar environment. Because of their tendency to respond to separation with panic, hospitalization may exacerbate their symptoms. For some, however, hospitalization may mean getting away from an environment that was too difficult to live in, or it may mean the gratification of regressive needs, so that after entering the hospital they show a conspicuous remission of symptoms. Family members often misconstrue the symptomatic worsening or remission. They must therefore be informed about the possible meaning of the patient's behavior; otherwise they may either become distrustful of the hospital for making the patient worse, or believe that the patient is really not very sick. In either case they may interfere in various ways with the patient's subsequent treatment. There are other things the family members must be familiarized with. For instance, before hospitalization, a given schizophrenic-I or schizophrenic-II patient may

not have any history of an acute break with reality. Yet, in the course of his treatment, such a break may occur. In the case of schizophrenic-I and schizophrenic-II patients, the family members should also learn why the patient might go AWOL or resort to sexual acting out. The family of a schizophrenic-III patient should learn that before the patient can overcome his fear of trust, he will seem to be "frozen." For a long time to come, the patient simply will not seem to make any "progress."

In addition to informing the family members about these matters, their special ties to the patient should also be "studied". For instance, the alcoholic mother of a schizophrenic-I patient was very competitive with the patient. She could not stand to see her daughter getting well, and kept enticing her to leave the hospital prematurely. The mother of a schizophrenic-II patient was so enraged at learning from the patient that her doctor did not seem to be upset about her homosexual interests that she instantly arranged the patient's discharge from the hospital. The mother of a schizophrenic-III patient was so tied to her son that she let him stay in the hospital only because he tried to knife her. After a year in the hospital he showed an increased attachment to his therapist, as well as some remission of symptoms. Aware of this, the mother arranged for the patient to be transferred to another hospital, from which hospital we learned that a year later the patient was once again removed and transferred to a third hospital. Examples like these are abundant. Unless the family member's own emotional ties with the patient are clarified, it is often almost impossible to insure that the patient will receive optimum care in the hospital.

Admission to a mental hospital is a tragic event in the life of a schizophrenic. First of all, it means leaving a familiar environment and entering a strange one. For schizophrenic patients separation is reacted to not with anxiety, but with organismic panic. All their lives they have guarded against the re-experiencing of organismic panic (see Chapter 14).

When separation panic is imminent (in a schizophrenic-I patient, in making the final step of the second separation-individuation; in a schizophrenic-II patient, in loosening the ties with the primary object; in a schizophrenic-III patient, in heightened instinctual drive pushes, which necessitate withdrawing from the libidinal object), the defense organization is called on to order and modulate, and symptoms result. Since symptom formation reflects a compromise or the best possible solution the ego can achieve at a given time, the severity of a patient's symptoms is largely determined by the degree of organismic panic he is experiencing at a given moment. To leave a familiar environment for a strange one tends to intensify organismic panic. Conceivably, on admission to a hospital, the best possible solution is reformulated. A schizophrenic-I patient may resort to a flight to health, whereas a schizophrenic-II or -III patient may resort to further regression.

Because admission to a hospital strongly affects the later course of a patient's hospitalization, special attention must be given to it. If the patient is able to understand what is involved in hospitalization, the referring psychiatrist should apprise him of the purpose of his hospitalization. The hospital that is to receive the patient may invite him to visit and learn about the living situation there. Thus the patient need not feel "railroaded" into the hospital when he arrives there. For many a patient who is severely ill and unable to grasp the situation, the procedure described above will have to be foregone. But even with such patients, it would be good to explain fully to them the reasons for their admission. Although on the surface they do not appear to understand what is explained to them, there is always that healthy part of them that does understand what is happening.

Separation problems aside, patients may assign special meanings to admission to a hospital. Take Mrs. N. P., a 44-year-old divorced woman. After eight years in other hospitals, she was committed to Chestnut Lodge. Immediately after her admission, she established the reputation of being a terror.

She struck out, bit, kicked, and pulled other people's hair. Eight years later, she had recovered from her illness and re-established herself in the community. One day, when our conversation brought us to the time of her admission to Chestnut Lodge, she said, "When a person is sick, he doesn't *know* what is right and what is wrong." I asked her to give me an example. She said, "I pulled the head nurse's hair—I know I shouldn't have done it but I did it anyway." I pointed out that according to what she had said, she did seem to know right from wrong. She reflected for a moment and said, "You are right, but I didn't care—I really didn't. When I was committed to a hospital, I felt that was the end of me—all of society had discarded me. As a discard, I really didn't care what I did." Later, I asked her what alternative there might have been to hospitalization. After she thought for a moment and reviewed some of the things she had done before her hospitalization, she said, "There wasn't any. If I were my husband, I would have done the same thing." Although in retrospect she felt hospitalization had been absolutely necessary, at the time it happened her feelings had been very different. This woman is not alone in her reaction to hospitalization. Many a patient, after recovery, has said the same. As much as in the healthy corner of their minds they might have realized that hospitalization was the proper thing to do, they reacted to it as the end of their lives, as being discarded by society. In the hospital, therefore, they acted irresponsibly, for they no longer cared.

Admission to a hospital is often associated with the loss of hope. As long as one has hope, one will continue to strive for better ego functioning. But when one's hope is crushed, one "gives up"; the level of ego functioning then drops drastically. When symptoms begin to appear, the patient (even a schizophrenic-III patient) hopes that the psychiatrist will be able to avert the impending organismic panic. When the psychiatrist takes care of that threat—through prescribing drugs, say—the patient's hope is enhanced. His symptoms therefore disappear. But since the conflicts that caused the threat of organismic panic continue to operate, before long the patient again senses the threat of organismic panic and symptoms again break out. In the circumstances, the original drug is useless. A change of drug renews hope. But after several such rounds, hope can no longer be spurred. If hospitalization is recommended at this point, it will be associated with hopelessness in the patient's mind. Hospitalization will therefore be followed by more marked regression or dedifferentiation of ego functioning.

By the time hospitalization is considered, the patient is already in a regressed state. Hospitalization per se further promotes regression (owing to increased hopelessness, increased separation panic, etc.). As a result, the patient does not perceive the hospital ward as such, but regressively experiences it as "his home." The nursing staff and the other patients are assigned special roles—for example, as parental figures, siblings, servants. The patient not only develops various wishful expectations of them, but works toward actualizing his wishes through them (Sandler, 1976). For this reason, each member of the nursing staff must learn how to determine the meaning of the patient's behavior on the one hand and to scrutinize his own emotional response to it on the other. To achieve this goal, frequent, regular ward staff meetings, in which staff members can candidly exchange their views (sometimes with the assistance of the administrator, who also participates), are very useful.

The duration of hospitalization varies from patient to patient. Because their previous life experiences lacked continuity, most patients (with exceptions, of course) are better off staying on one ward for the whole duration of their stay in the hospital. On each ward the composition of the patient population is better when it is heterogeneous rather than homogeneous. By heterogeneous is meant that the group contains not only patients belonging to each subcategory of schizophrenia I, II, and III (and IV as well), but also each of the subcategories of acute, subacute, and chronic; by homogeneous is meant that the group consists almost entirely of patients of a single subcategory. In a heterogeneous group, at any given moment each patient's needs will probably be different. Among themselves competition will therefore be limited. Not only will there be less chance for animosity to develop among them, but there is also the possibility that the less sick patients will help the sicker ones. In the meantime, on such a heterogeneous ward the nursing personnel will have different concerns about different patients; for some patients they will be concerned with how to allay organismic panic; for others, with how to oversee personal hygiene; for still others, with how to plan (in conjunction with the activities service) daily activities outside the ward. Thus they will avoid the monotony attendant on caring for a single type of patient making the same demands all the time. If each ward is conceived of as a "home," and the whole hospital, which is composed of several wards, conceived of as a "community," each ward will be looking after the patients who have strong regressive needs, and turn to the community to work out a more constructive life for the patients who require less attention to their regressive needs.

In treating any type of patient intensively, the therapist will not only have to have overcome his own conflicts, but also to have reasonably thoroughly studied their nature and origin. In the treatment of neurotics, the therapist, having been analyzed himself, will be better able to listen to the patient's verbal production with an evenly hovering attention or to maximize the function of his "work ego" (Olinick et al., 1973). In the treatment of schizophrenics, the therapist cannot rely on the patient's verbalization. First of all, the patient may not talk. (This is especially true of schizophrenic-III patients, but many of my schizophrenic-I patients go through a phase of mutism lasting for weeks at a stretch.) Second, even if they talk, they often talk unintelligibly, or the content of a session may not be at all connected with that of the previous session. The therapist must therefore depend not on the patient's verbal production but on his own capacity for empathically reaching his patient. One of the surest ways for the therapist to enhance his empathic capacity, as Kohut (1957) has demonstrated, is through an understanding of his own narcissistic conflicts.

To maximize the use of his empathic capacity to understand his patient, the therapist must confine his work to "analysis" only—he must seek the assistance of a colleague in the management of the patient's living conditions in the hospital, as well as in dealing with the patient's family. As early as the early 1940's, the need for a division of labor between the clinical administrator and the therapist in the treatment of the schizophrenic was recognized (Bullard, 1940; Morse and Noble, 1942; Stanton and Schwartz, 1954). The therapist's task is to encourage the patient to tell him everything that concerns him. Because the therapist has no management role, the patient may find it easier to reveal to him his innermost thoughts without the realistic fear of punishment or disapproval. The patient has had very warped relations with others in the past—he has learned that he had better keep things to himself rather than share them with any need-satisfying object lest the latter not be interested (which would hurt the patient terribly) or be punitive and disapproving (which would devastate the patient). In his relation with the therapist, it is hoped that the patient will not only acquire a sense of basic trust but will also acquaint himself with his own distorted views about himself and others so that he can try to correct them. The clinical administrator, in collaboration with the nursing staff, social service worker, and activities personnel, maps out the patient's general care. As a team, they prevent the patient from hurting others or himself. They set limits on the extent to which his dominating needs are gratified. They weigh carefully how much responsibility a given patient can assume—for instance, whether he should go to his therapy session escorted or unescorted, make his own bed, clean his own room. They also work out a schedule for the patient's diversion, exercise, work assignments, etc. In addition, they work with the family members to make sure they understand the patient's need for hospitalization and the purpose of the hospital program. They also help the family to recognize some of their obvious conflicts in relation to the patient. (For their own emotional problems, the family members are encouraged to seek private help in their own community.)

Although the clinical administrator and the therapist have different tasks and often work independently to attain their goals, they must also work together so that they will not cancel out each other's efforts. Although the therapist does not report the details of the patient's communication to the administrator, he should periodically apprise the administrator of the patient-therapist relation. The administrator should in turn inform the therapist of each major decision he makes about the patient. Contrary to the usual theoretical assumption, schizophrenic patients (I, II, III, or IV) do resort to the defense mechanism of splitting. Often they see the therapist as the good person and the administrator as the bad person, or vice versa. Accordingly, they may be nice to one and mean to the other. It is therefore unavoidable that from time to time the clinical administrator and the therapist will not see eye to eye on certain issues. They must then try to work out their differences. When they are unable to do so, they may ask a third person to listen to their differences. They must not lose sight of the fact that the division of labor is to assure the patient of the best possible care, and is not intended to create complications.

Because of the nature of schizophrenic communication (see Chapter 18), to understand the patient the therapist has to rely more on his own empathic capacity than on the patient's verbalizations. After working with a schizophrenic for a while, the therapist may become quite strained and develop various countertransference responses. As a remedy, he may require regular consultations with a senior colleague. Such an arrangement is ideal, but it is not always practical. Because the patient's communication is so meagre, it is highly probable that the therapist will talk to the consultant essentially about his own emotional response to the patient. By and large, he may find the procedure difficult, or he may develop a special kind of "transference" relation to the consultant. If the consultant is concerned only with practicalities, the therapist may feel that he is not being offered very much. If the consultant chooses to speculate about the patient's "unconscious" communication, the therapist may feel that the consultant is marvelous (even if such speculations are difficult to apply in therapeutic sessions with the patient).

An alternative to seeing one regular consultant is to meet frequently and regularly with several colleagues in a group—some senior and some junior. At such a meeting, the therapist may speak of his problems with a patient, or he may listen to a colleague's problems with his patient. In such a give-and-take situation, the therapist may feel more like a participant than like a student or recipient. If the group meets long enough, all the participants will feel quite natural and share their countertransference experiences. Therapists are not the only ones who benefit from such meetings; the clinical administrator may also benefit. For instance, at one such meeting, a participant presented his problem as clinical administrator. He said he had been pondering the pros and cons of allowing one of his administrative patients to become an outpatient. Every time he was about to make his decision the patient violated the rules and regulations in some minor way. He had, therefore, over several months, repeatedly set and reset the date for the patient's change of status. As he described his problem, his colleagues were able to point out how strange it was that only he was burdened with the problem, for this patient's therapist was being completely left out of the decision. In the follow-up discussion, the clinical administrator reported his conversation with the patient's therapist, from whom he learned that the patient was in a phase of negative transference, that the therapist had in fact tried to avoid being the target of the negative transference, and that the therapist, identifying with the patient, was as uncommunicative to the administrator as the patient was to the therapist. In this case, the group meeting not only helped the clinical administrator, it also indirectly helped the therapist.

I have said that in treating a schizophrenic patient, I aim at improving his views about himself and his object world through modified psychoanalytic treatment, and that the use of the hospital is only one means of facilitating the treatment. Thus every hospitalization should have an end point as well as a starting point. So far I have considered how to prepare the patient for admission to a hospital and how the hospital can facilitate the treatment goal. Here I shall consider when and how to end hospitalization.

As I pointed out above, if the schizophrenic-I patient has been asymptomatic without medication for some time, can talk comfortably about his illness, is engaged in treatment, and intends to continue in treatment to further his understanding of his conflicts, he may be ready to leave the hospital. (See the case illustration in Chapter 23.) Since most schizophrenic-I patients are old enough to live away from their family home, they may go to live in a halfway house or in their own apartment if that is what they wish and if their families do not object. In the latter case, some family work may have to be done. Now if the patient is moving into his own apartment, he must immediately face living alone, housekeeping, and other problems. If, on the other hand, the patient is going to a halfway house, there will be no drastic change in his life—e.g., he will still be living with a group of people, and meals will be prepared by others. However, it is likely that he too will some day want to establish an apartment of his own. Therefore both patients, long before they are ready to leave the hospital, should be taught how to keep house if they do not know how. And once they leave the hospital, both patients should be amply helped out with the problem of loneliness, etc., by group therapy or a work program.

In general, the above criteria for the release of the schizophrenic-I patient from the hospital also applies to the schizophrenic-II patient. If the schizophrenic-II patient is still a minor at the time of his discharge, certain modifications may be required in the general plan for him after he leaves the hospital. If he is to return home to the family, there may be no need for him to learn to keep house nor any immediate concern about the problem of living alone. But it may be necessary to arrange family therapy.

In the case of the schizophrenic-III patient, the condition for release from the hospital is determined more by work with the family than with the patient. The schizophrenic-III patient's many deficiencies can be overcome only over a long period of time. Since all his deficiencies cannot possibly be made up during his hospital stay, he may leave the hospital when he is no longer in distress (even if he is still on drugs) and has a reasonable degree of trust in his therapeutic team. But it is imperative that his family genuinely stand behind his treatment. Otherwise he has no chance of staying in treatment.

The criterion for releasing the schizophrenic-IV patient from the hospital and preparing him for a posthospital adjustment varies from case to case: It may be similar to that of a schizophrenic-I, -II or -III patient depending on the circumstances.

When the patient's return home involves a reunion with a spouse, special work may be required. My work with Lichtenberg (Pao and Lichtenberg, 1960, and Lichtenberg and Pao, 1960) shows that the patient's prognosis is often influenced by conflict between him and his spouse. If a reunion of a hospitalized mother with her children is involved, it may be necessary to study the patient's immediate conflicts with her children (Pao, 1960).

CHAPTER 21

Countertransference, Empathy, Verbal Intervention

Long-term psychoanalytic psychotherapy of a schizophrenic patient can be defined as a continuous interaction of the total personalities of two persons—the therapist and the patient—within the limits of social, ethical, and professional mores. The interaction involves the verbal and nonverbal behaviors as well as the conscious, preconscious, and unconscious manifestations of the two participants. In addition to engaging the patient in the interaction, the therapist is also expected to understand the patient's and his own behaviors in terms of the theoretical framework of transference and countertransference, and to use his own empathy to bring about favorable changes, through verbal interventions, in the patient's symptoms or character. To fulfill what is expected of him the therapist must study his own self in great depth—that is, through his personal analysis. Not free from conflicts of his own, the therapist's interaction with the patient is perhaps no better than the blind leading the blind. The result of their interaction could be chaos, out of which the patient would certainly not reap any benefit. While the therapist's personal analysis should reduce the impact of his infantile conflicts on the therapeutic process, it cannot supplant individual supervision by a senior colleague, who identifies and clarifies on-the-spot transference-countertransference issues so as to enable the therapist to rely on his empathy and thereby make timely and appropriate verbal interventions. It is for these reasons that at Chestnut Lodge every therapist is expected to undergo a personal analysis and is provided with opportunities to discuss his patients with senior colleagues. In this chapter, I shall consider countertransference and empathy in the therapist's formulation of verbal interventions. I shall take up transference in Chapter 22.

Freud (1910b) defined countertransference as the analyst's unconscious feelings toward the patient because of his own infantile complexes, and said that "no psycho-analyst goes further than his own complexes and internal resistances permit" (p. 145). He therefore recommended that the analyst undergo a personal analysis before treating patients by analysis. "Since Freud's time," observe Laplanche and Pontalis (1973), "the counter-transference has received increasing attention from psycho-analysts, notably because the treatment has come more and more to be understood and described as a *relationship*, but also as a result of the penetration of psycho-analysis into new fields (the analysis of children and psychotics) where reactions from the analyst may be more in demand" (p. 92). Kernberg (1965) has observed that two contrasting approaches to countertransference have evolved, the "classical" and the "totalistic." The classical approach stays close to Freud's (1910b) use of the term, and limits countertransference essentially to the analyst's unresolved conflicts. The totalistic approach defines countertransference as all the analyst's emotional responses to the patient in the treatment situation. Since the analyst cannot avoid having emotional responses, he should strive to know what they are and to make active technical use of them. Among those who advocate the totalistic approach, Kernberg lists Winnicott (1949, 1960a), Fromm-Reichmann (1950), Heimann (1950), Little (1951, 1960), Cohen (1952), Weigert (1952), and Racker (1957).

Perhaps it is not a coincidence that those whom Kernberg lists as advocating the totalistic approach (Kernberg himself included) are those who seem to have long since adopted a widening scope of indications for psychoanalysis and who have attempted analytic treatment of narcissistic personality disorders, borderlines, and even psychotic patients. As a matter of fact, in the treatment of such patients, the analyst really cannot avoid experiencing intense emotional reactions. To suppress his own emotions or to be indifferent to them would only deprive him of valuable clues to understanding his patients.

However, even in the treatment of neurotic patients the distinction between the two approaches is perhaps only one of descriptive convenience. As Kernberg notes, many analysts tend to straddle the two approaches. Moore and Fine (1967), for instance, say that "in countertransference, the analyst has displaced on to the patient attitudes and feelings derived from earlier situations in his own life. . . .One of the cardinal purposes of the analyst's own analysis . . . is to make him aware of his own conflicts and derivatives, so that they do not distort his therapeutic work with patients" (p. 22). But they hasten to add that "the analyst's continuing scrutiny of his own countertransference feelings frequently provides correct clues to the meaning of the patient's behavior, feelings, and thoughts, and may facilitate more prompt perception of the patient's unconscious" (p. 22). That is to say, no matter how countertransference is defined, countertransference feelings can and should be made use of in the therapeutic situation.

In the treatment of schizophrenics, the therapist cannot help having strong emotional responses to the patient's intense emotional tumult. Those who have worked intensively with schizophrenics have all emphasized this fact. Through a detailed, on-the-spot study of countertransference feelings, Searles (1965, 1966, 1972, 1975a) has illuminated how a therapist registers and organizes his emotional responses to his patient as well as how he uses the material in the therapeutic setting. The illustrative case I shall present is intended to show how the therapist, by studying his own experiences, can become acquainted with the conflict the patient is struggling to resolve.

The patient, Kevin G., was a schizophrenic-I. For a long time he had tried to keep his therapist at bay by using various distancing maneuvers, including numerous love affairs and the fantasy of doing only preliminary work with the current therapist and switching to another therapist at a designated date. After having repeatedly been made aware of his behavior, Kevin declared one day, in all seriousness, that he should commit himself to working out his problems with the current therapist. Two weeks after this declaration, to prove that he was serious about his commitment, Kevin broke off his relation with a fellow patient, a girl, with whom he had spent a good portion of his waking hours in the past few months. Almost instantly he was no longer his "together" self, and in less than a week he drifted into a catatonic state with a moderate concretization of thought. In the meantime, he was not overtly hostile but, in a disjointed way, kept mentioning recent phone conversations with members of his family, who, he said, were very much dissatisfied with the hospital (not the therapist). He added that since he himself wanted to continue to work with the therapist, he had tried to convince his family that the hospital with which the therapist was associated was above reproach, etc.

As these events were unfolding, the therapist at first tried to concentrate on the patient's fear of commitment, but soon found himself a bit anxious and wandering from topic to topic—from the patient's loss of the girlfriend to his marked regression, etc. A little later the therapist began to feel both helpless and annoyed: helpless because he could not stop the patient's regression, and annoyed at both the patient and his family—at the patient because his symptoms had reappeared, and at the family because it had introduced an irrelevant issue during a phone conversation with the patient at a very inappropriate time. Although experienced and adept at his work, the therapist was unaware that his preoccupation was irrational and that his therapeutic work with Kevin was being compromised.

Then, one day on the way to lunch, the therapist found himself saying to a colleague that he was much annoyed with

Kevin's family and that he wished the colleague would get together with them to straighten things out. No sooner had he verbalized his thought than he realized (even before his colleague had caught on) that he was preoccupied with Kevin's family rather than with Kevin. Later, by himself, he reviewed the whole situation and became aware that his preoccupation with Kevin's family served a need to increase distance between Kevin and himself. This distancing maneuver paralleled Kevin's effort to place his family between the therapist and himself. After having committed himself to work seriously with his therapist, Kevin must be scared. In the past his anxiety about the symbiotic pull was made tolerable by flights to relations with girls or by his entertaining the fantasy of leaving the therapist. But the commitment left him with no escape. As his anxiety mounted he had no recourse but to regress. At the regressed level, impaired ego functioning as well as deinstinctualization became marked. Now, overwhelmed by deneutralized aggression, he resorted to more primitive defense mechanisms. He denied the source of aggression in himself and projected it onto his family. As far as he was concerned, he was in alignment with and friendly to his therapist, whereas his family was hostile to the therapist. The temporary success of this defensive act led the therapist momentarily to counteridentify with the patient, feeling victimized by the patient's family as the patient was.

The therapist's review of recent therapeutic developments freed him from being a conspirator in the patient's defensive endeavor. As a result, the therapist was once again able to function as he was supposed to, that is, to observe the therapeutic situation and to articulate his observations to the patient. It must be obvious that the therapist cannot verbalize whatever he has observed, or, whenever he makes the observation. He must always be concerned with the patient's ego capacity to make use of his interpretations.

In this particular case, the unraveling of the therapist's countertransference snag appeared to be simple. With the impetus of a lunch-time conversation, the therapist was able to complete the task more or less alone. Usually more feedback from a colleague is required before the therapist can come to grips with his countertransference problems. Three other types of arrangements are available at Chestnut Lodge to facilitate feedback. (1) When the therapist feels that therapy is stagnating he may formally arrange a consultation with a senior colleague to talk about his patient. (2) If the problem cannot be clarified in a single consultation, the therapist may arrange supervision; that is, regular interviews with a colleague to talk about the patient for a period of time. (3) The last arrangement is what is generally called "small groups." The entire medical staff at Chestnut Lodge is evenly divided into several groups. Each group, which comprises six or seven doctors, meets regularly twice a week for three years or more. Since the group meets regularly and continuously, each participant soon feels free to talk about his patients and his own feelings about them. Thus, by and large, at each meeting the conversation will gravitate toward transference-countertransference issues related to a specific doctor and a specific patient. Then all members of the group make a concerted effort to help out with one another's "problems." These small groups are essentially working groups, and in the course of years, this arrangement has been found to be very valuable in identifying countertransference problems as soon as they arise.

Let us return to Kevin. After his review of recent events, the therapist was no longer feeling victimized by the patient's family and had no need to interpose Kevin's family between Kevin and himself. He felt rather free again to do what he was expected to do in therapy. The question is what he did and how he did it. In the treatment of a neurotic patient, the therapist's discovery of countertransference feelings may be readily transmittable to the patient. But in the treatment of a schizophrenic patient that is not the case. For instance, Kevin's ego was now functioning at a regressed level; he did not seem able to comprehend what he had comprehended a few weeks earlier, before he made the commitment. It is highly probable that he might not have understood the therapist at all if the therapist had told him all that was involved in the study of his own countertransference feelings.

In the case of Kevin, after the therapist's discovery of his countertransference feelings, the next few therapeutic sessions went as follow. During the first session Kevin continued in a slightly fragmented way to stress his alignment with his therapist, and mentioned repeatedly his family's dissatisfaction with the Lodge. By now, the therapist was able to discern the hostility (not fear, as before) in Kevin's remarks, but made no comment. A while later, observing Kevin's emotionally standoffish attitude, he asked Kevin if he at times felt hesitant about his commitment to the therapist. At first Kevin denied that he had any such thoughts. A few minutes later, however, he admitted that occasionally he did feel like going away from the therapist. At this point Kevin became visibly tense. The therapist commented that Kevin might be distressed by these occasional intruding thoughts. Kevin agreed, but with great hesitancy. The therapist decided not to pursue the matter further.

Kevin began the next session by announcing that he had not slept well the previous night and had woken up in a pool of sweat. His general behavior showed the effect of a sleepless night. He did not seem to be able to do the "analytic" work, as his thoughts showed evidence of concretization and he skipped from topic to topic. He expressed a belief that he might be physically ill, catching a cold or something. Halfway through the session he turned more "psychological," saying that sweating could be related to his nightmare, the content of which he had completely forgotten. The therapist connected the night terror and the conversation they had had in the previous session. This the patient agreed to. Before the session ended, the therapist briefly reviewed the conversation they had had the previous day, stressing the patient's own doubts, fears, and possibly other feelings that could have been stirred up by his commitment.

When the patient was seen the next day he was visibly

more "together." He reported that he felt better after the talk of the previous day. But he seemed instantly to have recoiled "emotionally" from the therapist. He acted a bit haughty, straightened himself up in his chair, and said that he had thought a great deal and had come to some conclusions. The therapist might be a good analyst but he was a lousy doctor. As far as Kevin was concerned, he did not need psychoanalysis but did need drugs. Therefore, the therapist was fired. The therapist responded matter-of-factly that he respected the patient's right to fire him. However, since the patient was not yet able to exercise his best judgment, he could not exercise the right to fire the therapist. The therapist would accept the firing when the patient regained his capacity for sound judgment. There was a faint smile on the patient's face but it was instantly wiped away. Now the patient climbed on the chair and tried to reach the ceiling. The chair had wheels. As it moved, the patient had a difficult time steadying himself to keep from falling. The therapist said, again matter-of-factly, that the patient did not have to fracture his bones to assuage his guilt feelings simply because of having openly expressed his hostility to the therapist and his daring act of firing him. The patient promptly climbed down from the chair. Although not sure whether the patient was responding to his comment or was himself scared when the chair moved under him, the therapist was pleased at the development of events.

However, he did not have the pleasurable feeling for long. In a split second, he saw the patient marching toward him, and felt his own physical safety momentarily threatened. As the therapist maintained outward tranquility, awaiting disaster, the patient stopped short before him and then made a 180-degree turn; his back was now to the therapist. Then and there the patient seemed frozenly "catatonic." The therapist collected his wits and said that evidently a part of the patient was trying hard to push the therapist away, and a part of him was trying to preserve his relation with the therapist. As far as the therapist was concerned, he hoped that the part of the patient that was trying to preserve their relationship would

prevail. With the relationship preserved, they could work together toward enabling the patient eventually to attain the
life goal he had striven so hard to achieve. The patient remained "catatonic," frozen at the same spot, for a long while.
Then, still with his back to the therapist, he said he had
decided to end *this session*. The therapist echoed that he respected the patient's right to end *this session*. The patient
thereupon walked out of the office.

Following a weekend, the patient arrived for his hour visibly distraught. His eyes were half closed. He moved very
slowly. Periodically he mumbled something that the therapist
was totally unable to make out. After a long time the patient
said haltingly, though in a slightly louder voice, something
like "Do you suppose. . ." and "weekend." Although unable to
grasp the full meaning of the patient's utterance, the therapist ventured that perhaps the patient was questioning the
therapist's reliability and was using the weekend interruption as proof of the therapist's unreliability. (At this point,
the therapist was thinking about the connection between the
patient's commitment, his general behavior after the commitment, and his immediate utterance during this session.
His comment was, in a way, a shot in the dark.) And he has-
tened to add that it was sound for the patient to ponder over
such an issue as the therapist's reliability, but it was not
sound to select weekend interruptions as evidence of the therapist's unreliability. The patient did not respond. The rest of
the hour was silent but calm.

From that hour on, the patient became, surprisingly, quite
verbal. His thoughts were more together and showed less evidence of concretization or fragmentation. In his verbalizations, however, there was evidence of projection-identification
or loss of self-boundaries, which seemed to be determined by
his ambivalence about the therapist. For instance, he chided
the therapist—"You are an analyst?"—as if an "analyst" were
the lowest worm in the world. He went on derisively, "How
many analysts would treat psychotic patients? You are an
elitist." After a brief pause, becoming visibly proud of himself,

he said, "For that matter, I am an elitist too." Apparently the proximity upset him. He asked, "May I have a cigarette?"— even though he lit the cigarette without waiting for the therapist to express consent. While the therapist was about to say something, the patient went on, "I am going to join some sports event. That's what you want me to do, isn't that right?" (This was not a thought the therapist was entertaining.) He immediately added, "There are just too many people telling me what to do. At twenty-five, wouldn't you like to be on your own? You're damn right you would. That is what I am going to be, to be free from anybody's influence," etc. (It is difficult to describe the way the patient uttered these remarks. They were said in quick succession. Obviously the patient was not looking for an exchange of thoughts between himself and the therapist. Therefore the therapist did not do anything.)

For the next few weeks Kevin continued to show some blurring of self-boundaries. But increasingly he appeared to be calmer, less hostile, and to have more ego capacity to make objective observations. It was then possible gradually to get across to him that his behavior of the recent past was related to his fear of commitment. And he was then able to recognize that "it makes me feel vulnerable" to be dependent on anyone. For "when you depend on someone you can be sure to lose him."

This clinical vignette is intended to illustrate that there is a difference between the treatment of a neurotic patient and that of a psychotic patient in the way in which the countertransference feelings are used. With a neurotic, the therapist can fairly promptly transmit his understanding to the patient, whereas with a psychotic, he may not be able to do so for an undetermined period of time. Because of the patient's regression and the concomitant loss of ego function, he can no longer understand what he could understand during his "normal" moments. It would be quite senseless for the therapist simply to speak his mind without considering the patient's capacity to make use of what is being said to him.

To decide when to say what to his patient, the therapist

has to rely on his capacity for empathy. Fliess (1942) defined empathy as a trial identification through which the therapist succeeds in understanding the patient. Olinick (1976) both refined and broadened the definition, asserting that "empathy is a phenomenon of two persons transacting; it entails processes both between and within each of the participants. . . . [Moreover,] the full empathic process is one that also calls on the integrative and synthetic functions of the ego. . . . only as a curtailed description may one say that empathy is a trial identification" (pp. 10-11).

During each hour, the therapist must gradually develop his empathic understanding of his patient. In the therapy of a neurotic patient who can verbalize his feelings and thoughts, what the therapist does is listen to the patient's verbalizations. From them he collates what the patient says and what he seems to be experiencing emotionally. He compares his own affective responses with the patient's speech and affects. He may say something or make some movements that in turn affect the patient in such a way that he raises or lowers his voice, slows or accelerates his speech, relaxes or becomes more tense, etc. A constant feedback system must be established between the two. Out of the back and forth reverberations (much of which is outside of consciousness) the therapist will understand the patient's predicament, and whenever appropriate will impart his knowledge to the patient. In the case of a schizophrenic who may not be able to verbalize all that occurs to him, the therapist can also expect to establish a feedback system of affective responses between the patient and himself. In this case, however, he must also make use of the patient's nonverbal behavior.

For instance, because of her assaultiveness, Ellen, a schizophrenic-IV patient, stayed behind the locked door of a quiet room most of the time. The therapeutic sessions were held in the quiet room; that is, the patient and the therapist were alone behind the locked door. One day, on the therapist's entry into the room, Ellen threw a quick glance at him and then turned to look out the window. He found a place to sit down. Since she chose to ignore him, he said nothing. Within a few minutes she began to turn her head toward him. When their eyes met, he said, "Hi." She quickly turned her head and looked out of the window again. He remained silent. She made a tapping noise on the window sill, obviously a bit nervous. Sensing that she might want to communicate with him, the therapist said, "How do you do." She nodded but said nothing, still looking out of the window. He said, "I told you yesterday I would be here [at a particular time]." She turned more toward him but said nothing; her eyes were fixed on the floor. He said, "I wish you could share with me why you are not allowed to look at me or to talk to me," emphasizing the word "allowed." She raised her eyes and met his, but instantly looked down at the floor again. He said, "It is puzzling that you should not be allowed to look at me." She began to stare at him.Instantly, she clamped her jaw tight and looked fierce. He said, "You must not try to send me away." A moment later she began to relax, and said, "When can I get out of this building?" Henceforth there were verbal exchanges, though her language was extremely obscure.

As a rule, empathic feedback loops between two persons are not established easily, although they break down easily. They can break down in the treatment of a neurotic patient, and even more so in the treatment of a schizophrenic patient. In the case of the neurotic patient, empathic exchanges between patient and therapist come to a standstill when the patient's resistance mounts. In the case of a schizophrenic patient, "resistance" in the form of to-get-together and not-to-get-together with the therapist is almost constant. Moreover, in the treatment of a schizophrenic, in contradistinction to the treatment of a neurotic, the therapist will, from time to time, experience very strong emotions in reverberation with the patient's. Such strong emotions (usually rage and hate) can diminish the therapist's capacity to use his empathy. For these reasons it is rather difficult for the therapist, as Jacobson (1967) observed, to establish an empathic understanding of a schizophrenic patient or to maintain it after it has been established.

Both empathy and totalistic countertransference involve

the therapist's affective response to the patient, and both are essential tools of the therapist in treating his patient. But they are not the same process. Totalistic countertransference feelings are often described as more intense, more conscious, and therefore more definable and identifiable than empathic feelings, which are more refined, more preconscious, more a product of the autonomous work ego, and usually not readily identifiable. In studying his countertransference feelings, the therapist may focus mainly on his own feelings, even though he knows that they were excited by someone else. Empathy, on the other hand, is the product of the back-and-forth emotional reverberations between two participants; it cannot be studied through the feelings of one participant only. Personal psychoanalysis, talking to a senior colleague, or discussions in a small group can all help the therapist immediately to identify and remove his countertransference feelings; these procedures, however, cannot really help the therapist *immediately* to improve his empathic capacity unless its impairment stemmed from countertransference feelings.

Olinick (1976) has warned that

> in the presence of empathy, the two participants are often—not always—persuaded that they work well together and belong together. This is so because empathy as a regressive experience relies on qualities of the transitional processes. . . . As factors in progressive development, the transitional processes have much that is valuable and durable. They may lead to the developing of sound relationships, reality-orientation, imaginative living and creativity. This is not so when they are fixated at a regressive level [p. 11].

In the treatment of schizophrenic patients, such a "fixation" is likely to occur. Often the therapist is persuaded that he and his patient work well together and belong together. Yet a bystander may disagree. The therapist may then have to review the situation and, if necessary, objectify his subjective experience through the help of another person (e.g., a senior colleague).

Everyone is endowed with the capacity for empathy. In the course of growth, one may or may not have furthered the development of this capacity. Thus, as Olinick (1976) puts it, "Empathy . . . is not a skill or talent possessed by everyone, though when present it can be refined and augmented" (p. 10). It is conceivable that the therapist's empathic capacity is highly refined and augmented, but is particularly in tune with only some patients and not others. In the treatment of schizophrenic patients, the therapist must especially know whether he can be empathic with the patients he works with.

In psychoanalytic treatment, interpretation is considered the ultimate tool. The analyst listens, organizes his thoughts, and waits for a propitious moment to make an interpretation that will make the patient's unconscious conflicts conscious. If the interpretation is correct and timely and, in addition, if it is properly worded, a change in the patient is to be expected: Not only will his symptoms disappear, but his personality will undergo structural changes. To make his interpretations, the analyst's work ego must be operating both consciously and unconsciously (Olinick et al., 1973), and he must be free of countertransference problems. To maximize the exactness of his interpretations, the analyst is expected to be "passive," meditative, and relatively silent. Except on occasions when he must act "humanly" (Greenson and Wexler, 1969), the analyst may say nothing to his patient except for his interpretations.

In the treatment of schizophrenic patients, the analyst may not be able to keep silent for long, as long silences are conducive to undesired regression. The silence allowed the analyst in treating a neurotic patient also allows him to confine his statements to interpretations; he does not need to make noninterpretative comments. However, when the analyst cannot maintain silence in treating a schizophrenic patient, he is forced to make noninterpretative comments. That is to say, in treating a neurotic patient the analyst can confine his verbalizations to one type—interpretation, whereas in treating a schizophrenic patient, the analyst must make two types of comment—the interpretative and the noninterpretative.

The distinction between an interpretation and a noninterpretative comment seems obvious in the above clinical material on Kevin. For instance, during the first hour after the
therapist's enlightenment about his own countertransference
feelings, his remark that Kevin might sometimes feel hesitant about his commitment was an interpretation. Two days
later, the patient declared that he wanted to fire the therapist. The therapist's refusal to be fired by the patient was
noninterpretative. If he had intended an interpretation, he
would at least have stated the patient's motivation in the
form of a question (Olinick, 1954)—"Do you want to fire me
because . . .?" But at that moment the therapist felt that the
patient was not quite "together enough" to be charged with
the burden of answering a question. However, a moment later
during the same session, the patient's psychological state
changed. The therapist accordingly tried to stop the patient's
antics on the chair not by an order, but by an interpretation.

In the treatment of patients sicker than Kevin, the noninterpretative comments may even seem like a kind of play.
Another brief clinical vignette about Ellen will illustrate this
point. She was alone in the quiet room where she and her
therapist had been meeting for some months. On this day she
seemed very self-engrossed, methodically tearing up a pile of
newspapers without showing any anger. Although she had
glanced at the therapist as he entered the room, now she
seemed to ignore him altogether. The therapist took a chair
five or six feet away from her. After a while she pushed part
of a newspaper toward him. He leafed through it while observing what she was doing. Without uttering a word, she
suddenly tore off a piece of paper and held it out in his direction. He accepted the paper, on which there was an ad for a
man's camel-hair double-breasted overcoat. He looked at the
picture and made comments about the style, material, and
color of the coat, while she remained silent and busy with her
newspaper. He suddenly recalled seeing an ad (it concerned
a woman's hat) in his pile of newspapers. He found the ad
and tore it out. He passed it to her, saying, "It should look
good on you." (He did think it would have, if it had been a

real one.) She grabbed the piece of paper from him, took a good look at it, and put it on top of her hair. (It stayed there the rest of the hour.) She continued to be busy with the newspaper. Then she suddenly asked him, "Do you want a drink?" He responded, "I don't mind," although he had no idea where she would get drinks since there were none in the room. Swiftly she dug out a small piece of paper and handed it to him. It was an ad for a certain brand of Scotch. He thanked her. Then he recalled that there was a food-store ad in the pile of papers she had pushed toward him earlier. He tore the ad out, gave it to her, and said, "Have some cheese with your drink." She thanked him. Then and there she was no longer as self-engrossed. He asked her if Scotch was her favorite kind of liquor. She said, "No." Soon they were quite engaged in talking about her family, who drank too much and who drove her crazy, etc. Some of the material was old, but some was quite new.

To reiterate, there are two types of verbal intervention: interpretation in the strict sense and noninterpretative comments. For a verbal intervention to be effective, it should be timely. In respect to interpretation in the strict sense, consideration should be given to its correctness,[1] proper wording (Loewenstein, 1957), and tactful delivery (Poland, 1975).

So far, I have described the importance of outwardly discernible therapeutic action in the form of verbal intervention, but I have not sufficiently emphasized the value of not-so-discernible therapeutic action in the form of the therapist's sorting out and mastery of the affects that are aroused in him by the patient's chaotic and intense affects. The two actions often occur together, but quite often the not-so-discernible therapeutic action is not followed by verbal intervention. Yet both actions are therapeutic.

As I pointed out earlier, "empathizing" involves establishing a continuous feedback system between the patient and

---

[1] The making and correcting of insignificant inexact interpretations cannot be avoided in the treatment of schizophrenia. Elsewhere (Pao, 1977) I have argued that they are actually helpful to the progress of treatment.

the therapist. In this process, the patient verbally or nonverbally imparts to the therapist intense chaotic affects related to his immediately experienced conflicts (e.g., anxiety, guilt, sadness). In reacting to the patient's affective tone, the listening and observing therapist experiences intense feelings, which give rise to certain nonverbal behavior. This silent behavior may, to a minute degree, alter the patient's affect. Subsequently, the patient's modified affect produces a new kind of affective reaction in the therapist. This goes on and on, until at some point the therapist becomes aware that he must take one of two courses of action: make a verbal intervention or not make a verbal intervention. In the first case the therapist gradually develops a relatively cohesive picture of what is going on. He "constructs" (Greenacre, 1975) what the patient might be going through. Then he waits for a propitious time to tell his "constructions" to the patient as tactfully as possible. From then on there will be what Greenacre (1975) calls "reconstruction" work between the patient and the therapist. In the second case the therapist continues to feel the impact of the patient's chaotic affect but feels increasingly comfortable with the feelings the patient stirs up in him. Being comfortable now, he does not want to run away from the patient in the therapeutic situation. He does not feel an urgency to do something or anything to change the atmosphere. As this happens, he witnesses a change in his patient as well, so that he begins to relax. All this time the therapist may have a "construction" that he finds himself unable to share with the patient. Or he may not be able to "construct" anything at all (his cognitive function cannot be fully used).

In the second case, the therapist does not appear to have done anything visible. Yet he is very active throughout. He receives the patient's communication, reacts to it with his own emotions, identifies himself with the patient, and finally sorts out and masters his own emotions. It is at that point that the therapist's trial identification with the patient ends. In Beres and Arlow's (1974) view, he is again separated from the patient after a period of temporary identification. The therapist's mastery of the emotions stirred up by the patient is therapeutic.[2] For when this mastery permeates the therapist's being, the patient feels it and begins to relax. As he relaxes, he also "feels" that he has mastered his intense chaotic affects. Even though in the whole process the cause of his feelings and the conflicts underlying them are still not identified, the act or the feeling of having "mastered" his emotions gives him a belief in his strength and an incentive to cope with similar affective crises. It is in this sense that the capacity to bear anxiety and depression (Zetzel, 1949, 1965) improves.

The quiet mode of therapeutic action occurs in the treatment of neurotics as well. For instance, the analyst sits through many hours of boredom, drowsiness, irritation, etc. But its importance becomes doubled in the treatment of schizophrenics because the latter are usually unable to verbalize their feelings. They simply have to live them out with their therapists. In commenting on the divergent theoretical constructs formulated by various authors (see Part II), I wondered why, despite differences in their theoretical positions, each could claim success in the outcome of treatment. Now, considering this quiet mode of therapeutic action, we can perhaps appreciate why this is so. For much that goes on in the treatment of schizophrenics really falls into the category of the quiet mode of therapeutic action. After all, the theoretical constructs of different schools can best be used in the verbal intervention.

To some extent, the quiet mode of therapeutic action described here resembles Klein's description of projective identification (1946). Klein, however, began her formulation from the patient, who in the therapeutic situation projects and then introjects, whereas I have been concerned with the action that the therapist takes in the therapeutic situation. Expanding

[2] This corresponds to what Mahler (1968) calls the "symbiotic corrective experience."

on Bion's (1968b) concept of "the therapist as the container," Langs (1976) suggests that not only is the therapist a container, he keeps what the patient puts into him, metabolizes it, and gives back to the patient what has been metabolized. In different language, Langs is describing something similar to what I have been discussing.

CHAPTER 22

Attachment, Therapeutic Alliance, Transference

In psychotherapy with schizophrenics, three kinds of doctor-patient relationships can be observed: attachment, therapeutic alliance, and transference. Attachment reflects the human tendency to be involved with one's fellow men. Despite his basic conflict in human relations—to move simultaneously toward and away from others—the schizophrenic patient, if given a chance, will form an attachment to someone. After he has become attached to the other person, the patient's relationship with that person is a transference phenomenon, as it reflects the patient's relations with important persons in the past. Therapeutic alliance denotes the joint patient-therapist effort to define the patient's problems and work toward their resolution. In this chapter, I hope to establish a therapeutically useful distinction among these three kinds of relationship.

Human beings are endowed with a tendency to form attachments to others; schizophrenics are no exception. However, the potentially schizophrenic person learned in infancy that the gratification of biological needs is accompanied by increased body tension. As far as he was concerned, the person who gave him pleasure was the person who caused him pain. In the course of time, he therefore developed an ambitendency about forming attachments to other human beings. To defend himself against attachment, he trained himself to experience intense hate toward the person who aroused in him a desire to become involved. For further defensive purposes, he may even have developed a preference for becoming attached to nonhuman objects, animate or inanimate, rather than to human beings (Searles, 1963). Yet even during his most defensive moments, such a patient may still maintain a very keen interest in becoming attached to some person in his environment. This is evidenced by such observations as that many a highly withdrawn, obviously out-of-contact catatonic or hebephrenic patient unfailingly fixes his gaze intently on a particular nurse working on the ward. If this nurse happens to have as much interest in the patient as the patient has in her, she may bring about a miraculous improvement in the patient's condition.

As stated, the patient erects all sorts of defenses to protect himself from becoming involved. One of the first tasks in psychotherapy with a schizophrenic patient is to overcome his fear of attachment. To do so the therapist must first understand the source of the patient's fear. He must also deal with the patient's defenses, including risking the patient's physical and emotional assaultiveness.

As for the fear, we have seen that the patient's early experiences have led him to develop an ambitendent way of relating to others. Subsequently, because of this ambitendency, he could rarely get his needs fully gratified. Unable to recognize that his own ambitendency was the reason for the nonfulfillment of his needs, he envisaged others as always trying to frustrate and deprive him. In the course of time his desire to get involved with others steadily diminishes. Now he begins to see others' interest in involving him as their intentional effort to lure him into frustration. To avoid disappointment, he resorts to hostile attacks on others —attitudinally, verbally, or even physically—when they try to tempt him. Since it took a long time for the patient to develop his fear of involvement, and to become resigned to expressing his fear in the form of actively repelling others, the therapist must not expect him to overcome his fear or defensive aggressiveness overnight. In therapy, the therapist must have a determination to help the patient overcome this fear, but he must exercise a great deal of patience in waiting for the patient to turn around.

Nevertheless, no matter how difficult the job of overcoming the patient's reluctance to form human attachments, it can usually be accomplished; for a part of the patient is always working on the therapist's side. In the hospital setting, this job can be greatly facilitated by the concerted effort of the whole therapeutic team. When one member makes a breakthrough, it will invariably "spill over" to other members as well. Take, for example, the case of Florette (detailed in Chapter 5). At the beginning of her treatment, the first therapist seemed to be the only person who was spared Florette's furious assaults. That was not only because of the therapist's great empathic understanding of the patient, but also because of her nonpressuring approach of sitting and waiting, which the therapeutic team let her take. Allowing the patient to maintain her "rituals" to regulate the discharge of her aggression (see Chapter 17) had a soothing effect, which in turn fortified the patient's good feelings toward the therapist.

But when the therapist was the only person the patient did not assault, she inevitably invited jealousy in those who in their dealings with the patient were constant targets of aggression. Therefore, to maintain her therapeutic approach, the therapist had to have the therapeutic team's mandate. This was arrived at through numerous meetings in which the team members exchanged and discussed their divergent observations of the patient. In the meantime, the patient had also allowed nurse A. consistently to see her as an extremely frightened person rather than as the unpredictably aggressive, threatening person she tried to make others believe she was. As this made nurse A. feel rather comfortable in approaching Florette, she succeeded in feeding Florette and in giving her baths and shampoos singlehanded. Some time later, nurse A. had further succeeded in getting the patient to accept food, help with her bath, etc., from anyone she recommended. All the time that the patient singled out nurse A. as favored, she was the most envied person. But the envy never got out of control, for each member of the team accepted that while nurse A. was favored by Florette, he or she was being favored by some other patient. Besides, when Florette was discussed in group meetings, the team soon learned that nurse A.'s success with her rested chiefly on the fact that she reminded Florette of a nursemaid of her childhood. In short, the therapeutic team members were very willing to support the therapist's and nurse A.'s efforts because they anticipated that through the therapist and nurse A. Florette would soon find it unnecessary to maintain her defensive, hostile, and assaultive attitude—as in fact turned out to be the case.

Witnessing the clinical course of any patient, we can appreciate why he resists forming an attachment to another person in the first place. For instance, once he has formed such an attachment, he begins to develop a much stronger reaction to that person's physical or emotional absences. Realistically, the therapeutic team members cannot avoid such absences. But the schizophrenic patient, who conceives such absences as willful withholding or rejection, tends to react with murderous rage. Since the patient cannot tolerate his aggressive impulses, he may become so terror-stricken that he retreats to symptoms again. Thus Florette, after physical "absences" of her therapist, nurse A., or others (because of holidays or vacations), started head-banging and assaultiveness all over again after a period in which she was free of symptoms. Once the symptoms have returned, they may last for some time. A period of time seems necessary for the patient to allow his rage and terror to subside or to reassure himself that neither he nor the other person is really dangerous. By the time he lets go of the symptoms, he may be ready to give the other person "another chance." If that happens, and after several repeated cycles, the patient may become more and more able to tolerate ambivalent feelings; the "absence" of the other person will cause less and less upset.

He may then branch out, willing to form relations with new persons. This happened to some extent to Florette. After having attached herself to both the first therapist and nurse A. for several years, she lost her first therapist. She was of course upset, but she did not have to resort to head-banging or assaultiveness. She fell back on nurse A. As it was, she was very hesitant to start a new relation with the second therapist. Her reluctance was reflected in her running away from him and in her telling nurse A. that "men are scary." However, through the assurance of nurse A., she did allow herself to meet and get involved with the second therapist, and eventually benefited from meeting with him.

In treatment, the establishment of the schizophrenic patient's attachment to his therapist or any other member of the therapeutic team is very important. In the case of Florette, the establishment of her attachment to her therapists, nurse A., and others resulted in the gradual subsidence of her disturbing symptoms and the subsequent formulation of a living plan. However, the therapeutic value of such attachments alone is limited. Florette, for example, could not go beyond an attachment to others—the preliminary step in the psychotherapy with schizophrenics. She would not conceptualize what she wanted and make plans to reach for it. She would only count on someone to get her what she wanted. She could not do any exploratory study of herself, and without it her basic views about her self and the object world could not be changed.

That Florette could not go beyond the preliminary step of attachment is not accidental. She had been ill since she was eight years old. Receiving no psychotherapy until she was 39, she had already been fixed in the chronic stage of her illness for a long, long time. But many a schizophrenic-I or -II patient would also prefer to stay at the therapeutically preliminary stage of attachment. Take Claudia, for example (see Chapter 24). After four years of therapy and well on the way to recovery, she confided that although she had consistently examined her problems in therapy, she had also made careful reservations "to not go too deep." She reasoned that if she did she would be really getting well, leaving the therapist, and worst of all breaking the close bond with her family or her mother. According to Mahler (1968), those who have not had a satisfactory experience during the symbiotic phase of development tend to strive for symbiotic union in their subsequent object relations. That seemed to be the case with Claudia. However, being a schizophrenic-I patient, Claudia did subsequently proceed with separation-individuation with the aid of psychotherapy.

In the literature, the schizophrenic patient's close bond with his mother (sometimes his father) has been repeatedly described (e.g., Fromm-Reichmann, 1950; Hill, 1955; Will, 1958; Stierlin, 1969). What is to be emphasized is that this bond with the mother often determines whether the patient can or will advance beyond the preliminary step of attachment in therapy. In a schizophrenic-I patient like Claudia, the bond is often dissoluble; the unfolding of separation-individuation is therefore possible in the course of treatment. But in schizophrenic-II, -III, and -IV patients, dissolving this bond through therapy becomes increasingly difficult; it is often impossible to anticipate what can be expected in treatment beyond so-called social recovery—that is, the patient is no longer psychotic, maintains his attachment to mothering persons, and allows no basic change of his views about self and object world. During one phase of treatment Tina (a schizophrenic-II patient; see Chapter 12) repeatedly described her mother as a bitch or witch who could drive, and had driven, everybody at home crazy. Yet six months later she accused the therapist of trying to kill off her mother and was most hostile to him; at this point, her symptoms returned. It then took months for her symptoms to abate and for her to reassess the situation so as to make further steps toward separation-individuation. Needless to say, the maintenance of this close bond depends on both parties involved. The mothers (or fathers) of schizophrenic-I patients tend to have less investment in the bond than the mothers (or fathers) of schizophrenic-II and -III patients. This fact no doubt accounts for the easier dissolubility of the bond among schizophrenic-I patients.

The concept of therapeutic alliance or working alliance or mature transference has been defined by Zetzel (1956b), Greenson (1965), and Stone (1961). When in alliance with the therapist, the patient is usually dimly aware that he must join forces with the therapist to identify and work through his emotional problems or conflicts. In addition to accepting that his problems or conflicts reside in himself, he must also have enough innate strength to work out his problem. Furthermore, he should have enough trust in his therapist, who in his view will know not only how to solve his problems but also how to guide him through the resolution of them without disturbing his background feeling of safety too severely.

Therapeutic alliance should be distinguished from attachment. In therapeutic alliance, the patient has a vision of past, present, and future, and is working toward becoming an individuated person, whereas in attachment the patient is concerned only with the present and aims at maintaining the status quo. When the patient is in alliance with his therapist, he is at the same time very attached to him. But a strong attachment to the therapist does not mean that the patient is ready to work collaboratively with him in treatment. If the therapist misidentifies attachment as therapeutic alliance, he will no doubt overestimate the patient's capacity and will expect too much from him. For instance, the therapist may try to give abstract interpretations before the patient is ready to make use of them. Sometimes he even gets so carried away by the patient's submissiveness—the prerequisite for maintaining attachment—as to see the patient as being truly in agreement with his interpretations. Such blatant dysfunctioning of the therapist's empathic understanding often leads to serious consequences. For instance, when his own overexpectations are disappointed, the therapist may get angry with the patient, because, despite the verbalized insight, he does not seem to make any forward movement. Or he may become disillusioned with his own work or even with his own value as a person. In either case he may do something that is not going to be useful to the patient, such as deciding that the patient is hopelessly ill and does not deserve his energy and time, or that the schizophrenic is constitutionally defective and requires esoteric forms of treatment.

Now it is a fact that not every schizophrenic patient is capable of establishing a therapeutic alliance. To establish a therapeutic alliance, the patient must have an adequately functioning ego. He must also experience a sufficient background feeling of safety and "trust" in the patient-doctor relationship. It follows that during the acute phase, when his ego is completely shattered, the patient cannot form a therapeutic alliance. During the chronic phase he is too crippled by his distorted views of his self and the object world to develop enough trust to establish a therapeutic alliance. Even during the subacute phase, schizophrenic-I and -II patients are potentially more capable of forming a therapeutic alliance than schizophrenic-III patients, who may be quite incapable of doing so.

Even when a schizophrenic patient is capable of establishing a therapeutic alliance, it is not easy for him to do so. Following his break with reality, his trust in others is completely shattered. In the absence of trust, he cannot allow himself to team up with anyone to solve any problem, least of all to solve his own problems. The therapist usually has to work very hard to first win the patient's trust,[1] especially with a schizophrenic-II or -III patient. Generally, the patient first develops an attachment to the therapist. Then, after another period of testing, he will dare bring to his hours such problems as those related to his living with people in the immediate surroundings. The clarification of such interpersonal problems is vital to his well-being, but in a sense they are relatively "superficial." However, if the therapist is helpful in solving them, the patient may eventually try to share with his therapist his most intimate feelings and thoughts.

---

[1] See Will's (1975) article, "The Conditions of Being Therapeutic."

When this proves to be gratifying and nonthreatening, the patient will finally allow himself to form a therapeutic alliance with the therapist, doing exploratory work. Thus, in the case of Claudia (Chapter 24), after she had established an attachment to her therapist, she only gave blow-by-blow reports of daily happenings, without much commentary. Over a year passed before she started to tell her therapist some of her intimate feelings—anger, jealousy—in the context of current events. Not for almost another six months did she admit that such feelings had had a deleterious effect on her throughout her developing years. Still another period of time had to elapse before she indicated a willingness to study the nature and origin of various emotional problems that had caused the break with reality to begin with, and had necessitated repeated hospitalization.

As difficult and tedious as is the therapist's job in helping the patient to establish a therapeutic alliance, the job of maintaining it is perhaps even more difficult. The patient has a limited trust in himself to work out his problems and a limited trust in the therapist's willingness to help him. Any rise in tension within him intensifies his distrust of both himself and the therapist. He therefore withdraws, and the previously established alliance is destroyed. To re-establish it the therapist has to work doubly hard.

To win the patient's trust—the prerequisite for a therapeutic alliance—the therapist may rely on both his skill and his "person." His skill involves mainly his empathic understanding of the patient's need. That empathic understanding invites trust is fully demonstrated in Fromm-Reichmann's work with Deborah (see Green, 1964) and Sechehaye's (1951) work with Renée. It is generally believed that the capacity for empathy differs in different persons, and that Fromm-Reichmann, Sechehaye, and others were endowed with a superior capacity to empathize with their patients. That may be true. But in the therapy of schizophrenic patients, the therapist need not be concerned with his endowment for empathy; rather, he should be concerned with the extent to which he has developed it. One can definitely learn to synchronize one's affective reaction with the patient's, and then to conceptualize one's own affect. Personal analysis and case supervision are helpful in developing the therapist's capacity for empathic understanding of his patients (see Fromm-Reichmann, Hill).

The therapist's "person" is difficult to define. Broadly stated, it is everything that represents the person—the sum total of the way he dresses and is groomed; the way he speaks, gestures, walks, and moves; the volume and color of his voice; the warmth he displays on the surface and the warmth he feels inside; his basic beliefs. If the therapist's person reaches the patient, there is often no need for him to do anything in a conscious way to win the patient. During my psychiatric residency training years, I had a colleague, Dr. W., in his late 30's, who had recently arrived in the United States from a southern European country. He was very charming and warm, and also commanding and authoritative. He was impeccably groomed and dressed. He had a deep, ringing voice that was further enriched by his accent. Very frequently, he patted his patients' backs and chucked their chins. Invariably, women patients, young and old, responded to his approach miraculously. In a short time he could make them leave their catatonic or hebephrenic positions and move on to "better" wards.[2] But after these patients had advanced to the ward next to the open ward, their progress was arrested. Looking back, it seems clear that his person or charismatic personality evoked the patients' trust and in turn enabled them to establish an attachment to him. Because they liked him, they tended to perpetuate their attachment to him. They did not want to leave him, and therefore they did not progress further.

While the person of this particular colleague seems to have had a therapeutic effect on most of his women patients, the person of any therapist can usually reach certain patients. In this respect, there has been growing interest in "matching"

[2] The segregation of patients according to the severity of their illness was the practice at the hospital where I received my residency training. It has not been the practice at Chestnut Lodge.

the therapist and the patient (Whitehorn and Betz, 1954, 1956; Semrad, 1975). For the past 10 years I have alloted a portion of my time to "matching patients with therapists." I have found that matching requires a very detailed knowledge of both patient and therapist. Not until I have worked closely with any therapist for a year or more do I get to know enough about him or her. As for the patients, I am always meeting them for the first time. Owing especially to the patients' reluctance to reveal anything about themselves, I have found that I can rarely make a "match" with real conviction that it will be satisfactory.[3] Yet only so much about human factors can be defined "scientifically." Many a match that I did not consider satisfactory at the time it was made turned out to be most gratifying; the reverse was also true.

While the therapist's person can evoke enough trust in the patient for him to establish a therapeutic alliance, it cannot be relied on to maintain the therapeutic alliance. To maintain the therapeutic alliance, all that counts is the therapist's skill. And his skill is not confined to his ability to empathize with his patient. He must constantly be aware of the patient's transference to himself and his own countertransference to the patient. He must also be able to make timely and tactful interpretations and help the patient work through his problems in the transference-countertransference matrix. All in all, his job seems infinitely more complex than the job performed by Dr. W., described above.

Freud declared that schizophrenics have no capacity for transference, but all those (far too many to name) who have worked intensively with schizophrenics have argued the opposite. I believe that to some extent the debate is really about the definition of the term transference.

In 1910, Freud defined transference as follows:

The patient, that is to say, directs towards the physician a degree of affectionate feeling (mingled, often enough, with hostil-

---

[3] On another occasion, I hope to describe my observations on matching.

ity) which is based on no real relation between them and which—as is shown by every detail of its emergence—can only be traced back to old wishful phantasies of the patient's which have become unconscious. . . .Transference arises spontaneously in all human relationships just as it does between the patient and the physician [1910a, p. 51].

If that is what transference is, then schizophrenic patients are indeed capable of it. In fact, Freud (1911) described Schreber's feelings about his physician, Dr. Flechsig, as a transference of the former's feelings about his father or older brother.

However, having in mind also that psychoanalysis is the preferred treatment for sufferers from hysteria, anxiety states, and obsessive-compulsive neuroses, Freud further defined transference taking the results of the treatment into consideration. Thus he qualified that via transference the psychogenic conflict is revived and subsequently worked through, and that transference is reliving without conscious memory, whereas psychoanalysis aims to make what is unconscious conscious, including the repressed conflict, now in the form of transference. With these qualifications, transference becomes the exclusive property of neurotics. For most of the patients[4] that Freud would have diagnosed as schizophrenic were not at all able to "work through" or "make conscious" their conflicts with physicians they hardly knew or knew for only a short time. Taking the results of psychoanalytic treatment into consideration, Freud (1916-1917) now defined transference more narrowly, writing:

> [Schizophrenics] have no capacity for transference or only insufficient residues of it. They reject the doctor, not with hostility but with indifference. For that reason they cannot be influenced by him either; what he says leaves them cold, makes no impression on them; consequently the mechanism of cure which we carry through with other people—the revival of the pathogenic conflict and the overcoming of the resistance due to repression—cannot be operated with them. They remain as they are. Often they have already undertaken attempts at recovery on

[4] Freud used a more stringent criterion than we use nowadays. See Chapter 1.

their own account which have led to pathological results. We cannot alter this in any way [p. 447].

In line with this conclusion, Freud would have to attribute Schreber's feelings about Dr. Flechsig not to "transference" but to delusions or something related to an attempt at recovery or restitution.

From the study of the transference phenomena of patients with narcissistic personality disorders, Kohut (1971) has suggested that the transferencelike phenomenon of narcissistic patients be distinguished from the transference proper of neurotic patients. The former is determined and shaped by narcissistic love, the latter by object love. Yet in both cases the configuration can be revived in the therapeutic situation and be worked through in terms of psychoanalytic procedures. He further suggests that in psychotics and borderline patients, because of their propensity toward a fragmentation of self, no stable transferencelike structure can be revived in treatment. Consequently, for them psychoanalysis is not applicable. Thus, in adhering to Freud's definition of transference that takes the results of treatment into consideration, Kohut also explains the schizophrenic patient's feelings about his therapist in terms of delusions.

From his wide experience with schizophrenic patients, Searles (1963, 1972) has documented that the schizophrenics, regardless of their self-fragmentation, definitely exhibit libidinal and hostile feelings about their therapists in the fashion of the transference of neurotic patients, and that in addition the transference of the schizophrenic represents a reactivation of specific psychological conflicts that had, to begin with, generated the psychotic process. Because schizophrenic transference is highly structured, he labeled it "transference psychosis"—a term that Rosenfeld (1954), Little (1958), and others had used before him.

According to Searles's definition, a transference psychosis will be encountered in the therapy of virtually any schizophrenic patient. Whether it can be worked through, it seems to me, is an entirely different issue. It may be said, however, that during the acute phase, the schizophrenic patient's ego is simply not able to maintain the objectivity necessary to study his feelings about his therapist as a transference phenomenon (that is, these feelings are determined largely by his own past experience). During the chronic phase so much effort in therapy must be directed to the patient's distorted view of reality that he may not be able to become oriented to the nature and structure of his conflicts and thereby to trace their origin and effect a working through. During the subacute phase only certain patients—especially those who were originally schizophrenic-I and -II—are really able to study and resolve the transference psychosis as neurotics are able to study and resolve the transference neurosis.

Although the transference in schizophrenics takes many forms,[5] its core is the simultaneous moving toward and moving away from the therapist, which, in the language of Burnham et al. (1969), is the "need-fear dilemma." In essence, every schizophrenic will develop this core transference phenomenon toward the physician or other persons as soon as he overcomes his reluctance to becoming attached to the person. Whether such a phenomenon is called transference, transferencelike phenomenon, or transference psychosis is merely a matter of preference. For that matter, arguments about whether the conceptualization of transference psychosis is correct seem unnecessary (such questions have been raised, for instance, by London [1973]); how transference psychosis is conceptualized, however, is important. Preferably, in

---

[5] Searles (1963) has distinguished four types of transference psychosis. (1) Transference situations in which the therapist feels unrelated to the patient, as the therapist is being treated as an inanimate object. (2) A clear-cut relatedness has been established between patient and therapist, but it is a deeply ambivalent one. (3) The patient's psychosis represents, in the transference, an effort to complement the therapist's personality, or to help the therapist-parent to become established as a separate and whole person. (4) The deeply and chronically confused patient, who in childhood had been accustomed to a parent's doing his thinking for him, is ambivalently (a) trying to perpetuate a symbiotic relationship wherein the therapist to a high degree does the patient's thinking for him, and (b) expressing, by what the therapist feels to be sadistic and castrative nullifying or undoing of the therapist's effort to be helpful, a determination to be a separately thinking, and otherwise separately functioning, individual.

speaking of transference we do not take the results of therapy into consideration. If we do, we must qualify the subcategories of schizophrenia as well. For a schizophrenic-I patient, as indicated earlier, the core transference phenomenon can be worked through; but for a schizophrenic-III, it might (for a long time to come) have to be totally bypassed in treatment.

As mentioned at the beginning of this chapter, transference and attachment are not synonymous. Attachment refers to a general human tendency to be involved with other human beings, whereas transference refers to the patterns of human relatedness determined by specific past experiences of relatedness with significant persons. Transference is usually preceded by the attachment. In treatment, attachment may lead to the abatement of symptoms, whereas working through the transference could lead to a healthier id-ego-superego balance. Nor are transference and therapeutic alliance the same. Via transference, conflicts and problems are worked through; but working through is possible only when there is a commitment to the task, which commitment is the therapeutic alliance. Once the patient establishes an attachment to his therapist, he will exhibit, in spite of himself, transference phenomena toward his therapist, whereas he can exercise (albeit unconsciously) a great deal of control over the development of a therapeutic alliance. Dictated by the patient's need for safety, the configuration of his transference may vary from tending more toward to tending more away from the therapist, or vice versa; nevertheless, the decathexis-recathexis mode of relation with the therapist is a constant phenomenon. On the other hand, the need for safety may lead the patient to withdraw from an established therapeutic alliance.

A clinical example from the treatment of Melissa may clarify these matters. Toward her therapist, Melissa was still characteristically exhibiting her moving-toward and moving-away pattern of relatedness. One Wednesday the therapist informed Melissa that he had to go out of town on Friday unexpectedly and would have to cancel her hour on that day. On the following day, Thursday, Melissa failed to show up for her hour. Yet, on Friday, she was waiting outside her therapist's office at the time when the canceled hour was supposed to take place. During her Monday session, Melissa sat through the hour without saying anything, and the therapist was not able to get her started no matter what he said or did—quite in contrast to her previous attempts to work on her problems. On Thursday, when Melissa was feeling very angry about being abandoned by her therapist, she moved away from him, lest the sight of him stir up uncontrollable rage that could disrupt her sense of self-cohesion. On Friday, when her rage had to some extent subsided, her attachment to her therapist propelled her to move toward him. (Perhaps the moving-toward tendency was also fortified by the knowledge that his office, unlike himself in person, could not stir up too strong a feeling in her.) However, on Monday, when they finally met again, Melissa had turned off her therapeutic alliance altogether.

B.

Approaches to
Different Stages of Illness

CHAPTER 23

Psychotherapy with Schizophrenic Patients during the Acute Phase

Once I have decided to work with a schizophrenic patient, I cease to think about whether he falls into the category of I, II, III, or IV, for such thoughts may be counterproductive. I do, however, determine whether the patient is in the acute, subacute, or chronic phase, for I believe that my therapeutic task varies according to the phase of the patient's illness.

Clinically, not every patient proceeds from the acute to the subacute to the chronic phase. Some patients, after brief acute and subacute phases, make a social recovery. Some stay in the subacute phase for a long, long time; others proceed rapidly into the chronic phase. Many a patient in the subacute or chronic phase re-experiences organismic panic and reverts to the acute phase; this is an especially common occurrence in the course of modified psychoanalytic psychotherapy. Properly handled, a return to the acute phase often proves not to be detrimental.

In this chapter, I shall discuss some issues in the treatment of patients in the acute phase. In the acute phase, we have to be concerned with the patient's lack of sense of self-continuity or its fluidity. Because the patient is in extreme terror, he must be given immediate relief. In the following, I shall describe what I as a therapist would do and would not do in the therapeutic situation via an illustrative case. In this discussion I shall omit the question of nursing care for such a patient.

Case Material

Bruce was admitted to Chestnut Lodge when he was 21. Two and a half years earlier he had dropped out of college at the beginning of his sophomore year. Throughout his life Bruce had periodically been unhappy and had felt unliked by others; this problem became greatly exaggerated in the last year of high school. However, as far as he and his family were concerned, his illness dated from the time he left college. Thereafter, he felt extremely ashamed of himself for having fallen off the pedestal his family had put him on. Following an attempt at suicide, he began to see psychiatrists. In the course of office psychotherapy, he was soon described as having looseness of association, inappropriate affect, and hallucinations. He was repeatedly hospitalized as he became increasingly irascible, recalcitrant, and bizarre. He had received several courses of antipsychotic drugs as well as ECT—all to no avail. Finally, 2½ years later, he was admitted to Chestnut Lodge for long-term therapy.

Bruce's history revealed that he was the first-born in a military family of five. There was no family history of mental illness. His father had successfully risen from the ranks; his mother was described as "depressed," especially when the children were young. Before Bruce was a year old, the family had made three moves; thereafter, they moved every three years. When Bruce was 16 months old, and being toilet trained, his next younger sister was born. The birth of the sibling was said to have complicated the training a great deal. Finally he was sent away to his mother's eldest sister to be trained. When Bruce was about four, his next brother was born. Shortly afterwards, the family moved to a foreign city where Bruce started kindergarten. Feeling unliked by his teacher (a woman), Bruce was said to have repeatedly lost his "control" and was often sent out of the classroom. At eight, after the

birth of his youngest sibling, a sister, he developed a persistent fantasy of being adopted by some other mother in the
neighborhood. (His view of his own mother as cold and indifferent was consolidated at this time.) Also at that time one
of his younger brothers fell and fractured his collar bone. Although according to the babysitter who was at the scene, the
incident had nothing to do with Bruce, Bruce blamed himself
for his brother's injury—this self-blame later became the core
of his psychotic delusional belief that he was a potential murderer.

Because his father changed his post every three years,
Bruce often changed schools. Although beset by various difficulties after each change (e.g., feeling unliked by his teacher
or classmates, becoming withdrawn at home), he succeeded
in distinguishing himself scholastically by his second year in
the new school. Outwardly, he was agreeable, a good listener,
and ready to do what others wanted him to do. Although he
kept up a heavy correspondence with many classmates from
previous schools, he constantly felt alienated and not close to
anyone. He entered a new school for his senior year of high
school. While still getting adjusted to the new situation, he
had to make another change when he went to college. He
would have preferred to go to a college recommended by his
teachers, but felt that he had better go to the college his father
and grandfather had attended.

At college he felt "numb" and did not know exactly how
he felt. He had simply "gone through the motions"—even
though he did all right scholastically. In essence, he felt he
was not the master of himself. By summer vacation, he decided to travel alone in Europe in order to get as far away
from home as possible. In Europe he "gazed at his navel" and
wanted to be an introspective poet. As the summer drew to
a close, he felt that he was untalented and would never amount
to anything. He gave up his ambition to be a poet and became
intensely involved with a European girl for a week. When
they bade good-bye, Bruce took to his bed in the hotel and
cried for three days. He did not eat. Finally he managed to

get himself back to the United States. His family was much upset to see him in a very disheveled, undernourished state, but did not feel that they could do anything for him and chose to leave him alone. However, within a week after his arrival home, Bruce was suddenly transformed. He became unusually exuberant and behaved as if he were on a pink cloud. It was in that state that he returned to college. In less than two months, however, he had to drop out, as he felt very confused and very reluctant to face the term examinations.

On admission to Chestnut Lodge, Bruce was on a large combined dosage of Mellaril and Stelazine. He looked apathetic, showing muscular stiffness and limitation of facial expression. He was "in contact." Although he volunteered nothing, he answered questions appropriately but laconically. This fact, plus long pauses, resulted in his giving very little information about himself. Yet he was able to ask questions about me. (This curiosity of his I took as a good omen.) At the end of the first session I asked him how he felt about our working together. He said "All right," and added, "You are very serious—you don't laugh at me—and you understand." Thus we began to meet five times a week. Now, under close scrutiny, he was found to be highly suspicious and tended to attach meanings to unrelated events. There was some concreteness in his thought processes, probably of a defensive nature, as it tended to come and go. He also spoke vividly of visual scenes of "violence," which he characterized as very frightening. These were actually fantasies, but his impaired reality sense made it impossible for him to distinguish the real from the imagined.

He was diagnosed as a schizophrenic-I, and the therapeutic program for him was intensive psychoanalytic psychotherapy in the hospital, without antipsychotic drugs. It was recognized that in the course of psychotherapy Bruce might regress and break with reality, but it was also predicted that if he did so, the break would not have an adverse effect on the prognosis.

Thus, in Bruce's case, within 10 days medicine was rapidly discontinued. For the next four months, despite the withdrawal of the drug, Bruce did not show any evidence of increased anxiety or any drastic change in behavior (except less muscular rigidity). He remained "in contact" and continued to be able to give sketchy accounts of his history. During these months my main goal in treatment was to help Bruce to learn to talk to me as freely as he could. By talking I mean that talking as a process is an end in itself and not a means to an end. In analytic treatment, interpretation, as Eissler (1953a) puts it, is the analyst's principal activity. In such a case, the patient's talking is conceived as a preparatory step for the analyst to make an interpretation. To maximize the accuracy of interpretation the analyst may try to channel the content of the patient's talk, and in this sense, in the analytic situation, talking is the means to an end. In listening to a patient like Bruce at this stage of treatment, I do not aim at interpretations. Of course, interpretative comments (more correctly clarifying comments) are sometimes unavoidable, but such comments are not my primary aim.

Since I did not aim at interpretation, I did not need to encourage or discourage any particular content of the communication. Bruce was allowed to start or stop whenever he wanted; in the circumstances what I did was merely to register how the rise and fall of anxiety might have dictated his stream of speech. This "conservative" position of mine was based on the rationale that any exploratory work could provoke anxiety. After having been protected from experiencing anxiety by the medicine for so long a time, Bruce might not be able to mobilize more effective defense mechanisms. In a state of extreme anxiety, he might then resort immediately to activities to get away from the treatment, either by acting out (e.g., AWOL, signing out, or inducing the family to take him out of the hospital) or by regressing (i.e., being physically present but emotionally unreachable).

Notwithstanding my "conservative" approach, Bruce

showed gross behavioral changes in about the fifth month of treatment. At that time, for consecutive sessions, he talked about his mother as being cold, distant, and never available; then he suddenly clammed up. Hour after hour he curled up motionlessly in the chair farthest from me and appeared utterly dejected and lost in his thoughts. No encouragement could get him to share his feelings and thoughts with me. I reviewed the recent events that had led to the present development, hoping to start him talking. But to no avail. He remained silent. Yet he came to my office regularly. In fact, he often reminded the ward staff to bring him to our meetings. (He had to be escorted by a staff member when he was away from the ward.)

His silence continued for over two months. Then I went away for my summer vacation. On my return I was totally taken aback to find that Bruce was a completely different person. He was no longer dejected, "withdrawn," and self-engrossed. Instead, he was very active, although seeming very tense and "pushed." During our first meeting he informed me, with an air of defiance and determination, that he was leaving the hospital, that his family had agreed to take him away since he was no longer ill, and that he had waited for my return in order to get my permission to leave. I thanked him for having chosen to wait for my return to discuss the matter with me. I suggested that his behavioral change was perhaps related to my long absence and to his decision to get away from me. Although these considerations did diminish his pressure to leave the hospital, he flatly denied that he had felt anything at all about my coming and going. In subsequent meetings, he was very restless in the office, moving from chair to chair, emptying ashtrays, dusting chairs, etc. He prevented me from completing a sentence; skillfully, he used activities or a new topic to interrupt me. I said that he was apparently ignoring me, and suggested that he study the reasons for his behavior. He paid no attention.

A couple of weeks later, rather unexpectedly, he went AWOL. He went straight to his parents' home 200 miles away, and succeeded in convincing his parents to call the hospital to negotiate a discharge. The same night he "spaced out." He left home after dinner, walked miles in the neighborhood, and entered other people's houses to hold "talks" with relative strangers. After repeated calls from the neighbors, his parents finally told the police to take him back to the hospital. Now he was in very tenuous contact with reality. At times he could carry on a reasonable conversation with other patients and staff members on the ward. But at other times he stared into space, and it was difficult to "arouse" him and get his attention. He grimaced and whispered as if responding to hallucinatory voices. In the office he was visibly fearful. His general behavior became steadily more and more childish, "purposeless," and disorganized. He was sitting on the floor at my feet. Suddenly he withdrew to the far corner of the room, looking frightened, oblivious to my existence, and not understanding what I said to him. He sometimes played with cigarettes instead of smoking them. He tore up Kleenex, called the ragged pieces "butterflies," and decorated the floor lamp with them. He babbled, gesticulated, and struggled to utter a sentence without syntax. Soon his ward behavior became increasingly disorderly. He wandered from one end of the building to the other. He disrobed, was incontinent, and smeared himself with urine and feces when unattended. He struck out or threw things at others. He did not eat when his tray was brought to him, but gobbled up food taken from the trays of other patients. Then one day he was completely immobile, rigid, and mute.

Now he was seen on the unit. During our meetings he maintained the catatonic position. His facial expression, however, was never static; it changed constantly and rapidly—from fear to anger to sadness. (I later learned that he had dreamlike experiences of being different people at different times and places.) Most of the time he seemed unaware of my existence. Yet at times he tried to relate to me, making an effort to step toward me or lift his arm in my direction. But as soon as he initiated any such movement he looked very fearful and immediately checked himself. The verbal exchange between us was very limited. He had practically nothing to say. I commented only when his facial expression showed a marked change or when he tried to start a movement but checked himself. In the first case, I expressed the hope that he could share his thoughts with me. In the latter case, I sympathized with him, saying that it must be awfully painful and distressing to have very mixed feelings—such as wanting to reach out to me but being unable to allow himself to do so. Perhaps he conceived that reaching out toward me was too assertive and was therefore forbidden. When at times I noted a little relaxation of his facial muscles, I assumed that either my tone or the content of my statement might mean something to him. But I had no way of knowing what had actually gone on in his mind. Therefore I could not pursue the topic very far. One thing that profoundly puzzled me was whether the catatonic position is in fact the best possible solution to deal with aggressive impulses, as is ordinarily postulated. For, in the case of Bruce, by being catatonic he was no longer running away from me. He stayed with me and even allowed me to say something to him. In contrast, before the catatonia he did everything possible to distract me from saying anything to him, nor did he allow himself to listen to me.

For the next four months he continued to be catatonic. He was not able to be concerned with eating, but ate some when a certain few nurses fed him. He had no concept of sleep, but when one of these few nurses put him to bed and sat with him he did not seem to have much trouble falling asleep. He was particularly sensitive to the absence (i.e., off duty) of these few special persons or me. There were consecutive good days and there were bad days. But no one could figure out how to account for the fluctuation. When everybody began to feel that he was making progress, he suddenly slumped for undeterminable reasons. When everyone began to feel discouraged, he suddenly perked up, again for undeterminable reasons.

I continued to see him regularly five days a week. Walking

from my hospital office to where he lived took seven or eight minutes. I used the time to dismiss from my mind whatever might be bothering me at the moment. I tried to establish the state of mind that Freud described as being able to give evenly hovering attention to the patient. When we met, we met alone in the silent room he now occupied. The door was usually closed but not locked. The ward staff was sitting nearby; in case Bruce and I should get into a struggle, the staff could immediately come to my rescue. (This help was, however, never needed.) During our meetings, I sometimes stood up and sometimes sat on the floor—essentially because at that time the patient was standing up or sitting on the floor. Because he was mute, I had to do the talking. My comments were limited in both quantity and content. When his facial expression changed repeatedly, with obviously no connection with what was going on in the external environment, I would comment on his difficulty in accepting me at that particular time. Even though I knew what his response would be (that is, no response), I would still suggest that he tell me what was troubling him. If I said something he seemed to disregard completely, I would wait a while before I made another attempt. If he showed signs of responding to my comments, I would elaborate a little on my first comment, without introducing new ideas. Considering his slowness to respond, I did not wish to plant so many ideas that he would become confused.

Almost four months passed before he gradually began to respond to my invitation to sit in a chair opposite me. But in the meantime, while remaining mute, he began to move about in the room, moving swiftly from one corner of the room to another. Sometimes he approached me with such lightning swiftness that I would be all tensed up. Generally he stopped suddenly a few feet away from me, kneeling and perhaps praying. My fear of being assaulted by him must have been obvious, for he began to assure me that he would not hit me. Thereupon I continued to recommend to him that he talk about his feelings. It must be stated that as he was emerging

from the catatonia and was beginning to move about, I experienced quick changes in my emotions while sitting with
him: They ranged from extreme fear to irrepressible rage to
very tender feelings. None of these emotions were in themselves unpleasant; the unpleasantness lay in too frequent and
too sudden changes.

After another two months I found him changing. There
was less darting about; he evoked less fear and more tender
feelings in me. Over-all, I felt his terror subsiding and his
rage dissipating. And he and I began to develop a "closer"
bond. Such a feeling of being closer is almost undefinable, but
working with severely ill patients like Bruce we intuitively
"know" it. In Bruce's case it was reflected in his increased
placidity and relaxation while he was sitting with me. His
facial expression did not unexplainably change nearly as often.
He was increasingly aware of my presence. He glanced more
frequently in my direction. In response to my comments, he
often parted his lips, even though he said nothing. On the
ward, he was no longer incontinent, and was able to brush
his teeth if a toothbrush was placed in his hand. He ate better.
He also began to seek out the company of other patients, although he could not yet communicate with them. He still had
setbacks, but he emerged from each setback rapidly.

More and more he acted like someone awakening from a
nightmare. He appeared to be more "with it." His smiles became more genuine. He began to talk about memories of his
life before he lost contact. He did not seem to be interested in
what happened immediately before he went out of contact. If
he began to speak of his view about himself and about the
object world, I welcomed it. But I had to continue to try to
keep his panic to a minimum. I therefore refrained from over-
zealously dispensing insights. Given enough time, I believe
that a patient like Bruce usually comes to understand or know
what he needs to understand or know. For example, after I
had been absent for a week, he did not speak to me for a week.
Then, during one hour, he said, "I heard you were sick." "Are
you well now?" "I am glad you feel good now." The next day

he said, "I killed a deer." It was not really very clear if he meant "deer" or "dear," but I decided to talk to him about "deer." So I said, "Oh, yes, there must be deer running across the vast estate of your family." (This was almost a fact.) He said, "I killed it on our own property." I said, "You must feel pretty bad, for having wanted to kill that deer." He was silent. I added, "You must talk to me more about how you feel about having ideas to kill the deer." He nodded but did not say anything for a long time. When he started again he was on another topic. During the next session he suddenly asked me, "Do you think the deer would recover?" I said, "From my conversation with you yesterday, I understand that you wanted to kill the deer but had not resorted to action. If the deer learned about your thoughts it would feel hurt but it would forgive you and the relationship between you and the deer would certainly recover." He smiled. He did not say much the rest of the session but tried to smile at me periodically. Three days later, when we felt very close to each other, he volunteered, "I didn't kill the deer."

In subsequent weeks, Bruce's condition became increasingly stabilized and his obscure language disappeared.

Discussion

1. Although my focus is the acute phase of the schizophrenic process, in order to present a cohesive view of the patient, I have described in some detail the therapeutic interaction between Bruce and me before he broke with reality. The period before the break with reality can be divided into two phases, and my activities during the two phases were somewhat different. During the early phase, I encouraged him to "talk" to me and did very little interpretation—if interpretation is understood as conveying to the patient the latent meaning of his psychic production (Laplanche and Pontalis, 1973). It was not until the fifth month that I began to make interpretative comments. Distinguishing the two phases would

not, in my view, be particularly necessary if the discontin-
uation of medication had not been an issue. In other circumstances, I would carefully have given each interpretation in
accordance with my evaluation of the patient's capacity to
understand and make use of it. However, when a drug is being
withdrawn from the patient, I feel I must take an ultracon-
servative position. On the surface, such a patient may appear
very much "together." Yet his actual experience of and capacity to make use of interpretation is very difficult to esti-
mate. I have often seen adverse results produced by inex-
perienced therapists who tried too hard.

For instance, an 18-year-old girl named Joy was transferred to Chestnut Lodge from a university hospital where
she was admitted after a break with reality and was made
behaviorally "normal" by heavy doses of medication. At
Chestnut Lodge the dosage of the medication was reduced,
with the plan of discontinuing it altogether. Joy reported to
her therapist in their second meeting that she had dreamed
of being at a seashore resort. As she walked on the beach, she
found herself swallowed by waves. She woke up, alarmed. The
transference aspect of the dream is obvious; therefore the
therapist eagerly suggested that perhaps she was concerned
about being engulfed in the treatment situation. Joy ignored
the interpretation, but later told a nurse that she was afraid
of her therapist. During the third meeting, the patient said
she was to have a dental checkup after the therapy session,
and that she was always afraid of going to dentists. They
looked for cavities and always found plenty; she was afraid
of drilling, etc. Once again the therapist was eager to make
a transference interpretation. Joy was at first unable to see
the connection; then she began to talk a bit in gibberish. That
evening she went AWOL.

If I had been therapist, I would have thought as this therapist did—that the patient's verbalized statement reflected
her effort to clarify her feelings about the therapist—but I
would not have made the interpretations this therapist made.
Taking into consideration that the removal of drugs is like

the removal of a crutch and can be quite an anxiety-provoking experience, I avoid doing anything that would increase the patient's feeling that our meeting is an unpleasant kind of experience. If she feels that way, she can hardly be expected to tell me with comfort what comes to her mind. (In fact, this patient tore herself away from treatment in less than a month.) During the early phase when a drug is being withdrawn, I prefer not to risk overburdening the patient and therefore do not interpret.

2. It has often been stressed that initial interviews with a schizophrenic patient are important and may determine the whole course of treatment. Here I shall not discuss the initial interviews with the patient in any detail, except to say this. Since I happen to be the person who comes into the patient's life at a time when he is in great distress, I should be able to feel with him that he is in extreme distress. I should also be able, through my questions and statements, to demonstrate to him that I am interested in him and, more important, why he is in such a predicament and in such distress. Beyond that, I offer him hope but no promises. I may convey to him that things can be looked at from a different angle and that I might be the person to help him to do that. But I will not impress upon him my own viewpoint or my own values. If, for whatever countertransference reasons, I cannot see myself being empathic toward the patient, I will not work with him; then I will do my utmost to withdraw from the case without further damaging his self-respect. If, for whatever unspecified transference reasons, the patient simply cannot warm up to me, I will also withdraw from the case and again try not to damage his self-respect. (Even if he takes the initiative in rejecting me, he could still feel rejected if I withdrew.)

The patient should be approached in a nonhurried manner. The treatment is going to last for years. There is no need to expect everything to be achieved right away. I have mentioned above that when the therapist tried too eagerly to make a transference interpretation he ended up chasing the patient away.

3. What is designated as the acute phase of schizophrenia refers to a period when the patient does not experience a sense of self-cohesion, and is therefore terror-stricken. And the terror further interferes with the re-establishment of self-cohesion. The vicious circle must be broken. To do so, it is essential to reduce the patient's terror. In the above illustrative case I have shown what I did and I did not do to achieve this purpose. Essentially, I tried to be all-attentive to the patient when I was with him—attentive to the rise and fall of his terror in response to internal or external stimuli. Especially when the stimuli were external and related to my interventions, I immediately modified my behavior so that his terror could be reduced. When the stimuli were determined to be within him, I made an educated guess at "identifying" them, also with the aim of allaying his anxiety. If my guess was wrong, I hoped to correct it in subsequent interchanges.

I considered verbal communication between us paramount and tried my utmost to establish it. Yet I realized that because of his mental condition the patient might not want to talk or be unable to talk. In that case I talked to him, hoping he might somehow respond. Silence between us was acceptable as long as during the silence I still felt I was with him. If during the silence I became preoccupied with my own thoughts or reverie, I would study my reveries and determine how they were related to the situation.

Sitting with the patient and watching his nonverbal behavior and facial expressions, I often experienced intense emotions—anger, hatred, loathing, perverted sexual feelings. Sometimes the change from one feeling to another was rather rapid. Even though I was certain that my feeling reflected the patient's, I was often unable to determine why he felt a certain way at a certain time. Whenever I could not determine the cause, I preferred not to inform the patient of what he might be feeling, for inaccurate identification without the possibility of further clarifying the cause could not help him. On the other hand, I believed that when the patient sensed my ability to tolerate the various intense feelings he was experiencing, he might himself learn to be more tolerant of them through the process Klein describes as projective identification. At least he might experience me as increasingly less dangerous. That could lead to the strengthening of an emotional tie between us as well as to the improvement of our verbal communication.

4. I consider that one of the core problems of schizophrenic patients is the fear of establishing a close emotional tie with another person. Because of this fear, they resort to all sorts of measures to avoid such emotional involvement. Sometimes the patient gets involved with another person in spite of wishing the opposite. He becomes beset with anxiety, and various symptoms may result. For instance, in the case of Bruce, five months after the beginning of treatment, when he became involved with me, he resorted to marked withdrawal (without breaking with reality). Another several months later, by the time of my vacation, he was more involved with me; he behaved quite desperately and tried to increase his distance from me by first attempting a flight into health and then assuming the catatonic position with a concomitant break with reality.

In Bruce's case, his break with reality turned out to be a useful one. Before it, he could not allow himself to be involved with me; afterwards, he did not seem to have the need to move simultaneously toward me and away from me. In other words, he became less ambitendent in his object relations. But although a break with reality can have positive aspects, it should not be recommended for every patient, for not every patient can make his way back to normality. The issue is not whether the patient does or does not want to return to reality because the environment is pleasant or unpleasant; it is whether his ego capacity is or is not inherently sufficient to re-establish a nonpathological self, regardless of his intention. Because the outcome is unpredictable, the fragmentation of self or the break with reality is a serious matter. Accomplished therapists like Federn, Fromm-Reichmann, and others have advised how to guard against its occurrence.

Generally speaking, a schizophrenic-I patient like Bruce stands quite a good chance to return to reality; a schizophrenic-II patient may have a 50-50 chance; whereas a schizophrenic-III or -IV patient may be unable to make his way back. In a schizophrenic-I patient, the demarcation between the acute and subacute phases is usually clear-cut. It is less clear in the schizophrenic-II and even less so in the schizophrenic-III or -IV patient.

5. During the acute phase every patient appears to be in a dreamlike state. Yet in this state the regression of ego functioning differs according to whether the patient is a schizophrenic-I, -II, or -III. A schizophrenic-I regresses more unevenly; a schizophrenic-III regresses across the board; a schizophrenic-II lies between these extremes. Because of these differences in regression, we may adopt a somewhat different approach to each type of patient—even though, as a general principle, our aim in therapy is always to alleviate the patient's extreme terror. With the schizophrenic-I, because he does not slip deeply into what Winnicott calls "noncommunication," most of the time we can maintain our position as a psychoanalyst making therapeutic interpretations. But with the schizophrenic-III, because of his readiness to become totally self-absorbed and to stay in the noncommunicative state, we may sometimes need to make "small talk" with him in order to be with him.

After coming out of the dreamlike state, the patient forgets a good deal of the experience anyway; but he retains a good deal of it too. However, he generally prefers not to look back to it, lest a peek at it bring back the terror he experienced; unless for research purposes (!), we should respect the patient's wish. From the therapeutic point of view, even if the patient could recall the experience in detail, we cannot make use of the material *immediately* for any meaningful insight anyway.

CHAPTER 24

Psychotherapy with Schizophrenic Patients in the Subacute Phase

The treatment of a schizophrenic patient in the subacute phase involves very different concerns and tasks from those involved in the treatment of a schizophrenic patient in the acute phase (see Chapter 23). In the subacute phase, the therapist aims at (1) helping the patient *not* to settle for the closure of a pathological viewpoint about himself and his object world, and (2) helping the patient to conceptualize that a symptom is a symptom, that it is related to his experience of anxiety or lack of sense of well-being, and that his anxiety or lack of well-being is rectifiable in the context of his object relations.

The second task is essentially similar to the task to be accomplished in dynamic psychotherapy with any neurotic patient, except that the postpsychotic patient is more afraid to commit himself to the study of the source of anxiety, lest he again be overwhelmed by anxiety and again become psychotic. In the treatment of a schizophrenic patient in the subacute phase, the therapist must respect this fear and not rush the patient into anything that he is not ready for. The therapist must remember that for the patient the difference between anxiety and panic is actually very small. An unannounced absence of the therapist may be merely one of those anxiety-provoking events for an average neurotic patient; in the schizophrenic patient, however, it could cause such separation panic that a very serious, if not irreparable, setback in therapy could result.

As for the first task (i.e., helping the patient not to settle for the closure of a pathological view of himself and his object world), it is a therapeutic problem encountered only in schizophrenic patients in the subacute phase. Unlike the second task, the first is not a major concern in the treatment of the neurotic patient. Of course, every neurotic patient has distorted views about himself and his object world. But the neurotic's distortions are essentially determined by the pleasure-unpleasure principle, whereas the schizophrenic's distortions are determined by his need for a background feeling of safety (see Chapter 14). More important, the neurotic's distortions at the time he seeks treatment are usually quite stabilized; they are no longer in the process of being formed. Thus, in the treatment the therapist need be concerned only with the gradual rectification of distortions. The situation of the schizophrenic during the subacute phase is quite different. During this phase, he has regained many of the ego functions he had momentarily lost during the acute stage, but he is still subject to the barrage of intense panic, and is desperate to establish a sense of well-being or safety. If his affective experience dictates that he drastically distort his views about self and object world, he will, in desperation, do so. If, in so doing, he succeeds in arriving at a sense of well-being or safety, he will then cling to the distortion for dear life. In treating a patient in such a state of mind, the therapist cannot be concerned with the gradual rectification of stabilized distortions. Instead, he must be concerned with distortions that are in the process of being formed. He must do his utmost to enable his patient not to settle for such distortions, which could severely handicap the patient's future living.

It is not an exaggeration to say that helping the patient not to settle for the most handicapping distortions about self and object world is a tremendous task, a task preferably not undertaken by the therapist alone. At the outset, the patient may periodically regress and return to his symptoms (e.g., confusion, concrete thinking, fragmented thought processes, outbursts of irrational rage), and he needs constant support from the ward as the good holding environment. His time should gradually become occupied by a variety of activities. A little later, he should take up some "work" that involves receiving orders, discharging responsibilities, etc. Still later, he will have to consider whether to resume the life plan he had before he became ill. All these moves have to be planned for the patient step by step. It is a postpsychotic phenomenon that without external guidance the patient will tend to maintain the status quo and not take up anything new and unfamiliar.

The therapist may be the person who plans for the patient, but ideally he should not be the person who helps the patient carry out the plan. If the therapist did the latter, he would risk becoming the permanent manager of the patient's life. Say that the therapist has assumed the management role for a while. Then he observes that the patient is ready to take over himself. Now, as he starts to change from the role of the manager who gives directions to the role of the therapist who helps the patient explore his conflicts, the patient may respond to the changed relationship with the therapist by feeling panic-stricken, and a crisis in treatment may be precipitated. But if the therapist has from the beginning confined his job to being the therapist, and has delegated the managerial job to a clinical administrator, no sudden void will be created and no therapeutic crisis will occur.

When the patient is admitted to the hospital, his family is usually willing to do anything at all to support the therapeutic program. When the patient begins to improve, they begin to establish more contact with him. However much they continue to want to help the patient, they need professional guidance. On their own, they can do many things to enhance the patient's interest in returning to the outside world, but they can also do many things that may impede his progress. The therapist might be the person who keeps in contact with the family members and offers them the needed professional guidance. But, if he is, he may often find himself caught in between the patient and his family. To forestall these problems, it is preferable that there be someone else (e.g., a clinical administrator who works with the family).

The clinical administrator and the therapist divide the labor. The clinical administrator will be concerned with the detailed planning for the patient and will help him carry out the plan, and he will also be concerned with giving professional guidance to the family. The therapist will, in the meantime, be concerned primarily with establishing a therapeutic alliance, with transference-countertransference manifestations and, most important, with the special task of the subacute phase (not to allow the patient to settle for his newly formed, perverted views about self and object world). This division of labor does not mean that each pursues his own goal without sharing his ideas with the other. The two must work together. At all times they must share their views about the patient. Should there be any marked difference in opinion, they must iron it out, leaving no possibility of pseudo-mutuality or working against one another's cause—the very situation that permeated the home in which the patient was raised.

Case Materials

To illustrate these points, I shall describe in detail the treatment of a schizophrenic patient during the subacute phase. The patient will be called Claudia. Claudia was a schizophrenic-I patient who was admitted to the hospital in an acute confusional state. She was in constant terror and was totally out of contact. After about three weeks she lapsed into a catatonic state. With her eyes closed, she had to passively be taken from one place to another. At times she was violent; such episodes were usually followed by even more pronounced passivity. She refused food but would eat some when spoon-fed. She was incontinent and at times smeared feces all over herself.

However, Claudia showed steady, though very, very gradual, improvement. From the fifth month onward, her confusion became increasingly less constant, and she was more and more a "definite person." Although she still had brief "out" moments in the next two months, they were most obvious in the therapeutic sessions. After another two months she seemed quite "together" superficially, yet she was extremely bland and reluctant to engage in any group activities, such as card games or sports. If she was coerced into participating in such activities, she responded passively and acted like an automaton. Left alone, she sat in an inconspicuous corner for long periods of time. Often she was in bed, with her head under the covers. Not particularly anxious, she was able to some extent to recount what she had gone through during the times when she seemed to others to be out of contact. Nonetheless, she gave the impression of reporting what she had observed rather than what she had experienced. She seemed to be uninterested in anything. Contrary to her previously expressed wish to complete her college education, she now said that she did not really care whether she did or not. Since she had nothing better to do she might consider going back to school some day. She felt, however, that her brain had turned into a concrete slab[1] and that she could never successfully complete college.

This drastically changed view of herself was total. She approached almost everything with the attitude that she did not measure up to it. Formerly, other patients had considered her a fairly good bridge player. Now she avoided playing bridge, feeling that others might enjoy a better game without her. She was also an above-average tennis player, but now she felt she could not even play with a beginner. The strange thing about it all was that she was not in the least disturbed about being so inferior.

The clinical picture exhibited by Claudia after she emerged from the disorganized state is not uncommon. If nothing is

---

[1] Even though at this stage this delusion seemed to be related to her "dampening" her emotions, no interpretation was made.

done about this changed view of self and object world at the right time, it may leave a permanent mark on the patients' personality, resulting in their actually being far inferior to what they had been before the disorganization. Bleuler asserted that there is never a total recovery (*restitutio ad integrum*) from schizophrenia. He could have been referring to this drastically changed view about self and object world.

Considering that the major task in treatment was to modify Claudia's distorted views, the clinical administrator encouraged her to participate in all the activities on the ward, and in certain noncompetitive activities, such as cooking, sewing, and painting, in the activity department. Three months later, when she appeared ready, she was encouraged to participate in the hospital work program; now she was entrusted with some responsibilities. After another three months she was given to understand that within a reasonable period of time she was first to get a job off the grounds and ultimately to move into a rented apartment near the hospital. In the meantime, since the administrator was the one who told the patient what was expected of her at each stage, I stayed with the role of scrutinizing with Claudia her reactions to the various "demands" made on her by the administrator.

When she was told to participate in the ward activities and noncompetitive activities in the activity department, she complied dutifully. Then she spoke of her own clumsiness and of not fitting into the group. As she talked, she mentioned that even in her "normal" days she had often felt she was clumsy and a misfit. I said that from her past experience she could be sure that the feelings she was having now would pass away as they had before. Later, when she was told to join the work program, she again obeyed without complaint. Among various available jobs, she chose to work in the patients' library. As she put it, she chose this job because there wasn't much interaction with people. I said that perhaps working in the library also reflected her desire to stay close to books. She was too polite to contradict me, but her reluctance to think about college was obvious.

As this led to further consideration of why she wasn't as definite as she had been before about completing college, she revealed her belief that her mind was wrecked and was still a slab of concrete. Essentially, she felt that since her mind was not now at her command, it would not be in the future. In describing how her mind was not at her command, she spoke of not being able to concentrate when reading. Then she confided that the last time she had found herself unable to concentrate on what she was reading had been at the beginning of her illness when she was still in school, several months before she came to Chestnut Lodge. After a brief review of the events preceding the onset of illness, it was not difficult to establish with her that she was now not as desperately panicky as she had been previously. When I finally indicated that her reading difficulty at the onset of her illness was related to her panic, she didn't say anything. Then, a couple of weeks later, she said (in a way as if our previous conversation had never occurred) that since she had nothing to do on her library job, she was compelled to read novels. I asked what she was reading, whether she enjoyed it, what type of novels she enjoyed most, who her favorite authors were, etc. During that hour I did not ask her directly about her ability to concentrate, nor did I remind her of our previous conversation about her lack of ability to concentrate. A week later, I learned that she was on her second novel. Still, I did not initiate any conversation about her ability to concentrate.

A few weeks elapsed. She was told by her administrator that she would have to look for a part-time job off the grounds. Her overt response to this expectation was none. She showed no fear and spoke of none. When the social service worker discussed with her what type of work she would like to get, Claudia said that she wanted to go back to work in a particular department store where she had enjoyed working as a salesgirl one summer while in high school. A week passed; she did not do anything. Another week passed; she had responded to ads at small stores and then declined interviews, complaining that these stores were not reputable enough. Then she found various reasons not to return to the department store she had worked in before, even though she believed her old boss, who liked her a lot, would undoubtedly take her back for the rush season.

At this point, she began to complain in the hours that the social worker was too pushy and why couldn't she be left alone. After going over the situation in detail she was able to see that her avoidance could be due either to her reluctance to take a sales job or to her fear of taking a new step, but considered the latter more likely. After a more careful study of her fear, she expressed concern that she would make a mistake in her figures, as her mind was no longer what it used to be. Now when she spoke of her inability to concentrate, I reminded her that she had only recently finished reading several novels. She retorted that she did read novels but did not recall what she read. With her brain like a concrete slab, she could never work. A few days later, when by chance I mentioned the ending of one of the novels she read, she corrected an error I had made. This convinced her that her ability to retain and concentrate was good. But although she no longer used her "concrete brain" as a rationalization, her phobia remained.

While she was working on her phobic attitude about anything new, she was visited by an elderly cousin who learned of her fear and volunteered to take her to an interview at the department store. At the interview, she obviously conducted herself well and got the wished-for job. Instantly she began to have nightmares. The consistent theme was that she got lost in a strange place, and looked desperately for her parents or her friends who had been in her company a moment earlier. Altogether, she was too anxious to associate to dreams. It was possible, however, to help her see that nightmares reflected her fear and that her fear could be related to going to work. The next day, she reported her preoccupation with suicide (she had attempted suicide before). I again spoke with her about her nightmares and helped her to see that her desire to end life was intimately related to her fear and that the nature of her fear required understanding. Now she recalled her recurrent experience of feeling small and helpless in the past whenever she went to a new school in a new city. (The family had moved frequently when she was young.)

She did go to work. (The administrator had in the meantime had several talks with her and had encouraged her to try out at work. He had arranged for an escort to take her to work and pick her up afterwards for several days until she said she was ready to come and go by herself.) The next day she reported that things were not as bad as she had anticipated. But a week later she said that she wished she had not started work but had gone back to school instead. She suggested that she be allowed to register for the next semester, which was less than two weeks away. Even though the appearance of this wish to return to school at this time seemed to be a way of getting out of work, I still considered its expression important. For since her break with reality this was the first time she had talked about college. I had to interpret the defensive use of the wish, but I felt I had to be cautious lest the wish be pushed aside. I said words to the effect that I was glad that overcoming her fear of working had possibly given her the courage to want to take up the long cherished but recently inhibited goal of returning to college. But I was baffled by why she did not allow herself a breathing space before taking the next step. After all, we had yet to understand why she had had so many nightmares before she took the step of going to work. She thought that was reasonable and decided to postpone returning to college for another semester. In the meantime, as she started to talk about her work, she revealed that she was anxious when there were too many customers, as well as when there were too few. In the former case she felt overwhelmed and feared making mistakes, and in the latter case she felt that she would be criticized for being lazy. This led first to some consideration of her concern about other people's opinions of her, and later to some discussion of her desire to get out of a situation where she anticipated no success. But she could not talk very much about either topic.

Eight weeks later, when the rush season was over, she was pleased to have been retained on the job.

At this time she began to consider moving out of the hospital. But the mere thought of it stirred up another series of nightmares. Thus, although she told her administrator that she would be looking for an apartment, she dragged her feet. Each of the apartments she and her social worker inspected was too swanky or too cheap-looking, lacking atmosphere or too far from busy streets, etc. After three months she finally found a place. When she was ready to move in, she became depressed, feeling sorry for herself for the years she had "lost" because of her illness. She was, however, able to see the defensive use of depression in this situation. She moved out of the hospital only a week later than originally planned.

After moving into her apartment[2] she had many dreams in which she or she in the disguise of a friend or relative was admitted to the hospital. Although her basic problem was related to separation, she conceptualized it as her inadequacy in coping with various situations. She could talk only about organizing her life around her apartment, when to go grocery shopping, when and what to eat, etc. I listened to her and learned a great deal about how she planned her daily living. Two months later, she seemed to have gotten accustomed to the routine, talked less of insurmountable daily tasks, and stopped dreaming of returning to the hospital. After another two months the administrator began to make occasional inquiries about her returning to college. A few months earlier she had shown such urgency about going back to college. Now she talked about college as if it were the remotest thing one could think of. As we studied her attitude in the context of her feelings of inadequacy, her interest in finishing college gradually heightened. Now I tried to establish a tacit agreement with her, that is, that once she started something she must finish it. Before she was sure she could do so, she had

[2] With some flexibility, most patients at Chestnut Lodge move into their own apartments gradually, beginning with one night a week and working up to seven nights a week.

better wait. And I tried to impress on her the disadvantages of starting and stopping.

Nine months later she re-entered college. At that time she had made a few friends at work and had also renewed friendships with a few high-school girlfriends, who had long ago earned their college degrees. She did well at college, although she was still obsessed with the idea that her brain was wrecked. At the end of the semester she was totally taken aback when her grades were higher than those of most of her classmates. Her success at college gradually put her feeling of inadequacy into proper perspective.

Claudia was an attractive young lady. Even when she was an inpatient and was markedly withdawn, her narcissistic air had attracted many young men, who paid special attention to her. She reciprocated only to those few who were extremely infantile, self-centered, and tended to set up a sadomasochistic relation with her. For some time the administrator had to take the position of telling her whom she should and should not associate with. This initially aroused some resentment in her. But as she became steadily involved in the study of her feeling of inadequacy, she became less concerned with male companions. Several weeks after she was established in her apartment, she ran into a young man who had dated her before she became ill. When he asked her out she instantly felt distressed and tried to avoid seeing him. She felt that he was a person whom she liked very much. Now, since she was not the same person she had been, she had better not see him any more. It is true that at a later date her fear of receiving attention from any young man whom she liked was a very deep-rooted problem, but at this time the problem must be seen in the light of her current subjective feeling of changed self. She was left to decide if she wanted to avoid him completely or, as an alternative, see him and find out where her problem lay. Fortunately she chose the latter course. For, in the near future, it was through dating him that her confidence was gradually and finally restored.

Now she felt very much like herself before her break with

reality. After a period of consolidating this feeling, her treatment became increasingly analytic. She associated freely, examining her defenses and conflicts.

Discussion

1. During the acute phase, the patient's clinical picture is rather uniform. If we do not have complete knowledge about him up to this point, we may not be at all certain whether he belongs to the category of schizophrenia I, II, III, or IV. In the subacute phase, however, even at the beginning, various types of clinical picture may become evident. (1) Along with the reestablishment of self-continuity, one group of patients has "normal periods." By "periods" I refer to times when the patient can hold on to his sense of self-cohesion, in contrast to times when he cannot. By "normal" I mean that the patient is free from hallucinations, fragmented thought processes, or other grossly psychotic symptoms. More often than not, the patient can hold a good conversation on a relatively neutral topic. In the further course of improvement, the patient shows less and less fluctuation between "normal" and psychotic. As the patient becomes increasingly "normal," he may develop pseudoneurotic symptoms such as phobias, and be obsessive-compulsive. Claudia, for instance, developed a diffuse phobic attitude. (2) A second group of patients remains psychotic, but with more psychotic moments and less psychotic moments. Even during the less psychotic moments, the patient retains psychotic symptoms (e.g., hallucinations, fragmented thoughts) in order to assure a maximum sense of well-being or safety.

Toward the end of the subacute phase, or the beginning of the chronic phase, both groups have less need for their pseudoneurotic or psychotic symptoms. In the meantime, they develop increasingly rigid viewpoints about themselves and the world around them. Henceforth, any therapeutic effort with the primary goal of changing his view about himself and his object world will not necessarily meet with much success. It is therefore imperative that we do what we can not to allow a patient like Claudia to settle for her pathological views about herself and her object world while she is still in the subacute phase.

2. In the early part of the subacute phase, because of his difficulty in maintaining a sense of self-cohesion, the patient lacks a sense of mastery and feels extremely vulnerable and helpless. He may experience both panic and depressive feelings—panic when he loses the sense of self-cohesion and depression when he possesses the sense of self-cohesion but realizes that he has but little power to maintain it. At this stage the patient is like a toddler taking his first steps, who can never be sure of keeping his balance; the difference being that the schizophrenic patient is usually very pessimistic and will not keep trying like the toddler. In treating a schizophrenic, the therapist must be aware of the patient's frustration over his lack of mastery and his readiness to give up. Aware of the patient's predicament, the therapist does not need to do anything more specific. As long as the therapist recognizes the patient's frustration, he can be more tolerant of the patient's narcissistic rages, neither punishing nor rejecting the patient. And as long as the therapist realizes that the patient is prone to pessimism, he will not be irritated and will be ready to inspire hope when the patient gives up.

In the treatment of Claudia I did no more than empathize with what she might be experiencing at different times. Several years later, when she was able to talk about this period, she considered that what was most helpful to her was that "you were very patient and hopeful."

3. In presenting the case of Claudia, I described only a fragment of her treatment, covering a period of about two years (the total treatment lasted for eight years) to demonstrate the phenomena and management of the subacute phase of schizophrenic illness. As is perhaps evident in the presentation, her basic problem with separation panic came through again and again, whenever she was called on to make a

change. While not neglecting the problems related to her separation panic,[3] I placed greater emphasis on the task of modifying her recently organized distorted view of herself and her object world. The emphasis on this task is based on the reasoning that while we have the entire time the patient stays in treatment to work on the problem of separation panic, we only have the subacute phase to work on the task of modifying distorted views. Such distorted views, which are formulated by the end of the acute phase, become "fixated" at the beginning of the chronic phase. Once "fixated," they are modified with difficulty, if at all.

Ordinarily, in treatment we tend to think a step ahead of the patient, but stay a step behind him. But during the subacute phase that should not be the case. If the therapeutic team simply thought a step ahead of Claudia but stayed a step behind her, she would probably have continued to view herself as undesirable and worse off than anybody else until such views became fixated. By then any attempt to modify them may threaten a return of symptoms. For example, in the past, Claudia had been reasonably comfortable in dating the old boyfriend. Now, after the break with reality, she no longer felt worthy of his company. If she had not been in treatment, she would probably have resorted to one of two courses—avoid seeing him, or go out with him but subtly discourage his further approach. In either case, she would gradually have developed a conviction of her own undesirability.[4] Because of this conviction, she would stubbornly have to maintain a position of not getting close to anyone ever, lest any intimacy stir up excessive anxiety and cause a return of symptoms.

4. In treating a patient during the subacute phase, the therapeutic team must therefore stay a little ahead of the patient. In Claudia's case, for example, the clinical adminis-

---

[3] Elsewhere (Pao, 1973) I have dealt more fully with the issue of separation panic.

[4] Most patients in the subacute phase, like Claudia, manifest feelings of inferiority. But some patients tend to be self-aggrandizing. With the latter type of patient the therapeutic team would have to take a different approach.

trator, whose action was in complete harmony with the whole therapeutic team, was constantly in the lead, slowly but steadily encouraging her to take such steps as joining activities on and off the ward, working in the library, working as a salesgirl at the department store, and returning to school. He also openly expressed his opinion about when and whom she could date, etc. In all this the therapeutic team's primary purpose was to enable the patient to bring her views about herself and her object world as close as possible to what they had been before the reorganization of self occurred. This purpose could be accomplished only through her mastering each little step she took. To avoid unnecessary discouragement, each step had to seem achievable to her. Once this purpose was attained, the therapeutic team revised its approach. The clinical administrator no longer actively set up little steps for the patient, expecting her to fulfill them. Henceforth, the patient was allowed to work out her problems gradually, at her own pace.

The combination of little steps that the clinical administrator expected Claudia to take was of course not chosen at random but carefully and specifically designed for Claudia. The choice was partly guided by his knowledge of her past aspirations, but mainly by what he learned directly from Claudia each time about her interest in taking a certain step. For instance, if he had known that Claudia definitely had no interest in returning to college, he would not have guided her in that direction. Or if she had expressed a desire to return to college instead of to work in the department store, she would not have been encouraged to go to work. Nor was the breathing space the clinical administrator allowed after she had made each step decided on at random. He evaluated each situation carefully and certainly tried not to throw the patient into a panic.

With the clinical administrator assuming the active role of encouraging the patient to take different steps toward changing his views, the therapist can be relatively passive and neutral in helping the patient study and thus minimize the emotional tumult stirred up by the clinical administrator's gentle but firm pressure to move on. The therapist and clinical administrator must, however, be in constant consultation so that the latter will have the needed information about whether the patient can be started on a new step, whether a certain step is worth taking, etc.

The therapist himself may sometimes have to assume a more active approach. The following excerpt from a therapeutic hour with a patient may illustrate this point.

Within three years, Robin had been hospitalized twice because of catatonic symptoms. Since the second psychosis, four years earlier, she had shown steady improvement. About a year and a half before, she had moved out of the hospital but was still associated with the hospital work program.[5] This particular work program consisted of Robin, who was a patient, and four regular part-time hospital employees, all of whom were young college students.

During the hour in question, Robin began by reporting that she felt very distraught. The other workers on the program were planning a luncheon out together and did not seem to intend to include her. Robin recalled with some resentment that they had not included her at their last luncheon out either. But the last time her exclusion was forgivable, for after all she was new and they didn't know her well. This time, however, things were different. They had known her for a while and they all seemed to have indicated their liking for her. Still she was not included. Bitterly, she said that they were prejudiced against her because she was a patient. They were not supposed to be prejudiced but they were. She could just imagine how people outside the hospital would feel toward her, a previously hospitalized patient. Returning to the immediate situation, she said she felt like talking to the other workers and asking them to include her. (The last comment

[5] Note that Robin's association with the hospital work program continued after she left the hospital. Claudia, however, worked in a department store before she moved out of the hospital. This contrast exemplifies the individualized nature of each patient's program.

had a hollow ring to it, and was obviously intended to sound out the therapist's opinion.)

If Robin were a neurotic, the therapist might, at this point, simply leave the whole matter up to her to work out. If she did subsequently talk to the others and get herself included at the lunch party, it would be great. If she did not ask, her reasons for not asking would probably be taken up in the next hour. If, however, Robin continued to press the therapist for his opinion, then he would comment on her behavior, or if her behavior was of a transference nature, then he would have to make a transference interpretation.

But with the modification of Robin's distorted views about her self and others as his primary goal, the therapist may have to do more. He must assess the whole therapeutic plan, and gauge his own action in accordance with what the clinical administrator intended to do at that moment. In the actual situation, the administrator had, for a couple of months now, wanted Robin to get a job outside the hospital, and Robin had been dragging her feet. Besides, the therapist was also aware that while the hospital personnel and the patients did eat in the same dining room, they ate during different shifts. In other words, Robin and her co-workers did not regularly eat together. In the circumstances, the therapist might do something on the order of the following. While being sympathetic with the patient, he must remind her that she was in an impossible predicament. If she did succeed in getting the others to include her at the luncheon, the solution could only be temporary. Practically never having eaten together, the others might also find themselves in a quandary about whether to include her at the luncheon. Later on, when she worked at a job outside the hospital, where everyone would feel more on an equal footing, similar social complications could perhaps be avoided. These comments by the therapist might momentarily make Robin feel rather unhappy. But they would give the patient some impetus to move on. In the long run she might derive more self-confidence from them than from winning the small battle of being included at the luncheon party.

5. It has been noted that phobia, obsessive-compulsive-ness, and depression[6] are common symptoms after the patient has emerged from the acute phase of illness. In Claudia's case, all three occurred in a mild form. Since she was able to talk about her "problems," these symptoms did not reach severe proportions. In patients who cannot talk about their problems as freely as Claudia did (e.g., schizophrenic-III patients, and many schizophrenic-II patients), these symptoms can become extreme.

Phobia, obsessive-compulsiveness, and depression may be related to what I have described as rituals. Elsewhere (see Chapter 17) I defined rituals as automated defensive measures that the patient resorts to in regulating the discharge of aggression. The patient's excessive concern about aggression is due partly to his past conflicts about aggression, which have now become incorporated into the reorganized self- and object representations. For instance, in the case of Claudia, in the further course of treatment she was able to study her conflicts about aggression, which dated back to the early rapprochement period of the separation-individuation phase and became represented by the memory of a scene of a power struggle with her mother corresponding to the time of the birth of the next sibling. However, in addition to the internal conflict and the reorganized views about self and object world, the patient's concern about aggression, which results in the symptoms, may also have something to do with coping with the here-and-now external environment. At a time when the integrative function of the ego is still liable to paralysis by overwhelming panic, the patient has organized himself in such a way as best to protect himself from external stimuli. Warding off external stimuli may necessitate the mobilization of aggression, and thereby intensify the internal conflicts. From the therapeutic point of view, the symptoms must be dealt with dynamically. Usually, as in the case of Claudia,

---

[6] Here the term depression refers to the clinical picture of sadness plus slowness in thinking and motility.

our therapeutic effort need not be directed specifically to the symptoms.

6. In this chapter I have not considered the nursing support and the family work. Especially during the early part of the subacute phase the patient, now comparable to the toddler in the process of hatching (Mahler, 1975), wants gradually to get away from the nursing staff on the ward, but still has high hopes of their continual interest in him and concern about his welfare. To deal with such a patient, the nursing staff must learn how to be attentive to his needs and how not to be carried away by their own sensitive feelings about separation or sometimes outright rejection. As for work with the family, it is never more important than during the subacute phase. Many a family needs professional guidance. To alleviate the burden of the other team workers, the social service worker may have to take the onus of facilitating communication between the family and the therapeutic team.

CHAPTER 25

Psychotherapy with Schizophrenic Patients during the Chronic Phase

The chronic phase refers to a time when the patient's distorted views about himself and his object world, organized since the recent break with reality, have become solidified and are not easily modified. During the chronic phase the therapeutic team must reconcile itself to the fact that these distorted views are by now practically unchangeable and that any strenuous attempt to change them may not only be unsuccessful but may also risk serious complications, including the possibility of another total break with reality.

During the chronic phase the therapeutic team must make a concerted effort first to help the patient make known his wishes and then to help him fulfill them if that is possible. By the time of the chronic phase, the patient has established a firm belief that the object world he lives in is hostile and that with it he can never successfully gratify his wishes. He therefore learns not to wish. Or, if he must wish, he fulfills his wish through hallucination. He has decided that it is simply meaningless to tell others of his wishes. Perhaps because of the unsuppressible nature of his wishes, however, he feels compelled, against his will, to tell them to other people. At such moments, as he anticipates denial of the fulfillment of his wishes, he experiences hopelessness, rage, and therefore panic. He thereupon accentuates the use of the special lan-

412

guage—schizophrenese[1]—by means of which he succeeds in simultaneously revealing and hiding his wishes. He realizes that his language is unintelligible. But he does not care. For he has discovered that he can derive a maximum sense of safety by adopting the policy that it is not his responsibility to communicate to others what he wants, it is the duty of others to "know" what he wants. In the process he has completely lost sight of the fact that while his policy may maximize his sense of safety, it forfeits his right to have his wishes fulfilled by others. In treating such a patient, therefore, the primary therapeutic task is to help him overcome his distrust of others. Once that is accomplished, the patient will rectify his communication problem so that his wishes can be studied in terms of the possibility of their being fulfilled.

To help the patient overcome his distrust of others is a tremendous task, and to achieve it is so time-consuming that it often becomes the only thing that can be accomplished with a schizophrenic patient during the chronic phase. When the patient has relearned how to trust others, explicitly to express his wishes to others, and to get the needed help in fulfilling his wishes, his views about his self and the object world will, of course, be significantly changed. Still, this change is quite restricted in scope, as the patient tends to preserve many of his fundamental eccentric views and behaviors. Besides, the limited change that occurs takes place without the patient's conscious recognition of what his original views were. In this respect, this change is quite different from what is expected to occur in the treatment of a schizophrenic patient during the subacute phase.

Case Material

Florette arrived at Chestnut Lodge when she was 39 years old and had already been hospitalized for 15 years, episodi-

---

[1] In the rare instances when patients are extremely gifted, they can explain, in retrospect, the logic of their highly personal language. See, for example, Deborah's use of language in *I Never Promised You a Rose Garden* (Green, 1964).

cally at first but continuously for the last eight years.

Little was known about Florette's infancy, except that she was looked after by a number of nursemaids. From the age of three, when all her sisters were at school and she was alone at home, Florette was drawn very close to her mother. The long-standing mother-daughter relationship was epitomized in the mother's statement on meeting Florette's therapist at Chestnut Lodge: "Florette and I feel and think the same way. We don't have to say anything to each other and I know what she wants." Moreover, while Florette was at Chestnut Lodge, the mother regularly sent clothes to her; once she sent two slippers of the same kind but of different colors. It turned out that the mother had kept the other unmatched pair. Florette was never close to her father, who was a public figure and little known to the family except for his discipline. Still, he spent a good deal of time with his oldest child and only son. When the son died of a tetanus infection, the father had intense headaches that also "went to his stomach" (whatever that meant). He died four years later at the age of 50. Following the father's death, Florette's mother took over, ran the family business, and multiplied the family fortune several times. Efficient as a business woman, she was, however, described as not knowing what to do when any of her children acted sassy to her. The mother had a nervous breakdown after the birth of her third child, and was said to have overcome her depression through her husband's insistence that she ride horseback several hours a day. Florette was the youngest of four daughters in a family of five. As already mentioned, her only brother died when she was eight. Of the sisters, the oldest married, although not until she was in her middle 30's, the second was described as an ambulatory schizophrenic, and the third went to a convent in her 30's, but left and got married when she was around 50 years old.

For as long as her family could remember, Florette had been extremely jealous and had terrible tantrums; through the tantrums she got what she wanted, and was therefore nicknamed "Queen." In kindergarten she established a pattern of taking a great fancy to a particular girl and then dropping her. After the death of her brother, Florette for a while would go into a room by herself, pull down the shade, and perform a ritualistic dance. At this time she also locked herself up in her room and dressed herself up as a queen. One day a few months later, while she was playing checkers with her mother, Florette shook all over at the sight of a boy whom her oldest sister, then 16, had brought home. There was no explanation for all these events. At around 12, she developed into a good-looking young lady, and for the first time her father warmed up to her. Not quite a year later, he died. After his death, she was described as becoming lifeless and emotionless for a year or so. At that time, she did not cling as much to her mother, who read aloud to her a lot. She recovered but did not seem as carefree, always having "that sour, sallow look that was later associated with her illness."

At 17, already very withdrawn and isolated, she was sent away to a finishing school in the East. A year later, she had become increasingly withdrawn, rude, and given to frequent outbursts of rage, such as yelling at her mother, "I hate you, I hate you." She had a few blind dates; no boy asked her out a second time. She was obsessed with being a homosexual. Although visibly troubled, she nevertheless managed to graduate from college at the age of 22. She was never gainfully employed.

At 24, when one of her sisters had an out-of-town boyfriend staying at their home, Florette began to act strangely. She mimicked him at the table, said she hated him and might kill him, and then acted hostilely toward the whole family. One day she put a veil over her face and wouldn't look at them. At this point she was taken to see a psychiatrist and was briefly hospitalized. For the next few years she made a marginal adjustment at home. When she was 28, her oldest sister married. Florette acted very antagonistically toward her brother-in-law, saying things to him like "you leaned on the table, you knew it was going to make me feel something." Soon she began to assault him. Presently, she was hospitalized. Ever since, she had been transferred from hospital to hospital and had received many ECT's and IST's. But her symptoms did not abate.

The deaths of her brother and father seem to have had such tremendous emotional impact on her that on both occasions she seems briefly to have lost her ability for reality testing. Considering how her mother's post-partum depression was overcome, it is not surprising that in this family no outside help was sought until she was 24, by which time her illness had advanced almost to the chronic phase. Fifteen years later, when she was transferred to Chestnut Lodge, she was described as looking like a witch without a broom, or a corpse, or a holy terror, or the meanest and ugliest person on earth. Whenever she was upset (which she was almost constantly), for reasons not immediately identifiable, she either struck out at others or banged her head against the wall. She clung to the bed and covered her head with blankets; she declined food and had to be tube-fed. She neglected her personal hygiene and fought ferociously against an army of nurses who tried to give her a bath or shampoo.

Florette's treatment involved a long list of therapists, administrators, nurses, activities workers, and social workers, and it would be impossible to identify whose contributions were most conducive to the outcome of the treatment. In general, the whole therapeutic team met regularly, exchanged their observations, and tried to approach Florette in a coordinated way. Here I shall describe the course of the treatment in terms of the work of her four therapists; I shall also give mention to nurse A.'s effort.

Her first therapist was a woman. In the beginning, when the therapist went to see Florette, Florette either hid under the blanket or ordered the therapist to leave her alone. A couple of months later, Florette began to sit through the hours with her therapist, but simply had nothing to say. Gradually the therapist succeeded in getting Florette to weave and do needlepoint with her. A year later Florette was able to do needlework with persons other than her therapist. She also began to paint. For a long time her paintings were stereo-typed, and consisted of a barn standing all alone in an open field. Much later she began to populate her pictures with hu-man beings. While they were weaving and doing needlepoint together, the therapist at first limited her comments primar-ily to their work. Slowly and occasionally, the therapist began to make connections between the patient's behavior on the ward and the possible emotional reasons for her behavior. For instance, the therapist questioned if the patient's assaultive-ness on the previous night might be related to her scary feel-ings or if the scary feelings were related to her anger, jealousy, etc.[2] Initially the patient did not answer, but gradually she started to say "yes" and "no." The therapist would then sug-gest that some day the patient should talk about those fright-ening experiences instead of acting on them.

Gradually the symptoms subsided. As Florette began to talk a little about what scared her, her language proved to be so obscure that both therapist and patient had to exercise a great deal of patience to decode it. For instance, she said she was frightened on the previous day by the color yellow, and in a long, dragged-out conversation, it turned out that a virile man had sat on a yellow chair on the ward. Evidently while it was sometimes possible to clarify her immediate concern, a dynamic understanding of transference was out of the ques-tion—partly because of the scantiness of her associations and partly because of the obscurity of her language. Six years later, the first therapist left the hospital feeling quite good about her work with the patient. Most of the work had been done at a nonverbal level. By allowing the patient to relive a long period of symbiotic existence (similar to the patient's life with her mother after the death of her father), the ther-apist had reawakened the patient's hope and trust in the re-establishment of human relations.

Florette's next therapist was a man. He observed that

[2] Obviously Florette used the "scary" feeling to conceal all sorts of emotions. Because of the defensive use of this feeling, Florette never allowed herself to define what it was about, except to say that it was uncomfortable.

Florette was very shy and aloof in all interpersonal situations. She never initiated a conversation but did respond appropriately. Usually, however, her answers were very simple sentences, often consisting of only "yes" or "no." She was currently engaged in several projects at the activity department. In the past year she had been allowed to come and go within the hospital grounds with an escort, and had often gone on escorted shopping trips in town. She had also visited her home. The visit went very well. Now, in the therapy, she arrived for her hours at the appointed time, sat for an undetermined period of time, usually 5 to 15 minutes, and then ran out of the office, screaming, "He is a man, I don't know what to do with him. It is scary."

Months later, when she could sit more calmly and for longer periods of time in his office, she would relate, in a disjointed way, something about her brother, and that after his funeral she had thrown a pitchfork at one of her brother's friends. Any attempt to consider these isolated memories, in terms of establishing continuity with her past or even in terms of her current fear of hurting the therapist, was met with blandness. As it was, these and many other memories were therapeutically unusable. However, they must have served some important function. The presence of the therapist obviously brought forth a limited degree of derepression of past events, such as the death of the brother. Since she was not yet ready to deal with the emotions attached to the events, she promptly rerepressed them. Perhaps the brief resurfacing of the unresolved conflict paved the way for a possible working through in the future. Perhaps the rerepression offered her a sense of mastery which could in turn enhance her self-esteem. At any rate, the therapist was pleased that the patient could report these disconnected fragments without fear. Given the fact that the patient's language was still very obscure, he was not eager to make connections for himself or for the patient. In addition, the patient harped on a theme of rebirth. The original theme was of being physically reborn as a baby; it gradually changed into an "emotional" rebirth. Things seemed to go as well as could be, and it was unfortunate that two years later the second therapist also left the hospital.

Florette showed some, but manageable, reservations about establishing a relation with the third therapist, who had a very relaxed approach to his patients. This therapist noted at the outset that Florette was extremely phobic and had many rituals. For instance, she started her day by traversing the same route, beginning with the cottage where she resided, to a seat in another building, to a second seat in yet another building, to a third seat in still another building, smoking a cigarette at each place and watching the surrounding hubbub; arriving for her hour, she walked to the threshold of the door and waited for an invitation to come in; and if for any reason the therapist was not aware of her arrival, she stood motionlessly for a long time without uttering a sound, until she was recognized. During the therapeutic sessions, Florette timidly went over daily events, obviously expecting the therapist to select a topic to elaborate on. Inquiry about the origin of the extreme caution she exhibited before the therapist yielded no results; nor was any meaningful verbal exchange initiated by such comments as, "It was scary for you to have voted for Roosevelt instead of the candidate your mother voted for? Perhaps you feel you should be very cautious with me like you were with your mother, whose will you felt you should not contradict." It did seem that the patient was still thinking at a very concrete level; she was completely baffled by abstract thinking.

The therapist therefore decided as his initial step to go along with the patient and picked topics to establish some sort of conversation between them. Slowly and steadily, he subtly allowed the patient to take more and more initiative in deciding what she wanted to talk about. There were silent hours during which the patient felt there was nothing to talk about; but then on direct questioning she said her mind was not blank, nor was it crowded with conflicted thoughts. She was too scary to tell the therapist what she was thinking. He worked on the sharing. Gradually she told him that during the silent moments she often heard the voice of one of her sisters criticizing her. Accepting that any discussion of her having hallucinations in order to keep distance from himself might further drive her away from him, he chose to talk with her about the voices. Together they compared the differences between the content of her sister's voice and what she herself would think about. Further along, the difference between what she thought and what her sister said to her became narrower. Moreover, the voice now resided in her head, instead of coming from outside. As the therapist continued to talk with her about the difference between her own thoughts and her sister's voice, the patient finally announced one day that the voice was actually her own thoughts. (There followed a period when this belief of the patient's was not firm.)

By now, the patient seemed increasingly to know what she wanted and to tell the therapist about her wishes. For instance, she wanted to revisit the South Sea islands where she had traveled with her family in her early teens (perhaps after her recovery from her psychosis following her father's death). However, while she was unequivocal about her decision, she was not able to give reasons for it. In the circumstances, the therapist did not interpret, but explored with her the realistic problems involved in carrying out such a plan.

Six years after the beginning of their work together, the patient expressed a wish to move out of the hospital. At a very slow pace, she investigated different facilities in the vicinity of the hospital, and concluded that she liked none of them, for "outside life was too scary and lonely." She now declared that she would go home to live with her mother, but her mother did not want her there. She then expressed a wish to move back to the psychiatric hospital in which she had been an inmate before coming to Chestnut Lodge and which was situated very close to her home. She insisted on revisiting this hospital. After the visit, she decided that she could not go back there, but offered no reasons why not. At this point, her third therapist went into private practice near the hospital. Florette decided to continue working with him and to see him in his office. She went back and forth on her own, by taxi. Facing a new situation, she was flabbergasted, and spoke of "men in the elevator," but soon settled into the routine. Then her mother died. By way of mourning for the loss of her mother, she mourned, perhaps for the first time, the loss of her father and her feeling about his preference for her siblings. She acknowledged that she was jealous. For the next year or so, she continued to decide whether to live near Chestnut Lodge or to move back to her hometown. In the midst of this indecision, the patient declared one day that she would not continue to work with her therapist any longer and that her mind could not be changed.

Now she began to work with a fourth therapist, whose selection she had a voice in. In the beginning the fourth therapist noted that since the patient reported in such fragments, it was very difficult to distinguish current events from past ones, and quite impossible to see how statements were related. When anxious, her use of a primitive type of metaphorical thinking (e.g., to characterize an aide's behavior as authoritarian and unreasonable, she had to say that she was upset by an aide who had something to do with Hitler's Nazis), as well as her inability to understand abstract thought, were conspicuous. Ideas of reference also recurred—e.g., she received vibrations from another woman patient—but she could recognize them as her ideas and was not compelled to do anything about them. Because of the latter quality, her grasp of reality seemed solid, and hence her judgment was reasonably sound. In general, her maintenance of thought and language peculiarities seemed to have a lot to do with her limited social intercourse. Yet, on questioning, she made it clear that she was perfectly satisfied with her seclusive life.

Even though Florette had more or less one-sidedly decided on the change in therapists, she did express some regret and remorse afterwards. She could not grasp the similarity between this dropping of a therapist and her early pattern of dropping her friends. Soon she began to talk about her wish to go back to her hometown again. Since her mother had recently died and her sisters were not blocking her return, her wish seemed to stand a good chance of being fulfilled. Now she could certainly buy her mother's old home and take up residence there; but for her to live there without a companion was inconceivable. Where to find this companion? She thought of nurse A. Fortunately, nurse A. was agreeable. Henceforth Florette initiated meetings with her trust officers, step by step realized her plan, and after talking about going home for almost six years, she finally did. A two-year-follow-up revealed that she was quite happy with her present life and that she had recently relearned how to drive and was driving a car. She remained reticent but made decisions about her living, and in making her decisions she showed reasonably sound judgment.

In regard to nurse A., ever since Florette's admission to Chestnut Lodge nurse A. had been very much involved with her. On Florette's admission, while other persons were afraid of her, nurse A. saw her as a frightened child. Nurse A. was the first person to succeed in singlehandedly bathing and shampooing Florette after her admission. Later, Florette would accept a bath or shampoo from anyone that nurse A. recommended. When Florette made her first trip home she asked nurse A. to accompany her. Ever since, a very strong bond had existed between them. Shortly before Florette began to work with her second therapist, she went with her fears about him to nurse A., who suggested that she relate those fears to the therapist, which Florette did. Thereafter, nurse A. became, as it were, Florette's traveling companion. Whenever Florette wanted to go home, to the beach, to the South Sea islands, to Europe, she asked nurse A., who accommodated her whenever possible. On trips, nurse A. left decisions to Florette, and took over only when she intuitively felt Florette really wanted her to. She never seemed to block Florette's initiative, and that was perhaps the reason why Florette was very comfortable with her. For several years nurse A. had invited Florette to spend nights at her home, and Florette seemed to be rather comfortable with nurse A.'s husband. The final living arrangement seemed to be quite ideal.

Discussion

1. The case of Florette is intended to demonstrate what can and cannot be accomplished in the treatment of a schizophrenic patient during the chronic phase. At the end of the treatment, Florette was capable of communicating her wishes to others and was thus able to get the needed help from others to fulfill some of her fulfillable wishes (for instance, returning to her hometown and establishing a household at her mother's old home). Yet, despite her solid grasp of reality and sound judgment, she still had strong paranoid tendencies. And, more significant, the core of her concept about her self and her object world had not been changed at all in the course of treatment. She used to believe she was a queen. As a queen, she was entitled to have her every whim carried out by others. She owed no one any explanation why she wanted what she wanted. Toward the end of the treatment she continued to act queenly. She left the third therapist without explaining why, even though she could have felt that she had given him enough time and he had not yet worked out ways to fulfill her wish to live in her hometown. As far as she was concerned, she had only to say what she wanted, others would then have to carry it out and deliver it to her on a silver tray. To a large extent, the realization of her going-home plan was worked out in this way. Even though she did the talking with nurse A., with her trust officers, etc., others had to work out for her with whom she should be talking.

Florette seems to have derived a good deal of safety from the queenly approach. As early as eight years of age, after her brother's death, she seems to have made use of a formerly adaptive technique to establish some sense of security. It is therefore understandable that she would hardly budge from her attitude during the whole course of treatment, in spite of the fact that it had cost her dearly. She started to speak of returning to her hometown six years before she actually went. One can easily conceive that if she had not maintained the queenly attitude—"Here is my wish, help me figure out how to fulfill it"—things might have worked out quite differently.

As it was, when her wish was blocked by her mother's reluctance to have her in town, her queenliness was challenged
or her sense of safety was threatened, so that she gave up
talking about going home. Her subsequent desire to go to
another hospital seemed to be a face-saving device; yet her
seriousness in approaching this goal necessarily consumed a
great deal of time that she could have used more construc-
tively.

Truly, it was sheer luck that she finally fulfilled her dear-
est wish, i.e., to return to her hometown. If nurse A. had not
retired and had not consented to live with her, it is hard to
conceive how she could have gone home by herself. Her mother
was no longer alive and her sisters had their own lives to live.
Any other companion would probably not have been able to
understand her special kind of queenly attitude. Without such
an understanding, other companions would probably have
been dropped by the patient before they even knew why—just
like the third therapist and her numerous girlfriends of earlier years. But how would the repeated loss of companions in
the end have affected the patient? By then, would she have
chosen to retreat to the hospital?

2. The interaction between patient and therapist in psychotherapy is determined by the personalities of the two participants. In Florette's case, all the therapists seem to have
been made "passively" responsive to the patient. Two questions may be raised: Were these therapists chosen because
they could respond passively to the patient? (The patient had
no voice in the selection of the first three therapists.) And
what would have happened if the therapist had insisted on
being very active, for instance, driving home interpretations
about the patient's unconscious motives?

Regarding the first question, the first three therapists were
actually very different in their personalities as well as in
their theoretical and philosophical leanings. All of them, however, agreed on one issue: They believed in talking with the
patient, hoping to establish conversation with her instead of
bypassing her ego and making an effort to delve directly into

her unconscious. As for the second question—What would have happened if the therapist had insisted on giving her deep interpretations?—in Florette's case, when the therapist attempted to make an abstract statement, she chose not to understand it, and also not to feel anything about not understanding it. In this way she forced the therapist to change his course. If the therapist had ignored her cue and insisted on driving home his point, he could have torn down her defenses. If a complete break with reality had resulted, there was no telling whether Florette could have returned to reality. Otto Will once told me about a colleague of his who had believed in stripping off the patient's old defenses and aiding him to rebuild new ones. When she put this belief into practice, she succeeded in causing quite a few patients to break with reality. But the rebuilding fantasy never materialized.

3. During the early years of Florette's illness, antipsychotic drugs were not available. (Therefore, she had ECT and IST.) When the drugs finally became available in the last several years of treatment, their use seemed unnecessary. The question may be raised: If drugs had been available, what would have happened to Florette, who began treatment when already in the chronic phase of her illness? My own experience with similar patients leads me to conclude that drugs can make many of these patients appear "normal" on the surface. Consequently, they can return to the community after a much shorter hospital stay than Florette's. However, as in the case of Florette, therapeutic attempts to modify their grossly distorted views about the self and the object world still do not meet with much success.

For reasons of space, I can only mention the case of Mrs. Estelle C. At 18, she had an acute schizophrenic episode that lasted for about three years. She was kept at home, and her mother was said to have been instrumental in her recovery. When the mother was asked what she thought she did that helped Estelle's recovery, she said, "I agreed with her. For instance, it was snowing outside but if she said 'it is hot here,' I would agree with her and opened all the windows. It was very quiet in the room, but if she said 'it is too noisy here,' I'd agree with her and make the place quieter," etc. A few years after her recovery, Estelle married; she was then 24. Immediately she had two children. However, at 29, she had to be hospitalized because she was confused, bewildered, and violent. In the hospital, she giggled and made no sense. She tore all her clothes into shreds and occasionally hit people. She hallucinated and was at times incontinent. After some time, antipsychotic drugs were prescribed, and her outward behavior became "normal" pretty readily.

Several months later, she returned home and continued her psychotherapy sessions. Although she never missed a session (she was chauffeured to the hour), she only sat and stared. Months later, with much encouragement from the therapist, she began to give a five-minute resume of what had happened the previous night. When asked how she had felt about what she had just reported, she was completely lost. Once, after she said she had discovered lipstick on her husband's shirt, she was asked if she had been angry or jealous. Her answer was that she was neither angry nor jealous. She was upset. Gradually it became clear that she could not differentiate such feelings as anger, jealousy, envy, joy, delight. As far as she was concerned, she was either feeling all right or she was upset. This lack of ability to identify her emotions seemed to serve a very useful defensive purpose. If she was angry, she had to do something about it, whereas if she was upset or panicked, she became paralyzed and did not have to do anything at all.[3] Thus, for nearly two years of office treatment, much effort was devoted solely to helping her identify her emotional response to various events. By then, she began to be able to describe clearly how she was angered by her husband's criticism. Some time later, she recognized that her husband's criticism angered her because her mother too was critical of her. One would hope that with this realization, Estelle would not be half as upset when her husband criticized

[3] Estelle's defensive use of "upset" was like Florette's defensive use of "scary."

her. But that was not the case. In fact, Estelle began to expect her husband to behave like her mother, who praised Estelle after having criticized her. What this amounted to was that no change was supposed to occur within her; the world had to change to make her feel better. This attitude had apparently been greatly reinforced by her mother when her mother was supposedly bringing Estelle out of her psychosis. Incidentally, despite improvement in other aspects of mental life (e.g., reality testing, judgment), she was still blind (after eight more years of treatment) to the fact that she always expected the world to change for her.

References

Abelin, E. L. (1975), Some further observations and comments on the earliest role of the father. *Internat. J. Psycho-Anal.*, 56:293-302.

Abraham, H. & Freud, E. (1965), *A Psycho-Analytic Dialogue: The Letters of Sigmund Freud and Karl Abraham, 1907-1926.* New York: Basic Books.

American Psychiatric Association (1952), *Diagnostic and Statistical Manual of Mental Disorders, DSM-I.* Washington, D.C.: American Psychiatric Association.

―――― (1968), *Diagnostic and Statistical Manual of Mental Disorders, DSM-II.* Washington, D.C.: American Psychiatric Association.

Applegarth, A. (1971), Comments on aspects of the theory of psychic energy. *J. Amer. Psychoanal. Assn.*, 19:379-416.

Arieti, S. (1974), *Interpretation of Schizophrenia,* 2nd ed. New York: Basic Books.

Arlow, J. A. (1966), Depersonalization and derealization. In: *Psychoanalysis: A General Psychology,* ed. R. M. Loewenstein et al. New York: International Universities Press, pp. 456-478.

―――― & Brenner, C. (1964), *Psychoanalytic Concepts and the Structural Theory.* New York: International Universities Press.

―――― ―――― (1969), The psychopathology of the psychoses: A proposed revision. *Internat. J. Psycho-Anal.*, 50:5-14.

Bak, R. (1954), The schizophrenic defence against aggression. *Internat. J. Psycho-Anal.*, 35:129-134.

―――― (1970), Recent developments in psychoanalysis: A critical summary of the main theme of the 26th International Psycho-Analytical Congress in Rome. *Internat. J. Psycho-Anal.*, 51:255-264.

Bateson, G., Jackson, D., Haley, J., & Weakland, J. (1956), Toward a theory of schizophrenia. *Behav. Sci.*, 1:251-264.

Bellak, L. (1958), *Schizophrenia: A Review of the Syndrome.* New York: Logos.

―――― et al. (1974), *Ego Functions and Schizophrenics, Neurotics and Normals.* New York: Wiley.

Beres, D. (1956), Ego deviation and the concept of schizophrenia. *The Psychoanalytic Study of the Child,* 11:164-235. New York: International Universities Press.

429

———— & Arlow, J. A. (1974), Fantasy and identification in empathy. *Psychoanal. Quart.*, 43:26-50.

Bergmann, M. (1963), The place of Paul Federn's ego psychology in psychoanalytic metapsychology. *J. Amer. Psychoanal. Assn.*, 11:97-116.

Bibring, E. (1947), The so-called English school of psychoanalysis. *Psychoanal. Quart.*, 16:69-93.

Bion, W. R. (1956), Development of schizophrenic thought. *Internat. J. Psycho-Anal.*, 37:344-346.

———— (1957), Differentiation of the psychotic from the non-psychotic personalities. *Internat. J. Psycho-Anal.*, 38:266-275.

———— (1959), Attacks on linking. *Internat. J. Psycho-Anal.*, 40:308-315.

———— (1968a), Notes on the theory of schizophrenia. *Second Thoughts.* New York: Basic Books, pp. 23-25.

———— (1968b), *Second Thoughts.* New York: Basic Books.

Birns, B. H. (1965), Behavioral inhibition in neonates produced by auditory stimuli. *Child Devel.*, 36:639-645.

Bleuler, E. (1903), Dementia praecox. *J. Ment. Pathol.*, 3:113-120.

——— (1911), *Dementia Praecox, or the Group of Schizophrenias.* New York: International Universities Press, 1950.

Blos, P. (1962), *On Adolescence.* New York: Free Press.

——— (1970), *The Young Adolescent.* New York: Free Press.

Blum, H. P. (1974), The borderline childhood of the Wolf Man. *J. Amer. Psychoanal. Assn.*, 22:721-742.

Boverman, M. (1955), A factor in "spontaneous" recovery. *Bull. Menninger Clin.*, 19:129-134.

Boyer, L. B. & Giovacchini, P. L. (1967), Psychoanalytic treatment of character disorders. In: *Psychoanalytic Treatment of Schizophrenia and Characterological Disorders.* New York: Science House, pp. 208-234.

Brenner, C. (1957), The nature and development of the concept of repression in Freud's writings. *The Psychoanalytic Study of the Child,* 12:19-46. New York: International Universities Press.

———— (1974), On the nature and development of affects: A unified theory. *Psychoanal. Quart.*, 43:532-556.

Breuer, J. & Freud, S. (1893-1895), Studies on hysteria. *Standard Edition,* 2. London: Hogarth Press, 1955.

Brierley, M. (1951), *Trends in Psycho-Analysis.* London: Hogarth Press.

Brunswick, R. M. (1929), The analysis of a case of paranoia (delusions of jealousy). *J. Nerv. Ment. Dis.*, 70:1-22, 155-178.

Bullard, D. M. (1940), The organization of psychoanalytic procedures in the hospital. *J. Nerv. Ment. Dis.*, 91:697-703.

Burnham, D. L. (1955), Some problems in communication with schizophrenic patients. *J. Amer. Psychoanal. Assn.*, 3:67-81.

———— (1973), The restitution function of symbol and myth in Strindberg's inferno. *Psychiat.*, 36:299-343.

———— Gibson, R., & Gladstone, A. (1969), *Schizophrenia and the Need-Fear Dilemma.* New York: International Universities Press.

Cameron, N. (1944), Experimental analysis of schizophrenic thinking. In: *Language and Thought in Schizophrenia,* ed. J. S. Kasanin. Berkeley:

University of California Press, pp. 50-64.

Carpenter, W. T., et al. (1976), Another view of schizophrenia subtypes: A report from the International Pilot Study of Schizophrenia. *Arch. Gen. Psychiat.*, 33:508-516.

Chomsky, N. (1965), *Aspects of the Theory of Syntax.* Cambridge: M.I.T. Press.

Cohen, M. B. (1952), Countertransference and anxiety. *Psychiat.*, 15:231-243.

Eissler, K. R. (1953a), The effect of the structure of the ego on psychoanalytic technique. *J. Amer. Psychoanal. Assn.*, 1:104-143.

—— (1953b), Notes upon the emotionality of a schizophrenic patient and its relation to problems of technique. *The Psychoanalytic Study of the Child,* 8:199-251. New York: International Universities Press.

Eissler, R. S. & Eissler, K. R. (1964), Heinz Hartmann: A biographical sketch. In: *Psychoanalysis: A General Psychology,* ed. R. M. Loewenstein et al. New York: International Universities Press, 1966, pp. 3-15.

Ennis, J. (1971), *Reconstruction in Psychoanalysis,* Kris Study Group Monogr. 4. New York: International Universities Press.

Erikson, E. (1959), *Identity and the Life Cycle. Psychol. Issues,* Monogr. 1. New York: International Universities Press.

—— (1968), *Identity: Youth and Crisis.* New York: Norton.

Escalona, S. K. (1965), Some determinants of the individual differences in early ego development. *Trans. N.Y. Acad. Sci.,* Series II, 27:802-817.

Fairbairn, W. R. D. (1952), *An Object-Relations Theory of the Personality.* New York: Basic Books, 1954.

Farber, L. (1977), Harry Stack Sullivan and the American dream. Review of *Harry Stack Sullivan: His Life and His Works,* ed. A. H. Chapman. *Times Literary Supplement,* April 1.

Federn, P. (1926), Some variations in ego feeling. In: Federn (1952), pp. 25-37.

—— (1929), The ego as object and subject in narcissism. In: Federn (1952), pp. 283-322.

—— (1932), Ego feelings in dreams. In: Federn (1952), pp. 60-89.

—— (1936), On the distinction between healthy and pathological narcissism. In: Federn (1952), pp. 323-364.

—— (1943), Psychoanalysis of psychosis. In: Federn (1952), pp. 117-165.

—— (1949a), Mental hygiene of the ego in schizophrenia. In: Federn (1952), pp. 184-206.

—— (1949b), Ego psychological aspect of schizophrenia. In: Federn (1952), pp. 210-226.

—— (1949c), The ego in schizophrenia. In: Federn (1952), pp. 227-240.

—— (1949d), Depersonalization. In: Federn (1952), pp. 241-260.

—— (1952), *Ego Psychology and the Psychoses.* New York: Basic Books.

Fenichel, O. (1945), *The Psychoanalytic Theory of Neurosis.* New York: Norton.

—— (1953), A contribution to the psychology of jealousy. *Collected Papers,* First Series. New York: Norton, pp. 349-362.

Ferenczi, S. (1911), On the part played by homosexuality in the pathogenesis of paranoia. *Sex and Psychoanalysis.* New York: Dover, 1956, pp. 154-186.

Fliess, R. (1942), The metapsychology of the analyst. *Psychoanal. Quart.,* 11:211-227.

Fort, J. P. (1973), The importance of being diagnostic. Paper read at the Nineteenth Annual Chestnut Lodge Symposium, October 5.

Freeman, T. (1970), The psychopathology of the psychoses: A reply to Arlow and Brenner. *Internat. J. Psycho-Anal.,* 51:407-415.

—— (1972), A psychoanalytic profile schema for the psychotic patient. *Brit. J. Med. Psychol.,* 45:243-254.

—— Cameron, J. L., & McGhie, A. (1958), *Chronic Schizophrenia.* New York: International Universities Press.

Freud, A. (1936), *The Ego and the Mechanisms of Defence.* New York: International Universities Press, 1946.

—— (1965a), Diagnostic skills and their growth in psycho-analysis. *Internat. J. Psycho-Anal.,* 46:31-38.

—— (1965b), *Normality and Pathology in Childhood.* New York: International Universities Press.

—— (1972), Comments on aggression. *Internat. J. Psycho-Anal.,* 53:163-171.

—— (1973), A psychoanalytic view of developmental psychopathology. Twentieth Annual Freud Memorial Lecture, Philadelphia, April 27.

Freud, S. (1894), The neuro-psychoses of defence. *Standard Edition,* 3:45-61. London: Hogarth Press, 1962.

—— (1895), Draft H: Paranoia. *The Origins of Psychoanalysis,* ed. M. Bonaparte et al. New York: Basic Books, 1954.

—— (1896a), Draft K: The neuroses of defence. *The Origins of Psychoanalysis,* ed. M. Bonaparte et al. New York: Basic Books, 1954.

—— (1896b), Further remarks on the neuro-psychoses of defence. *Standard Edition,* 3:159-185. London: Hogarth Press, 1962.

—— (1899), Letters to Fliess, No. 125. *Standard Edition,* 1:279-280. London: Hogarth Press, 1966.

—— (1900), The interpretation of dreams. *Standard Edition,* 4 & 5. London: Hogarth Press, 1953.

—— (1910a), Five lectures on psycho-analysis; fifth lecture. *Standard Edition,* 11:48-55. London: Hogarth Press, 1957.

—— (1910b), The future prospects of psycho-analytic therapy. *Standard Edition,* 11:141-151. London: Hogarth Press, 1957.

—— (1911), Psycho-analytic notes on an autobiographical account of a case of paranoia (dementia paranoides). *Standard Edition,* 12:9-79. London: Hogarth Press, 1958.

—— (1914a), On the history of the psycho-analytic movement. *Standard Edition,* 14:3-102. London: Hogarth Press, 1957.

—— (1914b), On narcissism: An introduction. *Standard Edition,* 14:69-102. London: Hogarth Press, 1957.

—— (1915a), The unconscious. *Standard Edition,* 14:161-215. London: Hogarth Press, 1957.

———— (1915b), A metapsychological supplement to the theory of dreams. *Standard Edition,* 14:217-235. London: Hogarth Press, 1957.

———— (1915c) A case of paranoia running counter to the psycho-analytic theory of the disease. *Standard Edition,* 14:261-272. London: Hogarth Press, 1957.

———— (1916-1917), Introductory lectures on psycho-analysis. *Standard Edition,* 15 & 16. London: Hogarth Press, 1963.

———— (1917), Mourning and melancholia. *Standard Edition,* 14:239-258. London: Hogarth Press, 1957.

———— (1920), Beyond the pleasure principle. *Standard Edition,* 18:3-64. London: Hogarth Press, 1955.

———— (1922), Some neurotic mechanisms in jealousy, paranoia and homosexuality. *Standard Edition,* 18:223-232. London: Hogarth Press, 1955.

———— (1923), The ego and the id. *Standard Edition,* 19:3-59. London: Hogarth Press, 1955.

———— (1924a), Neurosis and psychosis. *Standard Edition,* 19:150-152. London: Hogarth Press, 1961.

———— (1924b), The loss of reality in neurosis and psychosis. *Standard Edition,* 19:183-187. London: Hogarth Press, 1961.

———— (1924c), A short account of psycho-analysis. *Standard Edition,* 19:191-209. London: Hogarth Press, 1961.

———— (1924d), The dissolution of the Oedipus complex. *Standard Edition,* 19:173-179. London: Hogarth Press, 1961.

———— (1925), Negation. *Standard Edition,* 19:235-239. London: Hogarth Press, 1961.

———— (1926a), Inhibitions, symptoms and anxiety. *Standard Edition,* 20:87-172. London: Hogarth Press, 1959.

———— (1926b), The question of lay analysis. *Standard Edition,* 20:183-250. London: Hogarth Press, 1959.

———— (1927a), Fetishism. *Standard Edition,* 21:152-157. London: Hogarth Press, 1961.

———— (1927b), Humour. *Standard Edition,* 21:161-166. London: Hogarth Press, 1961.

———— (1930), The Goethe prize. *Standard Edition,* 21:206-212. London: Hogarth Press, 1961.

———— (1937a), Analysis terminable and interminable. *Standard Edition,* 23:209-253. London: Hogarth Press, 1964.

———— (1937b), Constructions in analysis. *Standard Edition,* 23:257-269. London: Hogarth Press, 1964.

———— (1938a), An outline of psycho-analysis. *Standard Edition,* 23:141-207. London: Hogarth Press, 1964.

———— (1938b), Splitting of the ego in the process of defence. *Standard Edition,* 23:275-278. London: Hogarth Press, 1964.

———— (1939), Moses and monotheism. *Standard Edition,* 23:3-137. London: Hogarth Press, 1964.

Fromm-Reichmann, F. (1948), Notes on the development of treatment of schizophrenics by psychoanalytic psychotherapy. *Psychiat.,* 10:163-273.

—— (1950), *Principles of Intensive Psychotherapy*. Chicago: University of Chicago Press.

—— (1959), *Psychoanalysis and Psychotherapy: Selected Papers*. Chicago: University of Chicago Press.

Frosch, J. (1964), The psychotic character: Clinical psychiatric considerations. *Psychiat. Quart.*, 38:81-96.

—— (1966), A note on reality constancy. In: *Psychoanalysis: A General Psychology*, ed. R. M. Loewenstein et al. New York: International Universities Press, pp. 349-376.

—— (1967), Delusional fixity, sense of conviction and the psychotic conflict. *Internat. J. Psycho-Anal.*, 48:475-495.

—— (1970), Psychoanalytic considerations of the psychotic character. *J. Amer. Psychoanal. Assn.*, 18:24-50.

George, G. & Gibson, R. (1959), Patient-staff relationships change with environment. Paper read at the Third Annual Chestnut Lodge Symposium, November 6, 1957. *Ment. Hosp.*, November, pp. 18-19.

Gillespie, W. H. (1970), Discussion: The psychopathology of the psychoses. Opening and closing remarks of the moderator. *Internat. J. Psycho-Anal.*, 51:160-162.

—— (1971), Aggression and instinct theory. *Internat. J. Psycho-Anal.*, 52:155-160.

Gitelson, M. (1957), On ego distortion. *Internat. J. Psycho-Anal.*, 29:245-257.

Glover, E. (1945), Examination of the Klein system of child psychology. *The Psychoanalytic Study of the Child*, 1:75-118. New York: International Universities Press.

Grauer, D. (1957), Some misconceptions of Federn's ego psychology. *J. Amer. Psychoanal. Assn.*, 5:282-292.

Green, H. (1964), *I Never Promised You a Rose Garden*. New York: Holt, Rinehart & Winston.

Greenacre, P. (1941), The predisposition to anxiety. In: *Trauma, Growth, and Personality*. New York: International Universities Press, 1952, pp. 27-82.

—— (1975), On reconstruction. *J. Amer. Psychoanal. Assn.*, 23:693-712.

Greenson, R. (1965), The working alliance and the transference neurosis. *Psychoanal. Quart.*, 34:155-181.

—— & Wexler, M. (1969), The non-transference relationship in the psychoanalytic situation. *Internat. J. Psycho-Anal.*, 50:27-39.

Guntrip, H. (1968), *Schizoid Phenomena, Object Relations, and the Self*. New York: International Universities Press.

Hampshire, S. (1951), *Spinoza*. Baltimore: Penguin Books.

—— (1959), *Thought and Action*. London: Chatto & Windus.

Hartmann, H. (1939), *Ego Psychology and the Problem of Adaptation*. New York: International Universities Press, 1958.

—— (1948), Comments on the psychoanalytic theory of instinctual drives. In: Hartmann (1964), pp. 69-89.

—— (1950a), Psychoanalysis and developmental psychology. In: Hartmann (1964), pp. 99-112.

———— (1950b), Comments on the psychoanalytic theory of the ego. In: Hartmann (1964), pp. 113-141.

———— (1952), The mutual influences in the development of ego and id. In: Hartmann (1964), pp. 155-181.

———— (1953), Contribution to the metapsychology of schizophrenia. In: Hartmann (1964), pp. 182-206.

———— (1956), Notes on the reality principle. In: Hartmann (1964), pp. 241-267.

———— (1964), *Essays on Ego Psychology*. New York: International Universities Press.

———— Kris, E., & Loewenstein, R. M. (1946), Comments on the formation of psychic structure. In: Hartmann, Kris, & Loewenstein (1964), pp. 27-55.

———— ———— (1949), Notes on the theory of aggression. In: Hartmann, Kris, & Loewenstein (1964), pp. 56-85.

———— ———— ———— (1951), Some psychoanalytic comments on "culture and personality." In: Hartmann, Kris, & Loewenstein (1964), pp. 86-116.

———— ———— ———— (1964), *Papers on Psychoanalytic Psychology. Psychol. Issues,* Monogr. 14. New York: International Universities Press.

Havens, L. L. (1962), The placement and movement of hallucinations in space: Phenomenology and theory. *Internat. J. Psycho-Anal.,* 43:426-435.

Hay, A. J. & Forrest, A. D. (1972), The diagnosis of schizophrenia and paranoid psychosis: An attempt at clarification. *Brit. J. Med. Psychol.,* 45:233-241.

Heimann, P. (1950), On counter-transference. *Internat. J. Psycho-Anal.,* 31:81-84.

Hendrick, I. (1938), The ego and the defense mechanisms. *Psychoanal. Rev.,* 25:476-497.

Hill, L. B. (1955), *Psychotherapeutic Intervention in Schizophrenia.* Chicago: University of Chicago Press.

Holt, R. (1967), Beyond vitalism and mechanism: Freud's concept of psychic energy. In: *Science and Psychoanalysis,* Vol. 2, ed. J. H. Masserman. New York: Grune & Stratton, pp. 1-41.

Inhelder, B. & Piaget, J. (1958), *The Growth of Logical Thinking from Childhood to Adolescence.* New York: Basic Books.

Jacobson, E. (1953), Metapsychology of cyclothymic depression. In: *Affective Disorders,* ed. P. Greenacre. New York: International Universities Press, pp. 49-83.

———— (1954a), Federn's contributions to ego psychology and psychoses. *J. Amer. Psychoanal. Assn.,* 2:519-525.

———— (1954b), Contribution to the metapsychology of psychotic identifications. *J. Amer. Psychoanal. Assn.,* 2:239-262.

———— (1954c), The self and the object world. *The Psychoanalytic Study of the Child,* 9:75-127. New York: International Universities Press.

———— (1957), Normal and pathological moods: Their nature and functions. In: Jacobson (1971), pp. 66-106.

——— (1964), *The Self and the Object World.* New York: International Universities Press.

——— (1967), *Psychotic Conflict and Reality.* New York: International Universities Press.

——— (1971), *Depression.* New York: International Universities Press.

Joffe, W. (1969), A critical review of the status of the envy concept. *Internat. J. Psycho-Anal.,* 50:533-545.

Jones, E. (1952), Preface to Fairbairn (1952).

Kafka, J. S. (1971), Ambiguity for individuation. *Arch. Gen. Psychiat.,* 45:233-239.

Kasanin, J. (1944), *Language and Thought in Schizophrenia.* Berkeley: University of California Press.

Katan, A. (1951), The role of 'displacement' in agoraphobia. *Internat. J. Psycho-Anal.,* 32:41-50.

Katan, M. (1954), The importance of the non-psychotic part of the personality in schizophrenia. *Internat. J. Psycho-Anal.,* 35:119-128.

Kernberg, O. (1965), Notes on countertransference. *J. Amer. Psychoanal. Assn.,* 13:38-56.

——— (1967), Borderline personality organization. *J. Amer. Psychoanal. Assn.,* 15:641-685.

——— (1969), A contribution to the ego-psychological critique of the Kleinian School. *Internat. J. Psycho-Anal.,* 50:317-333.

——— (1970), A psychoanalytic classification of character pathology. *J. Amer. Psychoanal. Assn.,* 18:800-822.

Kety, S. (1974), From rationalization to reason. *Amer. J. Psychiat.,* 131:957-963.

——— (1976), Genetic aspects of schizophrenia. *Psychiat. Ann.,* 6(1):11-32.

Khan, M. M. R. (1963), The concept of cumulative trauma. *The Privacy of the Self.* New York: International Universities Press, 1974, pp. 42-58.

Klein, M. (1932), *The Psycho-Analysis of Children.* New York: Norton.

——— (1933), The early development of conscience in the child. In: *Contributions to Psycho-Analysis, 1921-1945.* London: Hogarth Press, 1948, pp. 267-281.

——— (1935), A contribution to the psychogenesis of manic-depressive states. *Internat. J. Psycho-Anal.,* 16:145-174.

——— (1946), Notes on some schizoid mechanisms. In: *Envy and Gratitude & Other Works, 1946-1963.* New York: Delacorte Press/Seymour Lawrence, 1975, pp. 1-24.

——— (1957), *New Directions in Psychoanalysis.* New York: Basic Books.

——— (1975a), *Love, Guilt and Reparation and Other Works, 1921-1945.* New York: Delacorte Press/Seymour Lawrence.

——— (1975b), *Envy and Gratitude & Other Works, 1946-1963.* New York: Delacorte Press/Seymour Lawrence.

Kohut, H. (1957), Introspection, empathy, and psychoanalysis. *J. Amer. Psychoanal. Assn.,* 7:459-483.

——— (1971), *The Analysis of the Self.* New York: International Universities Press.

Kraepelin, E. (1919), *Dementia Praecox,* trans. M. Barclay. Edinburgh: Livingstone.

Lagache, D. (1950), Homosexuality and jealousy. *Internat. J. Psycho-Anal.,* 31:24-31.

Laing, R. D. (1964), *Sanity, Madness and the Family.* New York: Basic Books.

—— (1967), *The Politics of Experience.* New York: Pantheon Books.

Langs, R. (1976), *The Therapeutic Interaction.* New York: Aronson.

Laplanche, J. & Pontalis, J. (1973), *The Language of Psychoanalysis.* New York: Norton.

LeFever, H. (1961), To antipodes and back: Some observations on the LSD experience. Paper read at the Seventh Annual Chestnut Lodge Symposium, Novmber 3.

Lewin, B. D. (1968), The pictorial past. *Selected Writings,* ed. J. A. Arlow. New York: Psychoanalytic Quarterly, 1973, pp. 385-399.

Lichtenberg, J. D. (1975), The development of the sense of self. *J. Amer. Psychoanal. Assn.,* 23:453-484.

—— (1978), The testing of reality from the standpoint of the body self. *J. Amer. Psychoanal. Assn.,* 26:357-385.

—— & Pao, P-N. (1960), The prognostic and therapeutic significance of the husband-wife relationship for hospitalized schizophrenic women. *Psychiat.,* 23:209-213.

—— —— (1974), Delusion, fantasy and desire. *Internat. J. Psycho-Anal.,* 55:273-281.

—— & Slap, J. W. (1971), On the defensive organization. *Internat. J. Psycho-Anal.,* 52:451-457.

—— —— (1972), On the defense mechanism: A survey and synthesis. *J. Amer. Psychoanal. Assn.,* 20:776-792.

Lichtenstein, H. (1961), Identity and sexuality: A study of their interrelationship in man. *J. Amer. Psychoanal. Assn.,* 9:179-260.

—— (1963), The dilemma of human identity. *J. Amer. Psychoanal. Assn.,* 11:173-223.

Lidz, T. (1973), *The Origin and Treatment of Schizophrenic Disorders.* New York: Basic Books.

—— Fleck, S., & Cornelison, A. R. (1965), *Schizophrenia and the Family.* New York: International Universities Press.

Little, M. (1951), Counter-transference and the patient's response to it. *Internat. J. Psycho-Anal.,* 32:32-40.

—— (1958), On delusional transference. *Internat. J. Psycho-Anal.,* 39:134-138.

—— (1960), Countertransference. *Brit. J. Med. Psychol.,* 33:29-31.

Loewald, H. (1971), On motivation and instinct theory. *The Psychoanalytic Study of the Child,* 26:91-128. New York: Quadrangle.

Loewenstein, R. M. (1957), Some thoughts on interpretation in the theory and practice of psychoanalysis. *The Psychoanalytic Study of the Child,* 12:127-150. New York: International Universities Press.

—— (1966), Heinz Hartmann: Psychology of the ego. In: *Psychoanalytic*

Pioneers, ed. Franz Alexander et al. New York: Basic Books, pp. 469-483.

London, N. J. (1973), An essay on psychoanalytic theory: Two theories of schizophrenia, parts I and II. *Internat. J. Psycho-Anal.,* 54:169-193.

Lustman, S. L. (1956), Rudiments of the ego. *The Psychoanalytic Study of the Child,* 11:89-98. New York: International Universities Press.

Mack, J. (1970), *Nightmares and Human Conflict.* Boston: Little, Brown.

Mahler, M. S. (1952), On child psychosis and schizophrenia. *The Psychoanalytic Study of the Child,* 7:286-305. New York: International Universities Press.

———— (1968), *On Human Symbiosis and the Vicissitudes of Individuation.* New York: International Universities Press.

———— (1975), *The Psychological Birth of the Human Infant.* New York: Basic Books.

Menninger, K. A., Mayman, M., & Pruyser, P. (1963), *The Vital Balance.* New York: Viking.

Meyer, A. (1938), *Proceedings of the Fourth Conference on Psychiatric Education.* Baltimore, Maryland, April 8-10, 1936. New York: National Conference for Mental Hygiene.

Modell, A. H. (1958), The theoretical implications of hallucinatory experiences in schizophrenia. *J. Amer. Psychoanal. Assn.,* 6:442-480.

———— (1975), A narcissistic defence against affects and the illusion of self-sufficiency. *Internat. J. Psycho-Anal.,* 56:275-282.

Moore, B. E. & Fine, B. D., eds. (1967), *A Glossary of Psychoanalytic Terms and Concepts.* New York: American Psychoanalytic Association.

Montagu, M. F. A. (1962), *Prenatal Influences.* Springfield, Ill.: Thomas.

Morse, R. T. & Noble, D. (1942), Joint endeavors of the administrative physician and psychotherapist. *Psychiat. Quart.,* 16:578-585.

Niederland, W. G. (1974), *The Schreber Case.* New York: Quadrangle.

Nunberg, H. (1920), On the catatonic attack. *Practice and Theory of Psychoanalysis,* Vol. 1. New York: International Universities Press, 1948, pp. 3-23.

———— (1925), The will to recovery. *Practice and Theory of Psychoanalysis,* Vol. 1. New York: International Universities Press, 1948, pp. 75-88.

———— (1929), The synthetic function of the ego. *Practice and Theory of Psychoanalysis,* Vol. 1. New York: International Universities Press, 1948, pp. 120-136.

Olinick, S. (1954), Some considerations of the use of questioning as a psychoanalytic technique. *J. Amer. Psychoanal. Assn.,* 2:57-66.

———— (1976), Parallel analyzing functions in work ego and observing ego: The treatment alliance. *J. Phila. Assn. Psychoanal.,* 3(1/2):3-21.

———— Poland, W., Grigg, K. A., & Granatir, W. L. (1973), The psychoanalytic work ego: Process and interpretation. *Internat. J. Psycho-Anal.,* 54:143-151.

Palombo, S. R. & Bruch, H. (1964), Falling apart: The verbalization of ego failure. *Psychiat.,* 27:248-258.

Panel (1974), The influence of theoretical model of schizophrenia on treatment practice. *J. Amer. Psychoanal. Assn.,* 22:182-199.

Pao, P.-N. (1960), Young schizophrenic mothers' initial posthospital adjustment at home. *Arch. Gen. Psychiat.*, 2:512-520.

—— (1965), The role of hatred in the ego. *Psychoanal. Quart.*, 34:257-264.

—— (1968a), On manic-depressive psychosis: A study of the transition of states. *J. Amer. Psychoanal. Assn.*, 16:809-832.

—— (1968b), Depressive feeling, depressive illness, despair. Paper read at the Fourteenth Annual Chestnut Lodge Symposium, October 4.

—— (1969a), The syndrome of delicate self-cutting. *Brit. J. Med. Psychol.*, 42:195-206.

—— (1969b), Pathological jealousy. *Psychoanal. Quart.*, 38:616-638.

—— (1971a), Psychopathological considerations of a case of recurrent manic psychosis. *Brit. J. Med. Psychol.*, 44:239-248.

—— (1971b), Elation, hypomania, and mania. *J. Amer. Psychoanal. Assn.*, 19:787-798.

—— (1973), On the defensive flight to a new object. *Internat. J. Psychoanal. Psychother.*, 2:320-337.

—— (1977), The experience at Chestnut Lodge on long-term treatment of psychotic states, with particular reference to inexact interpretations. In: *Long-Term Treatments of Psychotic States*, ed. C. Chiland & P. Bequart. New York: Human Sciences Press, pp. 314-331.

—— & Lichtenberg, J. (1960), Integration of husbands into the treatment program of hospitalized schizophrenic women. *Arch. Gen. Psychiat.*, 3:122-127.

Poland, W. S. (1975), Tact as a psychoanalytic function. *Internat. J. Psycho-Anal.*, 56:155-162.

Racker, H. (1957), The meaning and uses of countertransference. *Psychoanal. Quart.*, 26:303-357.

Rangell, L. (1965), The scope of Heinz Hartmann. *Internat. J. Psycho-Anal.*, 46:5-13.

—— (1974), A psychoanalytic perspective leading currently to the syndrome of the compromise of integrity. *Internat. J. Psycho-Anal.*, 55:3-12.

Rapaport, D. (1959), Introduction to Erikson (1959), pp. 5-17.

—— Gill, M., & Schafer, R. (1945-1946), *Diagnostic Psychological Testing*, 2 volumes. Chicago: Year Book Publishers.

Reichard, S. (1956), A re-examination of "Studies in Hysteria." *Psychoanal. Quart.*, 25:155-177.

Resch, R. C. (1976), On separating as a developmental phenomenon: A natural study. *Psychoanalysis and Contemporary Science*, 5:207-269. New York: International Universities Press.

Robbins, F. P. & Sadow, L. (1974), A developmental hypothesis of reality processing. *J. Amer. Psychoanal. Assn.*, 22:344-363.

Rolf, J. E. & Harig, P. T. (1974), Etiological research in schizophrenia and the rationale for primary intervention. *Amer. J. Orthopsychiat.*, 44:538-554.

Rosen, J. (1953), *Direct Analysis. Selected Papers*. New York: Grune & Stratton.

Rosenfeld, H. A. (1954), Considerations regarding the psychoanalytic approach to acute and chronic schizophrenia. *Internat. J. Psycho-Anal.*, 35:135-140.

—— (1965), *Psychotic States: A Psycho-Analytical Approach.* New York: International Universities Press.

—— (1972), A critical appreciation of James Strachey's paper on the nature of the therapeutic action of psychoanalysis. *Internat. J. Psycho-Anal.*, 53:455-461.

Rosenthal, D. (1963), *The Genain Quadruplets.* New York: Basic Books.

Sachs, H. (1942), The community of day dreams. *The Creative Unconscious.* Cambridge, Mass.: Sci-Art, pp. 11-54.

Sandler, J. (1960), The background of safety. *Internat. J. Psycho-Anal.*, 41:352-356.

—— (1976), Actualization and object relationships. *J. Phila. Assn. Psychoanal.*, 3:59-70.

—— & Joffe, W. G. (1969), Towards a basic psychoanalytic model. *Internat. J. Psycho-Anal.*, 50:79-90.

Sarnoff, C. (1976), *Latency.* New York: Aronson.

Schafer, R. (1968), *Aspects of Internalization.* New York: International Universities Press.

—— (1970), An overview of Heinz Hartmann's contributions to psychoanalysis. *Internat. J. Psycho-Anal.*, 51:425-446.

Schilder, P. (1935), *The Image and Appearance of the Human Body.* New York: International Universities Press, 1950.

Schneider, K. (1959), *Clinical Psychopathology,* trans. M. W. Hamilton. New York: Grune & Stratton.

Schulz, C. G. & Kilgalen, R. (1969), *Case Studies in Schizophrenia.* New York: Basic Books.

Schur, M. (1966), *The Id and the Regulatory Principles of Mental Functioning.* New York: International Universities Press.

Schwing, G. (1940), *A Way to the Soul of the Mentally Ill.* New York: International Universities Press, 1954.

Searles, H. F. (1959), The effort to drive the other person crazy. *Brit. J. Med. Psychol.*, 32:1-18.

—— (1960), *The Nonhuman Environment.* New York: International Universities Press.

—— (1962), The differentiation between concrete and metaphorical thinking in the recovering schizophrenic patient. *J. Amer. Psychoanal. Assn.*, 10:22-49.

—— (1963), Transference psychosis in the psychotherapy of chronic schizophrenia. *Internat. J. Psycho-Anal.*, 44:249-281.

—— (1965), *Collected Papers on Schizophrenia and Related Subjects.* New York: International Universities Press.

—— (1966), Feelings of guilt in the psychoanalyst. *Psychiat.*, 29:319-323.

—— (1972), The function of the patient's realistic perceptions of the analyst in delusional transference. *Brit. J. Med. Psychol.*, 45:1-18.

—— (1975a), Countertransference and theoretical model. In: *Psychotherapy of Schizophrenia,* ed. J. G. Gunderson. New York: Aronson, pp. 223-240.

—— (1975b), Violence in schizophrenia. *The Psychoanalytic Forum*, 5:4-89. New York: International Universities Press.

Sechehaye, M. (1951), *Symbolic Realization*. New York: International Universities Press.

Segal, H. (1950), Some aspects of the analysis of schizophrenia. *Internat. J. Psycho-Anal.*, 31:268-278.

—— (1954), A note on schizoid mechanisms underlying phobia formation. *Internat. J. Psycho-Anal.*, 35:238-241.

—— (1956), Depression in schizophrenia. *Internat. J. Psycho-Anal.*, 37:339-343.

—— (1964a), *Introduction to the Work of Melanie Klein*. New York: Basic Books.

—— (1964b), Fantasy and other mental processes. (Symposium on Fantasy.) *Internat. J. Psycho-Anal.*, 45:192-194.

—— (1972), A delusional system as a defence against the re-emergence of a catastrophic situation. *Internat. J. Psycho-Anal.*, 53:395-401.

Semrad, E. (1975), Alternative means of measuring change. In: *Psychotherapy of Schizophrenia*, ed. J. G. Gunderson. New York: Aronson, pp. 323-335.

Shapiro, R., et al. (1974), Family contributions to narcissistic disturbance in adolescence. *Internat. Rev. Psycho-Anal.*, 1:353-365.

Stanton, A. & Schwartz, M. S. (1954), *The Mental Hospital*. New York: Basic Books.

Stierlin, H. (1969), *Conflict and Reconciliation*. New York: Anchor Books.

—— (1973), Interpersonal aspects of internalization. *Internat. J. Psycho-Anal.*, 54:203-213.

Stone, L. (1961), *The Psychoanalytic Situation*. New York: International Universities Press.

Storch, A. (1924), *The Primitive Archaic Forms of Inner Experience and Thought in Schizophrenia*. Washington, D.C.: Nervous and Mental Disease Publishing Co.

Strachey, J. (1957), Editor's note to "On Narcissism." *Standard Edition*, 14:69-71. London: Hogarth Press.

—— (1958), Editor's note. *Standard Edition*, 12:3-11. London: Hogarth Press.

Sullivan, H. S. (1924a), The oral complex. *Psychoanal. Rev.*, 12:31-38, 1925.

—— (1924b), Varieties of repression. *Psychoanal. Rev.*, 12:333-334.

—— (1925), Peculiarity of thought in schizophrenia. In: Sullivan (1962), pp. 26-99.

—— (1926), Erogenous maturation. *Psychoanal. Rev.*, 13:1-15.

—— (1927), The onset of schizophrenia. In: Sullivan (1962), pp. 104-136.

—— (1929), Research in schizophrenia. In: Sullivan (1962), pp. 186-202.

—— (1931), The modified treatment of schizophrenia. In: Sullivan (1962), pp. 272-296.

—— (1940), *Conceptions of Modern Psychiatry*. Washington, D. C.: William Alanson White Psychiatric Foundation.

—— (1953), *The Interpersonal Theory of Psychiatry*. New York: Norton.

—— (1956), *Clinical Studies in Psychiatry*. New York: Norton.

—— (1962), *Schizophrenia as a Human Process*. New York: Norton.

———— (1972), *Personal Psychopathology*. New York: Norton.

Szasz, T. (1961), *The Myth of Mental Illness*. New York: Hoeber-Harper.

Tausk, V. (1919), On the origin of the "influencing machine" in schizophrenia. *Psychoanal. Quart.*, 2:519-556, 1933.

Tietze, T. (1959), A study of mothers of schizophrenic patients. In: *Advances in Psychiatry*, ed. M. B. Cohen. New York: Norton, pp. 159-179.

Tolpin, M. (1971), On the beginnings of a cohesive self: An application of the concept of transmuting internalization to the study of the transitional object and signal anxiety. *The Psychoanalytic Study of the Child,* 26:316-352. New York: Quadrangle.

Tolpin, P. H. (1975), On the regulation of anxiety: Its relation to "the timelessness of the unconscious and its capacity for hallucination." *The Annual of Psychoanalysis,* 2:150-177. New York: International Universities Press.

Von Domarus, E. (1951), The specific laws of logic in schizophrenia. In: *Language and Thought in Schizophrenia,* ed. J. S. Kasanin. Berkeley: University of California Press, pp. 104-114.

Waelder R. (1936), The problem of the genesis of psychical conflict in earliest infancy. *Psychoanalysis: Observation, Theory, Application,* ed. S. A. Guttman. New York: International Universities Press, 1976, pp. 121-188.

———— (1951), The structure of paranoid ideas. *Psychoanalysis: Observation, Theory, Application,* ed. S. A. Guttman. New York: International Universities Press, 1976, pp. 207-228.

Weigert, E. V. (1952), Contribution to the problem of terminating analysis. *Psychoanal. Quart.,* 21:465-480.

Weinshel, E. (1970), Some psychoanalytic considerations on moods. *Internat. J. Psycho-Anal.,* 51:313-320.

Weiss, E. (1952), Introduction to Federn (1952), pp. 1-21.

———— (1960), *The Structure and Dynamics of the Human Mind.* New York: Grune & Stratton.

Wexler, M. (1971), Schizophrenia: Conflict and deficiency. *Psychoanal. Quart.,* 40:83-99.

Whitehead, C. (1975), Additional aspects of the Freudian-Kleinian controversy: Towards a "psychoanalysis" of psychoanalysis. *Internat. J. Psycho-Anal.,* 56:383-396.

Whitehorn, J. C. & Betz, B. (1954), A study of psychotherapeutic relationships between physicians and schizophrenic patients. *Amer. J. Psychiat.,* 111:321-331.

———— ———— (1956), The relationship of the therapist to the outcome of therapy in schizophrenia. *Psychiat. Res. Rep.,* (5):89. Washington, D. C.: American Psychiatric Association.

Will, O. A. (1958), Psychotherapeutics and the schizophrenic reaction. *J. Nerv. Ment. Dis.,* 126:109-140.

———— (1975), The conditions of being therapeutic. In: *Psychotherapy of Schizophrenia,* ed. J. G. Gunderson. New York: Aronson, pp. 53-66.

Winnicott, D. W. (1949), Hate in the countertransference. In: Winnicott (1958), pp. 194-203.

—————— (1955), Metapsychological and clinical aspects of regression within the psychoanalytical set-up. In: Winnicott (1958), pp. 278-294.

—————— (1958), *Collected Papers*. New York: Basic Books.

—————— (1960a), Counter-Transference. In: Winnicott (1965), pp. 158-165.

—————— (1960b), Ego distortion in terms of true and false self. In: Winnicott (1965), pp. 140-157.

—————— (1963), Communicating and not communicating leading to a study of certain opposites. In: Winnicott (1965), pp. 179-192.

—————— (1965), *The Maturational Processes and the Facilitating Environment*. New York: International Universities Press.

Wyatt, R. J., Termini, B. A., & Davis, J. (1971), Biochemical and sleep studies of schizophrenia: A review of the literature, 1960-1970. I. Biochemical Studies. *Schizophrenia Bull.*, 4:10-66.

Wynne, L. & Ryckoff, I. (1958), Pseudo-mutuality in the family relations of schizophrenics. *Psychiat.*, 21:205-220.

—————— & Singer, M. T. (1963a), Thought disorder and family relations of schizophrenics. I. A research strategy. *Arch. Gen. Psychiat.*, 9:191-198.

—————— —————— (1963b), Thought disorder and family relations of schizophrenics. II. Classification of forms of thinking. *Arch. Gen. Psychiat.*, 9:199-206.

Yorke, C. (1971), Some suggestions for a critique of Kleinian psychology. *The Psychoanalytic Study of the Child*, 26:129-155. New York: Quadrangle.

Zetzel, E. R. (1949), Anxiety and the capacity to bear it. In: Zetzel (1970), pp. 33-52.

—————— (1953), The depressive position. In: Zetzel (1970), pp. 63-81.

—————— (1956a), Concept and content in psychoanalytic theory. In: Zetzel (1970), pp. 115-138.

—————— (1956b), The concept of transference. In: Zetzel (1970), pp. 168-181.

—————— (1965), On the incapacity to bear depression. In: Zetzel (1970), pp. 82-114.

—————— (1970), *The Capacity for Emotional Growth*. New York: International Universities Press.

Zilboorg, G. (1941), *A History of Medical Psychology*. New York: Norton.

Zuckerman, M. (1969), Hallucinations, reported sensations, and images. In: *Sensory Deprivation*, ed. J. P. Zubek. New York: Meredith, pp. 85-125.

Name Index

Subject Index

Adoptees, the study of Danish, 144-145
Affect(ive)
  distinguished from mood (Jacobson), 77, 81
  disturbances in; *see* Basic experiential disturbances, in affectivity
  indifference, 307-309
  see also Emotions; Feelings
Aggression
  conflict over, 190-193, 206-208, 410
  and libido, 97, 153-155, 228
  and neutralization, 64-65
  and primary autonomous ego defect, 65, 69
  propensity for, 12
  rituals against, 82, 265-280, 361, 410
  in schizophrenic process, 45, 65, 68, 76-77, 184-185
  treatment of, 91, 108, 265-266
Anxiety
  automatic, distinguished from signal, 219
  contagious, 156
  mastery of, 357
  and organismic panic, 217, 218
  see also Feelings of terror; Organismic panic; Panic
Attachment, 359-365, 381
  and therapeutic alliance, 359, 365
  and transference, 359, 373

Basic experiential disturbances, 144, 152-168, 185-186

in affectivity, 158
in communication, 158-159
and distorted self-image, 159-160
in libido-aggression balance, 153-155, 228
and maintenance mechanisms, 156-157, 224-225
modifiability of, 144, 161
mutual influence in, 160-161
and nature-nurture interaction, 143-148
in object relatedness, 152-153
and organismic panic, 155-156, 217
in perception, 157-158
relation to schizophrenia, 162
in sense of self-cohesion, 160
and thought disorders, 159
Basic trust, 335; *see also* Trust
Borderline personality disorder, 8, 18-19, 73
Break with reality; *see* Reality, break with

Catatonia
  as best possible solution, 225-226, 384; *see also* Symptom formation, as best possible solution
  and regression, 58
Classification of schizophrenia; *see* Phases of schizophrenic disorder; Subgroups, subtypes of schizophrenia
Cognitive development, 293-296
Communication, disturbances in; *see*

449